Countervisions

Asian American Film Criticism

MARCH 2001

TO CHARLES,

Who introduced me to
Crusin' J-Town, Wong Sing sang,
and Manzanar way back
when. Thanks for your
friendship and support.
Now, on to Yellow Erotica.

Dall Y.

C.S.U.L.B
Political Science, ~n.

In the series

Asian American History and Culture

edited by Sucheng Chan, David Palumbo-Liu, and Michael Omi

Countervisions

Asian American Film Criticism

EDITED BY

Darrell Y. Hamamoto and Sandra Liu

TEMPLE UNIVERSITY PRESS

PHILADELPHIA

Temple University Press, Philadelphia 19122
Copyright © 2000 by Temple University
All rights reserved
Published 2000
Printed in the United States of America

Library of Congress Cataloging-in-Publication Data

Countervisions : Asian American film criticism / edited by Darrell Y. Hamamoto
and Sandra Liu.

    p. cm. — (Asian American history and culture)

  Includes bibliographical references.

  ISBN 1-56639-775-8 (alk. paper) — ISBN 1-56639-776-6 (pbk. : alk. paper)

  1. Asians in motion pictures. 2. Asian Americans in motion pictures.

I. Hamamoto, Darrell Y. II. Liu, Sandra, 1967– III. Series.

PN1995.9.A78 C68 2000
791.43'6520395—dc21

                                    00-020630

The poem "No One Ever Tried to Kiss Anna May Wong," Copyright © 1989 by John
Yau, is reprinted on p. 31 from *Radiant Silhouette: New & Selected Work 1974–1988* with
the permission of Black Sparrow Press.

The poem "Thirty Years Under" is reprinted on p. 164 from *Camp Notes and Other
Poems* (Latham, N.Y.: Kitchen Table/Women of Color Press, 1992) with the permission
of Mitsuye Yamada.

To Donald Richie, film scholar, literary artist,
American expatriate, for showing me the way

—*Darrell Y. Hamamoto*

To my mother, Mariana P. Y. Liaw, who taught me
to love learning, and to the memory of my father,
Liaw A. Khim, who loved the movies

—*Sandra Liu*

Contents

List of Illustrations

Acknowledgments

Countervisions had its beginnings in the classroom, as we searched for relevant and academically rigorous texts for the students in our Asian American media courses at University of California, Berkeley, and University of California, Davis. They inspired us to take on this project and spurred us to finish it. We are, however, indebted to the contributors. It has been a privilege to work with them, and without them this volume would not have been possible. Their insights into Asian American film kept us excited and focused. We appreciate the interest and support expressed by many individuals along the way. Thanks to Janet Francendese for her patient shepherding, pragmatic outlook, and expert editorial advice. Michael Omi provided valuable feedback that made many of the essays stronger. Margaret Weinstein, Jennifer French, and the other professionals at Temple University Press helped us wade through seemingly endless details to bring the manuscript across the finish line. Pam Matsuoka and Julie Hatta at NAATA and Mijoung Chang at Women Make Movies were instrumental in our search for artwork for the cover.

Sandra Liu thanks Elaine Kim for her support, encouragement, and efforts. My thanks also go to Eithne Luibheid, who has been colleague, friend, task mistress, and counselor from start to finish; Caroline Streeter, Susan Lee, Nerissa Balce, and Jill Esbenshade, who were superlative cheerleaders; Norbert Hendrikse, who has been my constant partner and support; and Anja Hendrikse Liu, who kept me on my toes through the last stretch. And, of course, many thanks to Darrell Hamamoto. Your wise counsel and wit helped me maintain a healthy perspective.

Darrell Y. Hamamoto adds: All love to Gena Sayoko Hamamoto for tolerating an abberant father. Propers due to fellow Meyer Lansky fan Carl Boggs, who shared many of his insights into human sexuality prior to and throughout this project. In all his winning torment, Charles Igawa remains a touchstone to people, times, and places dear to me. Fred MacDonald fished me out of murky water. Appreciation to Leslie MacDonald for encouraging a career change. Rudy Torres threw me a towel. Kent Ono and Sarah Projansky were kind enough to let me test some of the ideas presented here one evening in a memorable film class at UC Davis in the aftermath of a fourteen-hour long-distance telephone conversation. Doug Kellner down at UCLA has got my back. Appreciation to Michael Omi at UC Berkeley and to Lisa Lowe at UC San Diego for reviewing *Countervisions* and offering valued insights. A salute to Janet Francendese for her unflagging advocacy and support of scholarship in Asian American Studies. Gratitude to Gina Marchetti for supporting my quest and having me take the gospel of Yellow eroticism to Ithaca College. Thanks to Elena Tajima-Creef and the honeez at Wellesley for enthusiastically receiving my vision for the Yellow Entertainment Network (YEN). Eddie Wong, Pam Matsuoka, and the staff at NAATA kindly made accessible the explosion of recent Asian American independent films. The Asian/Pacific/American Studies Program and Institute at New York University provided ideal conditions for me to complete the work at hand. Deepest thanks to Jack Tchen for inviting me to NYU as a visiting scholar. Risa Morimoto and the A/P/A staff made my stay both smoove and a groove. Adria Imada is the best teaching assistant one could ever hope to have. Props to multi-music man Masaki Yamagata for adding my funky guitar to the mix. Layin' tracks wit' da ban' in NYC was an unexpected bonus. The U.S. J-Pop kings Minoru Hasegawa, Masaki Yamagata, Mahbo Takigayama, and Gen Hasegawa of Halo Halo give me hope for the future of Japanese American society and culture. To Christina Fa. Brother Percy Sledge sang the truth: "Lovin' eyes can never see." A final word of thanks to Sandra Liu for her indefatigable efforts in bringing this anthology to fruition. 'Dra, you was a pleasure to work with.

Countervisions

Asian American Film Criticism

Darrell Y. Hamamoto

1   Introduction: On Asian American Film and Criticism

In the Critical Tradition

The art of independent Asian American film was forged in the crucible of the passionate political struggles and counter-culture practices that attended the new social movements of the 1960s and 1970s. Antiwar protest against U.S. military adventurism in Southeast Asia, domestic conflict over civil rights issues, widespread student revolt, counter-culture experimentation, and a generalized crisis of political legitimacy influenced much of the early independent media work of Asian American activist–artists. Although this early stage of development was often beset by sectarianism and ideological rigidity, it also embodied the liberatory idealism and commitment of the politically engaged cultural workers who stood at the heart of the Asian American movement. Independent film was but one of many expressive forms that artists adopted to oppose the cultural hegemony of the allied corporate and media industries. Along with film, self-consciously *Asian American* writing, music, theater, fine arts, and criticism began to assert themselves against the institutionalized racism that had marginalized or excluded creative and intellectual work by Yellow people in the United States.

These activist intellectuals belonged to a generation steeped in the controlling images of Asians and Asian Americans manufactured by network television and the Hollywood film industry. As such, they understood media criticism as a key component in the larger critique of racism, sexism, imperialism, and capitalism. In the essay "That Oriental Feeling" in *Roots: An Asian American Reader* (Tachiki, Wong, and Odo 1971)—the first comprehensive collection of oppositional essays that were directly influenced by radical intellectual currents within movement politics—the filmmaker Irvin Paik railed at racist representations of Asian Americans in film. Many of the essays in the anthology originally appeared in *Gidra*, an alternative newspaper with a revolutionary nationalist tilt that was staffed primarily by *Sansei* community activists based in Los Angeles (Wei 1993, 103–12). Radicals are not without a sense of humor:

The paper was named after a *"kaiju eiga,"* or "monster film," in which Godzilla and Mothra teamed up against the evil three-headed Ghidorah or "Ghidrah" (Weisser and Weisser 1997, 94–95). Also noteworthy for its seminal contribution to the formal discussion of controlling images in media was the 1971 essay *From Japs to Japanese: The Evolution of Japanese-American Stereotypes,* by Dennis Ogawa. This was followed several years later by a classic in the field by Eugene Franklin Wong, *On Visual Media Racism: Asians in the American Motion Pictures* (1978), which cleared a path for others to follow. By expressing their skepticism toward political orthodoxy and contravening official knowledge, these individuals assumed the role of what Edward Said calls the "critical intellectual" within a polity whose claims to legitimacy were badly in need of fundamental re-examination.[1]

The critique of the dominant media continued with *Counterpoint: Perspectives on Asian America* (Gee), an anthology that appeared in 1976. Like its predecessor *Roots, Counterpoint* was published by the Asian American Studies Center at the University of California, Los Angeles. Again, the essays—"Farewell to Manzanar," by Raymond Okamura; "Anna May Wong," by Judy Chu, and "Kung-Fu Fan Klub," by Irvin Paik—focused on stock media portrayals. The exception to the preoccupation with commercial media images was Ron Hirano's "Media Guerrillas." The article recounted the genesis of Visual Communications (VC), a community organization that was founded in the summer of 1969. The stylistically crude but grippingly powerful documentaries *Manzanar* (Nakamura 1971) and *Wong Sinsaang* (Wong 1971) were the fruits of these early efforts at making visible the hidden injuries of American racial politics. Visual Communications continues to nurture a vital Asian American independent film tradition as it enters its third decade.

Years later, the UCLA Asian American Studies Center and Visual Communications teamed up for a joint academic and community enterprise that resulted in *Moving the Image: Independent Asian Pacific American Media Arts,* an anthology edited by Russell Leong. Editorially inclusive almost to a fault and featuring striking graphics, the anthology's contributions ranged from scholarly essays to provocative rants by video artists, academicians, production technicians, archivists, writers, directors, graphic artists, and media activists. In an essay that followed Leong's introduction ("To Open the Future") and a detailed survey of independent media-arts centers by Stephen Gong, Renee Tajima provided needed historical perspective by meticulously charting two decades of Asian American filmmaking. Despite the unevenness in their quality, the contributions are unified by a shared vision of an alternative cinema practice that counters both the coded and overt anti-Asian racism seen in much of the product fabricated by the U.S. film industry.

In 1976, several years after Visual Communications came into being, Asian CineVision (ACV) was founded by Peter Chow, Christine Choy, and Tsui Hark (Gong 1991, 4). Initially, its organizational energy was directed toward video production by New York Chinatown residents for distribution through public-access cable television. In time, training and video production gave way to an emphasis on exhibiting and distributing independent films. The ACV also inaugurated publications such as the journal *Bridge,* further stimulating discussion of the nascent Asian American media-arts movement. The Asian American International Film Festival (AAIFF), which is sponsored by the ACV, grew to become a showcase for established talent and novices alike, giving career boosts to directors such as Wayne Wang and Ang Lee, both of whom later achieved crossover success (Xing 1998, 177–78).

In San Francisco, the National Asian American Telecommunications Association (NAATA) was founded in 1980 with funds provided by the Corporation for Public Broadcasting. This established an institutional support structure for independent film and video. One of NAATA's mandates was to develop original programming for broadcast on public television. In addition to funding film and video projects, NAATA distributes independent Asian American media to cable outlets, schools, and Public Broadcasting Service affiliates. Since 1983, NAATA has sponsored the San Francisco International Asian American Film Festival. Close to one hundred films have been exhibited at each of the more recent events. The San Francisco festival not only offers a needed venue for critics and scholars to view new work. It also serves as a forum for filmmakers, producers, distributors, educators, curators, and arts administrators to share observations and exchange information.

Return to Race

Asian American independent films have broadened considerably in scope subsequent to the media criticism that appeared in *Roots* and *Counterpoint*. Contemporary films address novel problems and integrate a host of fresh themes, including the feminist social revolution, gay men's and lesbian politics, the environmental movement, international human-rights campaigns, and a succession of single-issue initiatives that have caused seismic shifts within the larger society. In response to macro social change, academic film criticism has taken myriad theoretical and methodological turns in order to account for ever-emerging realities. Under the sway of poststructuralism, certain tendencies within theory and criticism have been unconscionably detached from political questions to a point at which "ideas and concepts circulate endlessly, with few if any external referents" (Boggs 1993, 132). But in the main, Asian American film criticism has avoided the excesses of psychoanalytic abstractions and theoreticism while holding to the primacy and determinate force of history and politics in explaining and understanding the impact of racial inequality on minority communities.

Until recently, much academic film criticism has side-stepped discussion of social conflict in favor of an elegant obscurantism, in the process under-theorizing race and ethnicity as analytical concepts.[2] Perhaps because of its "quasi-exclusive focus" on gender and psychic processes, film theory "has often elided questions of racially and culturally inflected spectatorship" (Shohat 1995, 168). But with the exhaustion of poststructuralist theory in a time of epochal crisis, a perceptible move has occurred toward regarding race and ethnicity as practical categories of analysis in the study of film, even extending to that of "White ethnics." Michael Rogin, for instance, describes how European immigrants (Jewish and Irish) used "racial masquerade" in early U.S. cinema to refashion their own "American" Anglo identity and secure "White privilege" (Rogin 1996, 128), even at the expense of Black and Asian American people. A more recent work re-evaluates such notable directors as John Ford, Frank Capra, Francis Ford Coppola, and Martin Scorsese as White *ethnics* whose films are suffused by values and attitudes that differ from (but are not necessarily incompatible with) those of the dominant WASP establishment (Lourdeaux 1990).

Yellow Criticism

The chapters in this anthology are grouped according to rubrics emerging from the productive interplay among such distinct fields as film studies, Asian American Studies, and, more broadly, cultural studies. The essays by Cynthia W. Liu and Peter X Feng, respectively, in Part I: Resignifying Asian American Bodies problematize the iconic status of Anna May Wong and Nancy Kwan in fresh ways that suggest a radical recasting and re-narrating of otherwise "Orientalist" representations.

In Part II: Negotiating Institutional Boundaries, Darrell Y. Hamamoto takes a cue from Marvin Gaye in proposing a full-frontal approach to sexual healing in racist society. Sandra Liu interprets Wayne Wang's career as one of pursuing success in the mainstream film industry in order to create space for his more politically grounded and aesthetically innovative work. Lindsey Jang offers a playful yet incisive seven-point plan of action to win Asian American filmmakers the same level of attention and respect that is accorded their overseas "cousins."

The sheer number of films on the removal and relocation of Japanese Americans during World War II makes this a genre almost unto itself. This is not to say that the multivalent meanings within each film have been exhausted, which is ably reflected in the essays gathered in Part III: Critical Approaches to Representing Japanese American Internment. In sifting through Rea Tajiri's film *History and Memory* (1991), Kent A. Ono contends that spectators participate in the production and validation of new historical knowledge. Glen Masato Mimura understands the work of Rea Tajiri, Janice Tanaka, and Lise Yasui, taken together, not as simply recovering the internment experience through documentation, but as a "generative, creative, *fictionalizing* act." Elena Tajima Creef expresses dissatisfaction with Hollywood films about the internment that feature White male characters and puts forth Steven Okazaki's Academy Award-winning documentary *Days of Waiting* (1988) as an advance over hackneyed narratives.

In Part IV: Exploring Form, the videomaker Valerie Soe draws inspiration from Guy Debord and the Situationist International's subversion of mass-mediated sign systems and places her own work in this context. Jun Xing surveys several experimental films and suggests ways in which "counter-memory" is deployed as a challenge to formulaic mainstream films and as a vehicle for forceful political statements. The dialogue between Gwendolyn Foster and Trinh T. Minh-ha explicating the director's (with Jean-Paul Bourdier) *A Tale of Love* (1995) tells of blurring the distinction between staged material and improvisation/documentary and narrative film, a legacy of the European avant-garde. Eve Oishi scrutinizes recent queer films and looks to them as harbingers of an enlivened Asian American cinema practice that forces the recognition of an integral gay men's and lesbian experience within straight, racialized, and sexualized society.

Marking a definitive break with the cultural nationalism of the early Asian American movement and many of the films it spawned, the essays in Part V: Beyond "Nation": Diasporas and Hybrid Identities both comment on and extend the refiguring of contemporary Asian American identity. Renee Tajima-Peña begins with a salutary chiding of those absorbed in the "culture of theorizing" to remind us that both "social change filmmaking" and theoretical practice must share in the commitment to political transformation. Theodore S. Gonzalves's interview with Celine Parreñas voices the necessity to move beyond the fabrication of merely "positive" images in filmmaking, which will make for a more fruitful exploration of power relations within a diverse Filipino American community aligned against the dominant society. Gina Marchetti offers keen insight into *The Wedding Banquet* (Lee 1993), a well-received film crosshatched with national, ethnic, sexual, class, and gender allegories that only incompletely resolve the dilemmas of Asian American society. Finally, Julian Stringer makes the compelling argument that recent Hong Kong films actually "represent Asian American screen identities that are in the process of formation."

Taken together, these critical pieces engage a plethora of themes and substantive questions that have occupied past and present independent Asian American filmmakers. The explosion of new and exciting work in recent years is collectively extending the Asian American filmmaking tradition by presenting novel glosses on queer identity, contemporary immigration flows, neo-imperial power relations in the Pacific, post-1965 transnationalism, and the role of politically engaged cinema. In addition, a number of films have begun grappling with one of the more dubious trends of the present: Asiaphilia. What follows is a survey of films that exemplify an evolutionary process whereby ever-changing political and historical realities inform the ideological content of cinema, which in turn feeds back into the system, ad infinitum.

Queer Identity Claims

The identity claims of gay men and lesbians that started to be voiced in the late 1960s as an extension of the civil rights movement, student protest, and counter-culture ferment have been assimilated into many recent independent films.[3] These range from an obsessive paean to the former Miss India and actress Persis Khambatta in *Love Song for Persis K.* (Kalal 1996) to a treatment of Asian American gay sexuality in the person of Andrew Cunanan, the subject of *Cunanan's Conundrum* (Gaffney 1997). The latter film archly recounts the ways in which the news media refashioned Cunanan's multiracial identity into that of a "gay narcissist" spree killer who was doubly threatening because of his ability to blend into all manner of social settings by assuming a variety of racialized personae.

While the documentary *There Is No Name for This* (Ma 1997) considers the taboo against homosexuality in both Chinese and Chinese American societies, an explicitly gay or lesbian political agenda is not necessarily foregrounded in other films. Instead, the strength of *Estrofemme* (Mah 1997) is seen in the frenzied performance of the director's San Francisco-based anarchic "queercore" band Tribe 8, while *Season of the Boys* (Tam 1997) is content to turn a voyeuristic gaze on the shirtless bodies of Asian American men playing basketball in New York City's Chinatown.[4] *Untitled (My Mama)* (Chan 1997) is a riotously affectionate characterization of a mother who dispenses advice to a lesbian daughter searching for romance in San Francisco. Ideologically explicit or not, these films put forth an aggressive counter-discourse that forces group recognition within the dominant public sphere and the ethnic communities that either devalue or disavow Asian American queer identities.[5]

Neo-Asian America

Recent immigration has increased the numbers and intra-ethnic diversity of Asian Americans, making the task of criticism—like that of mapping the shifting terrain of sexuality—more complex. This has broadened the field of films being made to reflect contemporary Asian American demographics and the multitude of issues that attend the marked change in population size, ethnic composition, and social-class origins (Hing 1997). As a direct consequence of U.S.-sponsored wars in Southeast Asia, about 830,000 Vietnamese refugees and immigrants have made their way to the neo-imperial core society. Adaptation to their collective new American destiny is of primary concern to filmmakers such as Trac Vu, whose offbeat *First Year* (1996) is a hilarious reminiscence of his exploration of homosexual identity in the land of Kmart and fatuous TV sitcoms.

By contrast, the mournful *Letters to Thien* (Trac Minh Vu 1997; Photo 1.1) lyrically reconstructs a murderous hate crime against a young Vietnamese American man at the hand of an avowed White supremacist.[6] The experience of dislocation, displacement, and deracination are themes common to many films by Vietnamese Americans. The documentary *I Am Viet Hung* (Bui 1997) captures the alienation of an elderly refugee—a master of *cai-long*, or traditional Vietnamese opera, and a respected artist in the home country—who today goes unappreciated by those within his own community.

Documenting the lives of under-represented Southeast Asian Americans is enriching the tradition of independent filmmaking. *Kelly Loves Tony* (Nakasako 1998) is a "camcorder diary" that chronicles the quotidian tribulations of two Iu Mien young people as they contend with problems of work, education, pregnancy, child-rearing, family life, and adaptation to a tough urban environment. The video shorts compiled in *Tenderloin Stories* (1996) reflect the ongoing connection between community organizations and Asian American independent media. The videos in *Tenderloin Stories*, which are without artistic pretense and technical polish, were directed by teenagers who participated in an eight-week production workshop sponsored by the Vietnamese Youth Development Center in San Francisco. *The Seven of Us* (Diep 1996) is

PHOTO 1.1.   Dao Huynh, mother of Thien Minh Ly, tells of his brutal murder in *Letters to Thien* (1997), dir. Trac Minh Vu. Photo: Fusion Pictures.

little more than a video vérité glimpse into the mundanely rich and vibrant lives of the fifteen-year-old director and her friends, who are in the process of self-discovery as they cruise the streets of San Francisco. But it is supremely effective in conveying the "suchness" of an urban underclass youth culture that is being conditioned by its members' lived experience as racial minorities, immigrants, refugees, and Southeast Asian Americans (Kiang 1995).

Consistent with the restructuring of the global capitalist economy, the U.S. Immigration and Naturalization Act of 1965 set the stage for the tenfold increase in the South Asian[7] American population between 1970 and 1990 (Sheth 1995, 169; Ong, Bonacich, and Cheng 1994, 3–35). The fourth-largest Asian American group in total numbers, foreign-born South Asian Americans are on average well educated and enjoy a level of income on par with their status as professionals. Yet Asian Indian Americans and South Asian Americans more generally suffer from relative social invisibility (Kar, Campbell, Jimenez, and Gupta 1995–96). Independent feature films such as *The Journey* (Saluja 1997), which dramatizes the spiritual crises of high-income professionals, and *Miss India Georgia* (Friedman and Grimberg 1997), a documentary in which nationality, gender, and ethnic identity are renegotiated through an annual Atlanta beauty pageant, offer necessary correctives to the fairly consistent disparagement of Asian Indian Americans in the commercial cinema. Their role in shaping U.S. regional and national history at the turn of the century only recently has been documented in film. Drawing heavily from the innovative research of Karen Isaksen Leonard (1992), *Roots in the Sand* (Hart 1998) recounts the little-known travails of Asian Indian American farmers who settled in California's Imperial Valley almost one hundred years ago.

Pacific Empire

The colonial relationship between the United States and the Philippines is basic to understanding recent films by Filipino Americans. With between 40,000 to 50,000 Filipinos entering the United States annually since 1976, and with the Filipino American population totaling about 1.4 million as of 1990, immigration from the Philippines has outpaced that of all other Asian groups (Espiritu 1995, 25). The deification of American popular culture by many Filipinos and its link with the larger system of imperial control is satirized in *Back to Bataan Beach* (1994) by Ernesto M. Foronda.

A spoof of the mindless 1960s beach movies that featured two wholesome Italian Americans (Frankie Avalon and Annette Funicello), the all-Filipino American cast in *Back to Bataan Beach* assume lead roles in a mock advertising trailer for the film. Of course, "Bataan" is associated with the infamous "death march" of American and Filipino soldiers captured in battle by the Japanese enemy during World War II. But through broad retro humor, the film suggests that life under U.S. neocolonial rule has been less than a pleasurable romp through surf and sand, even for those Filipino Americans who have managed to leave behind the dire poverty and political instability of their former homeland.

A poignant take on a different aspect of Filipino American immigrant life is captured in the ninety-minute feature *Disoriented* (1997; see Photo 1.2), directed by and starring Francisco Aliwalas. The son of a physician, Aliwalas grew up in Albany, New York, in relative isolation from a large Asian American community. But it is this sense of disconnection and alienation that provides both the underlying theme and the title for the film. Racial, gender, sexual, religious, and geographical tensions come into play in the movie, beginning with an absent husband and father who abandoned his devoutly Catholic wife, Lucia Cordova (Potri Ranka Manis), for a blonde woman. Danger Cordova (Wayland Quintero) is the prodigal son who has returned to Albany after working in New York City as a transvestite waitress at a Chinese restaurant.

While back at home awaiting the results of an HIV test, Danger renews his relationship to his younger brother West Cordova (Aliwalas), who holds a job as a delivery person for a local restaurant. Filial duty and personal inclination are at war in West, whose mother wants him to become a medical doctor. West, in the meantime, tries to rescue an aspiring Japanese model named Minako (Kayoko Takahashi) from her "rice king" boyfriend, Manny (Sutton Keany). Infatuated with Minako, West tries to prevent her from undergoing the blepharoplasty surgical procedure that she believes will advance her career.

PHOTO 1.2.   Potri Ranka Manis and Francisco Aliwalas with *lumpia* in *Disoriented* (1997), dir. Francisco Aliwalas. Photo: Taylor Morrison.

Once West finally declares to his mother that he will not pursue a career in medicine, and after Danger comes out to her, she too finds liberation in the person of Speedy Gonzalez (Jojo Gonzalez), a car-wash worker who, like her, hails from Leyte. "*Kabayan*," they exclaim upon learning of their common regional origins. Global diaspora, biculturality, border crossing, multiple locations, boundary violation, sexual politics, sociology of the body, postcoloniality, transnational identity, gender performativity: *Disoriented* is a textbook of poststructuralist sponge concepts sans discursive tedium.

Post-1965

Like *Disoriented*, the feature *Shopping for Fangs* (Lee and Lin 1997) brings to bear the material consequences of post-1965 Asian immigration to the United States. It depicts a hyper-cosmopolitan reality peopled by young, cellular telephone-wielding, transnational migrants living within a globalized popular culture in which both Hong Kong cinema and U.S. movies loom large. They hang out at ethnic mini-malls—from Alhambra in the heavily Chinese American-immigrant, suburban San Gabriel Valley to the substantially "Whiter" community of Westwood in Southern California—while mired in a therapeutic culture characterized by sexual repression and romantic entanglement. In contrast to films of an earlier vintage, *Shopping for Fangs* reflects the postmodern, global cosmopolitan "deterritorialization of culture" and the transnational character of memory and "home" among the post-1965 generation of Asian Americans (Buell 1994, 196). Indeed, the recomposition of the contemporary Asian American community is seen in the personal histories of the film's directors, Quentin Lee and Justin Lin, themselves. Lee grew up in Hong Kong and moved to Canada before coming to the United States, while Lin was born in Taiwan but raised in Orange County, California.[8]

The ninety-minute feature *Yellow* (C. Lee 1997) treads more familiar ground in its depiction of intergenerational conflict between Sin Lee (Michael Daeho Chung) and his immigrant father (Soon-Tek Oh). After Sin fails to win a college scholarship, his nutty friends devise harebrained schemes to raise tuition money for their beleaguered buddy. Underlying the many uproariously loopy comedic moments—such as when the none-too-bright Yo Yo (Jason J. Tobin) has difficulty remembering his access code while trying to withdraw money from an ATM—is a pathos derived from the sacrifices of the immigrant generation and the children upon whom they pin their hopes for success in American society. The lovingly re-created milieu and the characters who populate it have been drawn from the director's own experience working at the grocery store operated by his parents for more than twenty years.

Transnational Identity

Explorations of identity have been integral to Asian American film from its inception. In racist society, the ceaseless self-interrogation of identity is not merely an idle intellectual exercise or a salve for hurt feelings, as right-wing and even supposedly progressive critics are wont to imply. Nor does it necessarily signal the abandonment of a class-based radical politics, as some leftists bemoan (Gitlin 1996).[9] Rather, it is a matter of social survival. Both politically and at the level of individual psychology, the twin questions of identity and nationality have presented an ongoing dilemma to Asian Americans. For Asian American history—marked by a pattern of exclusion, relocation, deportation, and containment—has been shaped by the group identity imposed and enforced by the "racial state."[10] Perhaps it is for this reason that an earlier generation of political activists, artists, and intellectuals who had direct experience of deliberate misrecognition by the racial state sustained the illusion of a unitary "American" self rooted exclusively in U.S. society. The classic case is that of Japanese Americans who, bearing the face of the "enemy," were interned during World War II.[11]

In contrast to the earlier push to privilege "Americanness," many post-1965 directors revel in the fluidity of social identities and permeability of national borders. Unlike old-school Asian American films, these post-1965 films often simply assume a manifestly transnational identity. The director M. Trinh Nguyen, for example, has made Vietnam the subject of her films *Xích-Lô* (1995) and *Tiger's Apprentice* (1998). The latter takes as its subject Nguyen's great-uncle, a revered folk-medicine specialist whose craft has fallen into disrepute among government officials who deride such traditional practices because, they believe, the practices diminish the stature of Vietnam in the eyes of the advanced nations from whom they seek approval. Other than the directorial presence of Nguyen herself, the documentary has no specifically Asian American component. But in tallying the direct and hidden costs of the Vietnam War borne by the Vietnamese people at home and dispersed overseas, *Xích-Lô* and *Tiger's Apprentice* cannot help but expose the double-consciousness of refugee identity.

Han Chee/Sweet Potato (Cheng 1998) is directed by a second-generation Taiwanese American, yet the documentary revisits her parents' homeland and its history. Taiwan's tortuous history is shaped by European colonization, Japanese occupation, domination by mainland immigrants via the Guomindang (Chinese Nationalist Party), U.S. military clientage, and the current tenuous status as a nation-state vis-à-vis the People's Republic of China. Jean Cheng, who had little knowledge of Taiwanese history and politics before starting *Han Chee,* suggests that the film "tells us something about democracy and about nations and personal identity and how you choose collective identity" (Loh 1999, 47). Similarly, a dispossessed local named Tseng Tso Choi who leaves hand-painted anti-government screeds in public spaces, as seen in *King of Kowloon* (Egan and Shen 1998), would have escaped the attention of those outside Hong Kong were it not for the transnational orientation of the film's co-director.

A Canadian film by a former revolutionary propaganda artist from the People's Republic of China offers yet another perspective on displacement and dislocation. Through the deft use of bold graphics and animation to complement its narrative line, the serio-comic *Sunrise over Tiananmen Square* (1998) traces the road that the director, Wang Shui-Bo, traveled from committed revolutionary to Buddhist-inspired filmmaker. Recent films such as these evince the transnational orientation and bicultural consciousness held by a substantial segment of the contemporary Asian American population as a consequence of recent immigration. Linked to the new immigration from Asia is the increased presence of binational global professionals ("astronauts") and large numbers of students ("parachute children") pursuing educational opportunities in the United States (Wong 1998).[12]

Yellowphilia

As an expressive form integral to Asian American cultural politics since the late 1960s, independent films to varying degrees have confronted the basal anti-Yellow racism of the dominant society. The historical struggle against White racism has been the unifying, if not always the manifest, theme of independent Asian American film, whether documentary, narrative, or experimental in form. In the "post–Civil Rights" era, however, Asian Americans face an insidious twist on the traditional antipathy toward "Yellows": Asiaphilia. The fetishization of all things Asian in popular culture—owing in part to the rise of Hong Kong cinema, with its commanding, action-oriented personalities; the ubiquity of female Asian American television-news anchors and fashion models in the U.S. media; Asian food fadism among many urban professionals; and the acceptance by young people of such imports as *anime* (Japanese animation)—seemingly has neutralized the more virulent manifestations of Asiaphobia.[13]

Whereas "Orientalist" discourse in cinema once helped mobilize and sustain support for U.S. and European imperium in the Near East and Asia, Asiaphilia is a deceptively benign ideological construct that naturalizes and justifies the systematic appropriation of cultural property and expressive forms created by Yellow people. The classic colonial system of unequal exchange was based on the theft of human and material resources from the underdeveloped countries of the periphery and its removal to the imperial core society. The politics of cultural appropriation extends this history of exploitation into the "post-industrial" information economy, in which the expressive art of subaltern peoples is commodified and converted into corporate wealth. The commodity postmodernist celebration of ludic semiosis, cultural hybridity, and textual poaching ignores the unequal and exploitative power relationship between corporate media and communities of color responsible for the creation of oppositional cultural practices and novel expressive forms. "While it is true that no culture is fixed and that exchange among cultures has taken place throughout history," writes Coco Fusco (1995, 71), "not to recognize historical imbalances and their influence is *the* strategical evasion that enables the already empowered to naturalize their advantage." In this statement, Fusco objects to certain strains within contemporary cultural theory that in effect give license to appropriative acts committed against historically exploited non-White communities in the name of an anti-"essentialist" philosophical critique.

Recent films such as *Seeking Beautiful Asian Women* (Wong 1997) and *Take-Out* (Lei 1997) expose the benevolent racism that underlies contemporary Asiaphilic White desire, a new twist in what Frank Chin and Jeffrey Paul Chan (1972) identified as "racist love." In *Take-Out*, boorish White diners finally get their comeuppance at a Chinese American restaurant, courtesy of a disgruntled worker who decides that he has had his fill of condescension and racial servitude. *Seeking Beautiful Asian Women*, a witty short film, tries to disentangle the knotted strands of gender, racial, and sexual politics. *Beyond Asiaphilia* (Soe 1997) poses the question of whether an Asian American woman of suburban origins—after a lifetime of racialized lust for blue-eyed White men—can consider herself an Asiaphile when she becomes enthralled by the Hong Kong movie stars Chow Yun-Fat and Jet Li, thereafter dreaming desirously of at least these Yellow men. "I live with a blue-eyed man and I dream of Chinese movie stars," says Soe in her autobiographical meditation.

Asian American adoptees are at once the victims and beneficiaries of U.S. military adventurism and capitalist underdevelopment of Asian countries. After thousands of children were orphaned during the Korean War, Holt International Children's Services "pioneered the concept of intercountry adoption," which now extends to China, Hong Kong, India, the Philippines, Thailand, and Vietnam (Holt International Children's Services 1999). The large-scale placement of Asian children with predominately Euro-American families has resulted in a critical mass of adoptees who are beginning to ask questions about their place within the larger U.S. society. The documentary film has proved effective in laying bare the conflicting emotions, loyalties, and affiliations of at least two Korean American adoptees. A work in progress by the UCLA film student Nathan Adolfson titled *Passing Through* (1999) takes a light-hearted approach to his life as the adopted son of White parents who raised their child as if his Asian racial identity was irrelevant. Adolfson is loving toward his mother and father nevertheless, despite their limited understanding of his search for origins, which takes him to South Korea for a reunion with members of his birth family. Tammy Tolle (Chu Dong Soo), director of *Searching for Go-Hyang* (1998), was adopted along with her twin sister Amy (Chu Ok Soo) by a White couple who tried to mold them into perfect Oriental children. She judges her parents harshly after having endured "mental and physical" abuse made bearable only through sharing the suffering with her sister.[14] In an emotional sequence brimming with tears born of separation and dislocation, the sisters reconnect with their Korean birth parents. Adopted children from China now outnumber those from South Korea, but Asians remain the preference of those seeking to adopt.

Engaged Cinema

While allowing for a politics of identity devoted to the more particularistic concerns of besieged racial minorities defending against the subsumptive dynamic of the world capitalist system, a fully mobilized Asian American cultural politics transcends narrow group interest and extends beyond national borders to recognize the plight of people held captive to tyranny overseas. This expanded notion of an Asian American critical practice drives the secretly filmed *We Are Not Beggars* (Qin 1996), which portrays the harsh existence of children sent by their impoverished parents to the city as street performers. This stark example of uneven economic development in China enables the viewer analytically to connect the local and the global, a necessary step in understanding the geographically distant but compelling social forces that impinge on the lives of Asians in the United States.

Similarly, the tragedy of 130,000 Tibetan refugees who have taken flight since the Chinese takeover of their homeland, as shown in *Strange Spirit: One Country's Occupation* (Novick and Novick 1997), forces a re-evaluation of contemporary global power politics and its relationship to international trade between the United States and the People's Republic of China, which totaled $75 billion in 1997. U.S. corporate investment stands at $20 billion, an eightfold increase since the 1989 massacre of pro-democracy demonstrators at Tiananmen Square ("Human Rights and Business as Usual" 1998). More directly, the documentaries *Islands on Fire* (1996) and *Indonesia: One Struggle, One Change* (1997) by Maria Luisa Mendonça and Medea Benjamin point to U.S. complicity with an authoritarian client state engaged in the routine violation of human rights to protect the investment interests of American transnationals such as Arco, Mobil, Merrill Lynch, Freeport-McMoRan, and the notorious Nike Corporation (Barnet and Cavanagh 1995, 323–28).[15]

Disengaged Cinema

Despite the almost thirty-year gap that separates their release dates, Robert Nakamura's early experimental film *Manzanar* (1971) and *Rabbit in the Moon* (1998), directed by

Emiko Omori, are connected by a straight line. Both films approach the internment of Japanese Americans as one of the defining moments in U.S. history, but they take different stylistic approaches in grappling with a shared trauma. The rough-hewn expressionism of *Manzanar* cries out with the pain of discovery at a treachery so profound that an entire generation suppressed it from memory. *Rabbit in the Moon* begins by recounting the injuries and losses sustained by the director's family, but it then broadens in scope to illustrate the redemptive effects of political opposition to the internment by Japanese American draft resisters. Interviews with Frank Emi, Hiroshi Kashiwagi, Yoshio Harry Ueno, and others bear witness to their running battles with both the U.S. government and collaborationist forces within the Japanese American community.

Films such as *Rabbit in the Moon* hew to the spirit and ideals of an independent Asian American cinema as envisioned by those who founded the movement; an emancipatory, progressive edge, however, is not necessarily evident in the work of more than a few current directors. An irony has emerged: By bringing the Asian American presence to the fore, the independent movement has helped pave the way for filmmakers whose aspirations are unapologetically mainstream and commercial in nature. Such is the case of *A Good Lie* (Eltanal 1998), a seventeen-minute student film that bears the hallmarks of a Hollywood audition piece. To the director's credit, the film does feature Yellow lead characters. But for all its high production values and suspenseful writing, it says precious little about Asian American life.

That recent directors have shown savvy in reaching beyond Asian American topics and themes to earn establishment validation is seen by the three successive Academy Awards won by Jessica Yu in 1997, Chris Tashima in 1998, and Keiko Ibi in 1999.[16] Indeed, the film produced by Tashima, *Visas and Virtue* (Donahue 1997), appropriates a *Japanese* story about the so-called Japanese Schindler, which has nothing to do with Japanese *Americans* as such. Conversely, Ibi is a Japanese national working in the United States who chose to document the lives of Jewish American senior citizens on the Lower East Side of Manhattan. Ironically, all three Oscar winners are members of a racial group that is more often the object of racist ridicule and scorn in the few Hollywood movies where they even appear at all.[17] For three years running, the Academy of Motion Picture Arts and Sciences has conveniently forgotten its history of anti-Asian racism in film and congratulated itself by giving token recognition to Yellows who have demonstrated a willingness to play by its rules. Rule number one: The life worlds of Asian and Asian American peoples must always be mediated by Whiteness.[18]

Beyond Hollywood, *Three Seasons* (Bui 1999) received all manner of accolades at the Sundance Film Festival. Strangely, the film effaces nearly all traces of the Vietnam War, save for the moody presence of James Hager (Harvey Keitel), a former U.S. marine in search of the daughter he sired while overseas. Each of the principal characters finds redemption in some fashion by the conclusion of the film, including the whore Lan (Zöe Bui) who beds foreigners at plush hotels under the protective eye of a *xích-lô* driver named Hai (Don Duong). Hai offers prize money that he has won in a race against other pedicab drivers to Lan in order to sleep with her. But beyond all credulity, he declines sex and instead asks only to watch Lan as she slumbers. Later, she returns the money when Hai comes calling for her.

If Vietnam is symbolized by a fallen woman who is compromised during the war out of sheer self-survival, then *Three Seasons* helps restore her to grace by dramatizing the redemptive decency of the common man as represented by the *xích-lô* driver. With an aesthetic deriving from what might be described as "market socialist realism," the film applies a dreamy chamber-of-commerce gloss to a post-imperial Vietnam that is ripe for higher-order pimping out to transnational corporations such as those whose lurid signs are shown as already dominating the Saigon cityscape.

The career trajectories of filmmakers such as Wayne Wang and Ang Lee illustrate the impossibility of pinning down (even if this were desirable) the idea of an Asian American cinema. They began by making exceptional films that brought the textures of Asian American lived experience to the screen in highly original ways, but both then made self-conscious moves to break out of the ethnic ghetto. That meant directing movies with White Americans or White Englishmen as the primary focus.[19] Those directors who decide not to foreground Asian American characters and themes have made a political choice to hide behind the mask of a "color-blind" race-neutrality in the name of a false universalism and bourgeois humanism that nevertheless defers to Whiteness as the presumptive standard of superiority. This holds true even for alterna-director Gregg Araki, who has shunned popular acceptance but whose movies *The Living End* (1992) and *The Doom Generation* (1995) dwell exclusively on outer-edge White teen/young adult angst (Araki 1994).

Countervisions

As suggested by this survey of recent narrative, documentary, and experimental films, the restructuring of the world capitalist system under U.S. leadership has been of singular relevance to the social, political, and cultural life of Asian Americans. During the course of this thoroughgoing upheaval, the art of independent Asian American film has been a strategically visible and active presence in the running battle against racial oppression, political–economic exploitation, marginalization within the dominant culture, and related inequalities that define U.S. society. Moreover, the independent counter-media have done much to revitalize the public sphere, which has been made moribund by the sheer volume of news and entertainment simulacra generated by anti-democratic, corporate mega-media combines (McChesney 1997).

Within a postmodern political project aligned against the local and global predations of techno-capitalism with its corporate-sponsored spectacle commodities, a radical cultural politics "attempts to undo the enculturation of the dominant culture by providing new ways of seeing, feeling, thinking, talking, and being" (Best and Kellner 1997, 277). The cultural criticism of expressive forms such as film are part and parcel of a greater transformative political project guided by grounded social theory. For this reason, the critical enterprise requires not only formal and aesthetic considerations of cinema, but also the identification, explication, and activation of the latent political meanings inherent in all film. From the germ of critical awareness springs progressive political activity that forces further democratization of culture and society.

Evolving in tandem over a period of thirty years, Asian American independent film-making and criticism have helped forge an oppositional cultural practice that contests a mutually reinforcing system of race, class, and gender oppression within national borders. At the same time, the films and the practice of criticism extend the critique to include the global system of inequality between the capitalist metropole and the underdeveloped world. Against the monopoly of news and entertainment by global media conglomerates, these efforts become all the more crucial in carving out political space for heterodox visions and voices.[20] This collection of critical essays, and the array of films that the essays discuss, fall within this tradition in that they aspire to advance the truths, little and great, that coalesce to subvert regimes of control. By posing a direct challenge to the interlocking formations of subordination, the cultural politics of an engaged Asian American film and criticism adumbrate the emancipatory strategies that move us closer toward the realization of democratic ideals.

Notes

1. Said (1996, 11–12) writes: "The intellectual is an individual endowed with a faculty for representing, embodying, articulating a message, a view, an attitude, philosophy or opinion to, as well for, a public. And this role has an edge to it, and cannot be played without a sense of being someone whose place it is publicly to raise embarrassing questions, to confront orthodoxy and dogma (rather than to produce them), to someone who cannot easily be co-opted by governments or corporations, and whose *raison d'être* is to represent all those people and issues that are routinely forgotten or swept under the rug. The intellectual does so on the basis of universal principles: that all human beings are entitled to expect decent standards of behavior concerning freedom and justice from worldly powers or nations, and that deliberate or inadvertent violations of these standards need to be testified and fought against courageously."

2. A historical survey of "race" and "ethnicity" as explanatory concepts can be found in Banton (1998).

3. A popular account of the cultural, social, and political currents influencing the "gay awakening" is given in Berman (1997, 123–94).

4. Mah speaks to issues of identity, sexuality, and subculture in Alcantara, et al. (1997).

5. For a discussion of the "politics of identity and recognition," see Calhoun (1995, 193–230).

6. Note that the directors Trac Vu and Trac Minh Vu are two different people.

7. The regional descriptor "South Asian" here refers to India, Pakistan, and Bangladesh.

8. Panel discussion, San Francisco International Asian American Film Festival, March 8, 1997.

9. A response to conservative and leftist critiques of so-called identity politics is found in Kelley (1997, 123): "Although identity politics sometimes works as a fetter on genuine multiracial/multicultural alliances, I believe it has also enriched our conception of class, not moved us away from it."

10. The concept of the "racial state" owes to Omi and Winant (1994).

11. See Chapter 3, "Looking Like the Enemy," in Ancheta (1998).

12. The U.S. State Department issues 13,000 visas each year to Chinese students, 90 percent of whom do not return home (Farley 1999).

13. More than 2,000 *anime* titles are licensed for distribution in the United States (Server 1999, 84–89).

14. Panel discussion, San Francisco International Asian American Film Festival, March 14, 1999.

15. Organized protest against human-rights abuses in Indonesia yielded a victory in July 1998, when the U.S. Senate unanimously passed a resolution (led by the Democrats Russ Feingold of Wisconsin and Jack Reed of Rhode Island) requesting that President Bill Clinton pressure the regime "to promote and protect the human rights and fundamental freedoms of all the people of Indonesia and East Timor" ("A Senator to Praise" 1998).

16. Respectively, the films are *Breathing Lessons: The Life and Work of Mark O'Brien* (Yu 1996); *Visas and Virtue* (Donahue 1997); and *The Personals: Improvisations on Romance in the Golden Years* (Ibi 1999).

17. The actor Michael Douglas enjoys the distinction of being Hollywood's top Asian and Asian American basher, beginning with *Black Rain* (Scott 1989). In *Falling Down* (Schumacher 1993), the hostility leveled at a Korean American storekeeper by Bill Foster—also known as D-FENS—(Douglas) stands as a "doubly racist attempt to court an African American audience alongside angry white males" (Davies and Smith 1997, 37). The authors also argue that the subtext of the film *Disclosure* (Levinson 1994) is rooted in the anxiety over the threat to the United States of "Pacific Rim economies" (ibid., 39).

18. Prior to the recent run of Asian and Asian American Oscar winners, *Days of Waiting* (Okazaki 1988) told the story of 120,000 imprisoned Japanese Americans from the perspective of Estelle Ishigo, a White woman who voluntarily accompanied her husband to the Heart Mountain, Wyoming, concentration camp. The film was given an Academy Award for Best Documentary Short Subject in 1990.

19. See Wang's *Smoke* (1995) and *Blue in the Face* (1995), and Lee's *Sense and Sensibility* (1995) and *The Ice Storm* (1997). Although his earlier projects bear the stamp of Taiwan, Lee is regarded in these pages as an Asian American filmmaker. Not only is he a longtime resident of the United States, but his early films address Asian American themes. Indeed, Lee embodies the transnational nature of Asian American life ways within a globalized system of film production (Ma 1998, 144–58).

20. Schatz (1997, 101) observes, "The concentration of media control in the hands of a conglomerate cartel grows increasingly worrisome, due less to any fears of the political clout of the new media moguls and their communication empires, than to their blithe disregard for the political—i.e., for the free and open flow of information so crucial to social and economic justice."

Works Cited

Alcantara, Margarita, Leslie Mah, and Selena Whang. 1997. "Yellowdykecore: Queer, Punk 'n' Asian." Pp. 216–32 in *Dragon Ladies: Asian American Feminists Breathe Fire*, ed. Sonia Shah. Boston: South End Press.

Araki, Gregg. 1994. *The Living End/Totally F***ed Up*. New York: William Morrow.

Ancheta, Angelo N. 1998. *Race, Rights, and the Asian American Experience*. New Brunswick, N.J.: Rutgers University Press.

Barnet, Richard J., and John Cavanagh. 1995. *Global Dreams: Imperial Corporations and the New World Order*. New York: Touchstone.

Banton, Michael P. 1998. *Racial Theories*. 2nd ed. Cambridge: Cambridge University Press.

Berman, Paul. 1997. *A Tale of Two Utopias: The Political Journey of the Generation of 1968*. New York: W. W. Norton.

Best, Steven, and Douglas Kellner. 1997. *The Postmodern Turn.* New York: Guilford Press.

Boggs, Carl. 1993. *Intellectuals and the Crisis of Modernity.* Albany: State University of New York Press.

Buell, Frederick. 1994. *National Culture and the New Global System.* Baltimore, Md.: Johns Hopkins University Press.

Calhoun, Craig. 1995. *Critical Social Theory: Culture, History, and the Challenge of Difference.* Cambridge, Mass.: Blackwell.

Chin, Frank, and Jeffrey Paul Chan. 1972. "Racist Love." Pp. 65–79 in *Seeing Through Shuck,* ed. Richard Kostelanetz. New York: Ballantine.

Davies, Jude, and Carol R. Smith. 1997. *Gender, Ethnicity and Sexuality in Contemporary American Film.* Edinburgh: Keele University Press.

Espiritu, Yen Le. 1995. *Filipino American Lives.* Philadelphia: Temple University Press.

Farley, Maggie. "Shanghai Youths Test Welcome Mat in U.S." *Los Angeles Times* Online (http://www.latimes.com/HOME/NEWS/NATION/UPDATES/lat_students990503.htm), May 3.

Fusco, Coco. 1995. *English Is Broken Here: Notes on Cultural Fusion in the Americas.* New York: New Press.

Gee, Emma, ed. 1976. *Counterpoint: Perspectives on Asian America.* Los Angeles: Asian American Studies Center, University of California, Los Angeles.

Gitlin, Todd. 1996. *The Twilight of Common Dreams: Why America Is Wracked by Culture Wars.* New York: Henry Holt.

Gong, Stephen. 1991. "A History in Progress: Asian American Media Arts Centers 1970–1990." Pp. 1–9 in *Moving the Image: Independent Asian Pacific American Media Arts,* ed. Russell Leong. Los Angeles: UCLA Asian American Studies Center and Visual Communications, Southern California Asian American Studies Central.

Hing, Bill Ong. 1997. "Making and Remaking Asian Pacific America." Pp. 315–23 in *New American Destines: A Reader in Contemporary Asian and Latino Immigration,* ed. Darrell Y. Hamamoto and Rodolfo D. Torres. New York: Routledge.

Holt International Children's Services Web site. 1999. "Introduction to Holt" (http://www.holt-intl.org/intro.html). May 15.

"Human Rights and Business as Usual." 1998. *Progressive* (August): 8–10.

Kar, Snehendu B., Kevin Campbell, Armando Jimenez, and Sangeeta R. Gupta. 1995–96. "Invisible Americans: An Exploration of Indo-American Quality of Life." *Amerasia Journal* 21, no. 3: 25–52.

Kelley, Robin D. G. 1997. *Yo' Mama's Disfunktional! Fighting the Culture Wars in Urban America.* Boston: Beacon Press.

Kiang, Peter Nien-chu. 1995. "Bicultural Strengths and Struggles of Southeast Asian Americans in School." Pp. 201–25 in *Culture and Difference: Critical Perspectives on the Bicultural Experience in the United States,* ed. Antonia Darder. Westport, Conn.: Bergin & Garvey.

Leonard, Karen Isaksen. 1992. *Making Ethnic Choices: California's Punjabi Mexican Americans.* Philadelphia: Temple University Press.

Leong, Russell, ed. 1991. *Moving the Image: Independent Asian Pacific American Media Arts.* Los Angeles: UCLA Asian American Studies Center and Visual Communications, Southern California Asian American Studies Central.

Loh, Grace. 1999. "A Land Between: Jean Cheng's *Han Chee* Explores Taiwanese Nationhood and Identity." *Release Print* (March): 38, 39, 47.

Lourdeaux, Lee. 1990. *Italian and Irish Filmmakers in America: Ford, Capra, Coppola, and Scorsese.* Philadelphia: Temple University Press.

McChesney, Robert W. 1997. *Corporate Media and the Threat to Democracy.* New York: Seven Stories Press.

Ma, Sheng-mei. 1998. *Immigrant Subjectivities in Asian American and Asian Diaspora Literatures.* Albany: State University of New York Press.

Ogawa, Dennis M. 1971. *From Japs to Japanese: The Evolution of Japanese-American Stereotypes.* Berkeley, Calif.: McCutchan Publishing.

Omi, Michael, and Howard Winant. 1994. *Racial Formation in the United States: From the 1960s to the 1990s.* New York: Routledge.

Ong, Paul, Edna Bonacich, and Lucie Cheng, ed. 1994. *The New Asian Immigration in Los Angeles and Global Restructuring.* Philadelphia: Temple University Press.

Rogin, Michael. 1996. *Blackface, White Noise: Jewish Immigrants in the Hollywood Melting Pot.* Berkeley: University of California Press.

Said, Edward W. 1996. *Representations of the Intellectual: The 1993 Reith Lectures.* New York: Vintage.

Schatz, Thomas. 1997. "The Return of the Hollywood Studio System." Pp. 73–106 in *Conglomerates and the Media,* ed. Erik Barnouw, et al. New York: New Press.

"A Senator to Praise." 1998. *Progressive* (September): 10.

Server, Lee. 1999. *Asian Pop Cinema: Bombay to Tokyo.* San Francisco: Chronicle Books.

Sheth, Manju. 1995. "Asian Indian Americans." Pp. 169–98 in *Asian Americans: Contemporary Trends and Issues,* ed. Pyong Gap Min. Thousand Oaks, Calif.: Sage.

Shohat, Ella. 1995. "The Struggle over Representation: Casting, Coalitions, and the Politics of Identification." Pp. 166–78 in *Late Imperial Culture,* ed. Román del la Campa, E. Ann Kaplan, and Michael Sprinker. London: Verso.

Tachiki, Amy, Eddie Wong, and Franklin Odo, ed., with Buck Wong. 1971. *Roots: An Asian American Reader.* Los Angeles: Regents of the University of California.

Wei, William. 1993. *The Asian American Movement.* Philadelphia: Temple University Press.

Weisser, Thomas, and Yuko Mihara Weisser. 1997. *Japanese Cinema Encyclopedia: Horror, Fantasy and Science Fiction Films.* Miami: Vital Books.

Wong, Bernard. 1998. *Ethnicity and Entrepreneurship: The New Chinese Immigrants in the San Francisco Bay Area.* Boston: Allyn and Bacon.

Wong, Eugene Franklin. 1978. *On Visual Media Racism: Asians in the American Motion Pictures.* New York: Arno Press.

Xing, Jun. 1998. *Asian America Through the Lens: History, Representations, and Identity.* Walnut Creek, Calif: AltaMira Press.

Films and Videos Cited

Adolfson, Nathan. 1999. *Passing Through.* In progress.

Aliwalas, Francisco. 1997. *Disoriented.* Pinatubo, Inc.

Araki, Gregg. 1992. *The Living End.* October Films.

———. 1995. *The Doom Generation.* UGC/Teen Angst.

Bui, Diep N. 1997. *I Am Viet Hung.* No distributor.

Bui, Tony. 1999. *Three Seasons.* October Films.

Chan, Lynne. 1997. *Untitled (My Mama).* No distributor.

Cheng, Jean. 1998. *Han Chee/Sweet Potato.* Sweet Potato Productions.

Diep, Sarah. 1996. *The Seven of Us* (from *Tenderloin Stories*). NAATA Distribution.

Donahue, Chris. 1997. *Visas and Virtue.* NAATA Distribution.

Egan, Martin, and Joanne Shen. 1998. *King of Kowloon.* No distributor.

Eltanal, Ronald. 1998. *A Good Lie.* University of Southern California.

Friedman, Daniel, and Sharon Grimberg. 1997. *Miss India Georgia*. Urban Life Productions.

Foronda, Ernesto M. 1994. *Back to Bataan Beach*. NAATA Distribution.

Gaffney, Stuart, 1997. *Cunanan's Conundrum*. Fever Films.

Hart, Jayasri. 1998. *Roots in the Sand*. Hart Films.

Ibi, Keiko. 1999. *The Personals: Improvisations on Romance in the Golden Years*. Home Box Office (HBO).

Kalal, David Dasharath. 1996. *Love Song for Persis K.* Third World Newsreel.

Lee, Ang. 1993. *The Wedding Banquet*. Good Machine.

———. 1995. *Sense and Sensibility*. Mirage/Columbia.

———. 1997. *The Ice Storm*. Good Machine/Fox Searchlight.

Lee, Chris Chan. 1997. *Yellow*. Yellow Productions.

Lee, Quentin, and Justin Lin. 1997. *Shopping for Fangs*. de/center communications inc.

Lei, Jeffrey. 1997. *Take-Out*. Take-out Productions.

Levinson, Barry. 1994. *Disclosure*. Baltimore/Constant/Warner Bros.

Ma, Ming-Yuen S. 1997. *There Is No Name for This*. No distributor.

Mah, Leslie. 1997. *Estrofemme*. Wooden Dragon Productions.

Mendonça, Maria Luisa, and Medea Benjamin. 1996. *Islands on Fire*. NAATA Distribution.

———. 1997. *Indonesia: One Struggle, One Change*. NAATA Distribution.

Nakamura, Robert A. 1971. *Manzanar*. Visual Communications. NAATA Distribution.

Nakasako, Spencer. 1998. *Kelly Loves Tony*. NAATA Distribution.

Nguyen, M. Trinh. 1995. *Xích-Lô*. NAATA Distribution.

———. 1998. *Tiger's Apprentice*. M. T. Nguyen Productions.

Novick, Ronny, and Rebecca Novick. 1997. *Strange Spirit: One Country's Occupation*. Two Bat Productions.

Okazaki, Steven. 1988. *Days of Waiting: The Life and Art of Estelle Ishigo*. NAATA.

Omori, Emiko. 1998. *Rabbit in the Moon*. Wabi-Sabi Productions.

Qin, Wen-jie. 1996. *We Are Not Beggars*. Documentary Educational Resources.

Saluja, Harish. 1997. *The Journey*. New Ray Films.

Schumacher, Joel. 1993. *Falling Down*. Warner Bros.

Scott, Ridley. 1989. *Black Rain*. Paramount.

Soe, Valerie. 1997. *Beyond Asiaphilia*. Oxygen Productions.

Tajiri, Rea. 1991. *History and Memory: For Akiko and Takashige*. Electronic Arts Intermix.

Tam, Ho. 1997. *Season of the Boys*. No distributor.

Tenderloin Stories. 1996. NAATA Distribution.

Tolle, Tammy (Chu Dong Soo). 1998. *Searching for Go-Hyang*. Women Make Movies.

Trinh, T. Minh-ha, and Jean-Paul Bourdier. 1995. *A Tale of Love*. Women Make Movies.

Vu, Trac. 1996. *First Year*. NAATA Distribution.

Vu, Trac Minh. 1997. *Letters to Thien*. Fusion Pictures.

Wang, Shui-Bo. 1998. *Sunrise over Tiananmen Square*. National Film Board of Canada.

Wang, Wayne. 1995. *Smoke*. Miramax/Nippon/Smoke.

——— , and Paul Auster. 1995. *Blue in the Face*. Blue in the Face/Miramax.

Wong, Eddie. 1971. *Wong Sinsaang*. Visual Communications.

Wong, Telly. 1997. *Seeking Beautiful Asian Women*. Electric Shadow Pictures.

Yu, Jessica. 1996. *Breathing Lessons: The Life and Work of Mark O'Brien*. Fanlight Productions/ Pacific News Service.

Part I

Resignifying Asian
American Bodies

Cynthia W. Liu

2   When Dragon Ladies Die, Do They
      Come Back as Butterflies?
      Re-Imagining Anna May Wong

Both reviled and revered, the actress Anna May Wong continues to pique the imaginations of global filmgoing audiences long after her death nearly forty years ago. As the inspiration for a cameo in a contemporary film, as the model for a doll, and as the muse to several contemporary literary interpretations of her work, Anna May Wong casts a shadow that extends to the present day. Yet it is not the facts of her life and film career but her ongoing importance to the writers David Henry Hwang, Jessica Hagedorn, and John Yau, all working in the aftermath of the Asian American movement rooted in the 1960s and 1970s, that I will be addressing.

These authors' responses as consumers and producers of Anna May Wong's iconic status complicate our understanding of how these images circulate. By examining Asian American depictions of Anna May Wong and her career, it is possible to trace the evolution of attitudes that critics have had toward the filmic images of Asian people generated by Hollywood. There are two distinct critical modes—one that I call the "dismantling stereotypes" approach, and the other interested in "refunctioning representation." In availing ourselves of both modes of critique, we can better account for the many ways in which performer and spectator occupy contingent, and sometimes compromised, positions in relation to each other. With respect to Anna May Wong, I argue that cross-media explorations of what she signifies enlarge the debate from one preoccupied with stereotypes to one that reveals contemporary writers, alongside Wong, as disrupting Hollywood's meaning-making machinery in unexpected and idiosyncratic ways.

For writers and critics since the 1970s, if not earlier, Wong's body of film work constitutes one kind of half-life radiating beyond her death in 1961. As a frame for her artistic choices, the biographical details of her career constitute another sort of afterglow, and her importance to contemporary writers forms a third. To show how Anna May Wong's artful self-fashioning reveals her as refunctioning her own representation, much like the poems and plays of contemporary Asian American artists, it will be necessary to rehearse the critical histories of dismantling stereotypes and refunctioning representation.

This chapter will unfold in three main sections. The first focuses on diegetic analyses of Wong's roles. I define the "dismantling stereotypes" approach, recapitulating some of the findings of this critical endeavor, and define what I mean by those artists and writers engaged in "refunctioning representation." The second section addresses those extra-diegetic details of biography, constituting what Richard deCordova (1990) calls "the star system," and establishes Wong as someone who actively developed and sought roles for her acting career. The third section concludes with close readings of three Asian American artists and their reinterpretations of Wong's life and art.

Captured on/in Film

The idea of rebirth, implied in the title of this chapter, is a critical one for this pioneering actress, whose screen career was memorialized with the words "she died a thousand deaths," and for whom the twin legacies of "dragon lady" and "butterfly" were too much to live down within her own lifetime. A bit player in a number of silent films beginning in 1919, when she was fourteen, Wong appeared in a body of work that paralleled the shift from the silents to sound, from black-and-white films to color, from the predominance of filmgoing among audiences to the rising popularity of television. Upon her death in 1961, *Time* magazine's obituary labeled her "the screen's foremost Oriental villainess" (AMPAS, quoted in *Los Angeles Times*, 7 December 1987), although she is perhaps best remembered now, if at all, for her co-starring role opposite Marlene Dietrich in *Shanghai Express* (von Sternberg 1932).

This oscillation between prevailing perceptions of Wong's characters as villainess and victim coincides with the limitations of many, if not all, of her roles. Renee Tajima (1989, 176) critiques images of the exotic Asian woman that promulgate crude "dragon lady"/"lotus blossom" or "butterfly" stereotypes. For example, Wong's personification of the "dragon lady" in the 1931 Lloyd Corrigan film *Daughter of the Dragon* (based on the Sax Rohmer novel *Daughter of Fu Manchu*) has roots in the character she played of a deceitful, sly gangster's daughter in *Old San Francisco* (Crosland 1927). As the "dragon lady," or progeny of Fu Manchu, Wong plays a monstrously "masculine" female figure who double-crosses the Asian man (Sessue Hayakawa) who loves her and uses her treacherously enticing wiles to exact revenge against the white man she vowed to her father she would kill. The "dragon lady" provokes and titillates early film audiences because she cloaks an almost masculine racial pride and anti-white race hatred in the mutually reinforcing "duplicity" of being Asian and being a woman.[1]

The "butterfly," a descendant of Giacomo Puccini's 1904 opera *Madama Butterfly* (to which David Henry Hwang's play *M. Butterfly* [1986] is now irrevocably linked), has a more predictable narrative fate than the generalized image of Asian women as fragile "lotus blossoms." With the "butterfly," personifying naïveté and self-abnegation,

Wong's characters conveniently "elect" suicide so as not to mar the future happiness of their white lovers and their white fiancées, in the process consoling Western audiences with a fantasy of colonial power over the ever-yielding East.[2] One example of Wong's early "butterfly" roles is in the film *Toll of the Sea* (Franklin 1922), in which Wong's character gives up her white husband to the white woman with whom he falls in love. Wong's lovelorn young character chooses to leap to a watery death rather than assert the validity of their interracial love.

Wong's career encompassed most variations of this binary and thus provides ample material for critics intent on identifying and dismantling stereotypes. However, even those critics engaged in dismantling, or detoxifying, stereotypes of Asian women on film recognize the defensiveness of their approach. Eugene Franklin Wong and Judy Chu did the necessary work of rounding out Wong's flattened cinematic personae with biographical details to place the reviewers and the actress within a shared Asian American history, but to a major extent they remained locked in the logic of positive–negative image critique. Chu (1976, 288) argued that

> in the past Anna May symbolized everything from cheesecake sexiness to exotic assimilation to droll camp. But Anna May is not just an object of the past; she is a very contemporary comment on the imposed roles of Asians in America and on the sexist expectations still internalized and acted upon by Asian women. With knowledge of her history, one finds that beyond the charming exotic imagery emerges an understanding and somehow a closeness to the very real woman labeled the "lady of mystery."

By arguing that recycled images of "dragon lady" and "butterfly" stereotypes persist well beyond their initial screening, Chu attempts to link the dominant audience's proclivity, and appetite, for racialized–sexualized types in popular culture with the enactment of racialized–sexualized types in the behavior and beliefs of contemporary Asian women. In this way, the dominant culture's views of Asians in America, which are undeniably damaging and distorted, come to control both the tenor of critical Asian American film studies and what it is that Asian Americans themselves are purported to think, say, and do.[3]

Chu's powerful, if unidimensional, critique presupposes a number of conditions that, upon closer questioning, are more complex than her paradigm would allow. How, for example, does the dominant culture shift from a taste for "dragon ladies" on the one hand to "butterflies" on the other, and from era to era? Does "real" behavior exist that contradicts the binary that Wong represented for so long? (How would she or any other critic begin to describe that "realness" before prescriptive criteria began to creep in?) If Asian women act in ways that bear out either stereotype, then according to Chu's logic, they must be victims of "internalized" racism or sexism.

For Wong (1978), the necessary project of exploding pernicious and heavy-handed stereotypes of on-screen Asians can easily slip into the project of demonstrating that the exaggeratedly "femininizing" elements of Asian culture distort images of Asian American men and women unequally, violating tacit, supposedly "universal," norms of both femininity and masculinity. That is, the critic presents a survey of distasteful images whose genesis reveal more about the dominant culture than they do about

"Asia" and "Asianness." Wong asserts that "those roles which Asians do secure often call for stylized and patterned displays, requiring less in the way of acting than a series of directed Oriental affectations" (ibid., 15). Having established this, Wong then claims that filmic Asian American men are under a two-pronged attack: "Unlike the racist image of the threatening Asian rapist, white males are generally provided the necessary romantic conditions and masculine attributes with which to attract the Asian females' passion" (ibid., 27), because "in theory, non-white males have been positioned as threats. . . . In practice, because of the subservience to white male social power, non-white males have been credited with non-masculine, effeminate characteristics" (ibid., 24). In arguing that the racism of early Hollywood filmmakers maligns images of Asian American men even as the same racism "benignly" co-opts, sexualizes, and domesticates Asian American women's images, the implicit critical project becomes one of propping up hetero-normative, Asian-masculine desirability. Wong's examples show how romance plots can never be "satisfactorily" resolved between on-screen Asian American men and women. Although these conclusions are certainly borne out by the many ways in which Asian male bodies—animated by white "masking-tape actors" adorned with prosthetic eyelids and peculiar nail and hair additions—are monstrously conceived and caricatured through the practice of "yellowface," the critic who airs these grievances nevertheless bears the implied burden of articulating approved images that do not demean but instead uplift. I do not wish to suggest that Wong's critique lacks value or should never have been made. On the contrary: The emphatic denunciation of gross stereotypes of Asians perpetuated in film is, unfortunately, still needed, and if gesturing toward positive stereotypes of Asian Americans on film counters the vulgarity of the negative images, then to a large extent these corrective polemics have political and interpretive value. But to Wong and others who are temporarily enabled by dismantling these stereotypes of ethnic femininity and masculinity, I point out an unanticipated flaw in that approach: The tendency is to become entrapped in mimetic criticism's assumption that the primary task of filmic images—perhaps the sole task—is to reproduce the world faithfully.

Without becoming enmeshed in the unproductive ascertainment of which "real" behaviors, beliefs, and articulations make up Asian American culture, perhaps it is more productive to ask: Who among Asian American audiences have consumed and contemplated roles that Anna May Wong was asked to inhabit? On what terms have these particular Asian Americans understood Wong the actress and Wong's roles?

The three writer–critics discussed in this chapter—Yau, Hagedorn, and Hwang—anchor a reassessment of Wong's career in their own artistic interpretations of her life as a way to contend with the enduring power of the actress's image. It follows that a brief overview of shifts in film scholarship can help us understand how the writer–critics attribute new significance to Wong's iconicity by self-consciously regarding themselves as a newly constituted audience.

Janet Staiger's work on modes of cinematic production and consumption in *Interpreting Films: Studies in the Historical Reception of American Cinema* underscores the value of outlining "a contextual and materialist approach to the study of historical [film] spectators and [their] interpretative strategies" (Staiger 1992, xi). In addition to conducting audience ethnographies, examining publicity apparatuses, studio-production notes, and other trappings of what Richard deCordova calls "star discourse" constitutes a kind of "reception studies . . . [that] seeks to understand textual interpretations as they are produced" by particular audiences (ibid., 9). In naming pernicious stereotypes, critics such as Chu and Wong displace those types by turning to the reported words of Anna May Wong herself in order to get at the more accurate "truth" of her subjectivity. Having named those stereotypes, however, these critics are left with the difficulty of describing the manifestation of stereotypes (the "internalization" of those types) by real-life, if unspecified, Asian American women who ape models of behavior that they see in the movies. To posit a generalized category of "damaged Asian American women," for example, is to overlook how three actual Asian American writers have actually responded to, and complicated, the idea that images of Anna May Wong can signify only one thing.

Thus, the "dismantling stereotypes" school—critics of Asian American film culture such as Judy Chu, Eugene Wong, and Renee Tajima—mount their critiques from assumptions that differ from those of a second group of contemporary writer–critics. This group, which I call the "refunctioning representation" school, extends the project of dismantling stereotypes by posing media-crossing solutions to the problems articulated by the first group. To refunction representation, according to Walter Benjamin, is to transform a seemingly straightforward process by intervening in the "productive apparatus" (Benjamin 1978, 23). His famous example involves a photographer who goes beyond mastery of the craft of photography to document the world by instigating self-consciousness about the relationship that the photograph has to its viewer. That act can be as simple as attaching a caption to the photograph. What I'm suggesting here is that the artists I discuss perform the equivalent of "captioning" Wong's visual presence, sidestepping the ontological tangle that the dismantling of stereotypes yields. For Hagedorn, Yau, and Hwang, Anna May Wong's iconic importance is less a hurdle to representation in the realist mode—where it is thought possible to come closer, as Chu put it, to "the very *real* woman labeled the 'lady of mystery'" (Chu 1976, 288; emphasis added)—than it is an opportunity to intervene in a postmodern mode.

Those interested in refunctioning representation do so to take advantage of the flattening out of illusion and reality that Frederic Jameson's notion of pastiche (in some ways an inversion of the insistence that mimesis relies on an empirical reality), for example, implies (Jameson 1983).[4] That is, critics engaged in resignifying the meaning of Wong's career find it more productive to set aside hopes that the "real woman" can be found buried beneath layers of fictional representations. Instead, they focus on the fictivity of self-representation in the context of a range of representations. DeCordova (1990, 13) provides one context for conceiving of the actor/star's role in the cinema's enunciative apparatus by examining the post-structuralist turn to linguistic models in the following argument: "It is clear that the actor figures prominently in the film's production of meaning. It would be a mistake to view the actor/star merely as a signifier (an enounced). The pleasure and the process of the American film has in fact been dependent on the assumption that actors hold a productive, transitive relation to their images on the screen."[5]

To summarize, the dismantling stereotypes school of criticism is primarily concerned with deconstructing Anna May Wong as a signifier of exoticism, cruelty, and Asian despotism, and as the female embodiment of masochism. The refunctioning representation school, on the other hand, is concerned with intervening in the network of significations—in this essay, star discourse—in which the actor as a signifier is a small, but important, player whose meaning increases through the attention of fans and critics.

Not Only a Silent Film Star

For deCordova, the star system consists of discursive and economic practices—film appearances, posters, press books, personal appearances, fan mail, trade press, fan magazines, popular press, newspapers—that enable star discourse, or the management of celebrity, to take place. Within this system, "cinema as an institution and as an enunciative form produces this position from which the star can speak and be spoken" (deCordova 1990, 12).

Shirley J. Lim, the historian of Asian American youth culture before World War II, has amply demonstrated that Wong was far from being only a silent film star—that is, her reputed verbal ability smoothed her transition from an actor in silent films to those of the sound era. Lim (1997) argues that Wong's multilingual ease (in addition to speaking American English, she engaged a tutor to polish her Oxford English accent, learned and dubbed her films in German and French, and added Mandarin Chinese to Cantonese, the language her family spoke at home) allowed her to extend her film career beyond that of her less linguistically adaptable colleague Sessue Hayakawa.

Eschewing silence of another kind, Wong was also known to have complained publicly on several occasions that she was "tired of the parts" she had to play. Speaking directly to the Hollywood filmmaking community through fan magazines and interviews with gossip columnists, she withheld little of her dissatisfaction: "Why should we [screen Chinese] always scheme, rob, kill? I got so weary of it all—of the scenarist's concept of Chinese characters" (LOC, *Photoplay*, March 18, 1937; AMPAS, *Los Angeles Times*, July 12, 1987). Moreover, she campaigned vocally for the female lead, O-Lan, in *The Good Earth* (Fleming 1937), only to be offered a minor role as the second wife to the virtuous O-Lan.

There is an incident that I believe highlights the agency in Wong's public performance of self and underscores her adept use of mass-media outlets other than the Hollywood studio system to promote her celebrity persona. The incident illustrates how the process of refunctioning representation itself becomes a creative enterprise and represents a departure from realist assumptions that do not take into account "star discourse" because of the single-minded focus on eliminating stereotype.

In March 1936, after the bitter disappointment of losing out to the German actress Luise Rainer for the role of O-Lan, Anna May Wong decided to journey by ship to China, for the first time in her life, for what was supposed to be a year-long stay. Covering the well-publicized event were two Los Angeles city newspapers, the *Examin-*

er and the *Times,* and celebrity magazines such as *Photoplay* (LOC). A March 8, 1936, news article ran the headline, STRANGE HOMELAND BECKONS STAR: ANNA MAY WONG OFF FOR CHINA, WHICH TO HER WILL BE [A] NEW COUNTRY (AMPAS). The article also reported the third-generation, American-born Wong's goals: "I want to study the Chinese theatre—I'll be a neophyte there, for all my stage experience. I want to work with the old Chinese plays and, eventually, I want to select two or three of them, find good translations, and take a group of English speaking Chinese on a world tour" [AMPAS, *Los Angeles Examiner,* March 8, 1936].

Upon her return to the United States in September 1936, Wong told the *Los Angeles Herald Express,* "The possibilities of motion pictures in China are infinite." Far from being a willing puppet content to act out Hollywood's fantasies concerning Asian women, Wong, like other ambitious actors, actively sought out projects and attempted to develop those that would feature her in roles she liked. To some extent, she was successful: Production notes in the Paramount archives, in particular an April 28, 1937, treatment that became *Daughter of Shanghai* (and was for a time titled simply *Anna May Wong Story*), show the development of perhaps the most interesting film of her career specifically for her.[6]

Burned by her experience with Metro Goldwyn Mayer's casting of Luise Rainer in *The Good Earth,* Wong did not waste time bemoaning Hollywood's insulting attempt to cast her, an Asian American actress, in a minor role while awarding the lead roles to European and European American actors in "yellowface" makeup. In an attempt to generate better projects for herself, Wong used the September 1936 *Express* interview to urge Hollywood producers to "go to the Orient" for stories and not for mere background.[7] There is little question that late-1930s U.S.-China relations and Chinese American participation in Chinese nation-building endeavors (China relief efforts that could be legitimated as unequivocally "American" support for a wartime ally) created a groundswell of support for all things Chinese, which also benefited Wong's career. However, we can see the limits of American appreciation of Chinese subject matter in the way that Asian actors were passed over for lead roles, and in Hollywood's insistence that scenes filmed in China were for purposes of backdrop and local color as opposed to an opportunity for cross-cultural collaboration.

It is Wong's adroit manipulation of her celebrity while in China that is key. In a series of reports on her trip printed in the *New York Herald-Tribune,* Wong wrote that when she landed in Japan, a reporter wanted to know whether the rumors were true that she was to be married to a wealthy Asian businessman. "I replied that in fact, I am wedded to my art," was Wong's cagey response (AMPAS, *New York Herald-Tribune,* May 24, 1936). Wong, thirty-one years old and unmarried when she traveled to China in 1936, had had plenty of practice after some fifteen years in the film industry in deflecting questions about her marital status and romantic life in Hollywood. Later, a New York entertainment reporter who interviewed Wong gave this conclusion to the story: "Imagine her amazement, then, when the press carried the tale of her engagement to [a] 'wealthy Chinese merchant named Art!'" (AMPAS; Crewe n.d.)

Amusing and discreet as the story was about Wong's own desires, it reveals how audiences on both sides of the Pacific looked past the screen "truths" of Wong's roles to the details of her sexual life for either confirmation or refutation of the image. Of the kinds of identifications and fantasies audiences project onto and consume along-side the performances of screen stars, deCordova (1990, 140–41) writes,

> It's not surprising that a system of discourse driven by a logic of secrecy (and revelation) would light upon the sexual as the ultimate secret.... The star system, and arguably twentieth century culture in general, depends on an interpretive schema that equates identity with the private and furthermore accords the sexual the status of the most private, and thus the most truthful, locus of identity.... Foucault shows how sexuality has been constituted primarily as a problem of truth in modern western society and notes the ways a 'will to knowledge' elicited concerning sexuality has led to incessant efforts to uncover its 'truth.' In the process sexuality has become a particularly privileged site of truth, in some contexts no doubt the ultimate truth. This is certainly the case in the star system.... Truth is, at its limit, the truth of sexuality. The sexual scandal is the primal scene of all star discourse, the only scenario that offers the promise of a full and satisfying disclosure of the star's identity.

Wong's staging of her star persona in the Los Angeles and Chinese press, and even her encouragement of fans' speculation about her (hetero) sexuality for publicity's sake, can thus be seen as an attempt to expand the scope of her iconicity. Star discourse therefore provides supplementary narratives, themselves constructed, to the visual fictions that the actors project. Speculations about her sexual life, although annoying, intrusive, and trivial on one level, could be used to ensure continued interest in her career, and that continued interest could in turn be leveraged against studio politics regarding the development of worthwhile projects for the actor. Moreover, any implication among fans that Wong's interior life differed from the flat stereotypes she portrayed in her film roles was probably more desirable than the film industry's constant conflation of the actress with the roles she played. The commodification of her persona among fans held resistant potential when it came to pursuing her career within Hollywood.

"... Married to Her Art": Life as Art

What we know and what we want to know about celebrities—Anna May Wong, in this case—fosters a generative kind of unknowability that scratches at our imaginations and demands creative redress. In fact, the linkages between what we can possibly know about Wong and the limitations to our speculations have spurred David Henry Hwang, Jessica Hagedorn, and John Yau to re-imagine Wong's "inscrutability."

What *do* we know about Wong?[8] By culling from a number of sources that can be corroborated, it is possible to learn that she was born in Los Angeles shortly after the turn of the century. She made between fifty and eighty films that were distributed and shown in the United States, Canada, Germany, England, China, and France. She appeared in at least two plays (one with a then-unknown Laurence Olivier). She traveled to China in 1936, intending to live there for a year, but war between Japan and China may have forced her early return. She lived in Los Angeles for most of her life, with stints in England and Germany. She had her picture taken by Carl Van Vechten (patron saint of the Harlem Renaissance), and her clothes were designed by Edith Head, costumer to the stars. She never married or had children. And in 1931, she was photographed once by Alfred Stieglitz in Berlin standing between Hitler's favorite filmmaker, Leni Riefenstahl, and Marlene Dietrich. This last item speaks both to what we know about her and what we—1930s moviegoers and readers of fanzines as well as late-twentieth-century cultural critics, consumers of star discourse all—want to know about her. Were she and Dietrich ever lovers?[9] Compare that speculation with the other rumors about Wong that attempt to get at her "true" self: Did she drink a little too much? Did her father really have a first wife and family that he left behind in China, and did he return to that family when Wong's mother (the second wife) died in Los Angeles in the 1930s? Did Wong really direct a film, as some critics believe? What was all the gossip about Wong's possible engagement to her high-school friend Philip Ahn, especially since Ahn himself was rumored to be gay?

In the poem "No One Ever Tried to Kiss Anna May Wong," John Yau (1989) suggests that recourse to poetry complicates what a counter-image in film to Wong's screen stereotypes cannot: By using the poetic form, he can paradoxically unveil the act of looking and the kinds of positions occupied by those who look. In taking this approach, Yau can acknowledge the frisson of sexual "inscrutability" that Wong generated as part of the discourse of stardom, while, at the same time, he can examine the costs of her strategy.

No One Ever Tried to Kiss Anna May Wong

She's trying to find a way to turn her cup
upside down, while sequestered on a train
from Dublin to Vienna. Every angle
glistens from behind a celluloid scrim.
She's wearing a crescent scarf
and chilly snake high smile:
others claim she's all skin and eyes.
No longer lashed to this oily chatter
I enter her compartment.
    She's languishing
on a ledge, annoyed at all the times
she's been told to be scratched, kicked,
slapped, bitten, stabbed, poisoned, and shot.
Lightning flickers between the frames.
On the seat beside me I find a circle
smaller than one left by a wet apple.

Yau embeds in his poem references to the film *Shanghai Express,* starring Marlene Dietrich and Anna May Wong. In doing so, Yau experiments with refiguring Laura Mulvey's notion of fetishizing the feminine body through an implied masculine scopophilia that has "queer" implications (Mulvey 1989).

The early 1920s Hays Office Code regulating the depiction of "sexual content" in film speaks to the injunction implied by the poem's title, "No One Ever Tried to Kiss Anna May Wong." Ed Guerrero, historian and critic of African American film, describes the Hays Office Code as upholding a "strong sense of racial apartheid . . . by expressly stating that miscegenation, or the mixing of races, was to be portrayed as in no way desirable" (Guerrero 1993, 173). Incomplete repression of the undesirability of miscegenation is thereby "articulated through various narrative strategies of containment that filter it through the perspective, values, and taboos of the dominant white culture . . . [the most common being] interracial romance . . . between a white male and an exotic non-white female" (ibid.). Indeed, no one white ever tried to kiss Anna May Wong without penalty—and vice versa—because the films in which she starred set up all heterosexual romance between her white co-stars and herself as necessarily ill-fated and usually ending in suicide for Wong's character. In 1929, even British film censors removed an on-screen kiss between Wong and her co-star, Jameson Thomas, from the film *Piccadilly* (Dupont 1929). Hence, linkage between anti-miscegenation laws common to the period prior to 1950 and a concomitant interest in "decency" as regulated by the United States' Hays Office Code came to determine the narrative outcomes of her films—and, by extension, the bulk of Wong's career. Her "butterfly" deaths were as much a product of legislated morals as they were a product of Jesse Lasky's instructing his screenwriter specifically to include the plot twist involving Wong's character's suicide.

Yau's poem begins—as does its intertext, the film *Shanghai Express*—with Wong, playing Hui Fei, inhabiting a sleeper car on a long-distance train ride, sharing the car, the viewer discovers, with Marlene Dietrich's "Shanghai Lily." Of the two women, derided by another character as two "adventuresses" out to snare "victims" (USC-Para, release dialogue script, reel 3, p. 1), only Shanghai Lily owns up to her promiscuous past: "It took more than one man to make me Shanghai Lily." Chang, a mercenary half-European, half-Chinese revolutionary who is also on the train, discloses his identity at the same time that his confederates stop the train and take as their hostage a British surgeon. Shanghai Lily's moral reform occurs when she refuses to trade a night with Chang for the release of the surgeon, her old boyfriend. Hui Fei meanwhile is raped by Chang and later kills him, thus allowing the hostage situation to be defused and Shanghai Lily and her doctor to be reunited.

Although *Shanghai Express* departs from "Peiping"/Beijing and travels to Shanghai, Yau refigures Wong/Hui Fei's locomotive journey so that she proceeds from west to east, "from Dublin to Vienna," rather than from north to south. By beginning with her refusal and ending with her arousal, Yau's poem suggests that the exercise of the former is at least a precondition of the latter. In the poem, *Shanghai Express*'s narrative violence—a rape committed against Wong's character—is restaged as a lurking threat that may or may not be deflected. In the poet's imagined scenario, Wong forestalls coffee or tea service by turning "her cup upside down," signaling her rejection and telegraphing by implication her preferences, even if those desires are only a diffuse sort of negation. However, it is unclear whether the lip of the cup ever makes contact with the saucer in an unequivocal refusal. Wong as Hui Fei is in the act of "trying to find a way," perhaps constrained by her "sequestered" journey traversing Dublin and Vienna, west to east, East and West, the "twains" that are never supposed to meet.

Within the poem, the progression from "trying" to "wearing" to "languishing" all connote fatigue, a slow crushing of artistic spirit, in contrast to the vibrant energy and scintillating property of verbs such as "glistens" and "flickers" that are used elsewhere in the poem. The clarity implied by "glistens" (related to the wetness of the apple at poem's end) contrasts with its opposite, the viscosity of "oily chatter"—persistent Orientalizing—that characterizes Wong and "claims that she is all skin and eyes." The poet's use of the construction "is trying/is wearing/is languishing" highlights the constraints on Wong of the fashion for filmic Chinoiserie and implies stasis and failure, paralleling, perhaps, the containment of Wong's personae when the public's tastes changed after World War II, as China became a "Cold War enemy" and the old stereotypes were no longer enabling or palatable. Positioned "behind a celluloid scrim" or "between the frames," Wong is imagined by the speaker to be a desiring subject emanating both liquid erotic power and righteous anger through the lightning flashing between the frames. As Gina Marchetti (1993, 62) notes in her reading of *Shanghai Express*, Shanghai Lily's act of pulling the window screen down on the train compartment upon first meeting Hui Fei "keep[s] the camera at a distance [and] creat[es] a vague sense that their association may be somehow illicit." What the celluloid scrim hides, as well as what is projected upon it—again and again at twenty-four frames per second—contributes to the cinematic perception of "flicker" that the human eye, through the illusion of persistence of vision, merges into an apparently seamless whole. In this way, the poem alludes to the apparatus of cinema and comments on flashes of Wong's subjectivity that escape her film role and may even have exceeded her forays into managing the star system to her own advantage.

If the screen is a layer through which we see Wong, then it makes possible the idea that she herself no longer functions *as* the scrim permitting any and all of our fantasies and projections. Rather, we project our desires onto the screens that stand before the person, so that the possibility of a space of reserve remains. As I suggested earlier, Wong's participation in the shaping of her own "star discourse" in mass-media outlets apart from studio films may serve as the membrane separating the actor's subjectivity from that of the roles she purportedly embodies. Yet the scrim has dual properties, subjecting Wong/Hui Fei and Dietrich/Shanghai Lily to invasive viewing even as it partially shields them from it. In the poem, the liminal position that Wong/Hui Fei occupies on the "ledge" reproduces this ambivalence; there, she maintains a protective, slightly melancholy aloofness that accounts for the chilliness of her "snake high smile," indeed languishing in that she is forgotten or neglected by film historians. By dramatizing the scrim's placement between Wong and the audience reading this poem, Yau invites us to consider an analogous relationship between the film *Shanghai Express* and the poem, the poem at once critiquing and reassessing Wong's career. Further, if we can read this poem as a poem about Anna May Wong, as well as about the act of looking at Anna May Wong, then in some ways the poet also invokes our self-consciousness with regard to the pleasures of scopophilia.

The signal essay by Laura Mulvey, "Visual Pleasure and Narrative Cinema," (1989) lays out a way of thinking about scopophilia that Yau ultimately interrogates through his poem. It would seem that Wong is presented in the poem as sexual object, "the leit-motif of erotic spectacle. . . . She holds the look, plays to and signifies male desire," reminding us with her unavailable, but excited, vulva that she is the very embodiment of sexual difference, and therefore "implying a threat of castration and hence, unpleasure," according to Mulvey's formulation. Mulvey (1989, 64) goes on to specify two main responses to the specter of castration anxiety in men, whom she characterizes as the "active controllers of the look": "pre-occupation with the original trauma . . . or disavowal of castration by the substitution of a fetish object or turning the figure itself into a fetish." The latter, fetishistic scopophilia Mulvey identifies with von Sternberg's films, and the Dietrich films in particular.

It may be tempting to argue that, by positing a male viewer, Mulvey reinforces the same patriarchal organization of the gaze that she sought to diagnose and dismantle. I will bracket these major debates at this juncture, as well as more fundamental questions about the claims she puts forth about von Sternberg's visual economy (does the fetishization apply also to Dietrich's co-star, Wong, for example?). The point that I would like to take away from Mulvey's argument is that the positioning of owners of the gaze as male is a parallel conclusion that one might be tempted to find in Yau's poem—that is, one might mistake the poem's "I" for the autobiographical voice of the male poet. It would appear that within the poem, the owner of the gaze that consumes and creates Wong's desire is somehow heterosexually male. Yet, because the subtext of *Shanghai Express* ripples beneath our reading of the poem, we recall that Dietrich's character, "Shanghai Lily," is the one in the film who shares Hui Fei's, or Wong's, compartment, and could also be the narrator of the poem. Thus, not ever being allowed to "kiss Anna May Wong" is an injunction that does double duty: It works interracially to foreclose both miscegenation and same-sex desire. By imagining a scene in which both are possible, Yau defuses the taint of sexual scandal in deCordova's primal scene and refigures it with an invitation to speculate otherwise.

We are left with the kiss of Luce Irigaray's two moistened lips constituting the small circle "left by a wet apple" and an array of the traces of erotic pleasure experienced by Wong (Irigaray 1985). Is her moment of *jouissance* brought about through self-stimulation—masturbation? Is the object of fantasy herself having a fantasy? Or is the moment brought about through the close proximity to another desiring female subject, Dietrich's bisexuality or lesbianism iconic, which itself is the source of much speculation? In any case, the void created by the dearth of biographical detail about Wong's choices as a desiring subject, rather than a simple lapse into the stereotype of "*Asian* inscrutability," seems to be a useful enigma and an opportunity to transform a given celebrity's sexual selfhood into a larger epistemological question that attaches to all movie actors around whom star discourse swirls.

David Henry Hwang, the playwright and screenwriter who adapted his 1986 Tony-award winning play, *M. Butterfly*, into the 1993 David Cronenberg film of the same name, provides us with a glimpse of Wong as an iconic "tragic diva" embraced by a gay male figure who confounds national, gender, and sexual allegiances. Right after her first meeting with Gallimard in the film, Song Liling enters her apartment alone and picks up several movie fan magazines from beside her bed. The film cuts to a close-up of one magazine cover featuring a portrait of Wong—a moment of homage to an icon of Asian femininity that has interesting repercussions for Song, who is similarly isolated and for whom glamour and mystery together prefigure the "sexual scandal" of her espionage. Song's grasping of the fan magazine is an ironic comment on the elements of tragedy and glamour surrounding Wong that contribute to her embodiment of melancholy divahood, an embodiment of femininity that Song both mirrors and alters in the context of *M. Butterfly.*

That vision of tragic glamour is also the strongest emotion in Jessica Hagedorn's 1971 poem, "The Death of Anna May Wong" (Hagedorn rpr. 1993). In the poem, the unnamed narrator praises a mother figure who alternates among Dorothy Lamour, Wong, and the narrator's own mother. By superimposing the San Francisco neighborhoods of the Tenderloin and the Mission on a nameless motherland, the narrator layers spatial memory with auditory memory as experienced by his or her rhythm-inspired movement through those city streets.

For Hagedorn, "The Death of Anna May Wong" figures the actress as a fragile maternal presence, an Asian American woman who manages to "birth," however ambivalently, Asian American screen women in the jazz age. In the poem, the narrator imagines his or her mother as one way to summon the voice of Wong. The mother in the poem, like Wong, is imbued with remote glamour (like Dorothy Lamour) and adorned with "a beaded / Mandarin coat" signifying both her ethnicity and class. The mother, who owns a pair of "lavender lips," yet also "serves crêpe suzettes," nourishes the narrator's imagination with a smile as cryptic as Yau's "chilly snake high smile." In contrast with Dorothy Lamour, who "undrapes / her sarong" in the tropics, the narrator's mother wears her beaded jacket "in the dryness / Of San Diego's mediterranean parody" and maintains a sense of maternal propriety even as she later presides over a lush, junglelike urban scene based on San Francisco. By twinning Anna May Wong with Alice Coltrane, an avant-garde jazz musician in her own right as well as the companion to John Coltrane, the poet links the jazz-blues spectrum with other rhythms, such as "Mambo . . . Samba, calypso, funk and / Boogie," which pierce the narrator's being and function as an auditory mnemonic for the place to which the narrator knows she or he "can't go home again"—that is, the maternal body and the imagined motherland. Being unable to "go home again," as the American-born and -raised Wong's 1936 journey to China for artistic inspiration and cultural grounding shows, may very well be a paradoxical yearning that both drives and confines Asian American aesthetics, even today.

As I have argued, deCordova's and Staiger's theories present a number of advantages over the purely realist preoccupation with positive–negative image critique. Using their combined theories allows us to put Wong's stereotypes into perspective, taking into consideration the career limits and possibilities experienced by other actors of the time. We can better assess Wong's agency in her selection and cultivation of roles as contingent on studio control and the Hays Office Code. We can now view celebrity—the commodification of selves—as a way to assess the work of performed art, to paraphrase Walter Benjamin's formation, in the age of mechanical reproduction. We create a space for analysis that accounts for new formulations of these circulating images rather than placing us in the realist trap of proving and disproving them. We acknowledge Asian American writers and artists as part of the many audiences who actively consume Hollywood's images, reproducing and refunctioning them in ways that are idiosyncratic to their art, with Wong herself being one of those artists. And finally, by examining media-crossing resignifications of iconic images, we arrive at an open-ended analysis rather than an oppressively deconstructive one in which Orientalism is always and everywhere diagnosed.

Notes

Acknowledgments: This article would not have been possible without Sandra Liu's patient and attentive editing; generous research assistance from the film librarians Ned Comstock, Scott Curtis, Rosemary Hanes, Stuart Ng, Brian Taves, and Fay Thompson; research funding from the Kam Family Foundation, Huntington Beach, California; and plentiful support in the form of shared research and encouragement from such fellow Anna May Wong fans as Garland Richard Kyle, independent scholar and writer, and John Yau, poet and art critic. In addition, a very large bouquet goes to Beulah Quo for her time and her perspective on arts activism and Asian Americans in Hollywood.

1. A collection of critical essays on Asian American feminism, *Dragon Ladies: Asian American Feminists Breathe Fire* (Shah 1997), ridicules the stylization of uncontrollable, powerful Asian women as venal Oriental villainesses.

2. Not only were early American film audiences invited to regard Wong the actress as the mere embodiment of her characters; the studios also participated in conflating the actress with the "dragon lady"/"butterfly" sexual types she often played. For instance, a stipulation added to the contract she signed to do the Warner Bros. film *Old San Francisco* states that the "actress will provide own Chinese costumes" (USC-WB, file #2906, August 4, 1926, contract), the implication being that she need only "be herself" on-screen, with no "acting" required.

3. Fairly recent articles, such as Ito (1997), reproduce the "dismantling stereotypes" approach without attempting to account for the complexity of signification.

4. Film critics too numerous to document have reflected on the changes in film criticism and theory. This meta-theoretical discussion deserves its own lengthy discussion, especially as it relates to the use of ethnic studies and feminist analytical tools to "read" films by and about people of color. For an introduction to this discussion, see Sumiko Higashi's work on *The Cheat* (Higashi 1991); James Moy's study on performativity and ethnic identity (Moy 1993); Darrell Hamamoto's work on televised images of Asian Americans (Hamamoto 1994); and Gina Marchetti's discussion of the merits of a cultural-studies approach (Marchetti 1993).

5. DeCordova's arguments qualify the primacy of auteur theory, which, he argues, even Christian Metz may not be willing to support fully. See deCordova (1990) for a critique of Metz and the "problem" that Metz identifies of unruly enunciating subjects who break the spectator's primary identification. According to deCordova (ibid., 17), Metz attempts to account for the existence of "a figure exterior to the linguistic syntagm" by attributing this exteriority to the director. I agree with deCordova when he points out that the director is both a problematic producer of the enounced text and "a product produced by certain rules in a certain relation

to the film"—that is, subject to studio demands or other exigencies that modify his or her idealized auteur position (ibid., 18).

6. *Daughter of Shanghai*, a 1937 film directed by Robert Florey, began as a twenty-six–page treatment written by Garnett Weston, dated April 17, 1937, and titled *Honor Bright*. The protagonist at that time, named "Anna Sing," initiated little action in the mystery–thriller. After Anna May Wong committed to the picture, the writer revised her main character so that "Lan Ying" actively pursued the head of a criminal organization that was smuggling Chinese immigrants into the United States. By April 28, 1937, the property, in addition to being known as *Anna May Wong Story*, had been given the green light, and more than twenty-five days of shooting were done in September and October of 1937, with Philip Ahn as the male lead (USC-Para, *Daughter of Shanghai*, Paramount script files).

7. Incidentally, by capitalizing on growing U.S. sympathy for China (which was formally engaged in open combat with Japan soon thereafter, in 1937), Wong attempts to work the same conditions of transnationalism and "Chinese emergency" that in the 1990s have partially underwritten the successful migration of various Hong Kong Chinese filmmakers to the United States, including John Woo, Jackie Chan, Tsui Hark, and Ringo Lam.

8. I include Philip Leibfried's standard biography (1987), despite chronologies in his article that vary from other accounts. See also Nga (1995) for another overview of Wong's life and her importance to a contemporary filmmaker.

9. Weiss (1992) is a representative example of the deification of Marlene Dietrich as lesbian icon. Dietrich's photograph, in fact, graces the work's cover. See also Russo (1981) for an extensive examination of Hollywood's lesbian and gay actors, writers, directors, and producers.

Archival Sources

Anna May Wong clippings file, Margaret Herrick Library, Academy of Motion Pictures Arts and Sciences (AMPAS).

Anna May Wong clippings file, Motion Picture and Recorded Sound Division, Library of Congress (LOC).

Paramount Pictures production files, University of Southern California School of Cinema-Television (USC-Para).

Warner Brothers Archive, University of Southern California School of Cinema-Television (USC-WB).

Works Cited

Benjamin, Walter. 1978. "The Author as Producer." *Reflections: Essays, Aphorisms, Autobiographical Writings*, ed. Peter Demetz; trans. Edmund Jephcott. New York: Harcourt Brace Jovanovich.

Chu, Judy. 1976. "Anna May Wong." *Counterpoint: Perspectives on Asian America*, ed. Emma Gee. Los Angeles: Asian American Studies Center, University of California, Los Angeles.

Crewe, Regina. n.d. "Frosted Willow: Never Having Seen Homeland Before, Actress Has Many Varied Experiences." *New York American*.

deCordova, Richard. 1990. *Picture Personalities: The Emergence of the Star System in America*. Urbana and Chicago: University of Illinois Press.

Guerrero, Ed. 1993. *Framing Blackness: The African American Image in Film*. Philadelphia: Temple University Press.

Hagedorn, Jessica. 1993. "The Death of Anna May Wong." Pp. 12–13 in *Danger and Beauty*. New York: Penguin.

Hamamoto, Darrell Y. 1994. *Monitored Peril: Asian Americans and the Politics of TV Representation*. Minneapolis: University of Minnesota Press.

Higashi, Sumiko. 1991. "Ethnicity, Class, and Gender in Film: DeMille's *The Cheat*." Pp. 112–39 in *Unspeakable Images: Ethnicity and the American Cinema*, ed. Lester Friedman. Chicago: University of Illinois Press.

Hwang, David Henry. 1986. *M. Butterfly*. New York: New American Library.

Irigaray, Luce. 1985. *This Sex Which Is Not One*. Trans. Catherine Porter. Ithaca, N.Y.: Cornell University Press.

Ito, Robert B. 1997. "'A Certain Slant': A Brief History of Yellowface." *Bright Lights Film Journal* (March).

Jameson, Frederic. 1983. "Postmodernism and Consumer Society." *The Anti-Aesthetic: Essays on Postmodern Culture*, ed. Hal Foster. Port Townsend, Wash.: Bay Press.

Leibfried, Philip. 1987. "Anna May Wong." *Films in Review* (March), 147–52.

Lim, Shirley J. 1997. "Figures of Desire." Annual Association of Asian American Studies Conference (April 19), Seattle, Wash.

Marchetti, Gina. 1993. *Romance and the "Yellow Peril": Race, Sex, and Discursive Strategies in Hollywood Fiction*. Berkeley: University of California Press.

Moy, James S. 1993. *Marginal Sights: Staging the Chinese in America*. Iowa City: University of Iowa Press.

Mulvey, Laura. 1989. *Visual and Other Pleasures*. Bloomington: Indiana University Press.

Nga, Thi Thanh. 1995. "The Long March from Wong to Woo: Asians in Hollywood." *Cinéaste* 21, no. 4 (fall): 38–41.

Russo, Vito. 1981. *The Celluloid Closet: Homosexuality in the Movies*. New York: Harper and Row.

Shah, Sonia, ed. 1997. *Dragon Ladies: Asian American Feminists Breathe Fire*. Boston: South End Press.

Staiger, Janet. 1992. *Interpreting Films: Studies in the Historical Reception of American Cinema*. Princeton, N.J.: Princeton University Press.

Tajima, Renee E. 1989. "Lotus Blossoms Don't Bleed: Images of Asian Women." Pp. 308–17 in *Making Waves: An Anthology of Writings By and About Asian American Women*, ed. Asian Women United. Boston: Beacon Press.

Weiss, Andrea. 1992. *Vampires and Violets: Lesbians in the Cinema*. New York: Penguin.

Wong, Anna May. 1936. "Anna May Wong Relates Arrival in Japan, Her First Sight of the Orient," *New York Herald-Tribune* (May 24), n.p.

Wong, Eugene Franklin. 1978. *On Visual Media Racism: Asians in the American Motion Pictures*. New York: Arno Press.

Yau, John. 1989. "No One Ever Tried to Kiss Anna May Wong." In *Radiant Silhouette: Selected Poems: New and Selected Work 1974–1988*. Santa Rosa: Black Sparrow Press.

Films and Videos Cited

Corrigan, Lloyd. 1931. *Daughter of the Dragon*. Paramount Pictures.

Cronenberg, David. 1993. *M. Butterfly*. Warner Bros.

Crosland, Alan. 1927. *Old San Francisco*. Warner Bros.

Dupont, E. A. 1929. *Piccadilly*. British International Pictures Wardour.

Fleming, Victor. 1937. *The Good Earth*. Metro Goldwyn Mayer.

Florey, Robert. 1937. *Daughter of Shanghai*. Paramount Pictures.

Franklin, Chester M. 1922. *Toll of the Sea*. Metro Goldwyn Mayer.

von Sternberg, Josef. 1932. *Shanghai Express*. Paramount Pictures.

| 3 | Recuperating Suzie Wong: A Fan's Nancy Kwan-dary |

"I couldn't believe what she was telling me. It was straight out of some awful racist movie like *The World of Suzie Wong*," says Rose Hsu (Rosalind Chao) in the movie adaptation of Amy Tan's novel *The Joy Luck Club* (Wang 1993). In a movie avowedly concerned with illuminating the experiences of Chinese American women, this mention of *The World of Suzie Wong* (Quine 1960) meets the very definition of notoriety: The specific relevance of the movie is not explored; rather, a simple invocation of the movie's title suffices. *The Joy Luck Club* announces that *The World of Suzie Wong* is the film that Asian Americans love to hate. I would suggest that the film is something more: It is also the film we love to love.

The very notoriety of *The World of Suzie Wong* suggests that it is not a self-contained text studied in classrooms; rather, *Suzie Wong* has taken on a life of its own. The figure of Suzie Wong is both a character in a film and a character that is larger than film, a character that has had a pronounced and observable (if not measurable) impact on people's lives. In lieu of an empirical, sociological study of audiences, I propose to examine the next best thing: the ways in which audiences for *The World of Suzie Wong* have themselves been constructed in movies made by Asian American filmmakers.[1] Helen Lee's *Sally's Beauty Spot* (1990) and Deborah Gee's *Slaying the Dragon* (1987) do more than critique *The World of Suzie Wong:* They construct an audience of Asian American women with heavy investments in the character played by Nancy Kwan.[2] My aim in comparing these different conceptions of audiences (Lee's, Gee's, and my own) is to arrive at a preliminary understanding about the efforts by cinematic texts to stimulate and then reinvest spectator pleasure.[3]

Asian American filmmakers can recontextualize and thereby reinvest spectator pleasure by critiquing *The World of Suzie Wong* (the film we love to hate), but that begs the question of how *The World of Suzie Wong* produces pleasure in the first place (the film we love to love). The film's title suggests that it is an Orientalist text in Edward Said's sense of the term—this text constructs a vision of the Orient and implicitly jus-

tifies Western exploitation of that world.[4] As a thesis about the Orient, the text necessarily includes discourses that run counter to its ideological project—discourses
that it supposedly rebuts, discourses that may produce pleasure for the anti-racist,
feminist spectator. The cynical view of that pleasure is that it is at best mediated and
at worst co-opted by the text: If the film is constructed in such a way that both racist
and anti-racist spectators can enjoy it, then it is a truly successful consumer product.
An opposing view would celebrate an anti-racist reading by labeling it "resistant."
The fact that spectators can read the film as condemning racism suggests that the text
is not monolithic, after all. Rather than make one case or the other, I propose to seek
out a middle ground between these two positions. As Judith Mayne (1993, 93–94)
points out, each position depends on a restricted notion of how meaning is made:

> For many textual theorists of the 1970s, Raymond Bellour and the editors of *Camera Obscu-*
> *ra* in particular, the value of textual analysis was to demonstrate that classical narrative pro-
> duces a variety of ruptures, deviations, and crises only to recuperate them in the name of
> hierarchical closure or resolution. From this point of view, any validations of those ruptures
> is at best naive voluntarism and at worst a refusal to acknowledge what one does not want
> to know—that the cinematic appratus [*sic*] works with great efficiency to channel all desire
> into male, oedipal desire. The apparatus works; closure and resolution are achieved. Inspired
> in many cases by the work of [Stuart] Hall and cultural studies, others, like John Fiske . . . ,
> insist upon the social formations of audiences as the only ultimately determining factors. . . .
> The problem in each case is that the activity of making meaning is assumed to reside in one
> single source—either the cinematic apparatus, or the socially contextualized viewer.

I propose that we develop a theory of spectatorship that examines the give and take
between these two extreme positions, between the closure of the apparatus and the
openness of the audience. Audiences can take pleasure in opening up a text only if
they first perceive it as closed. Resistant spectators are necessarily aware of the dominant, racist message of *The World of Suzie Wong*; resistant readings are thus fleeting
and contingent by definition.

In staking out such a middle territory, we must beware what Mayne calls "Pollyan-
na dialectics" (ibid., 94): the banal observation that the text is racist, but that spectators do not have to give in to racist indoctrination. After examining the complex
dynamics of *The World of Suzie Wong*, I propose to shift the focus from the film to its
star. Star discourses are, of course, nowhere near as coherent as the narratives of individual movies. Stars are incoherent texts whose meanings are constantly contested.
Richard Dyer (1979, 3) describes the interpretation of star discourses as a "structured
polysemy." It is precisely at the intersection of the supposedly monolithic narrative
structure of *The World of Suzie Wong* and the structured polysemy of Nancy Kwan's
star discourse that Asian American spectatorial pleasure can be located.

Reading Suzie Wong: Resistance and Recuperation

Adapted from Richard Mason's 1957 novel and the 1958 Broadway play written by
Paul Osborn,[5] the film version of *The World of Suzie Wong* tells the story of draftsman

Robert Lomax (William Holden), who has decided to drop out for a year and establish himself as a painter. Robert rents a room at the Nam Kok hotel, a de facto brothel in Hong Kong's Wanchai District. He hires Suzie Wong, a prostitute, as his regular model, although he resists sleeping with her, ostensibly because he cannot condone the immorality of her "choice" of career. Robert realizes that he has fallen in love with Suzie at about the same time that he (an American) develops contempt for British hypocrisy toward the Chinese. Suzie becomes Robert's "permanent girlfriend" (the term connoting serial monogamy more than permanence), but because Robert has not sold any of his paintings, he cannot support Suzie and her baby for long. Robert refuses to use Suzie's money, and she leaves him. The couple is reunited in a failed attempt to rescue Suzie's child from a natural disaster, and as the film ends, the couple presumably is bound for the United States (as a seer had foretold), where Robert's career as a painter will support them (he has sold a painting in Suzie's absence).

The World of Suzie Wong is indeed a classic racist, sexist text. The only Chinese women we meet are prostitutes, and the few Chinese men we encounter are asexual. Robert's friend Kay is excoriated as a scheming white woman; in comparison, the submissive Suzie comes to embody desirable feminine attributes. William Holden's patented blend of world-weary cynicism and Yankee idealism is contrasted with British hypocrisy, underscoring the notion that Americans are not racist when compared with Europeans.[6] The movie's low point comes when Suzie's girlfriends coo enviously as Suzie announces that Robert beats her out of jealousy, in keeping with the movie's discourse about aberrant Chinese morality (in which Suzie's prostitution is characterized by Robert as a moral failing rather than the outcome of systemic racism and sexism in a neocolonial context).[7] And yet, this low point also occasions what I argue are moments of rupture, moments when "Suzie" threatens to break out of the "World" that has been constructed around her. The matter-of-factness with which Suzie describes Hong Kong's rampant poverty and the beatings she endures from British sailors might be read as indictments of the sanitized *World of Suzie Wong*. Robert's dumbfounded responses to Suzie's statements demonstrate both the character's fundamental incomprehension of Suzie's social reality and the movie's inability to articulate a coherent moral position. The movie works to contain these disruptive articulations, however: Suzie's matter-of-factness in the face of such horrors is offered as evidence of Asia's immorality and Asian women's submissiveness.

Another example: The beating that Suzie attributes to Robert comes at the hands of a sailor who is angry because he has been solicited merely to convey her into a bar that unescorted women may not enter legally. (The law is meant to prevent prostitutes from gaining access to clients.) The sailor's violence indicts not only the brutality of the colonial system that he enforces, but also his unfamiliarity with local laws and customs. This critique is quickly contained, however, when Suzie's white knight comes to her rescue,[8] prompting Suzie to tell her friends that Robert beat her. The spectator is simultaneously reassured that Asian women want to be beaten and allowed to displace revulsion onto the "Orient." After all, Western cultures would never equate violence with devotion.

Rupture, critique, containment. This is, after all, the classic apparatus model that Mayne describes. But it is too easy to argue that moments of critique are contained by the movie, for such an argument does not account for the pleasure that accompanies those isolated moments. We need to understand the nature of that pleasure before we dismiss it as delusional, co-opted, or mediated. How is it possible to sustain pleasure in a mediated text?

I want to turn to a particularly complex scene and explore the contradictions involved in attempting to read *The World of Suzie Wong*. Shortly after the midpoint of the movie, Suzie visits Robert wearing a Western-style dress; it is the first time we have seen her in anything but local costume. Robert is repulsed by Suzie's outfit, proclaiming that she has no idea what true beauty is. He pushes her down on his bed, strips the clothes from her body, and throws them off his balcony into the street. It is perhaps the most violent on-screen act in the film, yet it involves no bloodshed. It is definitely assault, but barely battery. The camera invites us to appreciate Suzie's form through conventional cinematic syntax (beginning with a low-angle shot of her feet and tilting up her body), then asks us to reject her allure. The film gives us a glimpse of Suzie in a half-slip, but salves any voyeuristic guilt by allowing us to condemn Robert for his aggression. Further, the film implicitly critiques Robert: His complaint is that Suzie "look[s] like a cheap European streetwalker." Judging from his actions, the key word would seem to be "European"— for tearing off her clothes does not make her look less like a prostitute, only less like a Western one. As long as Suzie is in her cheongsam or her lingerie, Robert is able to see her as Oriental first, prostitute second or not at all. But by attiring herself in Western clothing, Suzie breaks out of her purely Oriental image. Laura Marks notes that Suzie "threatens the American by underlining the fact that their relation is the sordid one familiar to him from 'home,' and by imposing her desiring subjectivity on his ideal image of her" (Marks 1991, 16). Indeed, this scene is the first indication the movie gives that the West has prostitutes, too, and that admission opens the door to a critique of Robert's exoticized perceptions of Suzie—and, by extension, a critique of the film as a whole. Of course, the film contains that critique simply by having Suzie accede to it. In the next scene, she returns to her Chinese mode of dress and greatly inspires Robert's libido.

This, then, is the nature of pleasure in reading *The World of Suzie Wong*—fleeting, contingent, and highly mediated. For all that, however, I do not want to deny that pleasure is there. I want to interrogate that pleasure, perhaps so I can break free of it, for as long as the movie gives me pleasure, it has a channel with which to speak its racist messages to me and potentially through me. It is a pleasure that has also been interrogated by *Sally's Beauty Spot* (Lee 1990), a film that quotes *Suzie Wong* in the course of a meditation about the cultural field in which Asian women negotiate their relationships to their bodies and their lovers.

Sally's Beauty Spot: A Cinematic Spectator and Fan

In *Sally's Beauty Spot*, written and directed by Helen Lee, a Canadian who produces her films on both sides of the U.S.-Canadian border,[9] the main character Sally scrubs at a mole on her breast in an attempt either to remove it or to massage it. The deep breathing on the soundtrack underscores that ambiguity. Off-screen voices quote cultural criticism—for example, this line from an interview with Homi Bhabha: "They will always conceive of the difference as that between the preconstituted, natural poles of black and white" (Photo 3.1). For the Asian woman caught between these two poles, the blackness of her hair and her mole become the terrain on which competing desires for her body are fought. When Sally is shown embracing first a white man, then a black man, it might be taken literally. The abstractness of the image track (with Sally and the two men shot in extreme close-up against a white background), however, suggests that these images are figurative expressions of the Bhabha quotation.

The construction of *Sally's Beauty Spot* is very dense and allusive. The soundtrack in particular offers a wide range of sounds that attach themselves to and detach themselves from the images in interesting ways (e.g., an image of Sally combing her hair is accompanied by sounds of waves crashing). This disjunctive use of sound seems

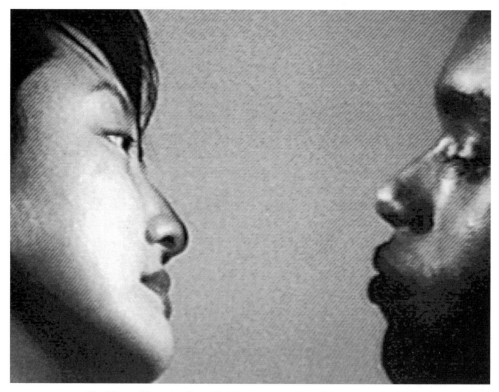

PHOTO 3.1. Is this a diegetic, literal image, or a non-diegetic, symbolic image? Sally kisses a black man in *Sally's Beauty Spot* (1990), dir. Helen Lee.

to underscore certain absurdities, as when the squeegee-like sound of obsessive scrubbing comments on Sally's application of so-called flesh-colored makeup to her beauty spot. The sound suggests she is not trying to cover up the spot so much as rub it out. Far from encouraging audience condescension toward Sally's actions, the humor evoked by the soundtrack suggests a knowing sympathy.

The World of Suzie Wong enters the equation by way of an off-screen voice that converses with Sally about her mole, then describes her favorite film, briefly encapsulating the plot of *Suzie Wong* in accented English. At one moment, Sally asks: "Why do you like the movie so much?" After a long pause in which no vocal answer is forthcoming, we hear Sally's voice say: "It's always been there—ever since I was a little girl." Sally might be describing her mole, but she might also be answering her earlier question—her friend likes the movie because it has always been there.[10]

Clips from *Suzie Wong* are presented in grainy color or in black and white with scan lines, sometimes accompanied by the sound of a projector. Different reception contexts are implied (a broadcast viewed on a black-and-white television set, a 16 mm print projected or perhaps viewed on an editing table), suggesting the pervasiveness of *The World of Suzie Wong*, but also emphasizing its variability. In particular, some of the contexts imply greater degrees of audience control over the conditions of reception. For example, the scene in which Robert strips off Suzie's dress is replayed upside down and in reverse, as if a print of the film had been threaded tail out through a 16 mm projector. In *Sally's Beauty Spot*, Robert is made to re-dress Suzie (forgive the pun), as if Lee's film were undertaking its own revision of an ambiguously pleasurable text (Photo 3.2). The sounds of projector motors whirring (as well as the scan lines, which suggest that an imperfect 16 mm dub was fashioned from a television broadcast) mark the effort involved in the revision. Rewriting *Suzie Wong* takes effort.

Theorizing the Spectator of Color

Sally's Beauty Spot shows us one way to find pleasure in a racist text—by upending, decontextualizing, and remobilizing it. This process gives rise to the intellectual pleasure of critique, but it does not necessarily account for the pleasure of seeing *The World of Suzie Wong* unaltered. Lee's film may provide us with another clue. At one point, Sally watches a scene in which Suzie instructs Robert on the proper use of chopsticks. (It is clear that Robert resents the implication that he is an uncoordinated child.) For a brief moment, Suzie takes charge, and Sally smiles. Of course, the movie as a whole tells us that Suzie is the child and Robert the adult; for the audience to take pleasure in Suzie's turning the tables on Robert, the audience must recognize that Robert set the table in the first place. Sally's fleeting appreciation of this scene suggests that a resistant reading of *The World of Suzie Wong* depends on maintaining a tension between awareness of the global and the local—that is, between understanding the film's overarching ideology and isolated moments of resistance to it. I believe that the figure of the star illuminates the global–local tension, but before elaborating my argument (itself influenced by James Baldwin's discussion of black

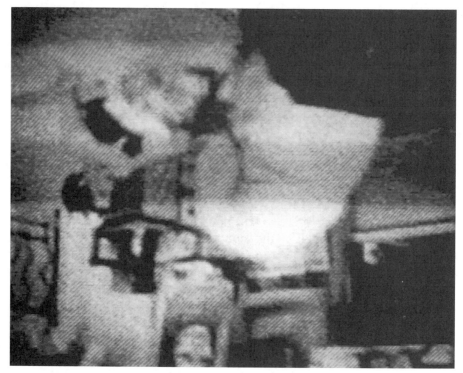

PHOTO 3.2. *Sally's Beauty Spot* (1990), dir. Helen Lee, runs *Suzie Wong*'s metaphorical rape scene upside down and backward, so that Robert "re-dresses" Suzie.

stars), I would like to place it in the context of previous writings on the complex relationship among star discourses, individual movies, and spectators, starting with Stuart Hall's conception of oppositional readings.

Hall's influential essay "Encoding/decoding" (1980) proposes three positions from which mass-media discourses are interpreted: dominant, negotiated, and oppositional. These terms emerge from Hall's description of mass communication,[11] in which he elaborates on the "sender/message/receiver" model with reference to Marxist notions of base-superstructure.[12] Hall points out that meanings go through a process of encoding before they can be transmitted by producers; those transmissions are then decoded by receivers. Certain codes are virtually transparent—that is, they are nearly universal within a given culture. These naturalized codes "appear not to be constructed" (Hall 1980, 132). More often, the processes of encoding and decoding are not symmetrical: *"lack of equivalence* between the two sides of the communicative exchange" results in misunderstanding or distortion of the producer's intended message (ibid., 131). Hall's three positions describe different degrees of equivalence between receiver and producer: the dominant position is the most symmetrical, the oppositional position is the most asymmetrical.

Judith Mayne renames Hall's decoding positions "decoding *strategies*" and argues that dominant and oppositional readings are "more usefully understood, perhaps, as

horizons of possibility" (Mayne 1993, 92). In Mayne's view, all readings are negotiated, because "it is highly unlikely that one will find any 'pure' instances of dominant or oppositional readings" (ibid., 93). Mayne therefore resists the tendency to
equate the existence of negotiated readings with "resistance to dominant ideology":
If all readings are negotiated, then negotiated readings are not inherently resistant.
In Mayne's words, "the sheer fact that a spectator or group of spectators makes unauthorized uses of the cinema is no guarantee that such uses are contestatory" (ibid.,
80). Further, the very notion of contestatory uses implies that readers are always
aware that their interpretations of the text are at variance with its intended effects:
"What Hall's model leaves relatively intact is the notion of a text's dominant ideology" (ibid., 92).

This statement begs the question of what text, precisely, we are talking about.
Although Hollywood films can be described as if they were a single text—a coherent
narrative—most Hollywood films can also be understood as the intersection of a
number of star texts (that is, an uneasy alliance of multiple incoherent narratives, with
stars as their protagonists).[13] Meaning is created from the spectator's efforts to resolve
the contradictions of these competing narratives. I suggest that the affection of the
spectator of color for a racist film is based on a strategy of selectively re-narrativiz-
ing elements of a star's performance. Thus, it is not a question of negotiating an oppositional reading of a film's narrative text. Rather, it is a matter of constructing an
entirely separate narrative from scavenged bits and pieces of a film.

Richard Dyer's discussion of alternative or subversive star types in *Stars* (1979)
investigates the relationship of the image of the "independent woman" to the narratives of the films in which such characters appear. "Do the narratives of the films they
appear in legitimate and promote this image [of independence], or undermine it?"
asks Dyer (64). Following Elizabeth Dalton's lead, Dyer notes that the narrative resolutions of most films involve the star's "climb-down"; therefore, "the narratives do
not appear to legitimize independence" (64–65). However, appearances can be deceiv-
ing: Molly Haskell has argued that (in Dyer's words) "What we remember is the
independence not the climb-down" (ibid., 65). Dyer summarizes:

> I think one could argue that in terms of emphasis, weighting within the film, perform-
> ance, *mise en scène*, etc., the independence elements are stronger, more vivid, than the
> climb-down resolutions. Two observations support this. One ... , the narratives do not
> seem invariably to point to inadequacies in the psychology of either the independent
> women stars or the people of their immediate environment to explain, and explain away,
> their independence. Two, because we are dealing with stars, and not just fictional char-
> acters, the specific details of what happens in the plot of the film may matter less than the
> 'personality' that the film as a whole reveals—the star phenomenon emphasizes the kind-
> of-person the star is rather than the specific circumstances of particular roles. [Ibid.]

Dyer's two observations deserve some examination. The first comment suggests
that narratives are not necessarily ideologically consistent or narratively coherent,
insofar as a Hollywood film may construct an independent character, then rein her
in without adequately accounting for psychological motivation.[14] The second obser-

vation suggests that star personae transcend the narrative resolutions in which they are developed.

In *The Devil Finds Work* (1990), James Baldwin describes the African American spectator's response to climb-down resolutions involving black stars. In his analysis of *The Defiant Ones* (Kramer 1958), Baldwin asserts that Sidney Poitier's performance, "which lends the film its only real distinction, also, paradoxically, smashes it to pieces. There is no way to believe both Noah Cullen *and* the story" (Baldwin 1990, 74). When Baldwin says "Noah Cullen," he is describing the character not so much as written but as performed ("no one, clearly, was able to foresee what Poitier would do with his role—nor was anyone, thereafter, able to undo it" [ibid., 74]). Baldwin points to certain psychological inconsistencies in the film, stating at one point: "It is unlikely that Noah Cullen would have sat still for this scene" (ibid., 77). Baldwin devotes most of his analysis to the final scenes of the film, especially the idiocy of Cullen's actions at the conclusion (he jumps off a train that his white cohort is unable to catch, despite the fact that they are no longer chained together). In describing this conclusion, Baldwin describes the reactions of two different audiences: "Liberal white audiences applauded when Sidney . . . jumped off the train in order not to abandon his white buddy. The Harlem audience was outraged, and yelled, *Get back on the train, you fool!*" (ibid., 75–76).[15]

Baldwin takes as his primary text the narrative of *The Defiant Ones*. Poitier's performance is his secondary text. But if these priorities were reversed—if we were to analyze Poitier's star persona and take the narrative of *The Defiant Ones* as just one aspect of it—I would like to suggest that what Poitier specifically transcends is the film's linear narrative. For the spectator of color to take pleasure in Poitier's star discourse, we must engage in a practice of selective remembering that refuses the linear development of *The Defiant Ones*. Poitier's star "personality" depends on our arresting the film before he jumps off the train. The last image we recall is Poitier reaching out to Tony Curtis, and we conveniently forget that he jumps.[16]

When we speak of resistance within texts, we are speaking about moments that work against our sense of the text's dominant ideology. These disruptive moments may, in the larger picture, be contained by the text. Worse, these moments may be a means for racist texts to tempt spectators of color to watch. But if we focus exclusively on the ways in which moments of resistance are recouped by the text, we are in part acceding to a narrative view of those moments, refusing to take them in isolation. When we speak of resistance within texts, we speak about moments. But when we speak of resistance within spectators, we speak of the mobilization of those moments into a new narrative space, one that transcends the narrative logic of the movies, avoiding the "climb-down resolutions." The novelist, poet, and critic Jessica Hagedorn had this to say about the images of Asian and Asian American women in film:

> When there are characters who look like us represented in a movie, we have . . . learned to view between the lines, or to add what is missing. For many of us, this way of watching has always been a necessity. We fill in the gaps. If a female character is presented as a mute, willowy beauty, we convince ourselves she is an ancestral ghost—so smart she doesn't have to speak at all. If she is a whore with a heart of gold, we claim her as a tough

feminist icon.... And if she is presented as an utterly devoted saint suffering nobly in silence, we lie and say she is just like our mothers. [Hagedorn 1994, 79]

Hagedorn describes a process of "filling in the gaps," wherein the spectator attempts to account for insufficient characterization by constructing stories that transcend the narratives offered by the film. Faced with a racist narrative and a character (or star personality), we recast those characters in an oppositional mold.

It could be argued that certain kinds of racist narratives are more amenable to oppositional recastings than others. Specifically, it is the preponderance of interracial romantic plots in Nancy Kwan's cinematic repertoire that allows and invites the renarrativization that I described. To take the film career of a contemporaneous Asian American actor such as Mako (or perhaps James Shigeta, whose career as a romantic lead is more comparable to Kwan's), one is immediately confronted with the different kinds of roles and plots that Asian American male actors were afforded. How would Mako's role as the "little brown buddy" in *The Sand Pebbles* (Wise 1966) be renarrativized? How can fans rewrite his performances? By contrast, the particular indignities inflicted on Nancy Kwan produce characterizations ripe for renarrativization. The combination of spunk and submissiveness that was Kwan's specialty results in a character that embodies both resistance and accession to the racist, sexist narrative that she inhabits. As an Asian American male spectator, my response to these narratives of interracial romance goes beyond frustration with the indignities suffered by the figure of Nancy Kwan, arriving at resentment that Asian and Asian American masculinity has been written out of these plots. My desire to renarrativize Nancy Kwan is therefore in part a romance of its own, a desire to write Asian American masculinity into the narrative by romancing Nancy Kwan away from the white male lovers that Hollywood fiction provides for her.

Star discourses involve more than the sum of roles performed by an actor. They also involve the narrativization of a star's career.[17] The spectator of color, confronted with a star who persistently takes roles in racist movies, must also renarrativize the star's career to remain a fan. Following Hagedorn, I'd like to suggest that when an actor continues to accept derogatory roles, we tell ourselves the star has a family to support, or that the exaggerated way in which the star conforms to stereotype is actually a parody of that stereotype.

Me and Nancy: Confessions of a Fan of Kwan

To argue that *The World of Suzie Wong* includes moments in which Suzie critiques the ideological project of the film is to claim that such moments are bold enough that they resist containment—it is to remember that Suzie points out that prostitution was the only option available to her and to forget that Robert replies dismissively: "Sorry I asked." (It is to remember Sidney Poitier reaching out with his hand while forgetting that he jumps off the train.) To be a fan of Nancy Kwan is to absorb her entire film career in this fashion, to remember her casting daggers with her eyes at a white racist and to forget that she falls for him a moment later (*Fate Is the Hunter* [Nelson 1964]),

PHOTO 3.3.   Nancy Kwan battles Sharon Tate in *The Wrecking Crew* (1969), dir. Phil Karlson. This flying kick clearly owes more to Kwan's dance training than to martial arts, perhaps ironically inflecting Kwan's dragon-lady role by emphasizing the substitution of Western dance moves for *Kung Fu.* Bruce Lee served as fight choreographer. © 1968 Columbia Pictures Industries, Inc. All rights reserved. Courtesy of Columbia Pictures.

to remember her gaining the upper hand in combat (Photo 3.3) while forgetting that Matt Helm blows her up in the next scene (*The Wrecking Crew* [Karlson 1969]). To be a fan of Nancy Kwan is to seize on the ludicrous intensity that she brings to her portrayal of a savage cannibal and muse that she is camping up an outrageously racist role (*Lt. Robin Crusoe, USN* [Paul 1966]). To be a fan of Nancy Kwan, the spectator of color has to forget more than she or he remembers, and to flatter oneself as a resistant spectator is to be forever aware of the narrative context from which one has mentally excerpted images of defiance. How else can I maintain my cathexis to Nancy Kwan in the face of such bubble-bursting movies as *Slaying the Dragon*?[18] Commenting on her role in *The World of Suzie Wong*, Kwan says: "She happened to be a prostitute. She could have been a nun [laughs], so then all the Asian women in America would have been identified as nuns! But she was a hooker—with a heart of gold." Kwan's comment reveals a simultaneously knowing and naïve position. She correctly notes that *The World of Suzie Wong* did not create the image of the hooker with the heart of gold, but she seems to think that the film's longevity is in no way attributable to its trafficking in well-known images. Suzie Wong did not just *happen* to be a prostitute; further, to suggest that the film would have been as successful as it was and is if Suzie were a nun is disingenuous.

Kwan's appearance in *Slaying the Dragon* runs completely counter to my attempts to read Nancy Kwan as a resistant actor. She reveals that she is smart enough to know that many Asian Americans are offended by her role as Suzie Wong and has developed a rote response to such criticism. In this, she resists the narrative of *Slaying the Dragon*, in which Asian American women are portrayed as universally decrying the lotus-blossom stereotype.[19] Kwan thus reveals herself as the ultimate resistant actor.[20] However, even Kwan's own words cannot sabotage a fan's rose-colored image. My desire to interpret Kwan's performances as feminist and anti-racist is already dependent on selective retention and disavowal of context; therefore, it is absurd to argue that *Slaying the Dragon* seriously undermines my reading. It merely underscores the contingency of such a reading practice. And I am not unique in continuing to like Nancy Kwan, even if she has never recanted her role as Suzie Wong. Nancy Kwan is the living link to the film that Asian Americans love to hate.

Notes

Acknowledgments: Portions of this essay were first presented at the Society for Cinema Studies Conference in Syracuse, New York, on March 6, 1994. I am grateful to Shari Roberts for organizing the panel, and to the audience and my fellow panelists for their comments on that draft. I am indebted to Marina Heung for sharing material on Nancy Kwan with me. A preliminary draft of this essay was presented at the University of California at Irvine on February 9, 1998; particularly helpful critiques were offered by John Liu and Valerie Chow. Michael Omi, Darrell Hamamoto, and Sandra Liu offered many useful suggestions that guided my revision of this essay for publication.

1. I do not claim to ground my theoretical speculations about audiences in empirical research; nor do I wish to substitute these cinematically constructed audiences for real audiences (if there are such things). I conceive of this essay as a dialogue between Asian American filmmakers and their spectators (including myself) in which we each construct an audience for *The World of Suzie Wong* for our own rhetorical purposes.

2. Kip Fulbeck's *Some Questions for 28 Kisses* (1994) also reveals a heavy investment in Nancy Kwan's character—or, rather, that investment is suggested by the structuring absence of *The World of Suzie Wong*. Fulbeck's video juxtaposes clips of white men kissing Asian women in twenty-two movies, with character-generated rhetorical questions aimed variously at white men, Asian American men, Asian American women, and so on, about interracial dating. The soundtrack consists of an audio collage of voices reading from articles and letters to the editor on the same topic. The piece concludes with Fulbeck's voiceover problematizing his own location: As the male child of a white father and an Asian mother, he can neither condone nor condemn these images.

The movies Fulbeck surveys range from documentaries (*Imagine: John Lennon* [Solt 1988]) to Hollywood comedies (*Mr. Baseball* [Schepisi 1992]), from independent features (the American

Playhouse-produced *Thousand Pieces of Gold* [Kelly 1992]) to mass-marketed teen-oriented movies (*Wayne's World* [Spheeris 1992]). Nancy Kwan (who, like the filmmaker, is *hapa*) is notably absent from the montage. Fulbeck cites the very notoriety of *Suzie Wong* as the reason for its omission. In his words, "I felt it had been done to death—like the *Year of the Dragon* [Cimino 1985] rape scene" (Fulbeck 1997).

3. The filmmaker Daniel Tirtawinata and the video maker Valerie Soe have also incorporated *The World of Suzie Wong* into their works. Tirtawinata's *Mail Order* (1989) and Soe's *Mixed Blood* (1992a) and *Picturing Oriental Girls: A (Re) Educational Videotape* (1992b) each feature *Suzie Wong* as one text among many that contribute to discourses about cross-racial desire. (Unlike these three pieces, Gee's *Slaying the Dragon* offers a discrete critique of *Suzie Wong*.)

Tirtawinata's *Mail Order* is a twelve-minute narrative film that depicts a white man's fascination with Asian women. In a brief sequence, excerpts from *Suzie Wong* on the soundtrack suggest that the main character is watching the film on his television set; a commercial for Singapore Airlines is treated in a similar fashion (the same commercial is shown in *Slaying the Dragon*), while a promotional tape for a fictional mail-order–bride service is presented directly, without specifying a diegetic audience. *Mail Order* thus constructs a white male audience for *The World of Suzie Wong*.

Picturing Oriental Girls offers what Soe (1997) describes as a "visual compendium" of images of Asian women in mainstream films, organized by categories suggested by quotations that scroll up the screen—notably, several excerpts from the original novel, *The World of Suzie Wong*. For example, Soe's video begins with an image of Suzie posing for Robert, accompanied by the following quote: "The creative impulse has its roots in sexuality and it was not mere chance that I enjoyed painting Malay women." Next we see a clip from *Shanghai Surprise* (Goddard 1986) in which Glendon Wasey (Sean Penn) paints Chinese characters on a woman's body, followed by a similar image from singer George Michael's "I Want Your Sex" music video. Thus, *Suzie Wong* is marked as the Ur-form of certain tropes of Asian female sexuality. The other quotations—from a "correspondence catalog" and a *GQ Great Britain* article labeling Asian women "the ultimate accessory"—suggest a white male audience for these images, somewhat akin to the white male character in Tirtawinata's film, while the subtitle suggests a metaphorical classroom, perhaps an Asian American Studies or Women's Studies class. In other words, *Picturing Oriental Girls* constructs a white male audience for the movies that it excerpts while evoking an anti-racist, feminist audience for the video itself.

Soe's *Mixed Blood* (originally part of an interactive installation) blends the compendium approach with found footage and "talking heads" (interviews). Asian American men and women, along with non-Asian men and women (who are always framed with their Asian American partners), talk about a variety of issues pertaining to cross-racial desire (fetishes for Asian women, parental disapproval, etc.). This testimony is intercut with images culled from mainstream movies and found footage (mostly from educational films) allusively juxtaposed with the talking-head testimonials (e.g., a bee colony is juxtaposed with testimony about the enclave mentality of Japanese American communities). The wide variety of perspectives, often mutually contradictory, suggest a diverse audience for *Suzie Wong* and the other Hollywood images. (A more complete consideration of the audience that the video constructs for itself would have to account for its context as part of an installation.)

4. Many theorists have extended the arguments that Said laid out in *Orientalism* (1978), notably Lowe (1991). For a cogent critique of Said's position, see Young (1990).

5. David Merrick produced and Joshua Logan directed the stage adaptation.

6. British hypocrisy in *The World of Suzie Wong* is expressed through the private acceptance of class hierarchies, coupled with the public disavowal of racism. For example, Robert Lomax's

patron enjoys puncturing the casual racism of his dinner guests by pretending he has a Chinese brother-in-law, but he later attempts to persuade Robert that he does not really love Suzie.

The American contempt for social hypocrisy is also illustrated by Holden's roles in *Stalag 17* (Wilder 1953) and *The Bridge on the River Kwai* (Lean 1957). In *Stalag 17*, Holden's opportunism makes him the scapegoat for the European officers with whom he is jailed, while his finely honed instinct for self-preservation in *The Bridge on the River Kwai* leads him to suspect immediately that the overly disciplined patriotism of the British officers will lead them to collaborate with the enemy.

7. For a more complete discussion of the displacement of racial discourses by discussions of morality in *The World of Suzie Wong*, see Harrison (1995). Harrison's project has much in common with mine—namely, the desire to reread the character of Suzie Wong as resisting the dominant logic of the film as a whole.

The discourse of morality is often inextricably bound to discourses about class. *The World of Suzie Wong*, however, mystifies class discourses by offering cultural explanations. Although Suzie continually declares that she turned to prostitution because she is poor and unmarriageable, she also insists on disguising her lack of culture and education in the name of "saving face." Class differences are thus subsumed by cultural differences, consistent with neocolonialist logic. Robert's all-American identity is affirmed as middle class, so the film's social hierarchy of British, Americans, and Chinese is congruent with class stratification.

8. Marchetti (1993) discusses the figure of the white knight in a chapter on the films *The World of Suzie Wong* (Quine 1960) and *Love Is a Many-Splendored Thing* (King 1955).

9. For the purposes of this discussion, I am speaking of Lee's film as if it belongs to an Asian American aesthetic. The fact that Lee counterpoises "Sally," her Korean Canadian sister, with the Chinese/Eurasian actor Nancy Kwan underscores the fluidity of these cultural and national labels. This should not, however, be taken as an excuse to conflate Asian Canadian and Asian American practices. Nor is it entirely appropriate to postulate an Asian North American aesthetic, for that ignores U.S. cultural domination of Canada. It would be fair to say that Lee's film circulates under an Asian American banner (as it does in the Women Make Movies catalog, for example), but that begs the question of the relationship between commercial categories and aesthetic discourses. (Lee is herself interested in preserving the possibility that her film might be both Canadian and American. Even when her films use identifiable landmarks, such as the dam in *My Niagara* [1992], Lee is aware that spectators will understand the film variously to be about Canada, the United States, and North America.)

For further discussion of the implication of these terms in constructing an audience for Asian American cinema, see Feng (1995).

10. The blackness of the mole, read through Bhabha's reference to "poles of black and white," also comes to stand for the very notion of racial difference. In this context, "It's always been there" refers to discourses of racialism. This reading is the one most favored by my students of Asian ancestry at the University of California at Irvine, who reminded me that moles are especially common among Asians.

11. Hall's specific point of departure is the analysis of what he calls "televisual communication," which might more precisely be called "television news reporting," because Hall's examples all refer to the encoding and decoding of representations of "news" events.

12. Many of Hall's formulations in this essay are indebted to Althusser (1971). Specifically, Hall notes that so-called misunderstandings between producer (sender) and consumer (receiver) have "a great deal to do with the structural differences of relation and position between broadcasters and audiences" (Hall 1980, 131). Althusser's version of "superstructure" also lurks behind Hall's argument that codes of professionalism reinforce hegemonic messages

(ibid., 136). "Encoding/decoding" is thus consistent with Hall's project to elaborate and theorize the concept of "false consciousness"; see Hall (1996).

13. Bakhtin (1981) discusses the ways in which contrasting socio-ideological languages serve to express ideological differences within a given culture. In emphasizing the "higher stylistic unity of the work as a whole" (Bakhtin 1981, 262), Bakhtin focuses our attention on the text's dominant meaning. Movies, more so than novels, feature stars that take on life beyond the bounds of their characters in a given text. Star discourses work centrifugally, challenging the stability of an individual text's dominant meaning.

14. Altman (1989, 17) argues that many U.S. genres—not just the musical—operate "only in part according to the [classical Hollywood] model of psychological motivation." Altman sees the musical as reconciling what Dyer would call "independence elements" into a "concordance of opposites" via the marriage plot (ibid., 27). This resolution can be sustained if one approaches musical narratives as dual-focus structures (alternating between contrasting characters) rather than causally motivated plots necessarily driven by one character (ibid., 21). By focusing attention on narrative structure, Altman accounts for what would otherwise be read as ideological contradiction.

My own argument suggests that all films convey multiple narratives—the movie's own narrative and isolated moments of the movie's narrative that serve as installments in the intertextual construction of a star. "Climb-down resolutions" belong to the former narrative structure, but not necessarily to the latter.

15. Arguably, Baldwin is comparing a hypothetical audience ("liberal white audiences" in the plural) with a specific, empirically observed one ("The Harlem audience"). It could just as easily be concluded that both audiences are hypothetical, however—"Harlem" being not so much a specific term as a general signifier of a segregated, northern audience—and I would caution the reader not to conclude that just because Baldwin is himself black, his references to black audiences are necessarily empirical.

16. At the 1995 Kennedy Center Honors, Sidney Poitier's career was summarized in a short film (co-produced by Sara Lukinson). In the excerpt from *The Defiant Ones*, Poitier reaches back for Curtis, who grasps his hand. The film then cuts to another movie, omitting Poitier's leap from the train. Thirty-seven years after the initial release of *The Defiant Ones*, another audience—surely a descendent of James Baldwin's liberal white audience—is spared from remembering that Cullen/Poitier jumped.

In theorizing the spectator of color, I acknowledge that my position as a straight male spectator must be taken into account. In lieu of a full discussion of Asian American queer spectatorship, allow me to discuss briefly the homoeroticism of the actual final scene of *The Defiant Ones*, in which Poitier cradles Curtis while eyeing a white police officer defiantly. It is intriguing that Baldwin does not propose a queer reading of this scene, a reading that privileges moments of homoeroticism over moments of heterosexual performativity. Baldwin's emphasis on race does not allow him to discuss sexuality. He alludes to queer spectatorship elsewhere in the monograph, when he notes that as a child he identified with Bette Davis because of their physical resemblance, noting the contradiction that this black boy was told he was ugly, while this white woman was told she was beautiful. This cross-racial, cross-gender identification serves both to critique cultural discourses of sexual attractiveness and to articulate a spectatorial position that does not fit into Laura Mulvey's sadistic male model.

17. One aspect of this narrative is the emphasis in U.S. magazines on Kwan's multiracial heritage. It is beyond the scope of this essay to consider how Kwan's biracial identity plays in the press. I will, however, speculate that the emphasis on Kwan's European ancestry is an attempt to recuperate and attribute her beauty to her whiteness, to assure white audiences that it is accept-

able to find Kwan attractive because she is not wholly other. For Asian American audiences, any Asian face is claimed as an Asian American icon (in the 1990s, Asian American audiences followed Dean Cain's acting career with great interest). If a *hapa* actor plays Asian roles, then she or he is usually accepted as Asian American. If that actor takes non-racially marked roles, Asian American audiences gossip and "out" these closeted Asians. Of course, *hapa* actors may be of special interest to *hapa* fans, as Amy Hill points out in her one-woman show, *Beside Myself*.

18. Deborah Gee's *Slaying the Dragon* (1987) is a sixty-minute documentary that provides a historical context for the representation of Asian women in mainstream U.S. media. *Slaying the Dragon* juxtaposes clips from Hollywood films, television programs and commercials, and other media with interviews in which media scholars, producers, and actors discuss these representations. *Slaying the Dragon* also features interviews with Asian American female spectators who discuss the impact of these representations; the documentary constructs a classroom audience akin to that implied by Soe's *Picturing Oriental Girls*. While *Slaying the Dragon* is arguably the most conventional of the Asian American films and videos discussed in this essay, its ambitious scope (e.g., its discussion of the Connie Chung "phenomenon" of Asian female news anchors alongside examination of advertisements and television drama) and the range of interviewees (including "normal" people as well as "experts") reveal a theoretical sophistication that belies its tone as an educational primer.

19. I borrow the term from Tajima (1989).

20. According to Phillips (1994, 27), "Kwan made public her disapproval for [*The Joy Luck Club*'s] bashing of her 1960 movie."

Works Cited

Althusser, Louis. 1971. "Ideology and Ideological State Apparatuses." Pp. 127–86 in *Lenin and Philosophy and Other Essays*, trans. Ben Brewster. New York: Monthly Review Press.

Altman, Rick. 1987. *The American Film Musical*. Bloomington: Indiana University Press.

Bakhtin, M. M. 1981. *The Dialogic Imagination*. Ed. Michael Holquist; trans. Caryl Emerson and Michael Holquist. Austin: University of Texas Press.

Baldwin, James. 1990. *The Devil Finds Work*. 1976. Reprint, New York: Laurel-Dell.

Dyer, Richard. 1979. *Stars*. London: BFI Publishing.

Feng, Peter. 1995. "In Search of Asian American Cinema." *Cineaste* 21, no. 1–2: 32–37.

Fulbeck, Kip. 1997. Letter to author. March 16.

Hagedorn, Jessica. 1994. "Asian Women in Film: No Joy, No Luck." *Ms.*, vol. 4, no. 4 (January/February), 74–79.

Hall, Stuart. 1980. "Encoding/decoding." Pp. 128–38 in *Culture, Media, Language*, ed. Stuart Hall, Dorothy Hobson, Andy Lowe, and Paul Willis. London: Hutchinson.

———. 1996. "The Problem of Ideology: Marxism Without Guarantees." Pp. 25–46 in *Stuart Hall: Critical Dialogues in Cultural Studies*, ed. David Morley and Kuan-Hsing Chen. London: Routledge.

Harrison, Taylor. 1995. "'Permanent' Girlfriend: Enabling Displacements in *The World of Suzie Wong*." *Iowa Journal of Cultural Studies* 14: 69–78.

Lowe, Lisa. 1991. *Critical Terrains: French and British Orientalisms*. Ithaca, N.Y.: Cornell University Press.

Marchetti, Gina. 1993. *Romance and the "Yellow Peril": Race, Sex, and Discursive Strategies in Hollywood Fiction*. Berkeley: University of California Press.

Marks, Laura U. 1991. "Desire and Dissolution." *Afterimage* 18, no. 9 (April): 16–17.

Mason, Richard. 1957. *The World of Suzie Wong.* Hong Kong: Pegasus Books.

Mayne, Judith. 1993. *Cinema and Spectatorship.* London: Routledge.

Mulvey, Laura. 1975. "Visual Pleasure and Narative Cinema." *Screen* 16, no. 3 (Autumn): 6–18.

Phillips, Gene. 1994. "Star Profile: Nancy Kwan." *She,* vol. 2, no. 2, 25–27.

Said, Edward. 1978. *Orientalism.* New York: Pantheon Books.

Soe, Valerie. 1997. Letter to author. March 19.

Tajima, Renee E. 1989. "Lotus Blossoms Don't Bleed: Images of Asian Women." Pp. 308–17 in *Making Waves: An Anthology of Writings by and about Asian American Women,* ed. Asian Women United of California (Diane Yen-Mei Wong). Boston: Beacon Press.

Young, Robert. 1990. *White Mythologies: Writing History and the West.* London: Routledge.

Films and Videos Cited

Cimino, Michael. 1985. *Year of the Dragon.* MGM/UA.

Gee, Deborah. 1987. *Slaying the Dragon.* NAATA.

Goddard, Jim. 1986. *Shanghai Surprise.* MGM.

Fulbeck, Kip. 1994. *Some Questions for 28 Kisses.* Electronic Arts Intermix, NAATA, Video Data Bank.

Karlson, Phil. 1969. *The Wrecking Crew.* Columbia.

Kelly, Nancy. 1992. *Thousand Pieces of Gold.* American Playhouse.

King, Henry. 1955. *Love Is a Many-Splendored Thing.* Twentieth Century-Fox.

Kramer, Stanley. 1958. *The Defiant Ones.* United Artists.

Lean, David. 1957. *The Bridge on the River Kwai.* Columbia.

Lee, Helen. 1990. *Sally's Beauty Spot.* Women Make Movies.

———. 1992. *My Niagara.* Women Make Movies.

Nelson, Ralph. 1964. *Fate Is the Hunter.* Twentieth Century-Fox.

Paul, Byron. 1966. *Lt. Robin Crusoe, USN.* Disney.

Quine, Richard. 1960. *The World of Suzie Wong.* Paramount.

Schepisi, Fred. 1992. *Mr. Baseball.* Universal.

Soe, Valerie. 1992a. *Mixed Blood.* NAATA, Video Out.

———. 1992b. *Picturing Oriental Girls: A (Re) Educational Videotape.* NAATA, Video Out.

Solt, Andrew. 1988. *Imagine: John Lennon.* Warner Bros.

Spheeris, Penelope. 1992. *Wayne's World.* Paramount.

Tirtawinata, Daniel. 1989. *Mail Order.* Daniel Tirtawinata (1234 Granville Ave. #2, Los Angeles, Calif. 90025).

Wang, Wayne. 1993. *The Joy Luck Club.* Hollywood Pictures.

Wilder, Billy. 1953. *Stalag 17.* Paramount.

Wise, Robert. 1966. *The Sand Pebbles.* Twentieth Century-Fox.

Part II

Negotiating Institutional Boundaries

Darrell Y. Hamamoto

4

The Joy Fuck Club: Prolegomenon to an Asian American Porno Practice

Getting Off

The students enrolled in "Theoretical Perspectives in Asian American Studies" at the University of California, Davis, were taken aback one class meeting when I posed the question of whether their collective sexual imaginary was indeed dominated by non-Yellow people. Without prurient intent on my part, I had them contemplate and discuss the content of their sexual fantasy life in trying to demonstrate how even the most intimate of thoughts are linked materially to social relations. What types of faces and bodies were conjured when trying to "get off"? Which media personalities made them "hard" or "wet" while indulging in fantasy? How comfortable did they feel in their Yellow skin? Why did the tired topics (unbidden by me) of "interracial" dating, "intermarriage," body image, and other *A. Magazine*-type editorial fodder keep working their way into classroom exchanges and written assignments, no matter how hard I tried to lead the students toward a more elevated and sophisticated level of theoretical inquiry?[1]

As I had expected, what few responses there were evinced equal measures of defensiveness and evasion. After all, the sexualized semiotic universe of these representative Asian American students is overwhelmingly inhabited by Euroamericans, to the virtual exclusion of all but a select few people of color.[2] Their subject position is not unlike that of ten-year-old Yoneko Hosoume (Tricia Joe) in the film *Hot Summer Winds* (1991), written and directed by Emiko Omori. The story is told from the perspective of the pensive child Yoneko, who looks at the outside world through the narrow windows of a cardboard playhouse whose walls are decorated with paper dolls and cutouts of White people. She marvels at the looming presence of White America even in the shack of the itinerant farmhand Marpo (Pepe Serna), whose rude walls are

An earlier version of this chapter was published in *New Political Science* 20, no. 3 (1998).

graced with pictures of 1930s-vintage Hollywood film stars with marcelled blond hair and a portrait of an Anglo-Saxon Jesus. The disruption in the Japanese American immigrant household caused by the sexual tension between Yoneko's mother Hatsu (Natsuko Ohama) and Marpo is ultimately signaled by a static shot of the toppled playhouse, with the White family of paper dolls strewn on the ground.

The Asian American introjection of oppressively omnipresent White racial imagery is a key theme that is deconstructed in *History and Memory* (Tajiri 1991) through the juxtaposition or sequencing of voiceovers, newspaper articles read aloud, scrolled text, dramatizations, Hollywood glamor pinups, family pictures, World War II battle footage captured from the Japanese enemy, U.S. government photographs and film propaganda, "home movies," film shot surreptitiously from within a U.S. concentration camp, and excerpts from the dominant cinema such as *Bad Day at Black Rock* (Sturges 1954). In the opening sequence, the director and narrator, Rea Tajiri, tells of a voyeuristic "sister" who was wont to photograph surreptitiously a young Asian American man while obsessively shadowing him as he walked.[3] This dramatization is intercut with still photos of (White) movie stars in romantic poses and celebrity couples such as President and First Lady John F. and Jacqueline Kennedy during the early days of "Camelot." Moreover, the sister possessed a box of treasured photos whose subjects were exclusively White. That the pictures were bequeathed to her by an aunt suggests a cross-generational fetishization of the White master race by Asian Americans.

As the narrator, Tajiri relates how her fictive sister took to "observing others at a distance," a quirk that she herself had adopted. Like the scopophilic infant born in a state of powerlessness and dependence, the narrator derives pleasure from the mere act of looking. For subordinated racial minorities who historically have been consigned to the margins of the dominant society, what begins at the individual level as scopophilia shades into what I call the "social voyeurism" of the powerless. Within the act of social voyeurism, however, resides an inchoate form of power and mastery over the subject being observed, a covert challenge to an exclusionary regime that keeps people of color at a respectable distance. It is the social voyeurism of the latter, affirmative sort that sustains the oppositional vision that imbues the best in artistic creation.

The constricted, almost exclusively White pictorial world shown by Omori and Tajiri is emblematic of the situation that my students face.[4] The reticence and general unease with which the students greeted my questions spoke volumes about a fundamental self-alienation that has its material source in a sex/race/power regime so total in scope and depth that it reaches into the unconscious, shaping the stuff of the erotic imagination. It is out of this classroom experience that I began thinking about ways to destabilize the hegemonic system of sex/race/power, wherein the denial of unalloyed sexual desire and carnal pleasure to Yellow people is coextensive with their social subordination.[5]

Cruising Tom

Following the theoretical trail blazed by Sigmund Freud, Wilhelm Reich (1897–1957) first made explicit the connection between society and sexuality. More specifically, as a Marxist attempting to integrate psychoanalytic insights into the critique of capital-ism, Reich devoted his energy to "filling in the theory of alienation as it applies to the sexual realm" (Reich 1972, xiv–xv). At the Socialist Society for Sexual Advice and Research, organized in 1929, Reich operated a politically engaged clinical practice for the benefit of working-class Viennese, who were led to understand the social basis of the psychic and behavioral problems they suffered. For his pioneering efforts, Reich bears the dubious distinction of having been expelled from the Communist Party in 1933 and the International Psychoanalytic Association the following year.

Although his reputation as a theorist has diminished somewhat since the "sexual revolution" of the 1960s, Reich and those influenced by him nevertheless must be acknowledged for stressing that the intrapsychic processes of the individual are irre-ducibly bound together with the social. Further, theorists influenced by Reich, such as Herbert Marcuse and Norman O. Brown, are beholden to him for "first insisting on the link between domination and sexual repression and for arguing for sexual lib-eration as a foundation of social liberation" (Chodorow 1989, 117). One such legatee of Reich, the lesbian-identified "sex radical" Pat Califia, strenuously defends indi-vidual liberty, uncensored expression, human rights, and sexual freedom by politi-cizing erotic pleasure. "Pleasure returns our sense of wonder about the world," she says. "I can't think of anything that gives people more energy or more heart or more hope when they need to face opposition and get through parts of their lives that are difficult and frightening" (quoted in Cusac 1996, 37).

Reich and other heirs to the Marxian–Freudian legacy who put psychoanalytic knowledge to the service of a liberatory social theory largely restricted themselves to the problem of alienation in class society. The question of race and racial oppression under the regime of capital was not seriously broached until the period of imperial decolonization following World War II. The issue of color came to the fore with the realization by so-called Third World intellectuals that the colonial legacy of psy-chosocial domination at the individual level needed to be theorized as part of the larg-er political project of national liberation. The foundational text cited to this day is Frantz Fanon's *Black Skin, White Masks*. Beyond Fanon, it has by now become a tru-ism that the pervasive "epidermal fetishism" observed in class society is sympto-matic of the basal White racism underlying the American republic (Wolfenstein 1993, 336).[6] That the knotted relationship among sexuality, race, and power is widely acknowledged (if incompletely understood) throughout U.S. society is seen in most of its popular culture, including the cinema. This in itself might present little cause for concern, were it not for the fact that social inequality based on racial identity plays out through the field of sexuality. And sexuality, at bottom, stands as "an especially dense transfer point for relations of power" between people (Foucault 1990, 103).

The transfixing power of White racial imagery as embedded within Asian Ameri-can sexuality is seen in the short but sensational criminal career of Andrew Phillip Cunanan of San Diego, California. The son of a Filipino American immigrant who once served in the U.S. Navy (he has since returned to the Philippines, having been implicated in an embezzlement scandal), Cunanan is alleged to have murdered five people, including the couturier Gianni Versace. The accused killer's former roommate

Erik Greenman speculated that it was Cunanan's obsession with Tom Cruise that helped set off the killing spree that had people across the nation riveted to news reports. According to Greenman, Cunanan was "passionately" in love with Cruise and told of bondage and Foucauldian power-exchange fantasies that involved the actor. "He had pictures of Tom plastered all over his bedroom," says Greenman. "He'd rent five Cruise videos in a single night and spend the whole evening stopping the films frame by frame, studying Tom's every nuance and gesture."[7] Cunanan also kept a carrying case full of visual material featuring Cruise, including photos, movie reviews, and articles. While making the rounds of cafes and leather bars at night—a routine he called "Tom Cruising"—Cunanan reportedly would seek out men who bore a physical resemblance to his Top Gun.[8]

The historical relationship between the United States and the Philippines is incarnated in the person of Andrew Cunanan's father, Modesto Cunanan, whose American citizenship is owed to military service in the navy of the colonial power—a pattern not uncommon among families of the approximately 160,000 Filipino Americans who live in San Diego (Espiritu 1995, 14–16). Although he grew up in the suburban community of Rancho Bernardo, whose Filipino American population is large enough for wags to refer to the enclave as "Rancho Filipino," Cunanan had no known ties to co-ethnics, including classmates at the Bishop's School, a private secondary institution located nearby in La Jolla (Guillermo 1997, 5). Instead, his social and erotic life was focused on the male ideal represented by Tom Cruise. Yet Cunanan often voiced the fantasy of dominating, humiliating, and inflicting torturous pain on this global symbol of White masculinity. Cunanan even spoke of killing Cruise's wife, Nicole Kidman, so he could have her husband for himself alone.

Colonizing the Sexual Imaginary

The historical legacy of U.S. imperial conquest, neocolonial occupation, dislocation, exclusion, relocation, and the depredation of global capitalism, have played a material role in shaping the multiform sexuality of Asian American men and women. Restrictive immigration legislation directed specifically against Asians has done much to distort and even prevent family formation. The so-called bachelor society of early Chinese American workers is but one material outcome of political oppression.[9] White, bourgeois, female moral crusaders, striving to preserve their status as exclusive sex providers to the patriarchal establishment, have instigated campaigns to devise laws to repress those few Asian American women allowed in the country, under the assumption that they were in the United States for illicit purposes.[10] Anti-miscegenation laws were enacted with the intention of maintaining White racial purity by containing Yellow male sexuality. Asian American men on occasion have been the target of sex panics, as seen in the 1929 Watsonville race riot, in which Filipino American men were demonized as a direct threat to White male sexuality. When a *manong* was observed in the company of a White teenager (his fiancée), a combination of "economic rivalry and sexual jealousy exploded in a bloody anti-Filipino race riot" (Takaki 1989, 327).

In the postwar period, the U.S. military presence in Japan, the Philippines, South Korea, South Vietnam, and Thailand is responsible for the large-scale immigration of Asian women to the United States as dependent spouses (Chan 1991b, 140). The documentary *The Women Outside* (1996) by J. T. Takagi and Hye Jung Park, for example, establishes the centrality of "war brides" to the larger pattern of Korean American immigration and community formation during the postwar period. A thriving nationwide network of "Oriental" massage parlors is also the direct product of U.S. military-base operations in South Korea.

Out of the legal, legislative, and moralistic strategies brought to bear in the regulation of Asian American sexuality, a system of psychosocial dominance has evolved that, to varying degrees, has been internalized by the objects of social control. In addition, Asian Americans—along with members of the dominant society—have been immersed in racial supremacist ideology from cradle to grave. The psychosocial domination of Asian Americans, although never complete and always contested, is compatible with the interests of ruling elites who hold political and economic dominion over communities of color, which are constrained to occupy the stratum of superexploited laborers who create social wealth for capital. At the same time, the White working class maintains its marginal advantage over non-White competitors on the basis of superordinate racial identity within a segmented labor market. With the regulation of erotic desire and expression inextricably linked to a comprehensive system of political–economic and sociocultural control, Asian Americans have grappled with a psychosexual self-alienation that stems from a racialized sexuality shaped and sometimes deformed by hostile social forces.

The deformation of Asian American sexuality is dramatized perceptively in *Eat a Bowl of Tea* (1989), directed by Wayne Wang. The film's premise rests on the failure of a mustered-out Chinese American G.I., Ben Loy Wang (Russell Wong), to produce an heir with his wife, Mei Oi (Cora Miao), due to inhibited sexual arousal once he returns home to the United States with his Chinese-born bride. Before long, a combination of social isolation and sexual frustration similar to that portrayed in *Hot Summer Winds* conspires to deliver the vulnerable Mei Oi into the grasping arms of a sleazy sporting man, Ah Song (Eric Tsang Chi Wai), who is intent on seducing her from the time they first meet. Although their marriage is nearly destroyed by job pressure and conjugal infidelity, Ben Loy and Mei Oi eventually reconcile; the reintegrated Ben Loy regains his sexual potency (with assistance from Chinese herbal medicine); and offspring are produced, much to the satisfaction of the family patriarch, Wah Gay Wang (Victor Wong; Photo 4.1).

The distortion of Asian American sexuality by the system of racial exclusionism is established at the very outset of the film, with the opening sequence set in the New York Chinatown of 1949. A voiceover narrative by Wah Gay Wang movingly recounts how discriminatory laws and legislation targeting Asians prohibited immigration to the United States, denied them citizenship, and separated husbands and wives. During the narrative, Wah Gay himself is seen visiting a local prostitute at her apartment. As he leaves, Wang is met by a long line of similarly situated overseas "bachelors" waiting their turn to be served. But the United States' overriding of select anti-Asian

PHOTO 4.1. Wah Gay Wang grabs his crotch for emphasis when quizzing Ben Loy about his failure to produce an heir. All photos in this chapter are from *Eat a Bowl of Tea* (1989), dir. Wayne Wang. All illustrations in this chapter courtesy of Wayne Wang.

immigration laws after World War II, in order to gain support for its foreign policy among its Cold War allies in Asia, breathed new life into Chinatown. Under the amended law, World War II veterans like Ben Loy were permitted to marry Chinese women and bring them to the United States as wives.[11]

Ben Loy is not quite ready to leave bachelorhood, despite Wah Gay's disapproval of his son's freewheeling life. Ben Loy appears to spend much of his time in the company of a White demimondaine who haunts Chinatown night spots. (Later, after Ben Loy is married, the White, female object of desire suddenly reappears at an ill-timed moment.) At the insistence of Wah Gay, Ben Loy returns to his father's home village to find a suitable wife, with the assistance of a *mui-yan*, or matchmaker. When Ben Loy is reunited with his mother (Hui Fun), who has not seen her husband in twenty years, her loneliness and isolation is palpable. She is anxious for her son to marry well and live contentedly with his family in the United States. But when they later discuss his marriage prospects, Ben Loy puts forth idealized White women as his erotic touchstone.

> *Mother:* If you don't like this girl, you can pick somebody else.
> *Ben Loy:* Right. I pick Rita Hayworth, but I'll settle for Betty Grable.

The extent to which Ben Loy's sexual imaginary is dominated by Whiteness does not surface until this phantasy comes into conflict with the reality of being married to a Yellow woman once the couple returns to the United States as husband and wife. It is only then that he becomes afflicted with social and sexual impotence, able to function effectively neither at the workplace nor in the marital bedchamber.

Lost Erection

The pivotal sequence in *Eat a Bowl of Tea* is nothing less than masterly in the way it dramatizes the romantic bond formed between Ben Loy and Mei Oi at an outdoor screening of the film *Lost Horizon* (Capra 1937). At the same time, the insertion of key scenes from the classic film serves as meta-commentary on the way in which the dominant U.S. cinema defines the meaning of White eroticism for people the world over: Even those living in a remote Chinese village are within the colonizing reach of Hollywood movies, whose potent White stars stand in demiurgic contrast to the alienated sexuality of those either demeaned or excluded for most of Hollywood's institutional history. It should be recalled that in *Lost Horizon*—a colonialist film in the guise of Christian pacifism—the head "Asian" representative of Shangri-La, Chang (H. B. Warner), is played by a White actor in "Yellow face." It is also worth noting that the founder of the utopian Asian society is a Belgian missionary named Father Perrault (Sam Jaffe). The stated goal of Perrault-turned-High Lama is to let the warring nations of the world destroy themselves so his earthly paradise can thereafter exist in peace. "When the strong have devoured each other," says the frightfully messianic High Lama, "the Christian ethic may at last be fulfilled, and the weak shall inherit the Earth."

Not coincidentally, the James Hilton novel *Lost Horizon* (1933) was published when the British colonial empire was being tested both by Chinese nationalist movements and by the threat posed by the triumph of Japanese imperial military forces throughout much of East and Southeast Asia. European colonialist sentiment resides in the person of Robert Conway (Ronald Colman)—"England's 'Man of the East,'" "soldier, diplomat, public hero"—who arrives at the town of "Baskul" to evacuate its White British subjects before they are "butchered" during a "local revolution," only to be kidnapped and taken to Shangri-La at the urging of the virginal Sondra (Jane Wyatt). For at age thirty, Sondra is in need of the virile Englishman to help replenish the vanishing White leadership caste, which has been lost amid the peaceable kingdom of Yellow people to whom it has brought Christian civilization. Well before the film adaptation of *Lost Horizon* was produced, the United States had staked a claim in China, along with other nations belonging to the coalition exercising White Western imperial rule throughout most of Asia. It is only fitting that the celebrated director Frank Capra went on to become a key participant in the production of the classic U.S. Army propaganda piece *Know Your Enemy—Japan* (1945) and other films that drew upon the vast reservoir of anti-Asian racist images that Hollywood periodically tapped into (Koppes and Black 1990, 250).[12]

The budding romance between Ben Loy and Mei Oi, and the marriage that soon follows, quite literally is mediated by the dominant cinema and its White actors (Photo 4.2). From the very beginning, the couple's most intimate moments together are superimposed against scenes from *Lost Horizon* as the film is being projected onto a makeshift screen outdoors. While an older villager (Lui Tat) translates the English-language dialogue, the aging matinee idol Colman and his sweetheart Wyatt are seen kissing, raising embarrassed titters among the audience. At that instant, the film is interrupted by an announcement that Ben Loy and Mei Oi have been found compatible for marriage after careful study of their respective horoscopes. The pair slip away and meet behind the translucent screen, reversed images of scenes with Colman and Wyatt from *Lost Horizon* serving as the backdrop for their mounting passion. Ben Loy asks Mei Oi, "How do you feel about me?" Before Mei Oi answers, both of them turn in unison toward the hovering screen image of White superego Ronald Colman as if waiting for his benediction before coming together in mad embrace (Photo 4.3). Mei Oi waits almost fifteen full seconds before rushing to Ben Loy, kissing him, then fleeing in coquettish elation as the ghostly presence of Wyatt in a diaphanous robe crosses the screen in a parallel kinetic gesture (Photo 4.4).

After consummating their marriage without apparent difficulty during their honeymoon, Ben Loy and Mei Oi return to New York. There they are feted at a large banquet, where, in honor of the newlyweds, the president of the North American branch of the Wang Family Association solemnly notes the historic importance of the wedding. He speaks of the "harsh laws" that once governed Chinese immigration to the United States: "A man came here and lived as an outsider in the beautiful country. He could not share it with his wife. He could not watch his children grow." This is a specific reference to Mei Oi's father Bok Fat (Lee Sau Kee), who left Hong Kong before her birth. Only after coming to the United States as the bride of Ben Loy does Mei Oi meet her father. The speaker praises the sacrifices made by Chinese American veterans such as Ben Loy, who have helped to hasten the end of discriminatory treatment in matters of immigration by serving in the military during World War II and proving their loyalty to the United States. In siring children with his wife, Ben Loy is made to accept personal and historical responsibility for reviving what Wah Gay has described in the opening voiceover narrative as a "dying" Chinatown community.

While Ben Loy endures the pressures of his new job as manager of a large restaurant, long-repressed psychosexual dynamics are resurrected at home in bed with his new wife. On the nightstand sits a framed photograph of a smiling Wah Gay (Photo 4.5), which the self-conscious Ben Loy turns face down before directing his amorous attention to Mei Oi. But with the burden of family and history weighing heavily upon his shoulders, Ben Loy is unable to perform sexually (Photo 4.6):

Ben Loy: I don't think I'm gonna be able to do this.
Mei Oi: What's wrong?
Ben Loy: I just feel like everyone's watching us.

Later, at the gambling parlor operated by Wah Gay, his friends are gossiping about Ben Loy's failure to produce an heir. The playful sage Old Lum (Michael Lee) offers

PHOTO 4.2.
The budding relationship between Ben Loy and Mei Oi is mediated by White racial imagery.

PHOTO 4.3.
The couple await benediction by the White imperial superego.

PHOTO 4.4.
Their union is consecrated at the altar of White visual domination.

PHOTO 4.5.
Ben Loy feels the
weight of family
and social history
after seeing a portrait
of . . .

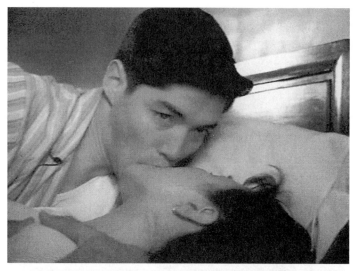

PHOTO 4.6.
. . . Wah Gay looking
on as his son
attempts to repopu-
late Chinese Ameri-
ca. Note fertility
symbols.

PHOTO 4.7.
The couple become
estranged as Ben
Loy's psychosexual
dysfunction persists.

a mocking but insightful comment suggesting that the couple's reproductive failure might lie in the lack of available examples to follow. "Hey, maybe they don't know how to do it. Back home, they watch the pigs, they get idea," says Old Lum.

Enter the Heavenly Dragon

Further psychosexual complications arising from Ben Loy's thoroughgoing social-ization by the dominant cinema are artfully dramatized in a downward spiral of sexual dysfunction. Upon experiencing further difficulties in the marital bed, Ben Loy and Mei Oi, following a physician's advice, take an automobile trip to Washington, D.C. Free of the oppressively familiar Chinatown ghetto, and rejuvenated by his pilgrimage to the seat of U.S. national government, Ben Loy finds renewed sexual vigor. While Mei Oi sits on his lap during love play in their hotel room, she is surprised by the Jade Stalk stirring in her husband's trousers. Jubilant congress of a sexual sort ensues. But immediately upon their return to New York, the couple is dismayed to discover that the Heavenly Dragon once more is unable to rear its head (Photo 4.7). It happens that only cinema-induced fantasies of the Anglicized actress Rita Hayworth can effect psychogenic arousal in Ben Loy.[13]

Without so much as a transition shot, the next scene, immediately following yet another of Ben Loy's erectile failures, opens directly into the extra-diegetic space and time of *The Lady from Shanghai* (Welles 1948). (The movie features sinister San Francisco Chinatown stock characters working in cahoots with the devious Elsa Bannister [Rita Hayworth], the "lady from Shanghai" who speaks fluent Cantonese and moves with ease through their *noir* alien world. Her dual White–Yellow identity makes her doubly treacherous to Michael O'Hara [Orson Welles], a seafaring rogue in pursuit of ill-gotten treasure.) Welles and Hayworth are kissing passionately at their rendezvous at San Francisco's Steinhart Aquarium. Sea creatures monstrously magnified through the glass of Tank #50 dart by in the background as the couple plot their next move, a visual allusion to the sensual dance of two individuals each maneuvering to outsmart the other while caught in the grip of primal sexual attraction.[14]

Only then, as the film cuts away from *The Lady from Shanghai*, do we see the beatifically illuminated, upturned faces of Mei Oi and Ben Loy, who are enraptured by what they are voyeuristically viewing on the movie screen. They are visibly excited by watching the White couple surrender themselves to unadulterated lust in so public a manner (Photo 4.8). So thoroughly aroused are Ben Loy and Mei Oi by witnessing the sexually charged exchange between Welles and the platinum blonde Hayworth that they shoot out of their seats without uttering a word and dash home to fuck (Photo 4.9). As they hurriedly disrobe in preparation for the coming together of Cinnabar Grotto and Jade Stalk, someone knocks on the door—just as Ben Loy has dropped his trousers. Standing suggestively at the threshold is none other than the White woman with whom he had frequented Chinatown nightclubs during his carefree days as a bachelor. After Ben Loy quickly ushers out his unwanted visitor, Mei Oi becomes angry, not believing him when he lies that the woman had come to the wrong apart-

PHOTO 4.8.
White racial imagery
is needed to fuel the
Yellow couple's
sexual desire . . .

PHOTO 4.9.
. . . as they view Orson Welles
and Rita Hayworth in a
steamy embrace.

PHOTO 4.10.
Ben Loy's White
demimondaine keeps
him from sexual
congress with his
Yellow wife.

ment. For Mei Oi, the mood for lovemaking has been broken by the White interloper (Photo 4.10). What the love goddess Rita Hayworth giveth Ben Loy, his former paramour taketh away. It is not long before the predatory Ah Song, sensing marital strife between the couple, begins a doomed affair with the sexually unfulfilled Mei Oi while Ben Loy is busy at work. When Mei Oi becomes pregnant, the entire community is elated. In the mind of Ben Loy, however, the question of paternity casts a shadow over the welcome news. But doubts over fatherhood are dispelled when he calculates that his wife's conception coincided with their motor trip to Washington, D.C.

During the closing moments of *Eat a Bowl of Tea*, the underlying themes of Asian American family fragmentation and deformed sexuality are reprised in a coda wherein a thoroughly demoralized Ben Loy pokes about the darkened apartment his father has abandoned. For Wah Gay has fled to Havana after avenging the cuckolding of his son by cutting off Ah Song's ear/penis with a cleaver. Ben Loy looks fondly at sepia-toned photographs of himself as a child with his mother (Photo 4.11). In another picture, he is a proudly uniformed G.I. with his father. A separate portrait of Wah Gay as a young man conveys a sense of confidence and great expectations in the new land. Significantly, there is not one photograph of father, mother, and son *en famille*. Ben Loy turns to look directly into a mirror. He sees *himself* as if for the first time, unmediated by the social gaze of others (Photo 4.12). Subsequent to this final act of self-recognition, Ben Loy is made whole again and recovers his procreative powers (Photo 4.13). The couple move to San Francisco, where Ben Loy will pursue a career in radio covering sports. With Ben Loy's social voice broadcast beyond the confines of Chinatown, he and Mei Oi become among the first full generation of Chinese Americans who can enjoy a semblance of "normal" family life.

White Porno Supremacy

Just as the "eroticization" of non-White peoples serves to "justify the control of entire communities," racism plays a constitutive role in the White masculinity complex (Kivel 1996, 63). As it affects Asian Americans in particular, the naked display of the White racist masculinity complex is found at its rawest in video porn, both gay and straight. The video-porn subspecialty featuring Yellow women has become so commercially popular that the actress Asia Carrera has achieved the distinction of becoming the only rookie to be named Female Performer of the Year (1994) by *Adult Video News*—this after being credited with nearly a score of feature appearances in her maiden season (Galt 1997). Along with Asia Carrera, Kia, Suzi Suzuki, Mimi Miyagi, Kitty Yung, Mai Lin, Tina Chow, Tricia Yen, Kobe Tai, Leanni Lei, and other up-and-coming Yellow female performers feed the growing appetite for the genre of video porn that the industry classifies as "Oriental." Vivid Video of Van Nuys, California, has become an industry leader in video-porn Oriengenitalia, as seen by its *Tongue Fu* (1994) compilation tape, which happily promises "Four Hours of Fellatio and Asialingus."

Born in Singapore, but currently residing in the United States, Annabel Chong was offered $10,000 in payment for setting a world record of 251 (forty-nine short of the

PHOTO 4.11.   Ben Loy gazes longingly at photographs of his fragmented family . . .

PHOTO 4.12.   . . . then peers into his self and becomes reintegrated.

PHOTO 4.13.   Ben Loy achieves psychosexual healing and at last recovers his virility.

300 she set as her personal goal) successive couplings and assorted stunts during one day of ambitious shooting for *The World's Biggest Gang Bang* (Bone 1995).[15] There is a brief on-camera interview with Chong before attempting the feat she herself had suggested be staged. Her prefatory comments concerning the event do not betray any sense of "victimage" that anti-porn feminists have often claimed for women performing "erotic labor."[16] Genuinely impressed by a stage set that is perhaps best described as Roman orgy kitsch, the deceptively ditzy Chong—who attends the University of Southern California as a student—seems more interested in knowing whether she can get one of the really neat commemorative T-shirts that crew members are wearing than in the impending sexual marathon.[17]

The director, John T. Bone, speaks through a bullhorn to the quietly expectant participants sitting in the bleachers, outlining gang-bang procedure and protocol as they pay rapt attention. After raising the possibility of situational impotence among attendees, his reassuring words are met with nervous laughter. Bone suggests that those so afflicted help themselves to a cup of coffee, have a sandwich, and take a moment to relax before getting back in line. Adding to the carnival of full-frontal absurdity is the former high-school teacher and witty porn legend Ron Jeremy, who as master of ceremonies interviews three "fluff girls" whose job it is to inspire the ardor of those in need of a lift.

It is quite telling that Yellow is the only color missing from the otherwise rainbow coitus coalition of more than one-hundred pro-am talent and porno-star wannabes from across the country who were enlisted to participate in *The World's Biggest Gang Bang*. The only Asian American in attendance seems to have been given the job of wiping Chong clean of spent pearl jam. A homophobic White journalist who reported on the follow-up gonzo extravaganza featuring Jasmin St. Clair—*The World's Biggest Gang Bang 2* (Bone 1996)—takes supercilious delight in having recognized from the earlier event an "overweight, faggy-looking Filipino in his early thirties" whose job it was to clean up "any and all spunk sprayed upon" the performers. "Wearing an actual pair of dishwashing gloves and an apron, Homo-Momo (as we'll call him) is also armed with sponges and towels to mop up the muck from Jasmin's cunt, ass, back, tummy, whatever. Blechhh! What kind of heterosexual would even *consider* doing this shit? . . . even for money?!!" (Petkovich 1997a, 28). For the White reporter, who is made anxious and perhaps even excited by the sight of so many cocks in various states of arousal all at once, it is convenient to "homosexualize" Momo both to allay his own fears of male-to-male attraction and to eliminate the thereby emasculated Yellow man from the ranks of heterosexual competitors.

Although Asian Americans are absent, African Americans and Latinos—two non-White groups that are more commonly associated with janitorial labor—are well represented among the gang-bang participants. For unlike Asian Americans, African Americans and Latinos, within the prevailing sex/race/power regime, are coded as hypersexual threats to the White male monopoly on all women, irrespective of color. "Sharing" women with supposedly preternaturally skilled Blacks and Latinos helps allay the performance anxiety of their White masters, however, because a pathetically large number of them have difficulty attaining, let alone maintaining, the degree of tumescence required to complete the copulatory act. For Momo, and the Yellow man in general, the desexualized function as custodial attendant and "homosexualized" eunuch denies him basic social agency.

Missing in Action

As seen in the "world's biggest" gang bangs (but on a far less epic scale), Asian American male performers are almost nonexistent in straight video porn, again reflecting their sexuo-erotic subjection within the White supremacist complex. In one of the few porn films to feature an Asian American man, *Once upon Annette* (Haven 1978), a White woman (Tina Orchard) and her mate (James Fong) are shown blithely romping through a meadow, both wearing only animal skins, in Neanderthal fashion.[18] As pseudo-Sinitic music plays in the background, the couple pause to caress each another. Across the way, a similarly clad White caveman (David Blair) spies the couple making out. He sneaks up on the two and, shouting caveman gibberish (the inter-title translation reads, "Eat Chinese—and half-hour later you want more"), runs off the Yellow man with a club before he can deposit Asian genetic material into the White woman. An extreme long shot shows White man and White woman going at it, troglodyte-style, until the dirty deed appears to be done. Thus does White man prevail over Yellow man, from prehistory to present.

The exclusion of the Yellow man from video porn on the basis of his Asian racial identity is simply assumed in the industry, contrary to the denials of at least two prominent insiders. Asia Carrera says, "I'd love it if there was an Asian actor," after first joking that there are no Yellow men in video porn, "'cause they all have small dicks." The porn director Hal Morton disingenuously contends, "If there was an Asian guy with the right equipment and a desire to be in this business, he'd get work" (Greenfeld 1995, 36). Truth be told, the absence of Asian American men in video porn has nothing to do with having the "right equipment" and the "desire" to be in the business. The reason is found in the obdurate anti-Asian racism of the dominant society, which is reproduced intact by the thematic conventions of U.S. video porn. The multivolume *Tokyo Blue* (various dates) series, imported from Japan and therefore free of the pervasive White-supremacist race/sex/power ideology of U.S. product, supplies ample evidence of the "right equipment" and "desire" among Asian male performers. Regrettably, the poor-quality *Tokyo Blue* tapes, the almost equally dismal *Ultra Call Girls* (1995), and more recent imports from Taiwan such as *Wonderful Desire* (1996)—complete with unintentionally humorous English-language subtitles—are indicative of the limited opportunities Asian Americans have in their power to view on video other Yellow people reveling in the joy of their own sexuality, without White intervention.[19]

Sum Yung Men

Concerning gay video porn, the filmmaker and theorist Richard Fung has observed that the sole function of the "eroticized Asian" in most commercial productions is to serve White male pleasure (Fung 1991). As evidence of the White racism found in much gay community life, according to one observer, Asian American men in gay video porn until recently have appeared almost exclusively as "feminized bottoms who serve White studs with their asses in bed and as literal servants in the nonsex scenes" (Browning 1994, 196). A study that advances gay video porn as a potent form of political practice, but nevertheless acknowledges that a dominant "sexual-racial discourse" lies within the subgenre that debases Asian American men in specific, reached a similar conclusion: "Although gay porn may radically rewrite much of history," the author concluded, "it unfortunately has not radically positivized the situations of gay men of color in this country" (Burger 1995, 57).

Through such work as *Dirty Laundry* (1996)—where the erotic encounter of two Yellow men on a passenger train parallels a larger historical meditation on the homosocial nature of nineteenth-century Chinese immigrant life in the Americas—Fung himself gamely has supplied a needed corrective to the gross disparity in sex/power as mediated by race. Yet his experience in producing an educational "safer-sex" porn video featuring two Asian actors met with contradictory responses from three Chinese Canadian men whom he interviewed.[20] While they were not necessarily attracted to the performers (who defy the racial and body conventions of commercial porn), they still said that it was important that "Asian features and bodies be shown as desirable" (Fung 1993, 365). This only reaffirms Fung's professional interest in eroti-cizing gay Yellow men by creating imagery that he hopes will rewrite a sexual script that otherwise degrades or excludes them.

John Hayman and Oggi are two directors who have carved out a specialty niche by filming overseas with Thai performers. Yet it is obvious that their work caters to White men who fancy Yellow men, or "rice queens." The review blurbs for such films as *Passage to Spring* (Hayman 1995a), *Room Service* (Oggi 1995b), *Sexual Healing* (Oggi 1995c), and *Thai Take-Out* (Hayman 1995b)—saying, "Great fantasy fodder for dad-dies with a yen for Asians"; "Appreciation may depend on your attraction to Asian men"; and "Rice queens will O.D."—suggest that it is the White, not the Yellow, male viewer who is being courted (Lawrence 1996, 122, 132, 135).[21] Rather than as offering an alternative to White-dominant gay video porn, such specialty titles are better understood as an extension of the Asian sex-tourism industry, in which Thailand plays a prominent part within the capitalist world economy.

Recently, however, there are signs that White racial domination as represented in gay porn is being renegotiated ever so slightly, if only at the pre-political level. The otherwise undistinguished Catalina Video production *Pacific Rim* (Dunne 1997) fea-tures an exclusively Asian American cast who exist for the pleasure of themselves alone, without the usual dynamics of unequal power stemming from White racial superiority and Yellow subordination. The producer, director, and writers, however, bear Anglo-Saxon surnames. Thus, overall power and control over content remain in the hands of White men.[22] This singular failing might account for the mildly Orien-talist script and cheesy but admittedly funny opening credits, with "Godzilla" men-acing a smog-shrouded Los Angeles. Apart from demonstrating that bad acting in video porn truly cuts across sexual modalities and racial, gender, and class lines, the all-Yellow ensemble in *Pacific Rim* might offer a foretaste of a future Asian American porno practice whereby beauty, desire, pleasure, and orgastic potency are conjoined with an integrated sense of self that makes its presence felt in the realms of social, cultural, and political power.

Porno Pop Culture

This brief survey establishes the way in which the massive video porn industry—like its mainstream "Hollywood" counterpart, which is also based in the Greater Los Angeles area—reproduces the assumptions and prerogatives of the White-suprema-cist complex. Its social sweep and widespread cultural influence is beyond dispute. The "adult video" market is both varied and extensive, reaching into every corner of U.S. society. The 7,852 "hard-core" titles released in 1996 generated sales and rental revenues of $3.9 billion (Fishbein 1996, 75). And these numbers do not even include mail-order sales. Once stigmatized as servicing the warped needs of an antisocial, deviant subculture, the products and services spawned by contemporary porn busi-nesses have moved to the vital center of U.S. industry. According to a positively glow-ing cover story that appeared in *US News and World Report*, the porno industry is a shining example of "free market" principles as extolled during the Reagan–Bush years (Schlosser 1997).

Last year, Americans plunged more than $8 billion into the "sex industry," an amount that far outgrossed the domestic earnings of Hollywood films and most of the recording industry combined. The sale of pornography has become a lucrative revenue stream for the mainstays of U.S. business, from family-owned video stores to large corporate entities such as the long-distance carrier AT&T and cable-TV companies such as Time Warner. Major hotel chains, including Holiday Inn, Hyatt, and Marriot, "now reportedly earn millions of dollars each year supplying adult films to their guests" (ibid., 44). At home, viewers last year ordered porno via pay-per-view services from Cablevision Systems Corporation; Continental Cablevision; TeleCommunications, Inc.; and Time Warner to the tune of $150 million. Neither is the consumption of video porn exclusively a male activity. A survey conducted by *Redbook* magazine, a publication that epitomizes middle-American domesticity, "found that almost half of its readers regularly watched pornographic movies in the privacy of their homes" (ibid., 46). Periodicals whose respective editorial focus is decidedly more sexually adventurous than *Redbook*'s, such as *Cosmopolitan* and *Mademoiselle*, probably would report an even higher percentage of video porn usage among its readership.

In late 1995, the genteel readers of *The New Yorker* were treated to a lengthy article by the noted author Susan Faludi, who plumbed the lower depths of the porno industry in the San Fernando Valley area of Los Angeles County. There she discovered a curious inversion of male–female power relations in a business in which women command greater respect by benefit of their markedly superior earning power as performers, making about 50 to 100 percent more in fees than do men. "But then she is the object of desire," says Faludi, while the man is "merely her appendage, the object of the object" (Faludi 1996, 65–66). This apparently is a commonly held prejudice among almost all male directors of heterosexual porn, according to "sexpert" Susie Bright. When asked by Bright why "most straight porn looks so uninspired," the director Andrew Blake answered that he considers the male actor to be a mere prop, a "piece of furniture" (quoted in Bright 1995, 85).

Faludi views the stable of top-drawer male porno performers such as Jeff Stryker, T. T. Boy, Nick East, and the late Cal Jammer as emblematic of the wider crisis in masculine identity caused by the disappearance of well-paid occupations that sustained male privilege until a generation ago. With women entering the workforce and competing for economic position, a shift has taken place in historically unequal gender relations that many men find threatening. Michael S. Kimmel makes an almost identical point when he connects the disappearance of meaningful work and community for men with the rapid decline of male domination in society. He also advances the notion that the gain in women's rights has been "accompanied by an increase in pornographic images" (Kimmel 1991, 316).

However questionable this argument may be, Faludi implies that this supposed turnabout in power is symbolized by the tragic story of Cal Jammer. He retired from performing in porno films (he was having difficulty "getting wood" on the movie set), only to have his wife, Jill Kelly, enter the business and begin outearning him. Having been unmanned in this way, Jammer went to his estranged wife's house one day and shot himself dead outside her door. Consistent with her perspective on male porno stars—they are portrayed as a pathetic lot—Faludi seems to relish the irony that while men might enjoy ejaculatory "money-shot" visual supremacy, female performers reap far greater monetary rewards than their male counterparts.[23] Beyond this, Faludi fails to develop the more profound implications of video porn in the popular culture.

By contrast, although sometimes overstating her case, Laura Kipnis (1996) understands pornographic expression as imbued with a common-sense "political philosophy" whose transgressive values threaten the stability of an inherently repressive social order. The anarchy of the imagination through porno fantasy permits otherwise forbidden exploration into the complex and often conflicting meanings attached to the limitless variety of sexual desire and practice that are formative constituents of human subjectivity. According to Kipnis, with pornographic fantasy a "crucial political space" is created wherein "different possibilities for individual, bodily, and collective fulfillment" can be imagined and perhaps realized in the future (Kipnis 1996, 203). Katha Pollitt, however, chides Kipnis for exaggerating the counter-hegemonic potential of porno by writing, "[O]nly a postmodern academic could seriously propose that a skin magazine offers a serious challenge to 'state power'" (Pollitt 1997, 9).

As an ardent proponent of a "sex-positive culture" who has fought as a self-described "partisan of desire" on the front lines of the contemporary sex wars, Carol Queen takes issue with certain antiporn activists, including John Stoltenberg, Andrea Dworkin, and Catherine MacKinnon, who have decried the "objectification" of women in sexually explicit erotica and its role in supposedly maintaining male dominance through violence. Queen jokingly argues that the current "absexuality" embraced by many progressive and conservative critics of pornographic literature is itself a kind of "kink" stemming from a compulsive need to impose their own sexual mores upon those whom they self-righteously condemn as benighted reprobates. Doing Kipnis one better by offering insights from a revealingly intimate perspective, Queen writes,

> Porn let me come to terms with what I was uncomfortable about. Watching a lot of it introduced me to the best-quality stuff. And an amazing thing happened to my politically correct uptightness—it turned into wet panties and multiple orgasms. I discovered the purpose of porn: to produce and enhance sexual feeling. Deconstructing it makes for interesting mental masturbation, but it can't hold a candle to the old-fashioned kind. [Queen 1997, 142]

Queen considers the use and sharing of porno to be on par with the pursuit of social knowledge through poetry or philosophy. Once she discovered the liberatory aspect of reading and watching porno, Queen went on to record herself on videotape as a performer. "Seeing my sexuality captured on videotape was the kind of leap in sexual development that having my first orgasm or tasting my first pussy had been," she writes. "It gave me a new sense of myself as a sexually powerful being" (ibid., 143).

In a similar fashion, after Lisa Palac first investigated video porno in search of "political theory instead of a sexual experience," she became "sexually autonomous" and in control of her "erotic destiny" by learning "how to use porn and come" (Palac 1995, 245). She credits the VCR with making pornographic sexual imagery more wide-ly available to women and men alike, placing perhaps even a bit too much faith in advanced electronic technology that promises to enhance "erotic communication" both locally and on a global scale (ibid., 251). Like Queen, Palac calls for the self-pro-duction of video erotica that can be made cheaply and disseminated widely.

The sex worker Nina Hartley, who appropriately has a featured role in the film *Boo-gie Nights*, views her career as a self-conscious response to the radical politics of the 1960s and 1970s. Hartley's decision to engage in public sex for a living was motivat-ed by a combination of financial need (she was pursuing a degree in nursing), poli-tics, and the desire to explore sexuality on her own terms against the neo-Victorian absexual orthodoxy of 1980s feminism. Hartley is critical of the "erotophobic logic" advanced by her detractors, who view her as a gender traitor of sorts. By contrast, Hartley revels in the affirmative aspects of sex work, including "enhanced self-image, sexual variety, creating a platform for my ideas about sex and society, creative erotic expression, exhibitionism, fantasy fulfillment, and economic gain" (Hartley 1997, 58).

Candida Royalle, the former porn star who founded Femme Productions to reflect her own aesthetic in film erotica, celebrates the values of "sharing" and "egalitarian-ism" that she believes are central to sexual experience. "The sex in my films shows how everyone deserves to be pleasured," says Royalle, who also takes enormous per-sonal pride in operating her own production company (quoted in Bell 1995, 26). With trenchant sarcasm, Royalle attributes the "new censorship" to the realization in cer-tain quarters that pornography is no longer the exclusive property of dirty old men who visit seedy theaters. As she asserts, "It is being brought into middle class homes to the wives and mothers, the madonnas. Now it is really going to corrupt society. We are going to corrupt women. We are giving women permission to enjoy sex. This is what Femme is doing" (quoted in ibid., 30). Against the possibility that the eroti-ca produced by women will deliquesce into romanticized soft-focus tableaux geared toward "couples," Sallie Tisdale holds out for a "low-brow, hard-core" porn that by necessity must be "politically incorrect." She writes, "If it's not outside acceptable con-ventions of family and culture, it's not porn" (Tisdale 1995, 157).

Naomi Wolf (1994) is less effusive than Royalle, Palac, and Queen in her praise of porno, both on ethical grounds and in the belief that those involved with it might be exposed to harm or suffer pain in some unspecified way. Although Wolf does not seem attracted to the utopian possibilities of sexually explicit art, her words are a far cry from the condemnatory rhetoric spewed by Louise Kaplan, who rejects the claim that women can free themselves of "sexual repression" through the "aesthetics of male pornography" (Kaplan 1997, 322).[24] Nevertheless, Wolf remains adamantly opposed to the idea of placing restrictions on pornographic work. Rather, in mapping the "dark continent of female fantasy and desire," women must take responsibility for making "better and more magical erotic material than the images that disturb many of us" (Wolf 1994, 105). Wolf issues a militant call for women to take up the "tools of the master" in rendering the provocative sexual images and erotic art that will help bring down the edifice of male supremacy.[25]

Toward A Yellow Porno Practice

Within a White-supremacist system of social recognition and power relations, Asian Americans historically have taken it upon themselves to represent their respective communities visually within and against the dominant symbolic order. Whether through the humble family snapshots taken by nameless thousands using mass-produced cameras or through the internationally acclaimed photographic portraits and Manzanar scenes of Toyo Miyatake, the soulfully poignant paintings of Henry Sugimoto, the kinetic line drawings of Miné Okubo, and the minimalist eloquence of the monuments fashioned and erected by Isamu Noguchi, Asian Americans have actively documented both the mundane aspects of community life and its grand occasions.[26] This is seen quite vividly in the "home movies" that serve as the basis for *Something Strong Within* (1994), produced and written by Karen Ishizuka and directed by Robert Nakamura.

Recently, the historical and cultural importance of Asian American visual memory was acknowledged when the Library of Congress inducted footage shot by the Topaz internee Dave Tatsuno into the National Film Registry (Yip 1997, 9).[27] Using a movie camera smuggled into camp after such items were classified by the U.S. government as contraband, Tatsuno gave little thought to the scenes that he filmed and that later proved to be such a compelling document of life behind barbed wire (Becker 1997). These examples of counterhegemonic visual resistance are by no means unique to Asian Americans: All people of color "recognize that the field of representation (how we see ourselves, how others see us) is a site of ongoing struggle" (hooks 1995, 57). The robust independent Asian American cinema that has developed over the past twenty-five years attests to the oppositional strength of community-based organizations such as the National Asian American Telecommunications Association (NAATA), Asian CineVision (ACV), and Visual Communications (VC), which help support media workers whose diverse visions of a pluralistic U.S. society stand at odds with corporate-controlled communications systems.[28]

Whereas the dominant media system of White racial supremacist representation alternately hypersexualizes and desexualizes Asian American women and men by controlling and containing their visual presence, an illustrious tradition of Asian erotica simply assumes Yellow people to exist at the center of desire and pleasure.[29] Because sexual satisfaction is considered within Asian societies to be one of the keys to health, well-being, and longevity, the art of the bedchamber has been studied and practiced over several centuries.[30] For instance, the oldest extant Japanese medical treatise—*Ishimpō* (*The Essence of Medical Prescriptions*)—was compiled in the late tenth century from even older Chinese texts.[31] The pursuit of bodily gratification for its own sake has been elevated to high art within certain strata of Asian societies, a fact that has been exploited by any number of popular authors who have made careers from writing books that promise to unlock "Oriental" love secrets for a sexually repressed American audience composed of individuals seeking permission to indulge in a life-affirming carnality within a sex-negative society.

While browsing the "sexuality" section at the Elliot Bay Bookstore in Seattle, Washington, during the May 1997 Association for Asian American Studies conference, I counted well over a dozen titles that owe direct inspiration to classics in Asian erotica.[32] Apart from certain high-end, Asian-manufactured devices that sex-toy retailers tout for their exceptional design, high-quality construction, and reliable performance, the books within this literary genre occupy the only domain within the popular culture in which Yellow sexuality is given prominence, and sometimes even conceded superiority.[33] Still, there is an underlying understanding among the White authors of such books that while Yellows can be admitted as gurus in matters of philosophically inflected "Oriental" sex technique, they (men in particular) are not to be taken seriously as practitioners. Yellow expertise in sexuality is strictly for the benefit of White pleasure.

In tandem with sustained efforts in the allied fields of law, politics, and education, a vital cultural politics is a critical force in securing a zone of freedom within an otherwise hegemonic White-supremacist regime of sex/race/power. In the visual arts, literature, theater, music, and film, Asian Americans have attempted to work through the contradictions of their racialized subordinate status within a putatively liberal democracy. It is important to understand that such counterhegemonic expressive cultural forms are crucial to the "formation of alternative social practices" and oppositional political activity (Lowe 1996, 172). Although Asian American feature films such as those that premiered at the 1997 San Francisco International Asian American Film Festival—*Yellow* (Lee 1996), *Shopping for Fangs* (Lee and Lin 1997), *Sunsets* (Idemoto and Nakamura 1997), and *Strawberry Fields* (Tajiri 1997)—hold promise for overcoming the institutional barriers imposed by the dominant U.S. corporate movie industry, the financing and distribution of independent cinema productions are still obstacles that limit their exposure to a wider audience.[34]

As long as Asian Americans are marginalized within, or excluded outright from, the dominant system of film representation, they will continue to embody an alienated sexuality conditioned by an oppressive system of White racial supremacy. Because independent feature films are prohibitively costly to produce, are difficult to distribute, return scant profit to investors, and often tiptoe around issues concerning sexuality anyway, the most efficacious and crudely direct strategy to assert an immediate visual presence is to take up the camera and turn it inward to capture the pleasures of the flesh as enjoyed by Yellow people: A "Joy Fuck Club."[35] Thousands of visually disfranchised people across the United States have done so already, leading to the proliferation of amateur-style video porn, which reportedly commands about 60 percent of the "adult" market (Mano 1996, 82).

No doubt there will be strident and harsh reactions to a politics of Asian American porno if the views of at least two censorial critics are indicative of a deeper absexuality among ostensibly progressive voices. The poet David Mura advances a set of absurd premises in a rambling essay that has porno stemming from "abuse," which therefore makes it degrading to the "soul." In keeping with the twelve-step temper of the times, he declares that the enjoyment of pornography is an "addiction" (Mura 1987, 16).[36] In her campaign against so-called assaultive speech, the legal theorist Mari J. Matsuda wrongly conflates sexually explicit expression, racist "hate speech," homophobic insults, and "Holocaust hoax claims," fallaciously equating "the batterer" and "the date-raper" with "the pornography addict" (Matsuda 1996, 115). There is cruel irony in the fact that their specious arguments contravene a constitutional principle that has protected the right of minority peoples to express political and cultural dissent. Matsuda in particular is adamant in her call for the abrogation of First Amendment guarantees as a salve for the wounded feelings of aggrieved individuals.

In revisiting and reclaiming Asian erotic arts traditions developed over centuries, by drawing from a demonstrated history of visual resistance, through the integration of the radical cultural politics of Asian American independent film movement, a Yellow porno practice can help recuperate a sexuality that has been distorted by the internalization of core racist values and beliefs that reach into the depths of individual psychology. Like other expressive forms, pornography is but one manifestation of the irrepressible urge to explore the oceanic possibilities inherent in the sexuality of our species-being. To engage more specifically in an Asian American porno practice is to take self-determined control of an unfixed, variable, malleable, but thoroughly racialized human sexuality, shaped and constrained over time by politically oppressive forces. I harbor no illusions that a self-conscious porno practice alone is sufficient to the task of destabilizing a near-hegemonic system of sex/race/power. But an Asian American cultural politics grounded in a radical *jouissance* that gives rise to the release of libidinal energy will remain an indispensable resource upon which to draw in the greater struggle against individual and group oppression.

Notes

Acknowledgments: The author thanks Asagiri Tomoyo, Carl Boggs, Itsuki Charles Igawa, Doug Kellner, Sandra Liu, Gina Marchetti, Pam Matsuoka, Kent Ono, Sarah Projansky, Donald Richie, and my students at UC Davis for their valued help in the development of this chapter. Thanks to C. F. for sharing her intimate and extensive knowledge of gay video porn.

1. The body self-image of Asian American women, for example, is dissected in Chen (1996). Almost as an afterthought, Chen observes, "Of course, many physical features now deemed beautiful in Asian culture are direct results of Western colonial domination." An advertisement for "eyelid surgery," or blepharoplasty, appears in a piece by Dr. Wes Young (1997).

2. In a breakthrough of sorts, the exclusion of eroticized Asian American men in the dominant media is subverted in the film *Boogie Nights* (Anderson 1997), where porno star Dirk Diggler (Mark Wahlberg) stands in open admiration of Bruce Lee and draws on the iconic image of the late martial-arts superstar to motivate himself before performing sex. Yet the documentary *Miss India Georgia* (Friedman and Grimberg 1997) captures one of the South Asian American beauty pageant contestants (struggling to reconcile ethnic identity with White supremacist norms) against a backdrop of advertisement photos featuring European American male models posted on her bedroom wall.

3. Tajiri admits that the voyeuristic "sister" is to a certain degree herself (Tajiri 1995).

4. However, Asian Americans have not passively accepted their exclusion from the dominant visual media and historically have sought other means of bringing to the fore self-validating images and depictions. There is a telling scene in *Picture Bride* (1995), directed by Kayo Hatta, where Japanese immigrant plantation workers in Hawaii enjoy a *chambara*, or sword-

play film, featuring the valorous actions of the "samurai hero" Nakayama Yasubei as narrated by a *benshi* played by Mifune Toshirō in a cameo appearance.

5. The empirical reality of visual White supremacy is verified through cross-cultural comparison with Japanese society, where the so-called *gaijin* (foreigner) complex arose from political, social, and cultural subordination, beginning in the Meiji era (1867–1912) and continuing to the present. The pervasiveness of U.S.-made films and television programs during the postwar period "led to the acceptance of White imagery as *atarimae*"—that is, "natural" (Creighton 1997, 216).

6. The phrase "epidermal fetishism" is given a somewhat narrow, economistic twist by Wolfenstein, but it has utility in the discussion of the White supremacist complex.

7. Cetner, Blackmon, and Blosser (1997, 33). See also Orth (1997).

8. Cruise is revered as both a gay and straight icon amid persistent public speculation concerning his sexual orientation.

9. The concept of "bachelor society" invoked in the standard historiography of Chinese Americans precludes consideration of other forms of erotic conjugality and familial organization within all-male sodalities. See Ting (1995). Richard Fung also speculates on the possibility of homosexual relationships within the homosocial communities of nineteenth-century Chinese immigrant workers in *Dirty Laundry* (1996).

10. See Cheng (1984) and Chan (1991a).

11. The amended law was the War Brides Act of 1947.

12. *Know Your Enemy* was withdrawn soon after its release and was not seen widely by the public until it appeared on PBS in *Films of Persuasion* (1977) (McBride 1993, 727).

13. Born in Brooklyn, New York, as Margarita Carmen Cansino, the actress adopted the Anglo "Hayworth" persona at the behest of her husband Edward Judson to boost an otherwise unpromising movie career (Keller 1997, 77).

14. Thanks to Steve Craig, chairman of the planetarium at the Academy of Sciences in San Francisco, for assisting in detective work concerning the filming of the Steinhart Aquarium scene in *The Lady from Shanghai.*

15. Although known today as "Annabel Chong," the actress introduces herself to Ed Powers in her first professional porno appearance as "Chung," in *More Dirty Debutantes* #37 (1995). She is credited as "Anabelle Chung" in the video.

16. See Chapkis (1997). For the contours of the feminist debate over pornography, see Mann (1994, 62–89); Duggan and Hunter (1995); and Strossen (1996).

17. In truth, Chong (Grace Quek) reveals herself to be an intelligent and thoughtful artist who describes her porn-performer role in part as a reaction to the repressive "eighties feminism" of McKinnon and Dworkin (Petkovich 1997b, 32).

18. Also titled *Once upon a Time/Cave Woman* (1978), the film was produced and directed by the former porn star Annette Haven, a White woman who apparently shares in the myths of primordial White male supremacy.

19. Japanese video porn for the domestic market is substantially better by all measures, but its erotic impact is blunted terribly by the state-enforced use of mosaic *bokashi* over genitalia. Like the *shunga* paintings of the *ukiyo-e* masters, even art films such as *In the Realm of the Senses* (1976) by Nagisa Oshima are unavailable for viewing in uncensored form (Oshima 1992).

20. One might also attribute the mixed response of the interviewees to the didactic purport of the "safer-sex" videos. According to one observer, who laments the "devolution" of homoerotic sexual pleasure and its utopian possibilities during the 1980s in response to the so-called AIDS crisis, gay pornography "became an integral tool in regulating men's sexual activity," and as a consequence "lost much of its status as purveyor of fantasies" (Hoffman 1996).

21. The same issue of the *Adam Gay Video 1997 Directory*, however, reviews *Lovespell* (1995a), Oggi's first U.S. production with established porn stars. The accompanying photo shows a Yellow man, Dustin Tye, being pleasured by a White man, Justin Side.

22. The producer of *Pacific Rim* is Josh Elliot; the director is Mitchell Dunne; and the writers are Mitchell Dunne and Danny Davenport.

23. Possibly complicating Faludi's analysis, the politics of "female ejaculation" has been explored by the performance artist Annie Sprinkle and others (Straayer 1996, 244–52). Similarly, multiple orgasms are being claimed for men by Chia and Arava (1997).

24. Kaplan's bizarre misrepresentation of "pornography" begs for more in the way of description: "Pornography is a male invention, a literature of harlotry designed to detoxify and repair the actual female body. Then, with the avowed aims of arousing erotic desire in men and freeing women from the bonds of sexual repression, female bodies are stripped, bent over, spread apart, twisted. Labia are pierced. Breasts are lassoed till they swell to an abnormal size. Nipples are pinched with clothespins. Breasts of pregnant women are shown expressing streams of milk. Buttocks are branded. The genitals of prepubescent girls are licked by dogs. Nymphomaniacs are sated unto death. Lesbians suck one another off. Virgins are subjected to exotic practices that turn them into groveling nymphomaniacs." Kinky indeed (1997, 322).

25. Wolf and others who advance ideas of "sexual agency" are dismissed out of hand as "retrofeminists" in Ebert (1996, 254).

26. See Miyatake (1984). On Sugimoto and Okubo, see Kuramitsu (1995). See also Okubo (1983). Okubo's illustrated narrative was originally published in 1946. Isamu Noguchi helped found the organization Nisei Writers and Artists Mobilization for Democracy in February 1942 and voluntarily entered the Poston, Arizona, concentration camp the following May, but won his release seven months later, in November, after finding conditions intolerable. Noguchi paid tribute to the pioneer generation in the sculpture *To the Issei* (1980–83), located in the Japanese American Cultural and Community Center Plaza in the heart of Little Tokyo. See Maeda (1994) and Ashton (1992).

27. Footage shot by Tatsuno is sampled in Tajiri's *History and Memory* (1991) and *Strawberry Fields* (1997). For other examples of work by interned Japanese American visual artists, see Gesensway and Roseman (1987).

28. See Leong (1991).

29. See, for example, the cultural history of eroticism in Japan by Bornoff (1991).

30. See Chu (1993). Despite its deceptively Orientalist title, the book's first two-thirds contain a well-researched social history of eroticism by an author who was born and educated in China and has translated many of the classic texts himself. More noteworthy is Chu's use of illustrations in the book's final "how-to" section, where Yellow men and Yellow women are shown pleasuring one another.

31. Tamba Yasunori, a Chinese physician living in Japan, was responsible for gathering the sources that composed the text of *Ishimpō*. See Levy and Ishihara (1989).

32. See Aldred (1996); Anand (1989); Chia and Chia (1986); Chia with Winn (1984); Dorra (1996); Douglas and Slinger (1979); Gach (1997); Hooper (1994); and Smith (1996).

33. The Xandria Collection—a large mail-order firm based in San Francisco—dedicates an entire section of its 10 May 1997 "Collector's Gold Edition" catalogue to Japanese-made sex toys. "Now you can experience the ancient traditions of skilled craftsmanship and oriental eroticism in products designed for ultimate female pleasure that are always discreet and reliable," says the section of the catalogue titled "Oriental Delights." Advertising text in a section that is whimsically titled "Erection Collection" brings a crosscultural perspective to bear in assuring

prospective purchasers that "references to Lingham rings abound in ancient Chinese, Japanese and Indian literature."

34. During a question-and-answer session at the 1997 festival, the directors spoke at length about problems associated with the finance, production, and distribution of Asian American feature films.

35. Not surprisingly—given the common practice of attaching parodic, punning labels to often-forgettable productions—a porno video titled *The Joi Fuk Club* (McCallum 1993) is in circulation. Other than wordplay with the title, it bears no resemblance to the mainstream film *The Joy Luck Club* (Wang 1993).

36. Funniest of all for its moralistic high seriousness is a poem (autobiographical?) that tells of a furtive, doobie-smoking wanker who returns home one day armed with skin mags and ready to spank the monkey after having visited the local adult-video arcade. When he hears his wife come home unexpectedly, the narrator hurries to get off in secret rather than invite her to join in the festivities.

Works Cited

Aldred, Caroline. 1996. *Divine Sex: The Tantric and Taoist Arts of Conscious Loving.* New York: Harper Collins.

Anand, Margo (pseud. M. E. Naslednikov). 1989. *The Art of Sexual Ecstasy.* New York: Tarcher/Putnam.

Ashton, Dore. 1992. *Noguchi: East and West.* Berkeley: University of California Press.

Becker, Maki. 1997. "Homemade History." *Los Angeles Times* (April 4), B4.

Bell, Shannon. 1995. *Whore Carnival.* New York: Autonomedia.

Bornoff, Nicholas. 1991. *Pink Samurai: Love, Marriage and Sex in Contemporary Japan.* New York: Pocket Books.

Bright, Susie. 1995. *Susie Bright's Sexwise.* Pittsburgh: Cleis Press.

Browning, Frank. 1994. *The Culture of Desire: Paradox and Perversity in Gay Lives Today.* New York: Vintage Books.

Burger, John R. 1995. *One-Handed Histories: The Eroto-Politics of Gay Male Video Pornography.* New York: Harrington Park Press.

Cetner, Marc, Robert Blackmon, and John Blosser. 1997. "Gay Killer and Tom Cruise." *National Enquirer* (August 5), 32–33, 36–37.

Chan, Sucheng. 1991a. "The Exclusion of Chinese Women, 1870–1943." Pp. 94-146 in *Entry Denied: Exclusion and the Chinese Community in America, 1882–1943,* ed. Sucheng Chan. Philadelphia: Temple University Press.

———. 1991b. *Asian Americans: An Interpretive History.* Boston: Twayne Publishers.

Chapkis, Wendy. 1997. *Live Sex Acts: Women Performing Erotic Labor.* New York: Routledge.

Chen, Joanne. 1996. "Through the Looking Glass." *A. Magazine* (April/May), 34–37.

Cheng, Lucie. 1984. "Free, Indentured, Enslaved: Chinese Prostitutes in Nineteenth-Century America." Pp. 402–34 in *Labor Immigration under Capitalism: Asian Workers in the United States Before World War II,* ed. Lucie Cheng and Edna Bonacich. Berkeley: University of California Press.

Chia, Mantak, and Douglas Abrams Arava. 1997. *The Multi-Orgasmic Man: Sexual Secrets Every Man Should Know.* New York: HarperSanFrancisco.

Chia, Mantak, and Maneewan Chia. 1986. *Healing Love Through the Tao: Cultivating Female Sexual Energy.* Huntington, N.Y.: Healing Tao Books.

Chia, Mantak, with Michael Winn. 1984. *Taoist Secrets of Love: Cultivating Male Sexual Energy.* Santa Fe, N.M.: Aurora Books.

Chodorow, Nancy J. 1989. *Feminism and Psychoanalytic Theory.* New Haven, Conn.: Yale University Press.

Chu, Valentin. 1993. *The Yin-Yang Butterfly: Ancient Chinese Sexual Secrets for Western Lovers.* New York: Tarcher/Putnam.

Creighton, Millie. 1997. "Soto Others and Uchi Others: Imagining Racial Diversity, Imagining Homogeneous Japan." Pp. 211–38 in *Japan's Minorities: The Illusion of Homogeneity,* ed. Michael Weiner. New York: Routledge.

Cusac, Anne-Marie. 1996. "Profile of a Sex Radical." *Progressive* (October), 34–37.

Dorra, Martine. 1996. *Kama Sutra in 3D: Add New Dimensions to Your Sex Life.* San Francisco: Thorsons.

Douglas, Nik, and Penny Slinger. 1979. *Sexual Secrets: The Alchemy of Ecstasy.* Rochester, Vt.: Destiny Books.

Duggan, Lisa, and Nan D. Hunter. 1995. *Sex Wars: Sexual Dissent and Political Culture.* New York: Routledge.

Ebert, Teresa L. 1996. *Ludic Feminism and After: Postmodernism, Desire, and Labor in Late Capitalism.* Ann Arbor: University of Michigan Press.

Espiritu, Yen Le. 1995. *Filipino American Lives.* Philadelphia: Temple University Press.

Faludi, Susan. 1995. "The Money Shot." *New Yorker* (October 30), 64–87.

Fanon, Frantz. 1967. *Black Skin, White Masks.* Trans. Charles Markmann. New York: Grove.

Fishbein, Paul, ed. 1996. *AVN: The 1997 Adult Video Entertainment Guide.* Van Nuys, Calif.: AVN Publications.

Foucault, Michel. 1990. *The History of Sexuality: An Introduction, Volume I.* Trans. Robert Hurley. New York: Vintage Books.

Fung, Richard. 1991. "Looking For My Penis: The Eroticized Asian in Gay Video Porn." Pp. 145–60 in *How Do I Look?: Queer Film and Video,* ed. Bad Object-Choices. Seattle: Bay Press.

———. 1993. "Shortcomings: Questions about Pornography as Pedagogy." Pp. 355–67 in *Queer Looks: Perspectives on Lesbian and Gay Film and Video,* ed. Martha Gever, Pratibha Parmar, and John Greyson. New York: Routledge.

Gach, Michael Reed. 1997. *Accupressure for Lovers: Secrets of Touch for Increasing Intimacy.* New York: Bantam.

Galt, Jay. 1997. "VideoGold's Exclusive Interview with Asia Carrera." *The Ladies of Risque Business* (February 15), http://www.risque.com/html/risque/interviewasia2.html.

Gesensway, Deborah, and Mindy Roseman. 1987. *Beyond Words: Images from America's Concentration Camps.* Ithaca, N.Y.: Cornell University Press.

Greenfeld, Karl Taro. 1995. "The X Files." *A. Magazine* (August/September), 31–37.

Guillermo, Emil. 1997. "We've Been Cunanized!" *AsianWeek* (July 25), 5.

Hartley, Nina. 1997. "In the Flesh: A Porn Star's Journey." Pp. 57–65 in *Whores and Other Feminists,* ed. Jill Nagle. New York: Routledge.

Hoffman, Wayne. 1996. "Skipping the Life Fantastic: Coming of Age in the Sexual Devolution." Pp. 337–54 in *Policing Public Sex: Queer Politics and the Future of AIDS Activism,* ed. Dangerous Bedfellows. Boston: South End Press.

hooks, bell. 1995. *Art on My Mind: Visual Politics.* New York: New Press.

Hooper, Anne. 1994. *Anne Hooper's Kama Sutra: Classic Lovemaking Techniques Reinterpreted for Today's Lovers*. New York: Dorling Kindersley.

Kaplan, Louise. 1997. *Female Perversions: The Temptations of Emma Bovary*. Northvale, N.J.: Aronson.

Keller, Gary D. 1997. *A Biographical Handbook of Hispanics and United States Film*. Tempe, Ariz.: Bilingual Press.

Kimmel, Michael S. 1991. "'Insult' or 'Injury': Sex, Pornography, and Sexism." Pp. 305–19 in *Men Confront Pornography*, ed. Michael S. Kimmel. New York: Meridian.

Kipnis, Laura. 1996. *Bound and Gagged: Pornography and the Politics of Fantasy in America*. New York: Grove Press.

Kivel, Paul. 1996. *Uprooting Racism: How White People Can Work for Racial Justice*. Philadelphia: New Society Publishers.

Koppes, Clayton R., and Gregory D. Black. 1990. *Hollywood Goes to War: How Politics, Profits and Propaganda Shaped World War II Movies*. Berkeley: University of California Press.

Kuramitsu, Kristine C. 1995. "Internment and Identity in Japanese American Art." *American Quarterly* (December), 619–58.

Lawrence, Doug, ed. 1996. *Adam Gay Video 1997 Directory: 7th Annual Edition*. Los Angeles: Knight Publications.

Leong, Russell, ed. 1991. *Moving the Image: Independent Asian Pacific American Media Arts*. Los Angeles: UCLA Asian American Studies Center and Visual Communications, Southern California Asian American Studies Central.

Levy, Howard S., and Akira Ishihara. 1989. *The Tao of Sex: The Essence of Medical Prescriptions (Ishimpō)*. Lower Lake, Calif.: Integral Publishing.

Lowe, Lisa. 1996. *Immigrant Acts: On Asian American Cultural Politics*. Durham, N.C.: Duke University Press.

McBride, Joseph. 1993. *Frank Capra: The Catastrophe of Success*. New York: Touchstone.

Maeda, Robert J. 1994. "Isamu Noguchi: 5-7-A, Poston, Arizona." *Amerasia Journal* 20, no. 2 (spring): 60–76.

Mann, Patricia S. 1994. *Micro-Politics: Agency in a Postfeminist Era*. Minneapolis: University of Minnesota Press.

Mano, D. Keith. 1996. "'I'm Ready For My Come Shot Now, Dear.'" *Playboy* (August), 81 ff.

Matsuda, Mari J. 1996. *Where Is Your Body? And Other Essays On Race Gender and the Law*. Boston: Beacon Press.

Miyatake, Toyo. 1984. *Toyo Miyatake: Behind the Camera 1923–1979*. Trans. Paul Petite. Tokyo: Bungeishunju.

Mura, David. 1987. *A Male Grief: Notes on Pornography and Addiction*. Minneapolis: Milkweed Editions.

Okubo, Miné. 1983. *Citizen 13660*. Seattle: University of Washington Press.

Orth, Maureen. 1997. "The Killer's Trail." *Vanity Fair* (September), 268–75, 329–36.

Oshima, Nagisa. 1992. "Theory of Experimental Pornographic Film." Pp. 251–64 in *Cinema, Censorship, and the State: The Writings of Nagisa Oshima, 1956–1978*, trans. Dawn Lawson. Cambridge, Mass.: MIT Press.

Palac, Lisa. 1995. "How Dirty Pictures Changed My Life." Pp. 236–52 in *Debating Sexual Correctness: Pornography, Sexual Harassment, Date Rape, and the Politics of Sexual Equality*, ed. Adele M. Stan. New York: Delta.

Petkovich, Anthony. 1997a. "This Way to the World's Biggest Gang Bang 2!" *Headpress* 14 (April), 23–29.

————. 1997b. "Get It On, Bang a Chong: A Conversation with Superior Porn Slut Annabel Chong." *Headpress* 15 (October), 26–41.

Pollitt, Katha. 1997. "Born Again vs. Porn Again." *The Nation* (February 3), 9.

Queen, Carol. 1997. *Real Live Nude Girl: Chronicles of Sex-Positive Culture*. Pittsburgh: Cleis Press.

Reich, Wilhelm. 1972. *Sex-Pol: Essays 1929–1934*. Ed. Lee Baxandall, trans. Anna Bostock. New York: Vintage Books.

Schlosser, Eric. 1997. "The Business of Pornography." *US News and World Report* (February 10), 42–52.

Smith, Gilly. 1996. *Asian Secrets of Sexual Ecstasy: Discover the Power of Bliss*. New York: Citadel Press.

Straayer, Chris. 1996. *Deviant Eyes, Deviant Bodies: Sexual Re-Orientations in Film and Video*. New York: Columbia University Press.

Strossen, Nadine. 1996. *Defending Pornography: Free Speech, Sex, and the Fight for Women's Rights*. New York: Anchor Books.

Tajiri, Rea. 1995. Telephone interview. February.

Takaki, Ronald. 1989. *Strangers from a Different Shore: A History of Asian Americans*. New York: Penguin Books.

Ting, Jennifer. 1995. "Bachelor Society: Deviant Heterosexuality and Asian American Historiography." Pp. 271–79 in *Privileging Positions: The Sites of Asian American Studies*, ed. Gary Y. Okihiro, Marilyn Alquizola, Dorothy Fujita Rony, and K. Scott Wong. Pullman: Washington State University Press.

Tisdale, Sallie. 1995. *Talk Dirty to Me: An Intimate Philosophy of Sex*. New York: Anchor Books.

Wolf, Naomi. 1994. *Fire with Fire: The New Female Power and How to Use It*. New York: Fawcett Columbine.

Wolfenstein, Eugene Victor. 1993. *Psychoanalytic-Marxism: Groundwork*. New York: Guilford Press.

Xandria Collection. 1997. Catalogue: "Collector's Gold Edition," May 10, n.p.

Yip, Alethea. 1997. "APA Archivist: Preserving Episodes of American History." *AsianWeek* (April 18), 9.

Young, Wes. 1997. "Taking a Second Look." *A. Magazine* (August/September), 24–25.

Films and Videos Cited

Anderson, Paul Thomas. 1997. *Boogie Nights*. New Line Cinema.

Bone, John T. 1995. *The World's Biggest Gang Bang*. Fantastic Pictures.

————. 1996. *The World's Biggest Gang Bang 2*. Fantastic Pictures.

Capra, Frank. 1937. *Lost Horizon*. Columbia Pictures.

————. 1945. *Know Your Enemy—Japan*. Signal Corps Army Pictorial Service.

Dunne, Mitchell. 1997. *Pacific Rim*. Catalina Video.

Friedman, Daniel, and Sharon Grimberg. 1997. *Miss India Georgia*. Urban Life Productions.

Fung, Richard. 1996. *Dirty Laundry*. Fungus Productions.

Haven, Annette. 1978. *Once upon Annette/Cave Woman*. International HVC (excerpt included in the compilation *Tongue Fu* [1994, Vivid Video]).

Hatta, Kayo. 1995. *Picture Bride*. Miramax.

Hayman, John. 1995a. *Passage to Spring*. Island Caprice Studios.

————. 1995b. *Thai Take-Out*. Island Caprice Studios.

Idemoto, Michael, and Eric Nakamura. 1997. *Sunsets*. A Cousins Film.

Lee, Chris Chan. 1997. *Yellow*. Yellow Productions.

Lee, Quentin, and Justin Lin. 1997. *Shopping for Fangs*. de/center communications.

McCallum, Robert. 1993. *Joi Fuk Club*. Western Visuals.

Nakamura, Robert A. 1994. *Something Strong Within: Home Movies from America's Concentration Camps*. Japanese American National Museum.

Oggi. 1995a. *Lovespell*. Exotic Productions.

———. 1995b. *Room Service*. Exotic Productions.

———. 1995c. *Sexual Healing*. Exotic Productions.

Omori, Emiko. 1991. *Hot Summer Winds*. One Pass.

Oshima, Nagisa. 1976. *In the Realm of the Senses*. Argos Films.

Powers, Ed. 1995. *More Dirty Debutantes #37*. 4-Play Video.

Sturges, John. 1955. *Bad Day at Black Rock*. MGM/UA.

Tajiri, Rea. 1991. *History and Memory: For Akiko and Takashige*. Women Make Movies.

———. 1997. *Strawberry Fields*. Ghost Pictures.

Takagi, J. T., and Hye Jung Park. 1996. *The Women Outside*. Camera News.

Tokyo Blue. 1996. Fat Dog Productions.

Tongue Fu. 1994. Vivid Video.

Ultra Call Girls. 1995. Excitement Video.

Wang, Wayne. 1989. *Eat a Bowl of Tea*. American Playhouse.

———. 1993. *The Joy Luck Club*. Hollywood Pictures.

Welles, Orson. 1948. *The Lady from Shanghai*. Columbia Pictures.

Wonderful Desire. 1996. Lasergram Audio Video.

Sandra Liu

---

5   Negotiating the Meaning of Access:
       Wayne Wang's Contingent Film
       Practice

In her article "Moving the Image: Asian American Independent Filmmaking 1970–1990," published in 1991, the independent filmmaker, media activist, and critic Renee Tajima urged Asian Americans to reexamine the political and representational goals articulated by Asian American filmmakers and activists in the late 1960s and early 1970s in order to assess the directions and development of Asian American media arts in the 1990s.[1] She characterized early Asian American filmmaking as socially committed: primarily concerned with entitlement and access to all aspects of American institutional and public life, redressing injustices and invisibility in mainstream media, and advancing the political struggles of Asian Americans and other racial minorities in the United States. By the 1980s, the focus of Asian American media activism had shifted to formal and technical improvement of films and to mass audience appeal, in part because access and entitlement were intrinsic to the struggle in the 1970s. Tajima noted that, ironically, "victories that were won in the 1980s such as access to funding and mainstream venues had an effect of coopting the work" (Tajima 1991, 21). The overall change in the outlook of filmmakers took place within the context of a swing toward conservatism in national politics, rapidly changing Asian American demographics and increasing reliance on film schools for professional training.

Tajima's article was groundbreaking as the first attempt to conceptualize a history of independent Asian American filmmaking. However, her bifurcated history reflects an understanding of the film industry that separates and judges independently produced films as occupying the political and artistic high ground, and mainstream or studio productions as being coopted and politically suspect. The reactions of many Asian Americans to the film version of *The Joy Luck Club* (Wang 1993) demonstrates that this is a common way to conceptualize the film industry. Columns, letters to the editor, and reviews in newspapers and magazines expressed a wary mistrust of, or directly denounced, the ways in which Chinese history, Asian and Asian American masculinity and femininity, Chinese American social- and economic-class standing, and mother–daughter relationships were being represented in the film.[2] Even positive evaluations of the film supported the dominant perception that studio productions automatically lead to the depoliticization of Asian American films. *The Joy Luck Club* was praised for depicting characters that transcend race, for having universal appeal, and—along with several other films being released at about the same time—for moving Asian American filmmaking into the mainstream.[3] Many Asian American critics read *The Joy Luck Club*'s ability to attract mainstream audiences as a sign of problematic assimilation, a realization of Tajima's concerns that Asian American filmmakers were achieving crossover success at the expense of their social and political vision. Even though all of the main characters in the film are Chinese and Chinese American, according to many reviews, their histories, cultural traditions, and socioeconomic issues were decontextualized, superficially depicted, or reduced to interpersonal conflict. In other words, *The Joy Luck Club* merely reiterated prevalent mainstream stereotypes in order to appeal to the widest possible audience.

However, the simple conclusion that filmmakers such as Wayne Wang, who directed *The Joy Luck Club,* have abandoned the representational and political aspirations of Asian American cultural activists in their reach for crossover audiences and profitability glosses over the social, economic, and political circumstances that Asian American filmmakers confront. To assess the state of Asian American filmmaking and to shape its future development, as Tajima urged us to do, Asian American cultural critics must take into account a complex of conflicting discourses and desires and continuously changing tactics in response to shifting material exigencies.

In this chapter, I propose to examine a film in the context of a director's body of work as one solution with several benefits. This approach alleviates some of the burden of representation—the often impossibly high expectations that one film will redress all past injustices and represent characters and situations that satisfy everyone—that any one Asian American feature film tends to bear because of the relative scarcity of these films, and by which *The Joy Luck Club* was certainly afflicted. Simultaneously, it offers assurance that Asian American filmmakers do not necessarily or inevitably gain access to the mainstream film industry—as modest as that access may be—at the expense of their artistic integrity or their social and political vision. Finally, it focuses on the tactics that filmmakers develop to negotiate complex and changing social and economic conditions.

By taking this approach, I seek to shift critical discourses about Asian Americans in film away from solely considering the supposed accuracy or realism of particular images[4]—the basis of many of the responses to *The Joy Luck Club*—to examining representations within structures and contexts that enable or restrict the practice of politically committed filmmaking in the United States. Thus, I read Wayne Wang's films as occupying contingent, strategic positions that contain periodic ruptures belying any simple mapping of his films on a continuum from politically committed social critique, beginning with *Chan Is Missing* in 1982, to supposedly depoliticized mainstream entertainment, with *Smoke* in 1995.[5] When considered within this framework,

Wang's filmmaking strategies can be seen as representing one example of socially and politically committed film practice.[6]

Wang's filmmaking career complicates and deconstructs the popular mythology that success as measured by Hollywood—that is, high profitability and a shelf lined with Oscars—is the pinnacle of filmmaking achievement. Thus, the objectives of a politicized Asian American filmmaking practice can be distinguished from a simple correlation with increased numbers of Asian Americans behind the scenes or in front of the camera in studio productions. Though some Asian American filmmakers have set their sights firmly on Hollywood-style success, market and media forces often collude to steer public attention toward the assumption that this is the goal of all narrative filmmakers. In contrast, I read Wang's filmography as revealing a canny ability to make strategic, self-conscious choices to create a balance of projects that support his reputation as a director who can make profitable films as well as movies that give primacy to his artistic and social vision. The combination of these two strategies has allowed Wang to negotiate the demands of a consumer- and profit-oriented system (with all the social inequities that this system also supports), and the desire to enact a socially committed and formally insurgent film practice.

Industrial Wang

You may be boss of your own trail, but the trail you take may not be your own choice. Sometimes you have to take the shit's trail. It's the only way out.
        Blind Man, Life Is Cheap . . . But Toilet Paper Is Expensive

Regardless of talent, several factors coalesced to create favorable conditions for filmmakers such as Wang to gain entrée into the film industry. First, in the late 1970s, film exhibitors thought that the number of movies available for distribution would increase. As a result, they built multiplex theaters to meet the expected supply. Contrary to expectation, however, the major distribution and production companies focused on financing and marketing a smaller number of high-priced blockbusters, such as *E.T.*, the *Star Wars* trilogy, and the Indiana Jones trilogy.[7] Throughout the 1980s, the markets for film grew at an exponential rate due to the introduction and wide adoption of VCRs and cable television. A shortfall of films was thus created. Small independent production and distribution companies were established during this period, stepping in to fill the vacuum with films by new directors (Rhines 1996, 11–13). Second, a sophisticated, affluent moviegoing audience made up of baby boomers and young college graduates demanding distinctive art house films emerged during this period (Rosen with Hamilton 1990, 265). Finally, filmmakers who had graduated from film schools, many of which were started in the 1960s, had opportunities to make at least one film in this relatively open field. In addition, filmmakers of color and white female filmmakers who were outside the traditional networks of funding and support took advantage of funds from federally funded arts programs that had been set up as part of the legacy of the civil rights movement. By the 1980s, some of these filmmakers had garnered enough experience to attract the attention of production and distribution companies.[8] Because of the burgeoning number of independent production and distribution companies, a supportive audience base, and the expansion of screening venues and ancillary markets, filmmakers had a relatively better chance of actually making their films and getting theatrical distribution.

This was the industry context in which Wang emerged as a filmmaker. Wang earned a master of fine arts degree in film and television from the California College of Arts and Crafts in Oakland in 1973. After working in film and television production in Hong Kong for two years, he returned to the United States to work as a community activist with Chinese immigrants in San Francisco's Chinatown. Wang was able to make his first film, *Chan Is Missing,* in 1982 with grants from the American Film Institute and the National Endowment for the Arts.[9] *Dim Sum: A Little Bit of Heart* (Wang 1985), his second film, was produced with a combination of funds from the profits from *Chan Is Missing* and from American Playhouse.[10] The films were distributed by two independent companies: New Yorker Films and Orion Classics, respectively. *Chan Is Missing* and *Dim Sum* were made and distributed during a particularly propitious time: The U.S. film industry was struggling to adjust to structural shifts; for a decade, Asian American media artists and activists had been protesting mainstream images of Asian Americans, creating original works, and demanding greater access to funding, the means of production, and screening venues; and the mainstream media was once again turning its attention to the significance of the Asian and Asian American population in the United States.[11]

Chan Is Missing and *Dim Sum* were independently produced by Wang and were therefore shielded from the pressure that major production companies might have brought to bear for the films to conform to mainstream production standards and narrative norms. However, the distribution companies that helped establish Wang as a filmmaker fell victim to the reassertion of control by the major studios in the mid-1980s. By the middle of the decade, the major studios were once again reclaiming dominance in film production and distribution. By enticing relatively established filmmakers of color and white female filmmakers to work for them, acquiring existing independent companies, and creating their own "boutique" studios to compete with the independent companies, they forced independent companies out of business or into specialty niches (Rhines 1996, 74–75). Some independent production companies began to resemble the major studios in terms of the types of projects they supported in order to remain competitive. Since it released *Chan Is Missing,* New Yorker Films has focused on producing and distributing international films, thus avoiding competition in the U.S. domestic market.

Orion Pictures, the parent company of Orion Classics, which distributed *Dim Sum,* ultimately was unable to compete with the major studios in this period. From its inception in 1982, Orion Pictures was promoted as an aspiring major production and distribution company, but by 1991, the company was forced to file for Chapter 11 bankruptcy, with more than $1 billion in debt. Since emerging from bankruptcy, Orion Classics, still under Orion Pictures, has distributed several small domestically and internationally produced independent films, but neither Orion Classics nor its parent company has been able to regain its former stature.[12] Similarly, Island Pictures, which produced (with Zenith Productions and Sho Films) and distributed *Slamdance* (1987)—Wang's third film—and other successful art house films during the 1980s,[13] was unable to remain competitive against the major studios and was forced out of domestic film distribution.

Wang was positioned fortuitously at the beginning of his career. By the time he had established himself as a filmmaker with *Chan Is Missing* and *Dim Sum,* the dominant film industry was closing ranks again. In the mid-1980s, Wang found that his options were limited. *Dim Sum* had earned mixed reviews, and its box office earnings were modest. Federal funding for the arts was already slowly drying up. Wang's choice to direct *Slamdance*—the only film thus far in his career for which he has worked strictly as a director for hire—may be read as a move to gain more credibility within the mainstream film industry, one source of funding that was not likely to dry up. *Slamdance* was a box office failure and was greeted by mixed, indifferent, and negative reviews. It cost $4.5 million to make, but earned less than $407,000 at the box office. Wang had pragmatic reasons for directing *Slamdance*: Concerned that he would be pigeonholed as a director who could make films only about Chinese American experiences, he felt that it was important to demonstrate his equal intimacy with other aspects of American life and cultures.[14] Also, directing *Slamdance* gave Wang an opportunity to learn how to navigate the mainstream film industry. The film's poor performance at the box office meant that Wang's struggle for funding would continue.

For his fourth film, *Eat a Bowl of Tea* (1989), Wang returned to filmmaking about Chinese American experiences. He also returned to American Playhouse, which had provided some of the funds to make *Dim Sum.* This time, his film was produced entirely by American Playhouse and Columbia Pictures. American Playhouse originally was established in 1980 as a nonprofit organization that would produce an original drama series of the same name for the Public Broadcasting Service (PBS).[15] It represented a unique opportunity: Its productions—plays, literary adaptations, miniseries, and original films—were chosen not because of their potential for mass market or broad audience appeal, and thus commercial profitability, but on the basis of how they expressed and visualized American perspectives, experiences, and lives. More than forty films (out of a total of 185 through 1994) by American Playhouse also received theatrical distribution in co-production deals that gave distribution companies the right to distribute a film theatrically before it premiered on the American Playhouse series on PBS. Though *Eat a Bowl of Tea* had a disappointing theatrical run that made less than $232,000 in the United States, Wang's association with American Playhouse reinforced his reputation as a competent, talented, and knowledgeable director with a strong artistic vision. It also demonstrated his continuing ability to attract funding for his projects.

Though American Playhouse was a nonprofit organization, it, too, was affected by the economic and social conditions in which Orion, Island, New Yorker, and other independent production and distribution companies were operating. American Playhouse was forced to privatize in the same environment of federal government deregulation of the mass media and celebration of market forces that has led to the ever-increasing concentration of corporate power over the media. In 1983, fifty national and multinational corporations owned the vast majority of the major media organizations in the United States. By 1992, that number had dropped to twenty (Bagdikian 1992, ix). Among other criticisms, conservative attacks on public television in the early 1990s were premised on the idea that all American media should be based on market principles (Hoynes 1994, 8).

American Playhouse's fortune was tied to that of the Corporation for Public Broadcasting (CPB) and PBS. Each time Congress successfully attacked funding for the arts and public broadcasting in the United States in the 1980s and 1990s, the CPB's—and consequently American Playhouse's—budget was cut. In addition, accusations by conservative leaders and politicians that the CPB and PBS were biased toward the left and liberal views, and that they funded projects that either were offensive or catered to a "minority" audience—presumed to be either poor non-white or rich white residents of major metropolitan areas, or gays and lesbians—took its toll.[16] After American Playhouse's third season, PBS pressured it to accommodate "broader audiences" who might be offended by portrayals of gay life or strong language in its productions.[17] Finally, in 1994, American Playhouse decided to form a new for-profit, independent production company in partnership with the Samuel Goldwyn Company. In its new incarnation as Playhouse Pictures, the company could no longer take the kinds of production risks that it did as a nonprofit organization in terms of the projects it chooses to produce and the practice of working with relatively unknown directors.

For Wang to remain in the game, his next project had to be a box office success. With the exception of *Chan Is Missing*, his films had been modestly successful, at best, and box office failures, at worst.[18] Though critics praised his work, Wang couldn't trade on his early success indefinitely. This was especially important in the politically and economically conservative climate of the late 1980s; within the context of a national economic recession, the movie industry was nervous about risky ventures. His fifth film was *The Joy Luck Club*.

Produced in 1993 for $10.6 million, *The Joy Luck Club* is an example of Wang's ability to navigate economic necessity and social perception. At the time, Wang said that, after *Eat a Bowl of Tea*, he did not plan to make another film about Chinese American experiences in the immediate future (Weinraub 1993). He continued to be concerned about being pigeonholed as a filmmaker who made films only about Chinese Americans; however, he was inspired to do *The Joy Luck Club* after reading the novel in 1989. In some ways, *The Joy Luck Club* was a risky project to take on. People told Wang that the story was too complicated: With characters who were almost all Chinese and Chinese American women, and with no stars or other obvious commercial hook (Dutka 1993), the film would have difficulty attracting a mainstream audience. It would have the biggest budget of any film that Wang had worked on thus far. And if the movie failed, Wang probably would find getting backing for future projects difficult. On the other hand, the risks were mitigated by the fact that Wang already had a solid reputation as a director of films with Chinese American themes. Here his reputation as a Chinese American filmmaker worked in his favor. The participation of other well-known, award-winning top team members—especially Ronald Bass (who had won an Academy Award with Barry Morrow for writing *Rain Man* [Levinson 1988] and who co-wrote the *Joy Luck Club* script with Amy Tan and Wang) and Oliver Stone (executive producer of *The Joy Luck Club* with Janet Yang)—gave the project added respectability. Hollywood Pictures agreed to produce the film, despite the fact that Wang insisted on retaining artistic control. For Hollywood Pictures and Buena Vista, both owned by Disney, the risk was moderate. The budget was relatively modest in an era when studio productions averaged $35 million, and as a historical drama, *The Joy Luck Club* was a bargain. And, of course, the novel's popularity would act as a built-in marketing tool.[19] Wang's risk paid off: *The Joy Luck Club* grossed almost $33 million in domestic box office receipts alone.

After his success with *The Joy Luck Club,* Wang directed *Smoke* (1995), produced and distributed by Miramax, which, like Hollywood Pictures and Buena Vista, is also owned by Disney. (Disney bought Miramax in 1993, after it had built a strong reputation as a producer and distributor of high-quality, profitable independent films.) The movie had been in development since mid-1991, when Wang approached Paul Auster about turning "Auggie Wren's Christmas Story," a story Auster had written for the Christmas edition of the *New York Times* in 1990, into a movie. An initial production deal between Nippon Film Development and American Zoetrope fell through in early 1992, but Auster continued to work on the script, with occasional input from Wang. *The Joy Luck Club*'s success helped to generate interest in *Smoke,* and in fall 1993, Miramax signed on as the co-executive producer with Nippon Film Development to make the movie.

About his decision to direct *Smoke,* Wang said, "I definitely want to step away from the Chinese thing for a while. I'll eventually get back to it—I'm sure I will—but at the same time, I feel I'm just as American as anyone else. There are stories and characters about America that I want to tell" (quoted in Weinraub 1993). This statement recalled his early concern about being pigeonholed as a "Chinese American" director, and making *Smoke,* whose cast was made up predominantly of African and European American characters, directly intervened in and challenged that assumption. If Wang's primary concern had been to consolidate his ability to command a large budget and to work within the bosom of the studio system, he could have chosen to make the movie version of *The Kitchen God's Wife,* Amy Tan's second novel, a potential project in which there was immediate interest in the wake of *The Joy Luck Club*'s success (Dutka 1993). In addition, in 1993, the media was giving marked attention to films with Asian and Asian American characters.[20] Wang could have ridden that wave of interest to make another film about Asian American experiences. Instead, he made *Smoke,* a character-driven art house film with a budget that was less than half the size of *The Joy Luck Club*'s. *Smoke* was a modest success in the United States, earning $8.4 million at the box office; overseas, it had a strong run, making $30 million.

Since *Smoke,* Wang and Hollywood have continued to dance around each other. While *Smoke* was still in production in late 1994, movie industry magazines began reporting on Wang's upcoming projects. Hollywood Pictures signed Wang to direct *The Kitchen God's Wife* (Busch 1994; Honeycutt 1994). Wang agreed to direct *The Big Nowhere,* a $20 million to $30 million movie for United Artists. He also was developing *Good Scent from Strange Mountain* for Oliver Stone's Ixtlan (Galloway 1994). Conflicting reports about what his next project would be continued after *Smoke* proved to be an art house success. In the second half of 1995 and into the first half of 1996, industry magazines were saying that Wang would next direct a trio of "erotic films for Miramax Films," each with a relatively low budget of approximately $3 million (Dunkley and Galloway 1995); that Wang had committed to direct *The Locked Room* for Fine Line Pictures (which would also distribute it) and a new independent production division of RKO Pictures for a $10 million budget (Cox 1996; Dunkley 1996a); that Wang was exploring the possibility of directing *Arkansas*, to be produced by Steven Spielberg and to star Brad Pitt (Busch 1996); that Wang was in negotiations to direct *The Good Shepherd*, a film produced by Francis Ford Coppola and American Zoetrope for Columbia Pictures (Dunkley 1996b); and that Wang had signed on to direct *Mrs. Wright* for Chestnut Hill Productions and Warner Bros. (Dunkley 1996c).

In short, since *The Joy Luck Club* and *Smoke,* Wang has had the cachet to make attractive deals with both the premier independent companies and the Hollywood studios.[21] However, he has defied conventional expectations about the types of projects an established filmmaker should make. Driven by a desire to make a film about the last days before Britain returned Hong Kong to Chinese rule at the end of June 1997, Wang put aside his other commitments to make *Chinese Box* in December 1996. The film was financed by European and Japanese companies, including Nippon Film Development, and as the film was being shot in Hong Kong, it still did not have a U.S. distributor.[22] *Chinese Box* was an experiment in filmmaking. Though the film had an outline, the script was being written as it was shot, so that the events that unfolded during the hand-over could be incorporated into the script. In essence, the film had fictional characters (played by Gong Li, Jeremy Irons, Maggie Cheung, Michael Hui, and Ruben Blades) nestled inside actual events occurring in Hong Kong. The plot's climax, and the shooting, coincided with the events on June 30, 1997, the day of the hand-over ceremony.

Superficially, Wang's career trajectory gives some credence to Tajima's contention that Asian American filmmakers may concentrate on bankability, and access to and assimilation into the centers of power in the film industry, to the exclusion of all else. Undeniably, Wang did ambitiously "locate and exploit particular, temporary imperfections in both national and industry-wide political and economic structures" (Rhines 1996, 2) in order to establish himself as a filmmaker. Reading Wang's films as simply charting a path to mainstream appeal, however, elides the changes that the industry itself was experiencing in the 1980s and 1990s. During this period, the film industry underwent tremendous changes as independent companies asserted themselves and then were absorbed into the studios and other entertainment conglomerates, blurring the distinction between independent and mainstream production. In this context, cultural critics can no longer divide films simply into two opposing camps: socially, politically, and artistically good independents on the one hand, and bad mainstream movies on the other. Instead, my reading of Wang's films highlights their contingent nature, acknowledging how each film might have increased or limited Wang's power to control his filmmaking efforts. Although they do not meet every expectation of progressive Asian American cultural critics, Wang's films offer varying levels of challenge to the mainstream film industry through their representation of Chinese and Asian American experiences and by pushing the boundaries of conventional mainstream narrative form.

Beyond "Dollars and Sense": Wayne Wang's Shadow Films

I'm only now realising that there is this constant theme in my work. There's always a journey, usually taken by characters who are not unique but commonplace, ordinary. . . . I do feel that what's really important for the ordinary person, not having a particular moral cause, but feeling an affinity deep down in the gut for something that is really and truly free, to do something about it even though it might compromise him. But there is a cynicism too, in this case that you kinda have to eat shit in order to do something right. And that's also true of film-making. You have to eat a lot of shit to make a movie.

Wayne Wang, quoted in Pannifer 1991

I turn now to three separate instances in which Wayne Wang made companion films that were inspired by or springboarded from a "mainstreamed" production on which he was working. *Dim Sum Take-Out* (1988) was made up of outtakes from a discarded story line for *Dim Sum. Life Is Cheap . . . But Toilet Paper Is Expensive* and *Blue in the Face* (Wang and Auster 1995) were inspired by the locations and situations surrounding the production of *Eat a Bowl of Tea* in Hong Kong and *Smoke* in Brooklyn, New York, respectively.[23] These films stand out among Wang's works because they represent distinct instances throughout his career (to date) in which his refusal simply to accommodate market demands have crystallized.

I have come to think of *Dim Sum Take-Out, Life Is Cheap . . .* , and *Blue in the Face* as shadow films because they were inspired by, exist in the shadows of, or portray a darker vision of parallel themes in their companion pieces. *Dim Sum Take-Out* was never distributed theatrically. It exists literally in the shadow of *Dim Sum. Life Is Cheap . . .* critically examined as a central theme the continuing importance among Chinese men of giving or having "face." This theme was sidelined in *Eat a Bowl of Tea* in favor of focusing on the romantic relationship and sexual tension between the newlywed couple, Mei Oi and Ben Loy. Both *Life Is Cheap . . .* and *Blue in the Face* represent contemporary social and political attitudes and conditions in Hong Kong and Brooklyn as central elements rather than as convenient backdrops to the main action, as in *Eat a Bowl of Tea* and *Smoke*.[24] Inspired by the actors' rehearsals for *Smoke, Blue in the Face* also is a study of the personalities and back stories of different characters (not always the central ones) that appear in *Smoke,* weaving in additional characters, as well.

Shadow films, by implication, are indelibly connected to their companion films, which can be conceived of as the shadow films' embodied, corporeal, or corporate complements. The shadow–body pair evokes the struggle surrounding the positioning of Asian Americans in the United States' cultural, social, and political spheres.

The fight to be acknowledged as bodies that count in terms of gaining the rights of naturalization, citizenship, and equal treatment in and access to institutional life has fundamentally shaped the history of Asians in the United States. Further, the implications of being a corporate body or being incorporated within the context of the U.S. economy also should not be ignored. Asian Americans' struggle for representation also can be translated into a struggle to be perceived as a significant market in the U.S. consumer economy (as problematic as achieving "market" status may be), a perception that is closely tied to political power. The struggle for embodiment or incorporation takes on a special significance in relation to being included and represented in the cultural landscape. As the documentary filmmaker Loni Ding (1991, 47) has observed, "It is somehow not enough that we've lived among a group of people, and see them every day in life. Something essential is missing when that existence is not also a confirmed public existence. The subtext of media absence is that the absent group 'doesn't count,' or is somehow unacceptable . . . . To be absent in T.V. imagery is a special kind of 'non-existence' or way of being 'non-American.'" The corporate films thus represent an extension of Asian American resistance against invisibility and disfranchisement. Corporate support of *Dim Sum, Eat a Bowl of Tea,* and *Smoke* in the form of production funds and distribution deals granted these films a level of visibility and allowed them (and by extension, Asian Americans) to have a greater presence in America's public life than would otherwise have been possible. The (in)corporation of these films thus suggests a (limited) measure of general cultural and social acceptance.

However, the shadows of the corporate films attest to continuing limits on the types of representations of Asian Americans that have become available in mainstream American movie culture. Wang's shadow films embody the experimental, critical, controversial, threatening, and incommensurate social, aesthetic, and political elements that could not find a place or voice in his corporate films. Notwithstanding the fact that *Dim Sum, Eat a Bowl of Tea,* and *Smoke*—not to mention Wang's other films—are all marginal relative to mainstream studio productions, the shadow films highlight the need for continued challenges to the mainstream movie industry. *Life Is Cheap . . . ,* in particular, expresses Wang's frustration with working within the constraints of that system. Wang recalled: "[*Eat a Bowl of Tea*] was very traditionally shot and I hated it. There was a certain anger in terms of not being able to make the film I wanted to make—I was under the reins quite a bit. Then in *Slamdance,* the producers changed my cut, which had been non-linear. So this film [*Life Is Cheap . . .*] is a kind of freeing process" [quoted in Pannifer 1991].

In other words, Wang was actively responding to the structural limitations that the mainstream film industry placed on him, wresting spaces for himself in which he could explore aesthetics and themes that would otherwise be suppressed. In the remainder of this discussion, I want to elaborate on the ways in which Wang's shadow films embody resistance to several systems of domination.[25] In particular, the films resist containment of the ways Asian Americans are represented in mainstream culture. They interrogate the concept of realism and challenge the artificial separation between documentary and fiction. Thus, Wang flouts formulaic and conventional

generic standards in film that censor critical perspectives and support dominant hierarchical social structures. [26]

Dim Sum Take-Out shows how the heterogeneity and complexity of Asian American experiences can be erased. It was literally cut together from film that was shot for
Dim Sum, which was conceived as a film about the ways in which five women of the
Chinese diaspora—three American-born (Laureen Chew, Amy Hill, and Rita Yee), a
naturalized citizen (Cora Miao), and a recent immigrant (Joan Chen)—try to balance
their personal goals and the expectations of the Chinese American community in
which they live (Seid 1983). The original story line was thought to be too complicated and ambitious, and, ultimately, significant portions of *Dim Sum* were rewritten and
reshot to focus on Geraldine, a second-generation Chinese American woman, and her
relationship with her immigrant mother.[27] However, footage that had already been
shot for the film was edited together to create *Dim Sum Take-Out*, an eleven-minute
film made up of narrative segments intercut with music video style segments, set to
English- and Chinese-language versions of the song "My Boyfriend's Back." During
the narrative sections, the characters talk candidly and humorously about a range of
topics: their relationships with one another; sex, gender roles, and stereotyping; their
feelings about and relationships with men; and their expectations about life and how
they have changed over time.

Dim Sum Take-Out does not offer an in-depth exploration of the ways in which the
five Chinese and Chinese American women negotiate their identities. In eleven minutes, however, it suggests the multiplicity of their identities in terms of women's gender roles, sexuality, class, and generation from immigration; the heterogeneity of
strategies of adaptation and acculturation; and the ways in which these various social
categories interact. The original set-up, the traces of which are captured in *Dim Sum
Take-Out*, subverted dominant binaristic ideology that distills and essentializes Asian
American experiences to the struggle between "Chinese tradition" and "American
modernism" while erasing or suppressing other significant social factors and incom-
mensurabilities. It foregrounds material exigencies that intersect with and complicate
the more commonly acknowledged theme of generational and cultural struggle.

Life Is Cheap . . . But Toilet Paper Is Expensive explores the complex position of Hong
Kong as, figuratively, the westernmost outpost of the United States and, literally, one
of the last remaining vestiges (at that time) of the British empire. The movie, shot and
edited during the events leading up to the June 4, 1989, massacre of pro-democracy
demonstrators in Beijing's Tiananmen Square, criticizes the fixation on saving face by
Chinese leaders and the blind materialism and willful political passivity that Wang
saw in a majority of Hong Kong residents at that time.[28] *Life Is Cheap . . .* presents the
story of the Man With No Name,[29] a naïve Japanese–Chinese American stable boy
dressed in a cowboy hat and boots (played by Spencer Nakasako, who also co-directed and wrote the screenplay), who is hired to deliver a steel briefcase to the Big Boss
(Lo Wai) in Hong Kong. The courier job turns out to be an elaborate face-saving
scheme by the Big Boss, who sets up the Man With No Name to take the blame for
his break-up with his mistress, a woman named Money (Cora Miao). In actuality,
Money has been discovered to be having an affair with the Big Boss's daughter (Bon-

nie Ngai). The daughter is married off to a dull Chinese American anthropologist to suppress the scandal.

The Man With No Name's efforts to find the Big Boss and uncover the reason for the apparently meaningless trip (he breaks open the briefcase to find trivial items such as a box of chocolates, a San Francisco street map, salami, and pornographic magazines) provide an opening for Wang to delve further into his profile of Hong Kong residents on the eve of the return of Hong Kong to Chinese rule. The people whom the Man With No Name meets address the camera directly in documentary-style monologues that interrupt the narrative and provide insight into the mind sets of a range of Hong Kong residents. By contrasting the aggressive passivity of Hong Kong residents and the Man With No Name's bumbling attempts to control and shape the course of his trip, the film challenges the residents of Hong Kong to stop being "sitting ducks"—to stop bowing to the traditions and political demands of China and to stop being seduced by the heritage from the United States and England.

The controversy that surrounded the release of *Life Is Cheap . . .* in 1990 is a compelling example of the way in which the monitoring and classification of supposedly universal morally and socially unacceptable representations can suppress political and social critique. The Motion Picture Association of America (MPAA) assigned *Life Is Cheap . . .* an X rating because of brief shots of a pornographic magazine depicting pregnant women, nightmare sequences in which a character's hand is chopped off, and two scenes involving bathroom humor and human excrement. Wang had the choice of cutting out the sequences to which the MPAA objected or accepting the X rating. Neither choice was acceptable. Wang defended the necessity of the scenes because they were integral to his critique of political passivity, "blind tradition, the abuse of power and the over-emphasis on 'face'" (quoted in Pannifer 1991) in Hong Kong and Chinese society in the late 1980s. Accepting the X rating also would have been tantamount to censoring the film. Because of the overwhelming association of the X rating with pornography, most major newspapers strictly prohibit or restrict the advertising of X-rated films. Most mainstream theaters also will not exhibit X-rated films. Wang and SilverLight Entertainment, the company distributing *Life Is Cheap . . .*, appealed the rating and lost.[30] Subsequently, *Life Is Cheap . . .* had a limited release in only a handful of cities under a self-assigned A rating, indicating adult themes that are unsuitable for people younger than eighteen. The institutional regulation of *Life Is Cheap . . .* in the form of the MPAA's assignment of an X rating, and the subsequent restricted distribution of the film (film copies of *Life Is Cheap . . .* currently are not in distribution, and the film has never been made available on video), resulted in containing the circulation of a complex, critical representation of the ambivalent relationship of Asian Americans to the intertwined legacies of ethnically and nationally defined identities, on the one hand, and of British and U.S. economic and cultural imperialism in Asia, on the other. The fight by Wang and SilverLight Entertainment to overturn the X rating is another example of the way in which shadow films represent resistance to categories defined by dominant institutions.

At first glance, *Blue in the Face* appears to be light mainstream entertainment, especially in contrast to *Life Is Cheap. . . .* Theatrical distribution in the same circuit of art house theaters as *Smoke*; the reappearance of the central character played by Harvey Keitel; and cameo appearances by mainstream and underground personalities such as Roseanne, Madonna, Michael J. Fox, Lily Tomlin, Lou Reed, Jim Jarmusch, and RuPaul contributed to the film's marketability and apparent accessibility. In fact, *Blue in the Face* offers aesthetic, formal, and social critiques that mark it undoubtedly as a shadow film.[31]

The social, cultural, economic, and historical context of Brooklyn and the cigar store in which the plot of *Blue in the Face* unfolds is as important as—and often overshadows—the "main" plot and characters of the movie. The film presents a melange of improvised and scripted scenes involving different characters in the movie and nondiegetic sequences of hand-held video footage of street scenes; interviews with Brooklyn residents; staged shots of people reciting statistics about Brooklyn; and newsreel footage about the former Brooklyn Dodgers and their old baseball field, Ebbets Field. However, *Blue in the Face* ostensibly is about Auggie (Harvey Keitel), the manager of the Brooklyn Cigar Company; his girlfriend Violet (Mel Gorham); the owner of the cigar store, Vinnie (Victor Argo); and his wife, Dot (Roseanne). The plot revolves around whether Auggie and Violet will stay together after Auggie cancels an important date with Violet; whether Dot and Vinnie will stay together and take a long-delayed trip to Las Vegas; and whether Vinnie will sell the store. The plot is so banal that one is forced to consider the possibility that the resolution of this narrative is not the filmmaker's main concern.

Asian Americans are only marginally on screen in *Blue in the Face*. Their traces are represented, particularly in the video segments, as part of Brooklyn's urban landscape, with signs on stores showing Asian national and ethnic origins and people of Asian descent appearing as statisticians, interview subjects, and passersby on the street. The appearance of Asian Americans, whether literally or iconically, often marks moments of critique of, or departure from, the limited world views of the characters in the diegesis, sometimes merely suggesting and sometimes forcefully showing the larger context in which the diegesis takes place. The margins in this case do not replicate familiar relations of racialized power; instead, they complicate and challenge what is usually considered the center of the film. Therefore, the marginalization of Asian Americans on screen can be understood within the larger context of my examination of Wang's shadow films and the goals of politicized Asian American filmmaking. The filmmaker and critical theorist Trinh Minh-ha (1992, 157) sums up this position:

> If it is a point of redeparture for those of us whose ethnicity and gender were historically debased, then identity remains necessary as a political/personal strategy of survival and resistance. But if it is essentialized as an end point, a point of "authentic" arrival, then it only narrows the struggle down to a question of "alternatives"—that is, a perpetuation, albeit with a reversed focus, of the notion of "otherness" as defined by the master, rather than a radical challenge of patriarchal power relations.

Though Trinh is referring to feminist challenges to patriarchal power, her insights can be applied equally to racialized contexts. A politically oppositional Asian American film practice should not be limited to corrective representations of Asian Americans;

rather, it should be defined strategically and provisionally. *Blue in the Face* therefore barely represents Asian Americans on screen, but through its critical examination of race, community, historical change, consumer culture, and relationships marked by gender and class, and through its deliberate disregard for the conventions of mainstream narrative fiction and documentary filmmaking, it opposes dominant paradigms in the social and cultural milieu that encompass, but also exceed, the purview of Asian Americans as a racial group per se.

The repeated, periodic appearance of shadow films in Wang's filmography is perplexing if one assumes that a filmmaker's goal is to reach the pinnacles of Hollywood-style mainstream studio production. But if one assumes instead that Wang, among other filmmakers, is struggling within the constraints of a binding system of movie production and distribution to present a social, political, and aesthetic vision that challenges the mainstream—and that he feels compelled to do so despite these constraints—then the shadow films take on added significance. They can be read as examples of defiance and resistance and, more important, as efforts to articulate alternative ways of creating culture and constructing social relations that are an integral and definitive part of Wang's politicized film practice.

A Point of Redeparture

> *Don't be fooled, things aren't what they seem to be.*
> Blind Man, *Life Is Cheap . . . But Toilet Paper Is Expensive*

To answer the question about whether Asian American filmmakers have been assimilating into the mainstream movie industry, Asian American cultural critics must look beyond measuring popular releases such as *The Joy Luck Club* according to how well they fulfill (problematic) notions of representational "accuracy" and "realism." Admittedly, "authentic" screen representations are one measure of Asian Americans' ability to create and define our images. However, popular movie releases usually indicate a certain level of cultural generality and conservatism that is likely to be incommensurate with the expectations of cultural activists. Referring to recent debates about public television, the sociologist William Hoynes (1994, 10) observed that

> The discussion has focused on narrow questions of "bias" and "objectivity." These questions are ultimately problematic, for they serve to obscure the broader questions about the reasons for creating a public television system, the structural arrangements necessary to maintain one, and the constraints imposed on public television by both internal and external forces. By focusing on the product and ignoring the process, the "bias paradigm" tells us little about the causes of supposed shortcomings, nor can it provide a theoretically informed analysis of how to move public television forward or, for that matter, where it should go.

Hoynes's observations about criticism of public television are equally applicable to debates about supposedly accurate or stereotypical representations of Asian Americans in film. Instead of reacting merely to the representations of Asian Americans that are offered, one must take the very structure in which filmmakers work into account, on two levels. First, we must understand that the film industry itself has changed and continues to change, simultaneously offering more opportunities, and regulating and limiting them as well. Second, as long as filmmaking occurs primarily within a corporate–capitalist entertainment system (even within so-called public sectors such as public television), filmmakers will be forced to make compromises in order to keep producing films. Some filmmakers continue to subvert, challenge, and resist the status quo in as many ways as they can, but the system itself will continue to be fundamentally conservative. This does not absolve us of the need continuously to resist the status quo, and it should inform cultural critics' evaluations of Asian American filmmaking efforts.

Just as Asian American cultural critics demand more specifically situated and contextualized representations of Asian Americans, their demands also should be situated and contextualized. If we want to see more films that challenge tired paradigms and that explore different aesthetics and experiences, such as the scenarios in *Dim Sum Take-Out, Life Is Cheap ... But Toilet Paper Is Expensive,* and *Blue in the Face,* then we need to understand the social, economic, and cultural reasons that these types of films are rarely made or narrowly distributed—because it surely is not due to lack of talent or interest.

My exploration of Wayne Wang's films illustrates these points, showing how the filmmaker may have made choices based on a range of criteria. Wang's film projects can be interpreted as strategic choices that have allowed him to keep making films—a privilege that cannot be taken for granted—and, over time, to increase his ability to maintain artistic control over them. This, in turn, has enabled him to experiment with film forms and explore themes and ideas that have not been represented in mainstream productions, without seriously jeopardizing his credibility.

Wang's shadow films demonstrate his commitment to producing films that critique social and narrative hierarchies. On balance, his filmography shows at least an equal concern for maintaining and even increasing his ability to access the resources of the filmmaking industry and for making films that are socially and politically meaningful. Access to the full range of resources in the mainstream film industry and socially committed independent filmmaking should be seen as two complementary strategies that work together to challenge and subvert dominant ideologies and structures. In actuality, Wang's films do not fall into neat categories. All his films have some element of the "shadow" in them.

Assuming that the United States will continue to be a consumption-oriented market economy, film activism cannot be the sole responsibility of filmmakers. The question that Tajima posed points to the activities only of Asian American filmmakers. She did not ask whether Asian American moviegoers have similarly assimilated into the mainstream movie culture. Filmgoers—the audiences—should also be film activists in their own sphere of action. This includes articulating our responses to movies with pickets, protests, reviews, and letters to newspaper and magazine editors, and showing our support for specific films through the box office. At the same time, we must also support film festivals, art houses and repertory theaters, public television, museum screenings, non-feature films and videos, and other non-mainstream venues. The combined activism of filmmakers, filmgoers, and cultural critics will pressure the filmmaking system to remain open to innovations by Asian Americans and other filmmakers on the cultural margins.

Notes

Acknowledgments: I am indebted to Eithne Luibheid, Caroline Streeter, and Laura Pérez for their insightful comments and careful reading of drafts of this chapter. Susan Lee, Nerissa Balce, and Elaine H. Kim also provided valuable advice. An earlier version of this essay was presented at the 1997 annual meeting of the Association for Asian American Studies in Seattle, Washington.

1. The information about Asian American media in this paragraph is summarized from Tajima's article.

2. See, for example, Aoki (1993), Danley (1993), Hagedorn (1994), Ling (1993), and Su (1993).

3. See, for example, Iwata (1993), Pimentel and Chung (1993), Wong (1993), and Wynter (1993). Other films that were often cited included *Dragon* (Cohen 1993), *Farewell My Concubine* (Chen 1993), *Golden Gate* (Madden 1994), *Heaven and Earth* (Stone 1993), *M. Butterfly* (Cronenberg 1993), *Map of the Human Heart* (Ward 1992), and *The Wedding Banquet* (Lee 1993). Note that some writers did not differentiate among films that were made by Asians, Asian Americans, and others, or among films that depicted Asians or Asian Americans.

4. Standards of "accuracy" and conceptions of what is "real" in film, as in any other discursive medium, are historically specific, socially constructed, and continuously contested, rather than essential, universal, or stable categories. However, most of the reviews I read problematically treated *The Joy Luck Club* as if it should offer an unmediated window onto reality.

5. This chapter was completed before *Chinese Box*'s theatrical release in May 1998 and does not take into account how Wang's career has continued to evolve since that time.

6. It is important to note some of the difficulties in practicing "socially committed" filmmaking in the feature-length narrative-film form, especially in the United States. Some of the interlocking difficulties are: the expense of working in the film medium; the lack of public funding for large-scale projects such as these; the reliance on private funding (and the concomitant assumption that not only must a film earn the money back, but it must make a profit for the film investors); a perceived small market for "social-issues" films and films featuring Asian Americans and Asian American issues; and the entrenched view that movies should be primarily an escapist, entertaining activity.

7. The *Star Wars* trilogy was produced by Twentieth Century Fox and Lucasfilms, and distributed by Twentieth Century Fox. *Star Wars* was originally released in 1977, *The Empire Strikes Back* in 1980, and *Return of the Jedi* in 1983. The Indiana Jones trilogy was produced by Lucasfilms and Paramount Pictures, and distributed by Paramount. *Raiders of the Lost Ark* was released in 1981, *Indiana Jones and the Temple of Doom* in 1984, and *Indiana Jones and the Last Crusade* in 1989. *E.T.* was produced by Amblin Entertainment and MCA/Universal, and distributed by MCA/Universal in 1982.

8. Some notable directors who became established during the 1980s are Jim Jarmusch, Spike Lee, and John Sayles. Although some European American women such as Susan Seidelman and Donna Deitch earned critical attention during the 1980s, men, regardless of race, continued to dominate the field of feature film production.

9. The National Endowment for the Arts (NEA) was created in 1965 as an independent federal agency to support the nonprofit arts sector in the United States. It awards grants to arts organizations, supports arts education, recognizes outstanding achievement in the arts, develops projects of national significance in the arts, and works to preserve the United States's cultural heritage. In 1967, the NEA "established the American Film Institute as an independent, nonprofit organization dedicated to: Preserving the heritage of film and television; identifying and training new talent; [and] increasing recognition and understanding of the moving image as an art form" (American Film Institute).

10. A more in-depth discussion of American Playhouse is offered in the analysis of *Eat a Bowl of Tea* (Wang 1989) in this chapter.

11. Among the stories covered in the first half of the 1980s, the U.S. mainstream media spotlighted sensational academic achievements of Asian American students and the role their families play in their success; unfair economic competition from Japanese companies, especially auto makers; growing tensions between Korean merchants who opened markets in poor, predominantly African American and Latino neighborhoods; and congressional hearings by the Commission on Wartime Relocation and Internment of Civilians, which concluded that the internment of Japanese Americans during World War II was a grave injustice. The media also covered the trials of Ronald Ebens and Michael Nitz, two European American men who beat Vincent Chin to death in 1982.

12. *Dances with Wolves* (Costner 1990) and *Silence of the Lambs* (Demme 1991) are two well known Orion Pictures releases. Orion Pictures emerged from bankruptcy in 1992 after it was bought by Metromedia International Group. The company was reorganized to be primarily a film- and television-distribution company (Wasko 1994, 66–67). In April 1997, MGM bought Orion Pictures from Metromedia, thus continuing the trend of consolidation within the movie industry (*San Francisco Chronicle* 1997).

13. Some notable Island Pictures releases included *The Trip to Bountiful* (Masterson 1985), *Kiss of the Spider Woman* (Babenco 1985), *Down by Law* (Jarmusch 1986), and *She's Gotta Have It* (Lee 1986).

14. Wang's concern about pigeonholing was well founded. In 1996, he said, "I would go up for jobs that were not related to Chinese-Americans and inevitably the question would come up, 'What makes you think you can make a movie about teenagers growing up in Minnesota?' I would always say, 'What makes you think Ridley Scott can make a film about American kids? I've been here a lot longer than he has,'" (quoted in Romney 1996). He reiterates this concern in other interviews (Chua 1993, Mandell 1990).

15. Some notable American Playhouse productions are *El Norte* (Nava 1983), *Stand and Deliver* (Menéndez 1987), *Longtime Companion* (René 1990), *Straight Out of Brooklyn* (Rich 1991), and *Daughters of the Dust* (Dash 1992). My discussion of American Playhouse is based on Day (1995), Collins (1994), Taylor (1983, 1984), and Weber (1992).

16. The supposed left or liberal bias of PBS has been shown to be greatly exaggerated. In a sample of PBS shows taken in the first six months of 1992, Croteau, Hoynes, and Carragee (1996, 46) showed that "examining public television's prime time programming in its entirety reveals that much of the [conservative] criticism directed at public broadcasting—which primarily has focused on public affairs documentaries—in fact involves only a small percentage (8.4%) of the evening schedule on PBS stations. . . . Much of the conservative critique was directed at individual programs, since there is no larger pattern at which to point."

17. Two examples of American Playhouse productions that were censored by PBS were *Tales of the City* (Reid 1993) and *Mrs. Cage* (Ackerman 1992). In *Tales*, shots of a woman's breasts were

"electronically obscured" (Bark 1994), and during reruns, in an unprecedented move, PBS provided a simultaneous feed of a different program to stations that considered *Tales of the City* "unsuitable for their markets" (Boone 1994). *Mrs. Cage* had an audible beep laid over offensive language.

18. *Chan Is Missing* is considered enormously successful in terms of the ratio of its box office return to its production budget—that is, about 66.7:1. The film grossed more than $1.5 million and cost about $22,500 to make.

19. *The Joy Luck Club*, by Amy Tan, was released in early 1989. By mid-1991, it had sold more than 233,500 copies in hardcover and more than two million copies in paperback (Donahue 1991).

20. See Corliss (1993), Iwata (1993), Pimentel and Chung (1993), and Wachs Book (1993). Media hype was based on speculation about a number of superficially related circumstances intersecting in 1993. They include the possible impact on U.S. markets and the film industry of filmmakers from the People's Republic of China, Hong Kong, Taiwan, and the United States, such as Chen Kaige, Ang Lee, Wayne Wang, John Woo, and Zhang Yimou, and the release of several U.S. films (see n. 3) made by non-Asian Americans featuring Asian and Asian American characters. Journalists variously conjectured about an Asian cultural invasion of the United States, whether so-called Asian-themed movies were a fad or a trend, and what kind of impact Asian directors might have in Hollywood.

21. According to Rhines (1996), the premier independent distribution companies are Fine Line, Goldwyn, Gramercy, Miramax, October, and Sony Classics. In 1994, these companies typically distributed films in the $3 million to $5 million range (Rhines 1996, 171). Though many of these companies are now officially subsidiaries of entertainment-media conglomerates or Hollywood studios, they continue to be referred to as independent companies because they distribute independently produced films.

22. *Daily Variety* reported on September 19, 1997, that Trimark Pictures had signed on to distribute *Chinese Box* in North America (Hindes 1997). *Chinese Box* was released in theaters in May 1998. In July 1997, Trimark was being characterized as "the last available [independent] film company [in the United States,] holding a sizable library of titles and a domestic theatrical and video distribution apparatus," even as it was looking for a buyer (Weiner 1997).

23. Though I refer to *Dim Sum, Eat a Bowl of Tea*, and *Smoke* as "mainstreamed" productions in this context, it is crucial to keep in mind that these films actually are art house films—in other words, marginal to the mainstream, independently produced and distributed, and with themes or narrative structures foreign to what is usually considered mainstream movies. Thus, I use the term "mainstreamed" in a relative sense.

24. *Eat a Bowl of Tea* was shot in Hong Kong because that location approximated the look and feel of New York City in the 1940s. Though neighborhoods are referred to in *Smoke*, the film is shot in such a way that the story could have occurred in other locations in New York City or in other urban locations in the United States.

25. Charles Musser and Robert Sklar (1990, 5) offer a potent definition of resistance: "Resistance implies exertion, force, effort. Its root meaning is to take a stand. It suggests ability, capacity, what historians frequently call *agency*. It means that people have the possibility to act on their own behalf, as opposed to being completely shaped by dominant classes and ideologies."

26. Generic conventions and other forms of categorizing and labeling films are taken for granted to such an extent that they seem like natural or essential aspects of films, rather than socially accepted ways of constructing meaning in films. Furthermore, their thematic and narrative conventions also support specific ideologies.

27. Wang's ex-wife Terrel Seltzer, who worked with Wang on his early projects, recalls that "one of the hardest things [about making *Dim Sum*] was, we'd write a scene and everybody had got [*sic*] to give their opinion—it had to pass a cultural test. Everyone was critiquing themselves in those days" (quoted in Romney 1996). Wang gained a reputation during the making of *Chan Is Missing* and *Dim Sum* as a democratic filmmaker, a legacy of his involvement in Asian American community politics during the 1970s (ibid.). He continues to maintain a more democratic style of directing than most successful filmmakers in the United States, although not to the same extent or in the same way as during his first two films.

28. According to Wang, the pro-democracy movement failed partly because of the students' unwillingness to give "face" to the Chinese government (Guthmann 1990).

29. The Man With No Name is a reference to Clint Eastwood's character in Sergio Leone's *Fistful of Dollars* (1964) and *For a Few Dollars More* (1965). Calling the character in *Life Is Cheap* . . . the Man With No Name supports a reading of Hong Kong as the westernmost outpost of the United States, into which the outsider, the lone cowboy, enters to resolve simultaneously a conflict within himself and a conflict in the community.

30. Mark Lipsky, then head of SilverLight Entertainment, and Wang composed a letter to Jack Valenti, then head of the MPAA, proposing a new A (adult) or M (mature) rating for films with adult themes that are unsuitable for people younger than 18. The letter was signed by prominent producers and directors, including Bernardo Bertolucci, Francis Ford Coppola, Jonathan Demme, Ron Howard, Spike Lee, Paul Mazursky, Sydney Pollack, Rob Reiner, John Sayles, Ridley Scott, and others. The letter was delivered to Valenti; it also appeared on July 24, 1990, in *Variety* and the *Hollywood Reporter* as "An Open Letter to Jack Valenti." In 1992, Valenti announced the NC-17 rating, which has been criticized by many people in all areas of the film industry as merely another term for an X-rated film (Lipsky 1992).

31. *Blue in the Face* was directed by both Wayne Wang and Paul Auster because Wang had bronchitis during part of the first three days of shooting (Auster 1995, 173–74).The film was shot in six days, three in mid-July and three in late October 1994.

Works Cited

American Film Institute. See http://afionline.org/home.html.

Aoki, Guy. 1993. "'Joy Luck' Movie Sends Old Message About Men." *Rafu Shimpo* (Los Angeles), October 5, n.p.

Auster, Paul. 1995. *Smoke & Blue in the Face: Two Films.* New York: Miramax Books, Hyperion.

Bagdikian, Ben H. 1992. *The Media Monopoly.* 4th ed. Boston: Beacon.

Bark, Ed. 1994. "Plenty to Provoke in *Tales of the City* on PBS." *Dallas Morning News,* January 10, final ed., 11C f.

Boone, Mike. 1994. "Local PBS Outlets Choose *Tales of the City*—and Liberty and Freedom." *The Gazette* (Montreal), May 1, final ed., C4 f.

Busch, Anita M. 1994. "'Club' Team Inks for 'Wife' Pic." *Daily Variety,* October 27, 4.

———. 1996. "Pitt, Spielberg Hot for 'Arkansas.'" *Daily Variety,* February 27, n.p. (Lexis-Nexis reQUESTer database).

Chua, Lawrence. 1993. "Wang Is Found." *Village Voice,* September 19, 66.

Collins, Glenn. 1994. "American Playhouse Is Moving Into Film." *New York Times,* March 29, late ed., C13 f.

Corliss, Richard. 1993. "Pacific Overtures: In Movies and Music Videos, in Fiction and Fashion, Asian Chic Takes America." *Time,* September 13, 68–70.

Cox, Dan. 1996. "Fine Line Locks Up 'Room'; Company Nabs Rights to Auster/Wang Film." *Daily Variety,* February 15, 7.

Croteau, David, William Hoynes, and Kevin M. Carragee. 1996. *The Political Diversity of Public Television: Polysemy, the Public Sphere, and the Conservative Critique of PBS.* Journalism and Mass Communication Monographs 157 (June). Columbia, S.C.: Association for Education in Journalism and Mass Communication.

Danley, Sharon Yamato. 1993. "'Joy Luck' Mothers Not Honest, Real." *Los Angeles Times,* October 11, home ed., F3.

Day, James. 1995. *The Vanishing Vision: The Inside Story of Public Television.* Berkeley: University of California Press.

Ding, Loni. 1991. "Strategies of an Asian American Filmmaker." Pp. 46–59 in *Moving the Image: Independent Asian Pacific American Media Arts,* ed. Russell Leong. Los Angeles: UCLA Asian American Studies Center and Visual Communications, Southern California Asian American Studies Central.

Donahue, Deirdre. 1991. "Tan Finds Joy and Luck: Second Novel Could Seal Good Fortune." *USA Today,* July 1, final ed., 1D.

Dunkley, Cathy. 1996a. "Smoke Folk Reteam on Room." *Hollywood Reporter,* February 15, n.p. (Lexis-Nexis reQUESTer database).

———. 1996b. "Wang to Guide Col's 'Shepherd.'" *Hollywood Reporter,* May 6, n.p. (Lexis-Nexis reQUESTer database).

———. 1996c. "Wang Has Date to Direct 'Mrs. Wright' for WB." *Hollyood Reporter,* May 13, n.p. (Lexis-Nexis reQUESTer database).

Dunkley, Cathy and Stephen Galloway. 1995. "Wang Bares Erotic Trilogy for Miramax." *Hollywood Reporter,* August 29, n.p. (Lexis-Nexis reQUESTer database).

Dutka, Elaine. 1993. "'Joy Luck': A New Challenge in Disney's World." *Los Angeles Times,* August 31, home ed., F:1 f.

Galloway, Stephen. 1994. "Wang on Road to 'Nowhere.'" *Hollywood Reporter,* November 30, n.p. (Lexis-Nexis reQUESTer database).

Guthmann, Edward. 1990. "Wayne Wang Wings It Wild." *San Francisco Chronicle,* September 2, 36 f.

Hagedorn, Jessica. 1994. "Asian Women in Film: No Joy, No Luck." *Ms.* (January/February), 74–79.

Hindes, Andrew. 1997. "Trimark Bags 'Box': Indie Buys Domestic Rights to Wang Romance." *Daily Variety,* September 19, 5.

Honeycutt, Kirk. 1994. "'Joy Luck' Team Back in 'Kitchen.'" *Hollywood Reporter,* October 27, n.p. (Lexis-Nexis reQUESTer database).

Hoynes, William. 1994. *Public Television for Sale: Media, the Market, and the Public Sphere.* Boulder, Colo.: Westview.

Iwata, Edward. 1993. "Asian Movies Take Flight: Filmmakers Making Move into the Mainstream." *Los Angeles Times,* May 13, home ed., F1 f.

Lexis-Nexis reQUESTer database. 1997. See http://web.lexis-nexis.com/requester.

Ling, Susie. 1993. "Reflections on *The Joy Luck Club* Phenomenon." *AsianWeek* (December 3), 4.

Lipsky, Mark. 1992. "New Rating for Movies Is the Same Old 'X' in 'NC-17' Undress." Letter to the editor. *New York Times,* December 18, late ed., A38.

Mandell, Jonathan. 1990. "Culture Clash." *Newsday* (New York), August 20, city ed., II:8 f.

Musser, Charles, and Robert Sklar. 1990. "Introduction." Pp. 3–11 in *Resisting Images: Essays on Cinema and History,* ed. Robert Sklar and Charles Musser. Philadelphia: Temple University Press.

Pannifer, Bill. 1991. "Outside Dealer: Bill Pannifer Talks to the Director Wayne Wang." *Independent* (London), May 24, 20.

Pimentel, Benjamin, and L. A. Chung. 1993. "'Asian Chic' Movies Make Money and History." *San Francisco Chronicle*, October 25, A1 f.

Rhines, Jesse Algeron. 1996. *Black Film/White Money*. New Brunswick, N.J.: Rutgers University Press.

Romney, Jonathan. 1996. "Wang's World." *The Guardian* (Manchester, England), March 30, weekend ed., 24–30.

Rosen, David, with Peter Hamilton. 1990. *Off-Hollywood: The Making and Marketing of Independent Films*. New York: Grove Weidenfeld.

San Francisco Chronicle. 1997. "Metromedia Sells Orion Pictures, Film Library to MGM," April 29, B1.

Seid, Steve. 1983. "The Chinatown Syndrome." *San Francisco Focus*, November, 26 f.

Su, Joanna. 1993. "Joy Luck No Luck—Suck?" *Slant* (November/December), 13.

Tajima, Renee. 1991. "Moving the Image: Asian American Independent Filmmaking 1970–1990." Pp. 10–33 in *Moving the Image: Independent Asian Pacific American Media Arts*, ed. Russell Leong. Los Angeles: UCLA Asian American Studies Center and Visual Communications, Southern California Asian American Studies Central.

Tan, Amy. 1989. *The Joy Luck Club*. New York: Putnam.

Taylor, Clarke. 1983. "'Playhouse' Funds Aid Independents." *Los Angeles Times*, June 17, VI:29.

———. 1984. "'American Playhouse' Finds Identity." *Los Angeles Times*, August 1, VI:10.

Trinh, T. Minh-ha. 1992. "Between Theory and Poetry," interview with Pratibha Parmar. Pp. 151–58 in *Framer Framed*, ed. Trinh T. Minh-ha. New York: Routledge.

Wachs Book, Esther. 1993. "The East Is Hot: U.S. Audiences Line Up for Films with a Chinese Flavour." *Far Eastern Economic Review*, December 23, 34–35.

Wasko, Janet. 1994. *Hollywood in the Information Age*. Austin: University of Texas Press.

Weber, Bruce. 1992. "Big Movies on Little Budgets." *New York Times*, May 17, late ed., H27 f.

Weiner, Rex. 1997. "Trimark Taps Bankers to Seek Buyers." *Daily Variety*, July 21, 1.

Weinraub, Bernard. 1993. "'I Didn't Want to Do Another Chinese Movie." *New York Times*, September 5, late ed., 2:7 f.

Wong, William. 1993. "'Joy Luck Club's Universal Appeal." *Oakland Tribune*, September 10, A15.

Wynter, Leon E. 1993. "Joy Luck's Good Luck Bypassed Ethnicity." *Wall Street Journal*, December 6, B1.

Films and Videos Cited

Ackerman, Robert Allan. 1992. *Mrs. Cage*. American Playhouse.

Babenco, Hector. 1985. *Kiss of the Spider Woman*. Island Pictures.

Chen, Kaige. 1993. *Farewell My Concubine*. Buena Vista.

Cohen, Rob. 1993. *Dragon: The Bruce Lee Story*. Universal Pictures.

Costner, Kevin. 1990. *Dances with Wolves*. Orion Pictures.

Cronenberg, David. 1993. *M. Butterfly*. Warner Bros.

Dash, Julie. 1992. *Daughters of the Dust*. Kino on Video.

Demme, Jonathan. 1991. *The Silence of the Lambs*. Orion Pictures.

Jarmusch, Jim. 1986. *Down by Law*. Island Pictures.

Lee, Ang. 1993. *The Wedding Banquet*. Good Machine.

Lee, Spike. 1986. *She's Gotta Have It*. Island Pictures.

Leone, Sergio. 1964. *Fistful of Dollars*. United Artists.

———. 1965. *For a Few Dollars More*. United Artists.

Lucas, George. 1977. *Star Wars*. Twentieth Century Fox.

———. 1980. *The Empire Strikes Back*. Twentieth Century Fox.

———. 1983. *Return of the Jedi*. Twentieth Century Fox.

Levinson, Barry. 1988. *Rain Man*. United Artists .

Madden, John. 1994. *Golden Gate*. TriStar Pictures.

Masterson, Peter. 1985. *The Trip to Bountiful*. Island Pictures.

Menéndez, Ramón. 1987. *Stand and Deliver*. Warner Bros.

Nava, Gregory. 1983. *El Norte*. Artesan Entertainment.

René, Norman. 1990. *Longtime Companion*. Samuel Goldwyn.

Reid, Alistair. 1993. *Tales of the City*. KQED.

Rich, Matty. 1991. *Straight Out of Brooklyn*. Samuel Goldwyn.

Spielberg, Steven. 1981. *Raiders of the Lost Ark*. Paramount Pictures.

———. 1982. *E.T., the Extra-Terrestrial*. MCA/Universal.

———. 1984. *Indiana Jones and the Temple of Doom*. Paramount Pictures.

———. 1989. *Indiana Jones and the Last Crusade*. Paramount Pictures.

Stone, Oliver. 1993. *Heaven and Earth*. Warner Bros.

Wang, Wayne. 1982. *Chan Is Missing*. New Yorker Films.

———. 1985. *Dim Sum: A Little Bit of Heart*. Orion Classics.

———. 1987. *Slamdance*. Island Pictures.

———. 1988. *Dim Sum Take-Out*. NAATA.

———. 1989. *Eat a Bowl of Tea*. Columbia.

———. 1989. *Life Is Cheap . . . But Toilet Paper Is Expensive*. No distributor.

———. 1993. *The Joy Luck Club*. Buena Vista.

———. 1995. *Smoke*. Miramax.

———. 1997. *Chinese Box*. Trimark.

———, and Paul Auster. 1995. *Blue in the Face*. Miramax Pictures.

Ward, Vincent. 1997. *Map of the Human Heart*. Polygram.

Lindsey Jang

---

6   Through the Mirror, Sideways

A little Asian invasion has been taking place in Hollywood. Asian filmmakers, espe-cially Chinese, are hot, hot, hot, Richard Corliss proclaimed in *Time* magazine. Well, they may not be exactly "hot," but Hollywood is definitely interested in doing busi-ness with them. Throughout the nineties, a string of art house hits has developed a following among American moviegoers and critics. Hollywood is courting directors such as John Woo and Tsui Hark from Hong Kong. There is even an infusion of Asian acting talent, as experiments with Chinese stars such as Jet Li, Chow Yun-Fat, and Gong Li are appearing in Hollywood films. Although Zhang Yimou, Chen Kaige, and Wong Kar-wai are not exactly the household names that Steven Spielberg is, they com-mand a measure of respect, and their films now generate positive anticipation.

This measure of acceptance of Asian films would seem to bode well for Asian Amer-ican filmmakers. If the art house audiences are willing to watch action movies and historical epics from Asia about characters with Asian faces, perhaps there is room in the American movie market for Asian American filmmakers who want to create films about Asian Americans. Alas, this may not be so. Although the past decade has seen a rising and maturing interest in contemporary Asian films, no concomitant rise in interest in Asian American films has taken place, even though a number of Asian American filmmakers have been toiling in their craft for decades. In fact, if we were to look just at the world of feature films in recent years, American society has learned more about Asians (in China, Hong Kong, Japan, Taiwan, and Vietnam) than it has about Asian Americans (in California, New York, Texas, or Washington). Although the American experience has a unifying effect on peoples who originated from the various corners of the globe, and although American culture tries to say that—in the-ory, at least—we are all the same once we enter, we, as Asian Americans, know that this is not wholly true. The great American narrative composed of American films is missing huge and interesting pieces because of the omission of the stories of women, gays, and people of color.

While Asian American students stream into film schools across the country, other Asian Americans are entering the film industry's workforce and are even beginning to approach the upper echelons of power. They are in every area of work, from the technical realms of production and post-production to the power-lunching realms of talent agencies and studio offices. Chris Lee and Teddy Zee have hold powerful positions at TriStar and Columbia Pictures, respectively. Janet Yang is an acclaimed producer in Hollywood. The employment growth of Asian Americans in the film industry is important as an issue of workforce diversification in an increasingly multiracial society. But it is equally important, if not more so, that there be a concurrent rise in cultural product: movies about Asian Americans. Without more movies, the problems of invisibility and misunderstanding—the ongoing symbolic annihilation of Asian Americans in American cinema—will continue to be perpetuated by a system that has no economic motivation to change.

"Quality is the key!" you scream. The adage about the cream rising to the top tells us that if the movies are good, they'll get seen. And that may be so. Perhaps in America we see only the best of Asian filmmaking. Zhang Yimou might represent the best of the Chinese Fifth Generation; John Woo the best of Hong Kong. Maybe it is just a matter of time before the Asian American filmmakers who are flocking to film schools develop their skills and can produce works of quality that the public, the industry, and critics will recognize. If the cream always rises to the top, this may merely be a numbers game that we can wait out as the Asian American community quietly, but expectantly, awaits its own Zhang Yimou or Steven Spielberg.

Fine. But what if merit alone does not determine studio green lights, theatrical bookings, favorable box office receipts, and critical praise for movies about Asian Americans? Suppose for a few short moments that other factors come into play. For the sake of argument, suppose that the legacies of racism, classism, and sexism have created a more difficult playing field for Asian American filmmakers to make and exhibit works about Asian Americans.

Assuming that these factors limit the ability of Asian American films to gain a foothold in the American movie-producing and movie-viewing milieus, what are Asian American filmmakers to think when they look in the mirror and try to answer their parents' questions, such as, "What the heck are you doing in such a risky business? You coulda had a nice job as a computer programmer like your cousin Kelvin. What kinda career you gonna have now?"

Indeed, while we may sidestep the first, rhetorical, question, the second one remains valid. As we look in the mirror, we might ask ourselves what hope we, as Asian American filmmakers, have for the success of our individual films, given what we know? What hope do we have to fashion long-lasting careers making movies about Asian Americans? What kind of image will we be able to craft of ourselves and our communities through our work?

It is possible that answers will come as we stare in the mirror. But some answers may surface by noticing a reflection that resembles us in some ways, but is different in many others. If, while looking in the mirror, we glance sideways, we may spy the countenances of our "cousin" filmmakers from overseas: the Asian filmmakers who have achieved respect and interest from American audiences. They look somewhat like us and share some roots with us, but their experiences have been drastically different from ours. If they appreciated our struggles to make films and get them seen, maybe they would give us advice from their experiences and perspectives in the United States.

Cousinly Advice: Getting on Screen

Get wise! our overseas cousins might tell us. If we really think Americans don't differentiate between Asian Americans and Asians, they might advise us, we might as well turn that myopia into advantages to get our films made and seen. To get your Asian American films on theater screens, they might say, try to:

1. Get fictional. Enough with the documentaries. You don't see documentaries from China, Japan, or Hong Kong getting big play in your theaters, right?
2. Get exotic—with places, people, or activities. Take the audience to a world it has never seen.
3. Get sexy—mostly if you're dealing with Asian women.
4. Get violent. The universal language is not mathematics, and it's not a "good story, well told." It's a good fight, full blown.
5. Get a trend going. Create a bandwagon. Hype a movement.
6. Get a new film language. Make audiences think they're watching something new and on the edge.
7. Get political. It's about scandal. Make a splash.

Let's explore some lessons that Asian American filmmakers can glean from the success of non-American Asian films. Though we'll take a lighthearted look, with tongues loosely planted in our cheeks, we may uncover serious dilemmas that face artists in the margins who want to survive in the mainstream without being engulfed by it. Unfortunately, there is no such thing as a free lunch. The seven tactics gleaned from our Asian cousin filmmakers may yield the desired benefit of more Asian American films playing in U.S. theaters, but can the tactics generate any negative effects? Surely.

1. Get Fictional.
You may have noticed that there has not been a great wave of new documentary films from Asia. If you want to be a filmmaker with a capital "F," stick to the realm of narrative. In this country, a documentary is barely considered a movie. It's more like a medicine—or, better yet, like a classic piece of literature that is supposed to be good for you, but that you really don't want to spend the time with. A friend, an Asian American graduate from UCLA film school, once told me to stick to fiction because "we already have enough documentary filmmakers." Perhaps this is true enough. The greatest exposure for Asian Americans on television has been through documentaries broadcast on PBS, such as *Forbidden City, U.S.A.* (Dong 1989), *Who Killed Vincent Chin?* (Tajima and Choy 1988), *The Color of Honor* (Ding 1987), *Sa-I-Gu* (Kim-Gibson and Choy 1993), and *a.k.a. Don Bonus* (Nakasako 1995).

The Asian American community has amassed so much experience in documentary filmmaking that its first breakthrough mainstream laurels have come in that discipline. The first Asian American to win an Academy Award for directing was Steve Okazaki, for the documentary *Days of Waiting: The Life and Art of Estelle Ishigo*, in 1990. Interestingly, this was a film about a white woman living in a concentration camp with Japanese Americans in World War II. The Asian American community's documentary-making talent was recognized in the mainstream again in 1995, when Freida Lee Mock shared the Oscar with Terry Sanders for the feature *Maya Lin: A Strong Clear Vision*, and in 1997, when Jessica Yu won an Oscar for the short film *Breathing Lessons: The Life and Work of Mark O'Brien*. For *Breathing Lessons*, an Asian American filmmaker once again won honors for a film about a non-Asian, this time a man in an iron lung.

Of course, documentaries have ethnographic and historical value. They provide a chance for Asian Americans to write their own history with the moving image. Ironically, though, narrative films often seem more "real" to ordinary audiences. Although audiences identify with on-screen people in documentaries, they do not lose themselves in the characters and stories as they do when watching fictional films. A positive result of this immersion effect is that fictional film audiences can come close to "experiencing" the characters by feeling as if they've walked that proverbial mile in another person's shoes.

Fictional films can also serve as ethnographic teaching tools and historical records. When audiences are faced with situations with which they have no experience, they believe they are learning something new and, implicitly, something true. For example, when audiences watch *Farewell My Concubine* (Chen 1993), they think they are learning something about Communist China and the Cultural Revolution. When they watch *Raise the Red Lantern* (Zhang 1991), they think they're learning something about old China.

The fictional piece allows filmmakers the opportunity to craft a story by manipulating the elements needed to create an engrossing drama. Similar to fiction, a documentary is subject to the biases and perspectives of the author; in documentaries, however, there is a greater need to adhere to objective facts. Thus, fiction offers more freedom than do documentaries (at least for the ethical filmmaker) to create works that will grab and hold an audience's attention.

On the other side of the argument, the "dramatic license" that gives the narrative form additional freedom can also call into question the cultural authenticity of a fictional work. For example, some Asian American critics have taken harsh views of Amy Tan's novels for overemphasizing, in their view, mystical aspects of Chinese culture, especially pertaining to the spirit world. These critics say that this feeds into Westerners' stereotypes of Asians. Though it is the prerogative of the artist to focus her work however she finds it most appropriate and meaningful, the "veracity" of her work may be challenged.

The subject of cultural authenticity, especially in the context of postmodern discussions, is worthy of greater in-depth treatment than can be offered here. But it is worth raising because of this chapter's interest in representations of Asian Americans and their relative harms and benefits. The right to claim cultural authenticity can be disputed, and it is a right that vying parties usually are not willing to share. Such disputes raise questions about "voice"—about who is allowed to speak for and about a particular community, even though the definitions of such a community get fuzzy around the edges. It is like the battle over determining history, only in the present tense. Though there can be a lot of destructive arguing, the debate can be used positively: Because intra-community scuffles usually contain some accusations of "selling out" or pandering to white mainstream stereotypes of marginalized communities, they can be used to draw attention to the mechanics of social oppression. Also, arguments between, say, white film-makers and Asian American community groups, such as those that occurred over the film *Rising Sun* (Kaufman 1993), can also be used to show how representations of Asians and Asian Americans affect the Asian American community.

People should not be turning to fiction as the best way of learning history and yet audiences continue to allow thremselves to be "educated" by commodities sold for entertainment, i.e., the theatrical feature film.

A downside of privileging fictional narratives over documentaries is that the history of Asian America may depend more on the documentary or personal video than on the feature film. When historians, and possibly our descendants, want to look into the stories that led them to their present, they may well prefer to look at such non-fiction pieces as *a.k.a. Don Bonus, Bui Doi: Life Like Dust* (Mishan and Rothenberg 1994), *The Fall of the I-Hotel* (Choy 1983), *Who Killed Vincent Chin?*, *Sewing Woman* (Dong 1982), *Forbidden City, U.S.A.*, or *Spirits Rising* (Diaz 1995) rather than such fictional works as *The Joy Luck Club* (Wang 1993), *Chan Is Missing* (Wang 1982), *Picture Bride* (Hatta 1995), or *The Wedding Banquet* (Lee 1993).

2. Get Exotic.

Play up the exotic angle. Make the liability an asset. If Asians can't escape being cast in an exotic light, use that light to your own ends. In a report for National Public Radio (NPR), Beth Accomando (1997) noted that Chen Kaige's project about China's first emperor, who ruled some 2,000 years ago (*The Emperor and the Assassin*, 1999), not only helped him avoid government censors; it also increased the exotic appeal of his film overseas.

Just as Asian films use the exotic allure of fascinating foreign backdrops (sweeping panoramas, gorgeous backgrounds, and so on), Asian American films can use the uniqueness of their communities. The result would be American films that look like a world that most mainstream audiences have never seen. The physical qualities of Asian communities can lend special visual qualities to Asian American films, arising from the use of distinctive forms, colors, or both. The idea is to capitalize on the Western fascination with the exotic Orient at least in look, if not in locale.

Asian American films can also play up the "exotic" social nature of Asian American communities. If you populate your films with Asian Americans, mainstream audiences can immerse themselves in a completely different world, without cumbersome subtitles.

Films from Asia can be implicitly or explicitly political—that is, they can critique their home society, and American audiences can comfortably watch them and ponder the inequities of, say, pre-modern China (e.g., *Raise the Red Lantern*). Perhaps one subconscious reason that many Americans are not drawn to films about people of color *in* America is because films from the margins often contain explicit or implicit critiques of American society. So steer clear in your stories of anything that approaches a critique of American society. Stories that show peculiarities of Asian American culture would be fine, and are actually encouraged, because they emphasize qualities of otherness without criticizing the mainstream.

On the other hand, playing up the exotic angle can perpetuate narrow stereotypes of Asian Americans. It can reinforce an audience's "need" to see Asian American characters only in the context of exotic settings and actions. Hasn't that, after all, been one of the problems in American cinema—that is, the use of Asians as exotic, mysterious, subservient, hypercruel caricatures? Therefore, those who want to play up the exotic will have to walk the fine line between particularity as authentic expression and otherness as tight constriction.

3. Get Sexy.
This is America. One of the basic rules, besides "It's a free country," is that sex sells. Marketers and advertisers use sex to sell everything, from cigarettes and beer to laundry detergent and hair coloring. Make movies that can be described as "Erotic!" "A Sexy Thriller!" or "Sizzling and Steamy!" Similar terms were used to market Chen Kaige's film *Temptress Moon* (1996). Some ads for the movie also included the outline of a woman's torso for added emphasis. Even Chen's *Farewell My Concubine* (1993)— practically a historical epic—got some of the sex-sell treatment. A quick survey of films in my local Blockbuster video store yields the following slogans for selling Asian films to potential viewers:

"An exotic oriental treasure" for *Raise the Red Lantern* (Zhang 1991)
"Erotic and beautiful" for *Red Firecracker, Green Firecracker* (He 1994)
"Erotic, intriguing" for *The Mystery of Rampo* (Mayuzumi and Okuyama 1994)
"Erotic tale of forbidden passion" for *Ju Dou* (Zhang 1990)

Well, you may say, marketers can slap the sexy label on almost any film just to sell it. Yes and no. The Asian American film *Picture Bride* went to the video shelves wearing a cover showing a woman with a naked back, but *The Joy Luck Club* could not be marketed with any such sexual innuendo. Although the image for *Picture Bride* was a result of wildly misconstruing a small bit of content for the sake of marketing, *The Joy Luck Club* did not provide even that opportunity. (And what is it with naked backs? The boxes for the video versions of *The Mystery of Rampo* and the American film *Golden Gate* [Madden 1994], starring Joan Chen, also feature Asian women baring their backs.) The point is, get some sex into the movie so you can use it to attract viewers.

Even if you can't get sex into your films, you can still use the exotic allure of Asian women to create interest. American culture in general, and some American men specifically, find that the Asian woman holds particular intrigue and sexual allure. Witness the attention paid to Gong Li, Maggie Cheung, and the action actor Michelle Yeoh. Yeoh, who starred with Jackie Chan in *Supercop* (Tong 1996), shows that there is always room for another sexy supporting female character. In fact, Yeoh has joined the long line of "Bond Girls," appearing in the James Bond film *Tomorrow Never Dies* (Spottiswoode 1997).

Remember, however, that using the age-old sex-sells tactic can divert attention from the more important themes and issues of a film. And if the tactic is successful, it can set up new stereotypes that can be limiting. African American men have long been used in American cinema as threatening, animalistic characters. Would it be progress to cast Asian American men in a similar light? Using Asian American women to lure American male audiences is the basest of all tactics and can be demeaning to the women's humanity. Taking this approach also works against attempts to show Asian Americans as people, as opposed to objects.

That caution aside, the Western fascination with the "Oriental" is best exploited when using female actors as publicity attractions. So use images of Asian American women to sell your movies, but don't expect the same results with Asian American men. Americans have yet to discover the sexiness of the Asian man, a dead Bruce Lee and a live Jason Scott Lee notwithstanding. Go ahead and use Asian men in sex scenes to get the steam factor up, but don't expect the image of men alone to sell your movie. Unless of course, they have big weapons. In that case, you can . . .

4. Get Violent.

See if you can inject whirling swordplay (as in martial arts) or "balletic" gunplay into your films. It is no secret that violence sells: Just look at samurai movies, Bruce Lee, Jackie Chan, and the films by John Woo. Critics claim that Woo has elevated the cinematic gunfight by evoking dance aesthetics through the use of unrealistically excessive gunfire, highly theatrical staging, and slow motion. Although the visual "text" of such scenes is hyper-violent, the presentation is so exaggerated that it seems actually to diminish the violent effect and distance the viewer from direct identification with it, like cartoon violence. Unlike cartoon violence, however, Woo's portrayals are considered cinematically beautiful. They are not, of course, just schlock fare. And even if they were, action and violence have the advantage of being easily understood by audiences. This was no doubt discovered early in the cinematic age, when silent-film directors—unable to take advantage of complex dialogue—found that they could present compelling, high-stakes problems via the simple revelation of physical danger.

Why is it that the most action-oriented—and in Woo's case, the most violent—of the Asian films, particularly those from Hong Kong, are the most accessible and popular in the United States? It seems that American audiences will accept Asian men as heroes or leading men only in the action genre. The action star Chow Yun-Fat is being courted by Hollywood, not Leslie Cheung. The first American hero with an Asian face was Bruce Lee, kung-fu superhero. In other words, the action genre holds the key to the creation of Asian American male stars.

But all the usual ethical arguments about violence in cinema aside, the problems with using violence in Asian American films go beyond over-sensationalizing. If violence is placed at the thematic or stylistic center of a film, the same problems that were attached to Bruce Lee as a hero will result—even if Asian Americans are triumphant through the carnage. When Asian American men must resort to hyper-physical tactics to emerge heroic, doesn't that feed back into limiting negative stereotypes of the Asian man as not fully human—that is, incapable of using intellectual, emotional, and creative qualities to rise to a challenge?

5. Get a Trend Going.

Instead of traditions, Americans revere trends. They even relive them and give them rebirth through "retro" and nostalgia crazes. For consumers, trends provide fun and enjoyment while setting a gauge against which to measure oneself. People can make personal statements by positioning themselves in any one of three places: "at the cutting edge" of a trend; in the midst of, or "riding," a trend; or in opposition to a trend. This love of trends is probably driven by business, which uses it to raise demand for consumer goods. In Hollywood, trends are driven by the studios' desire to lower their sense of risk and to capitalize on moneymaking opportunities via formulas that are perceived as sure audience pleasers or audience attractions.

Hong Kong films were "discovered" by American martial-arts enthusiasts, cool hipsters, and art house aficionados. The Chinese saw their Fifth Generation explode out of their film schools—though "explode" may be a term of embellishment. With Asian American enrollment in U.S. film schools at an all-time high, you can create a "Third Wave." Renee Tajima (1991, 14) has defined two earlier stages of Asian American filmmaking: 1) the late 1960s through the 1970s, which are characterized by "an urgent, idealistic brand of filmmaking" that is intimately connected with the politics of the Asian American movement of the time; and 2) the 1980s, a time of "institutionalization, pragmatism, and skills attainment" as Asian American filmmakers "focused their sights on a mass audience" and began "paying more attention to our right of access than the meaning of access." Tagged with a catchy name like the "Third Wave," the next generation of hot Asian American filmmakers could generate curiosity. Just make sure to be a highly publicized curiosity.

On the downside, although a correctly hyped trend can draw attention to itself and its "participants," it can also diminish the individuality of any one artist by shoving all artists inextricably into a category. Films that become part of the trend can be passed off as just more of the same, not judged on their own merits, again making the individual voice difficult to hear.

Also, trends are usually considered short-lived and devoid of substance. Being connected to a trend carries the danger of being easily dismissed, which would certainly be a detriment to filmmakers struggling for acknowledgment as serious artists.

6. Get a New Language.

The Chinese Fifth Generation employed, among other things, a new approach to fictional storytelling that was more metaphorical, symbolic, and visual, if less clear and melodramatic. It was partly this new filmic language that brought the Fifth Generation to prominence. Much attention was paid to the new style, but the Fifth Generation filmmakers were also exploring deviations from conventional Chinese film language. Such deviations can gain recognition even in films from Hong Kong, long seen as a synthesizer of Hollywood films, not a rebel. For example, Susan Morrison (1995, 38) viewed two films by Wong Kar-wai at the 1995 Toronto Film Festival and wrote: "Curiously enough, among all the films I encountered during the festival, it was *Ashes of Time* [1994a] and *Chungking Express* [1996] which stayed with me the longest, puzzling me in their strangeness, yet fascinating me by their difference from conventional forms." In the case of these films, the strangeness can be attributed to Wong's subordination of story to atmosphere and tone.

Asian American cinematic works could attract considerable attention if they were identified as having an exciting new style or language. Critics love to be the first to spot hot new trends. Of course, because critics and academicians alike enjoy recognizing trends and building categories—and almost need to do so—several works and artists would have to be identified with such a language in order to capitalize on the tactic.

A caution: Unlike the other tactics, this one can bring about a departure from convention that can make films less understandable and, if not well received, actually distance the work from viewers and limit its potential to reach mainstream audiences, who are leery of "art films." Being ghettoized in the world of art films may be slightly less frustrating then being ghettoized as being relevant only to Asian Americans.

7. Get Political.

Banning a film in China is a political act. In America, we have scandal and controversy. Maybe it's not fashionable in the 1990s, but how about advocating the overthrow of the U.S. government? No? How about creating something sexual that is worse than porn? Remember: There's no such thing as bad publicity. Get banned or cause a stir.

This worked when *The Blue Kite* (Tian 1993), *Farewell My Concubine*, and *Ju Dou* were banned by the Chinese government. In an interview with NPR's Accomando, Paul Pickowicz, professor of history and Chinese studies at the University of California at San Diego and co-editor of *New Chinese Cinemas*, spoke about strategies for contemporary Chinese directors such as Zhang and Chen. "It's absolutely essential that the film be banned in China," Pickowicz said. "They [the filmmakers] want that. They want to be able to find a way to say that, because this is what the distributors want" (Accomando 1997).

Zhang got an especially big ride on the publicity wave that the Chinese government's banning of *Ju Dou* generated. Even the Western filmmakers Martin Scorsese and Woody Allen decried China's censuring of the film. Even though the U.S. government doesn't offer the same kind of bans on which to capitalize, films that generate controversy often generate curiosity in equal measure. The 1993 movie adaptation of Michael Crichton's novel *Rising Sun* provides an interesting recent example. It was picketed by some Asian American community groups in an effort to expose its anti-Asian racist aspects. The movie's studio, Twentieth Century Fox, most likely did not want the negative publicity; nevertheless, the hue and cry gave the film a higher profile by thrusting it into the news, which in turn supplemented the movie's publicity campaign.

It may be possible to generate a buzz by offending foreign governments. China, for example, has expressed its disapproval of the Disney film *Kundun* (Scorsese 1997), which takes as its subject Tibet's Dalai Lama.

A domestic example of the use of controversy is Spike Lee, who, though not Asian, has gotten a lot of mileage from this tactic. Although his films and the issues they raise have contained implicit threats to the status quo, they nevertheless have generated discussion and, perhaps more important, media coverage. This undoubtedly has had a positive effect on the marketing of the films, which helps the studio's efforts to gain publicity. Knowing that there will be a requisite amount of buzz on a film can address a studio's concern for risk. Though controversy never guarantees box-office success, getting ticket buyers' attention is one of the primary steps in creating a chance for a film.

Being cast as a publicity hound or a controversy monger, however, can have limited use as a long-term career strategy. Continually crying wolf on the talk-show circuit can cause backlashes against an artist or group of artists.

For filmmakers, getting the metaphorical foot in the door is often the hardest task. Thus, extreme tactics are reasonable to consider. But if you are going to play with fire, be aware of the dangers. All of the problems mentioned here can, to a degree, be mitigated by films of outstanding quality, with stories and characters that are fully human and complex. One hopes that the content of the films—rather than the stylistic wrappings that are used to market them—will be strong enough ultimately to become the center of discussions.

Rebuilding the Mirror, Looking Straight at the Mirror

Trying to learn from our Asian cousins' success ultimately leads to the conclusion that, if you had any doubts about it in our post–affirmative action age, racism is still alive and working in American society and the American movie world.

All filmmakers face the constant tension between art and commerce. They also have to ask themselves hard questions about being true to their unique vision and making their films accessible to audiences. Because of the prevailing social forces of racism and sexism, Asian American filmmakers who look in the mirror and ask these questions may find that those tensions have more meaning and greater intensity.

Suppose that we adopt these strategies. What image might reflect back from our work when we look in the mirror? Would adopting strategies and tactics taken from overseas Asian films contribute to the development of a unique and meaningful style for Asian American cinema? Or would the films just end up conforming to another standard set up by non-Asian Americans? Our Asian cousins might argue that, whether self-determined or not, your style doesn't even have to be meaningful if all you care about is getting your foot in the door. Just find a marketable style. To varying degrees, all of the strategies drawn from the success of Asian film in the United States play with conventional notions of film marketing in America. They also play with mainstream stereotypes of Asians and Asian Americans. This means that care must be taken to insure that filmmakers follow a kind of movie-based Hippocratic oath—that is, at the very least, try to do no harm.

The number of Asian Americans entering American film schools seems to be rising dramatically. Although this appears to be an opening of American institutions to the unique visions of novice Asian American filmmakers, schools can also have a conforming effect. As Asian Americans compete for screen time in mainstream theaters, their work often will be judged by standards of classical Hollywood forms. Using Hollywood as the standard can push filmmakers toward that convention as a way to make their product commercially viable and accessible to the widest possible audiences. Thus, admission to the system via film schools can have an assimilating and de-specializing effect, for which there will always be costs and benefits.

Asian American filmmakers, like all minority filmmakers, also bear the extra burden of dealing with their relationships to their community or communities. The questions relating the artist to the community will persist, even for filmmakers who don't want to deal with them, because no art exists in a vacuum—especially film, which is so heavily based on stories about people. Take, for example, two hypothetical Asian Americans, one of whom makes films about Asian Americans, and the other of whom does not. For the former's art, questions will always arise about the impact that the work has on her community—either directly, via the community's reaction, or indirectly, via the mainstream's view of the community through her film. The whole question of connection to the Asian American community (or communities) underscores the importance of knowing about the history of the community and its portrayal (or absence) in American media.

For the Asian American filmmaker who chooses to present only non-Asian American stories, questions will always arise about why she has chosen not to present characters from Asian America and what that means about her and about the societal forces that push her to make that choice. And forces are at work, both large and small. When I was in graduate school, for example, a screenwriting teacher gave me a serious warning. I had proposed a story about a Japanese American man who struggles to come to terms with his sons' homosexuality. The teacher warned me that, if I had no compelling reason for making the characters Japanese American, I should just make them human— that is, white. Leaving aside the possibility that the story might be based on facts, I wondered what compelling reason there might be for the characters to be white. The only reason I found is that for a film to be just a film, in all its glorious possibilities—as opposed to a hyphenated film (Asian American, African American, etc.), with all its qualifiers and excuses and limitations—it has to be about straight white people.

Racism makes people suggest that ethnicity should be removed from characters. This not only de-ethnicizes film; it also reduces Asian Americans' screen representation (symbolic annihilation) and thus their power in the media. Thus, people who say that race doesn't matter and that it should be ignored have their heads in the sand. Granted, there is no reason that every film by an Asian American has to be about Asian Americans. But neither should every film *not* be about Asian Americans. That wastes the unique perspective of the Asian American artist.

Asian Americans should draw on their uniqueness as individuals and as Asian Americans to fuel the fire of their work. An old guideline for screenwriting says: Try to create unique and unusual characters. At far less than 10 percent of the country's population, Asian Americans—and, more pointedly, Asian American screen characters—are most definitely not run-of-the-mill.

Filmmakers can apply their uniqueness in at least two different ways: by diverging and by subverting. Diverging involves separating oneself from the pack of normal convention—by creating that new cinematic language, for instance. Films that use this technique can gain distinction and convey heretofore unseen stories in exciting and new ways. Subverting involves appropriatiung standard genres in order to tell stories about Asian America, thereby using the audiences' familiarity with common genres to pave the way for viewing characters and stories they might not otherwise have seen.

And so the battle rages, both out in the open and under the surface. Will Asian Americans' inroads into film-industry employment amount to changes in our on-screen representations? And again, what does the battle over image-making mean in the larger scheme of things? Critics of multiculturalism fear that a new tribalism will result in which people care only for their own small tribes, to the exclusion of others. But if we come to understand ourselves and other people better, a new tribalism will perhaps extend the care one has for one's small tribe to the larger tribes to which we all belong. The circles are endlessly overlapping and endlessly expanding. They all need care.

As Asian American filmmakers, our ultimate salvation may lie in refusing to allow self-interest to absorb us completely as we soldier on with our work. Being on the margin is not unique to Asian Americans. Working to promote the voices of other marginalized people will not only serve our self-interests; it will also provide the truer path to creating a society of inclusion that will benefit all people. The cross-fertilization that comes from working with artists who have different perspectives may advance the artistic development of all involved. Cross-fertilization in financial backing may enhance our collective commercial fortunes, as well.

Just as we as Asian Americans want our stories to be heard and accepted, so too must we use our perspective to try to hear and understand the stories of others who struggle to live that which should be their birthright. Because racism has so undeniably touched our lives, we should use that fact to appreciate the struggles of other cultural and religious minorities, women, and gay men and lesbians, and help them achieve what we want for ourselves. They are on journeys similar to our own.

Making the link between what we as Asian Americans have experienced and the oppression of others is not the same as giving in to the oppression. Rather, making the link can be a source of strength. I was fortunate to see this after I completed my first project, *Stolen Ground* (1993). In this nonfiction film, six Asian American men meet for dinner. During the meal, and in their later reflections, they share with one another, and the film's audience, what they have lost through racism and how racism has affected the lives of their parents, their children, and themselves. The original intent was to open the eyes of white America to the real-life fall-out of racism and to present a seldom-seen portrait of Asian American men expressing a full spectrum of emotions. This hope was realized. But we were surprised by other positive effects. I found that the film validates not only the heretofore silent experiences of Asian Americans, but also the experiences of other people of color, especially African Americans, who have identified very closely with the men's experiences in the film.

In my most recent documentary, *No Evidence* (1996), I was intent on exploring the positive effects that affirmative action can have on people in low-income communities, as seen through the life of a black man, Dr. Patrick Chavis. Instead of using the professional benefits of a medical education to escape his community in South Central Los Angeles, he chose to return. In documenting Dr. Chavis's and his patients' experiences, I saw similarities to the struggles in low-income Asian communities. Throughout the shooting and editing of the film, my mostly Asian American crew and I had to be mindful of exercising the same respect and care that we want for ourselves and our communities. That included trying to be aware of the stereotypes about the black community under which we were operating. Although we were outsiders to the Watts, Lynwood, and Compton communities, I had a guiding perspective as an Asian American who cares about issues of screen representation for all who have been shut out.

Other Asian American filmmakers hold this perspective, as well. We can draw on that to keep us going in what is, undeniably, an uphill battle. But by being true to a vision that goes beyond our self-interest, we can be satisfied with what we see when we look in the mirror, both literally and cinematically.

Works Cited

Accomando, Beth, and Bob Edwards. 1997. "China and Film." Morning Edition. National Public Radio, Washington, D.C., November 20.

Corliss, Richard. 1993. "Pacific Overtures." *Time,* September 13, 68–70.

Morrison, Susan. 1995. "Ashes of Time and Chungking Express." *Cineaction,* vol. 36 (February), 37–41.

Tajima, Renee. 1991. "Moving the Image: Asian American Independent Filmmaking 1970–1990." Pp. 10–33 in *Moving the Image: Asian Pacific American Media Arts,* ed. Russell Leong. Los Angeles: UCLA Asian American Studies Center and Visual Communications, Southern California Asian American Studies Central.

Films and Videos Cited

Chen, Kaige. 1993. *Farewell My Concubine.* Buena Vista.

———. 1996. *Temptress Moon.* Miramax.

———. 1999. *The Emperor and the Assassin.* Sony Pictures Classics.

Choy, Curtis. 1983. *The Fall of the I-Hotel.* NAATA.

Diaz, Ramona S. 1995. *Spirits Rising.* NAATA.

Ding, Loni. 1987. *The Color of Honor: The Japanese–American Soldier in World War II.* NAATA.

Dong, Arthur. 1982. *Sewing Woman.* NAATA.

———. 1989. *Forbidden City, U.S.A.* Deep Focus Productions.

Hatta, Kayo. 1995. *Picture Bride.* Miramax.

He, Ping. 1994. *Red Firecracker, Green Firecracker.* October Films.

Jang, Lindsey. 1993. *Stolen Ground.* No distributor (Lindsey Jang, 3758½ Colonial Ave., Los Angeles, CA 90066).

———. 1996. *No Evidence.* No distributor (Lindsey Jang, 3758½ Colonial Ave., Los Angeles, CA 90066).

Kaufman, Philip. 1993. *Rising Sun.* Twentieth Century Fox.

Kim-Gibson, Dai Sil, and Christine Choy. 1993. *Sa-I-Gu: From Korean Women's Perspectives.* NAATA.

Lee, Ang. 1993. *The Wedding Banquet.* Good Machine.

Madden, John. 1994. *Golden Gate.* TriStar Pictures.

Mayuzumi, Rintaro, and Kazuyoshi Okuyama. 1994. *The Mystery of Rampo.* Hallmark Home Entertainment.

Mishan, Ahrin, and Nick Rothenberg. 1994. *Bui Doi: Life Like Dust.* NAATA.

Mock, Freida Lee. 1994. *Maya Lin: A Strong Clear Vision.* Ocean Releasing.

Nakasako, Spencer. 1995. *a.k.a. Don Bonus.* NAATA.

Okazaki, Steven. 1988. *Days of Waiting: The Life and Art of Estelle Ishigo.* NAATA.

Scorcese, Martin. 1997. *Kundun.* Buena Vista, Touchstone.

Spottiswoode, Roger. 1997. *Tomorrow Never Dies.* MGM/UA.

Tajima, Renee, and Christine Choy. 1988. *Who Killed Vincent Chin?* Filmakers Library.

Tian, Zhuangzhuang. 1993. *The Blue Kite.* Kino International Video.

Tong, Stanley. 1996. *Supercop.* Dimension Films.

Wang, Wayne. 1982. *Chan Is Missing.* New Yorker Films.

———. 1993. *The Joy Luck Club.* Buena Vista.

Wong, Kar-wai. 1994. *Ashes of Time.* Scholar Productions.

———. 1996. *Chungking Express.* Miramax.

Yu, Jessica. 1996. *Breathing Lessons: The Life and Work of Mark O'Brien.* Fanlight Productions/ Pacific News Service.

Zhang, Yimou. 1990. *Ju Dou.* Live Home Vicks.

———. 1991. *Raise the Red Lantern.* Orion Classics.

Part III

Critical Approaches to Representing Japanese American Internment

Kent A. Ono

7   Re/membering Spectators:
     Meditations on Japanese American
     Cinema

Between about 1970 and 1990, many grass-roots, independent, fictional and nonfic-
tional films and videos were produced that tell stories about the incarceration of
Japanese Americans from a contemporary, post–World War II perspective. These films
and videos provide one specific site at which to examine the struggle with, contest
over, and interrelationships among Japanese American history, identity, and spectatorship. This chapter argues that, on the whole, these films and videos rely on particular versions of history that do not address larger social and cultural forces, even
as they produce new histories for public consumption.

   In order to make this argument, this chapter meditates specifically on the issue of
spectatorship in relation to these films and videos, especially as they have focused on
the historical trauma of the imprisonment of Japanese Americans during World War
II. Contrary to traditional spectatorship theory,[1] this chapter suggests that cinema
does not simply suture, or weave, the spectator into the film narrative. Historically,
spectatorship theory assumed that cinema had agency and that, by itself, cinema produced subjects. Such theory privileged the existential context of the spectator watching a film in the theater, while not fully addressing a larger social and cultural narrative—aspects of cinema that this chapter sees as historical processes that
simultaneously affect both the cinema and the spectator. Through a study of films and
videos about incarceration, I suggest that cinema interweaves particular versions of
history together with local memories in order to authenticate new versions of history. As a result, spectators participate dynamically in the history-making process that
films effect while also participating in the history out of which films are made. This
point illustrates cinema's contribution to a constitutive history—that is, making history what people later understand to be and refer to as history (e.g., that which leads
people to say, "This is history. Wouldn't you agree?"). In addition, this point shows

how the spectator participates not only in the particular versions of history cinema produces, but also in the historical context out of which cinema, itself, emerges.

Since Robert Nakamura's 1971 film *Manzanar*, film and video makers and artists have produced cultural works about the incarceration of Japanese Americans in the form of historical documentaries, fictional dramas, experimental films and videos, and "found footage" (such as home movies). These productions focus on the general history of incarceration and on specific themes of family, masculinity and heroism, women's roles in the incarceration narrative, as well as on specific concentration-camp themes. In each context, these productions involve spectators in the process of reconstituting their histories and identities. Each film or video has the potential to shape the way a spectator understands the history of incarceration and the spectator's relationship to that history and to the cinema. From avid students of film, to Nisei who were themselves incarcerated, to the mainstream public who might know little about Japanese American history, films and videos about incarceration have tremendous potential to shape the aftermath of the incarceration.

In short, I argue that these films affect spectators in two ways, as the title of this chapter implies: 1) by helping spectators remember the history of incarceration, and 2) by re-membering (or producing and bringing) new subjects into Japanese American history that heretofore have been either forgotten or simply overlooked. In its role of helping spectators remember, this cinema recalls the historical event and its associated traumas (one of which is the very loss of history) and acknowledges that these experiences did in fact happen. Sometimes, these films even recognize and praise committed and valiant struggles for survival, providing a context for a therapeutic recovery from the trauma. In its other role—of bringing new members together—this cinema first longs for a history that can replace the loss of history of Japanese Americans. Then it recruits spectators to become members of and participants within that constructed history. Overall, Japanese American cinema taps into, uses, reproduces, and shifts cultural-narrative processes of nation, gender, race, and sexuality, and thus reconfigures the representational landscape. For spectators, this cinema affects how they come to have substance—that is, how they come to be "articulated" within various domains of their lived realities.[2]

In part because they remain skeptical of mainstream depictions of Japanese Americans, and hence of cinema generally,[3] these films and videos offer counter-historical perspectives. Nevertheless, the counter-historical perspectives that shape the memory of Japanese Americans and Japanese American history in particular ways are simultaneously positioned within what I will identify as transnational, racial, and ocularcentric contexts. Moreover, the skeptical attitude taken by films and videos in depicting Japanese Americans and the history of incarceration, I argue, ultimately relies on an ethics with regard to understanding cinema that is affected by transnational, racial, and ocularcentric history and that itself affects a theory of spectatorship.

I examine how Japanese American cinema constructs history as a space for possible reconciliation with incarceration trauma. This desire for such a space, as demonstrated in these cinematic productions, exhibits a certain anxiety about the legitimacy of presence that I argue is informed by the cultural, historical, political, and social context of transnational migration, U.S. racial politics, and ocularcentrism. Thus, I examine the history of Japanese American and Asian American identities as part of a transnational historical project that understands the spectator not only as a recipient of direct address but also as a participant in the practice and production of history. By contextualizing contemporary Japanese American cinema in this way, the anxiety associated with representing history and spectators may become clearer. This anxiety may be necessary because films and videos necessarily leave out important historical details and facts that may, upon later discovery, be intrinsic to the very histories they tell. Because spectators exist within, and as part of, representation, requisite pause may have to be given to consider what kind of subjects emerge and what they ultimately "remember." I argue, then, that as a result of the transnational, racial, and ocular-centric context, scholars, spectators, and artists would be well advised to remain anxious about both cinema and history.

Japanese American Transnational History

Successive migrations of Japanese people to the United States not only necessitate theorizing a non-universal Japanese American community; they also demonstrate the senselessness of attempting to generalize around one fixed "sense of place." Acknowledging various transnational migrant experiences also means that, with each successive migration and each new generation of native inhabitants within a given locale, successive historical configurations surrounding identity and imagined productions of identities emerge. Thus, in order to understand the ways in which Asian Pacific Americans "migrate, regroup in new locations, reconstruct their histories, and reconfigure their ethnic 'projects'" as part of the process of "unyoking [the] imagination from place" (Appadurai 1991, 191), researchers will have to address the multiplicity, heterogeneity, and incommensurability of individual group experiences (Lowe 1991).[4] In Japanese American history—as in Asian American history generally, where particular forms of migration play definitive historical roles in the constitution of community and culture—groups cannot be conceived of as "tightly territorialized, spatially bounded, historically unselfconscious, or culturally homogeneous" (Appadurai 1991, 191). Thus, following Arjun Appadurai, it is important not to hold fast to an understanding of Japanese American history solely as it emerged within a U.S. context, for as students of Asian Pacific diasporas, we must be able to account for the transnational ideological and capital exchanges that operate just under the threshold of our understanding and that affect local present-day identities, relations, and processes.

Lisa Lowe (1996) takes up this project by describing the historical context underlying contemporary Asian American cultural politics. Lowe addresses the historical reality of shifting cultures and migratory patterns and their connection to U.S. policies, colonialism, the spread of imperialism, democracy, religion, and a particular understanding of modern nation-states, cities, and corporations subsidized by the U.S. government. That is, she describes the relationship between the situation in which we now find ourselves as Asian Pacific people and the conditions that account for our current condition, or, as Stuart Hall says, "positioning."[5]

Thus, historical narratives of colonialism and nationalism overdetermine discrete categories of identity. This renders histories that develop out of community activities within a given geographical space insufficient to account for the multiplicity of historical material relations at play. Narratives about communities and their histories rely on a particular reified understanding of group identity, as if we all know what that identity means. Understanding production, consumption, and culture, especially that associated with Japanese American spectatorship, makes little sense without addressing U.S. imperialism in Asian countries, Japanese colonialism of other Asian peoples, and the specific diasporic conditions that give rise to Japanese American cultural products that themselves refer to and rely on a relatively bounded conception of Japanese American history.

The larger Japanese diaspora emerged within the context of wide-ranging U.S. colonialism in Asia and the reciprocal colonial relationship between Japan and the United States. Moreover, in discussing the concentrated imprisonment of Japanese Americans in interior regions of the United States, precipitated by U.S. government responses to an attack by the Japanese military on Pearl Harbor,[6] one has to understand the community relations that evolved out of that history and the subsequent emergence of a late 1960s and early 1970s Asian American political identity. This identity is part of a discontinuous history that is deeply embedded in global politics—shifting alliances and conflicting identities caused by massive numbers of what I will call "tragic ironies" arising from historical intercultural encounters: when social and political activism and empowerment evolve from the horrors of oppression.

Japanese American history and identity are complicated for multiple reasons, not the least of which are Catholic Christian missionary movements in Japan beginning in 1549; the "opening up" of Japan to U.S. trade interests (1853); the Japan–Hawai'i friendship treaty (1871); Japanese imperialism in and colonization of Manchuria (1931–45), Korea (1910–45), and the Philippines (1941–44); the Gentlemen's Agreement restricting Japanese migration to the mainland United States (1907–08); the prohibition against further entry of so-called picture brides in 1920; closed trade practices prior to World War II; the bombing of Hiroshima (August 6, 1945) and Nagasaki (August 9, 1945) and subsequent U.S. colonization in Japan; Japan's favored-nation status vis-à-vis the U.S. "rebuilding" of Japan; the 1980s "bubble" economy (1986–91) and subsequent recession; and the increase in Japanese, West German, and U.S. transnational—primarily corporate—economic enterprises. All of these historical events, and many more, affect the migration patterns of Japanese people throughout the world, including to the United States; the demographic make-up of Japanese Americans during different periods; transnational economic, political, and familial ties; and generational experiences in the United States, for example. These specific events and their historical interconnectedness give rise to a particular "project" of Japanese American history and identity.

Hall's discussion of Caribbean cinema and spectatorship exemplifies the need to understand cinema within transnational and historical contexts. In order to do this, he suggests examining the common identity based on shared diasporic travel to the same geographical location and different unique identities of individual Caribbean groups prior to forced migration. In part, Hall is asking how it is that one begins to talk about a cultural history of descendants of slaves, when slave owners waged massive campaigns precisely to erase local histories and replace them with national histories of the inferiority of slaves and the superiority of themselves. He writes:

> We might think of Caribbean identities as "framed" by two axes or vectors, simultaneously operative: the vector of similarity and continuity; and the vector of difference and rupture. Caribbean identities always have to be thought of in terms of the dialogic relationship between these two axes. The one gives us some grounding in some continuity with the past. The second reminds us that what we share is precisely the experience of a profound discontinuity. [Hall 1989, 72]

Key to Hall's discussion is the notion that Caribbean identity is an effect of sometimes unwilled diasporic migrations, which, in this particular case, led to complex local identity formations that loosely coalesced to be read historically as *partially common* in origin. As he suggests, "The paradox is that it was the uprooting of slavery and transportation and the insertion into the plantation economy (as well as the symbolic economy) of the Western world that "unified" these peoples across their differences, in the same moment as it cut them off from direct access to that past" (ibid.).

Benedict Anderson (1983) suggests that the construction of "nations" and other "communities" was a result of a revolution in typographic print and reproduction technology, which allowed for the efficient exchange of visual, national models across time and space. Therefore, with print technology came the ability to imagine empires and map spaces elsewhere—thereby producing what Anderson calls "imagined communities." Although this may have been true for colonizers, the experience of community, even an envisioned one, for slaves, migrant workers, and other non–nation-builders, as Hall suggests, was very often an effect of, not a requirement for, diaspora. There is a profound difference between collectivizing in order to build an empire and collectivizing in order to survive the ravages of imperialism. The admixture of people coming together in one geographical space or place in order to take part in community activities contributes to a particular vector of history and memory that is much more like emergent unimagined communities than imagined ones.

Thus, for Japanese Americans, the concentration-camp experience created conditions for heretofore unimagined communities—the dispersion and subsequent reorganization of people into social spaces controlled and maintained by the U.S. government—out of which could emerge social and political networks. The concentration of people from different communities and different geographical regions, with cultural factors such as gender, race, class, nation, and sexuality coming into play—and the splitting of many families in the process—had both tragic and ironically empowering effects. This unimagined aggregation of communities and disaggregation of families and other communities, as another tragic irony, brought together for the first time Japanese Americans who would never have had the opportunity to know each other otherwise. To offer just one very specific example, concentration-camp life, as evidenced by oral-history testimony, often freed Issei women from domestic family duties and allowed for newfound friendships among women that, prior to incarceration, were not possible (Ono 1992).

I offer this brief discussion of the contemporary transnational economic, political, and cultural contexts in order to make it difficult (if not impossible) to read Japanese American cinema within a strict theoretical model that has been developed primarily to explain Hollywood film consumption (although aspects of a model, such as one that addresses the subject's desire for the "projected" image as a larger-than-life exemplification of a more perfect fetishized image, might be helpful in explaining some forms of Japanese American spectatorship).[7] As Darrell Hamamoto (1996) suggests, for Asian Americans and other marginalized people of color, Hollywood functions to produce narratives aimed at colonizing the mind. Thus, a film theory that depends on that colonization is necessarily too limited to explain fully counter-hegemonic film practices, such as the Japanese American cinema that I examine. The very act of talking about indigenous cinema resists a history that attempts to read all cinematic products into Hollywood history and which reads all non-Hollywood cinematic products as inauthentic, unauthorized, and inferior stories of unimportant people.

A U.S. Racial Context

Simply talking about indigenous cinema without addressing its politicized, racial specificity only takes us so far. "Asianness," like historically constructed concepts of "whiteness," "Blackness," "Indianness," and "Chicananess/Chicanoness," relies on a logic of power in numbers in order to make sense within a racially stratified U.S. society.[8] Ironically, new possibilities for collectivization and empowerment may emerge during disempowering moments. For instance, the concentration camps produced a sense of powerlessness in numbers, while simultaneously producing unimagined communities. Early European American migrants such as Italians, Irish, Jews, and Greeks, who experienced discrimination because of their deviance from mainstream ethnic history, religion, and culture, were very often willing to identify themselves as white or were willing to be labeled white, downplaying specific familial and ethnic identities in order to fit in with dominant white society.[9] As Alejandro Portes and Rubén G. Rumbaut (1990, 138) suggest, nation-states facilitate the "rise of ethnicity" by "treating groups differently."[10]

The benefits in consolidating a white identity went both ways. For the emerging white majority, adding members, even if they were "ethnic," decreased the potential for an ethnic, racial or other majority, especially after slavery, after World War II, and after the civil rights movement, as the potential for economic power for people of color grew.[11] And for those who now could be considered white, especially after years of discrimination because of their differentiation from the white majority, the ability to enter the white majority may have appeared as a sanctuary, an escape from racial and ethnic "others."

Similarly, and strongly as a result of slavery, abolition, the Harlem Renaissance, and the civil rights movement, histories of individual communities and traditions associated with diasporic migration patterns from various parts of Africa, the Caribbean, and Latin America were sacrificed or sublimated in order to become part of the larger "Black" community, whose power derived specifically from strength in numbers. The American Indian, Chicana and Chicano, and Asian American movements associated with the late 1960s and early 1970s all drew on the larger, dominant Anglo society's model of association, oppression, resistance, and empowerment struggles, which all relied on a concept of "group representation" (e.g., "nationhood"). Through appeals to group identity, these movements countered what came to be seen as a racially stratified United States, a white-supremacist environment into which racially marginalized groups entered very often as exploited laborers. Indeed, within a racist nation-state, appeals to whiteness function dialogically with appeals to Black, Indian, Chicana and Chicano, and Asian nationalisms.[12]

Appeals to the racial category "Asian American," which so often rest on individuals' giving up their ethnic histories for the power of Asian American numbers, may imply that political, economic, social, and cultural differences across ethnic groups do not matter. Although it has similarities to the history of the larger group of Asian Americans, Japanese American history deviates from that of Chinese Americans, Korean Americans, Filipina and Filipino Americans, Indonesian Americans, Vietnamese Americans, and Asian Indian Americans in fundamental historical, political, and economic ways. Japan's own domination of other Asian people should be evidence enough that a simple collapsing of ethnic identities into the larger racial one—Asian or Asian American—is insufficient to account for very specific relations of power at play, let alone empowerment struggles (Ono 1995).[13] As L. Ling-chi Wang's recent research on Chinese Americans suggests, a "dual domination" transnational model specific to Chinese Americans may account for the specific "ideological, theoretical, and public policy" issues affecting Chinese Americans (Wang 1995, 153). This dual domination model addresses both exclusionary aspects of U.S. life and the standard of "loyalty" that Chinese Americans and other members of the Chinese diaspora are held to in China. Such a model might be adapted specifically to individual Asian Pacific groups, or, as I would suggest, to specific families and communities.

Within migration patterns, and therefore within local U.S. communities, major differences among Japanese American experiences necessitate what Hall calls a dialogic understanding of the past. I would define this as a process of reciprocal interchange that is simultaneously shaping and being shaped by changing forces, or, as I have called it elsewhere, "*coming to terms* with ever-changing social conditions" (Ono 1995, 67). The past "is *something*—not a mere trick of the imagination. It has its histories—and histories have their real, material and symbolic effects. The past continues to speak to us. But this is no longer a simple, factual 'past,' since our relation to it is, like the child's relation to the mother, always-already 'after the break'" (Hall 1989, 72).

A genealogical approach to identity, history, and politics will be necessary to dismantle deeply ingrained racial configurations within a neocolonial U.S. context and to counter hundreds of years of racial oppression and indoctrination into Eurocentric, white, and Judeo–Christian ideas and values confronting racially marginalized groups within the United States. This kind of genealogy would account for individual family and community histories (not national, racial, or corporate ones), especially with regard to transnational events and migrations, within a complex relationship of power that emerges haphazardly. If we follow Hall's arguments, a genealogy would necessarily recognize that no preternatural moment of origin, no ultimate recovery, and no final sanctuary can be found, which means that genealogies would account for lived realities simultaneously within, in resistance to, and as a part of processes of representation. Appadurai (1991, 208) describes the effects of a similar self-conscious, albeit anthropological, project when he writes, "[T]he more we unravel these pasts, the closer we approach worlds that are less and less cosmopolitan, more and more local. . . . Once again, we need to be careful not to suppose that as we work backward in these imagined lives, we will hit some local, cultural bedrock, constituted of a closed set of reproductive practices, untouched by rumors of the world at large." Thus, the approach I employ in this chapter self-consciously attempts to account for assumptions and presumptions about daily living, especially in terms of that which is taken for granted, such as national context, relationships to history, geography, space, culture, and especially present historical conditions. Without radical scrutiny of such assumptions, especially as they affect what is constituted as history, legacy, and genealogy, we risk operating via a kind of willed blindness to the subjective nature of understanding the world and a presentist political perspective.

Identity Within Ocular-centricity

Underlying my discussion of cinema and Asian Americans lies my own deep-rooted suspicion of the prominent role that ocularcentrism (the idea that "what is seen is what is known") plays in the history of primarily Western representations of Orientalism, the West's exoticizing travel narratives and tourism, and the role that cinema has played within that history. As Judith Mayne (1993, 78) has argued,

> In the US alone, independent film and video, specifically addressed to a variety of markets—gay and lesbian, feminist, black, hispanic—continues to grow. One of the largest problems confronting spectatorship studies is the simultaneous affirmation of diversity and the recognition that "diversity" can easily function as a ploy, a way of perpetuating [sic] the illusions of mainstream cinema rather than challenging them. Put another way, there is no simple division between the cinema which functions as an instrument of dominant ideology, and the cinema which facilitates challenges to it.

Within the context of U.S. society today, it would be difficult for any film or video to break fully with the ocular-centric cultural context or with the aesthetics and consumption processes of U.S. cinema.

As products within a larger cultural context, for the most part, films and videos—and many of the critiques of films and videos—tend to privilege a certain form of spectatorship. In the 1980s, the issue of "spectatorship" was theoretically shaped by the discipline studying it: Film studies scholars studied spectatorship; speech communication scholars studied audiences; literature scholars studied reader responses; and communication and media studies scholars studied reception. In addition to the correlation between the discipline studying the phenomenon of spectatorship and the terms used to describe this research area, there was also a correlation between what the studies were called and the particular aspect of the body they tended to privilege through language. For instance, spectatorship emphasized the visual; audience studies privileged hearing or the aural; reader response privileged the visual (reading) and the vocal (answering or responding); and reception emphasized the passivity of the "receiver," which implies use of an archaic sender–receiver communication model, almost as if the receiver were an empty and open receptacle waiting to be filled. There indeed was an ambivalent politics around the issue of what to call and how to conceive of the spectator.

Although I could take up any one of these disciplinary approaches, I focus on *spectatorship*—and I make this choice somewhat arbitrarily—but use the term recognizing the multiple metaphysics of desire, stimulation, and pleasure that go beyond "viewing practices." But I also use the term to emphasize how films and videos about incarceration, while sometimes self-reflexively working against an obsession with spectation, nevertheless tend to privilege the ocular, thus popularizing only one aspect of spectatorship—watching. One reason for this is that Japanese American films and videos, in particular, criticize Hollywood for not putting forth an image that is representative of Japanese Americans. Japanese American cinema maintains a desire to see something other than the Hollywood construction. As Hall (1989, 70) notes about Caribbean cinema, "Such texts restore an imaginary fullness or plenitude, to set up against the broken rubric of our past. They are resources of resistance and identity, with which to confront the fragmented and pathological ways in which that experience has been re-constructed within the dominant regimes of cinematic and visual representation of the West."

Given its particular transnational and historical context, Japanese American cinema is perhaps less caught up in restoring "imaginary fullness or plenitude" than it is preoccupied with producing history in order to defy Hollywood's "logic of visibility," realizing that it can do so only by changing what is made visible.[14] As Feng (1996, 121) writes about *History and Memory* (Tajiri 1991): "While offering a critique of cinematic institutions (like Hollywood) that promote a representational logic whereby the visible is legitimated, the video hesitates to offer up images of its own since that would confirm that logic of visibility."[15] Nevertheless, that hesitation leads more often than not to the layering of images, not to an absence of them. For these films and videos, visibility is evidence of a confirmable past and of its accessibility via the medium of film. These films do call attention to the oral features of memory; every so often, the visual is juxtaposed to the oral in such a way that the shock of the visual evidence either discredits or calls into question that which has been orally given, rendering the image superior to the oral. In *History and Memory*, for instance, the narrator's visual perception betrays her sister's unconscious interest in and desire for whiteness: The story of the ghost's memory of the family's house disappearing following the family's incarceration appears to us narratively in scrawling white words. Similarly, archival footage of a "canteen" calls into question the mother's oral memory that no canteen existed at the Salinas Assembly Center. This scene appears simultaneously with the sound of the mother saying there was no canteen in Salinas, drawing attention to her failing memory. Feng (1996, 103) points to the lack of importance that the video implies "canteens" had for incarcerated Japanese Americans, as evidenced by the character's mother's having forgotten hers, and to the different cinematic objectives and foci between the U.S. Signal Army Corps' "official" government footage and Tajiri's reproduction of it. Thus, the spectator must "first perceive the image and then understand the soundtrack's relation to it, thus prioritizing the image" (ibid., 125). As my analysis of this video suggests, *History and Memory* does participate in fetishizing cinema as the medium that is best able to convey life experiences, even as it critically and self-referentially questions the history of mainstream depictions through its visual component.

In addition to privileging the ocular, which plays within and alongside overdetermined Western conventions, Japanese American films about incarceration often play the cinematic role of transporter. As Margaret Morse (1990, 193) suggests:

> Freeways, malls, and television are the locus of an attenuated *fiction effect,* that is, a partial loss of touch with the here and now, dubbed here as *distraction.* This semifiction effect is akin to but not identical with split belief—knowing a representation is not real, but nevertheless momentarily closing off the here and now and sinking into another world—promoted within the apparatuses of the theater, the cinema, and the novel.

What I call here a transportation, a "partial loss of touch with the here and now," is the translocationality effected by cinema generally: the experience of being swept up into an adventure, romance, melodrama, mystery, intrigue, or saga and being transported to a different space, place, and time in order to experience some other elusive life. Diaspora necessitates the translocation of a people from one geographical space to another. The only way that people can be transported from one location to another is via a medium—in the case of diaspora, via ships or other vessels. Thus, diaspora necessitates a history of dislocation from one place to another—a parallel experience to that of film viewing. Part of what film does is translocalize spectators, creating the experience of being in a different world. Like tourism, cinema informs desire and projects an imaginary approximation, or representation, of it through sound and image. These films and videos are caught within the desire for a Japanese American history: a desire for a place, space, and time *to be,* for reconciliation with a past elsewhere, and for a metaphorically empowered community in the United States. In this context, the spectator is transported into history, but it is a history that draws attention away from some aspects of the larger social context even as it attempts to highlight the social world. That is, even while the spectator may encounter the social issue of Japanese American incarceration for the first time, the spectator may also encounter that history through a nostalgia for U.S. military practices (e.g., in *The Color of Honor* [Ding 1987]). This is part of the problematic of Japanese American history within the context of diaspora. For although documentary and non-narrative independent films and videos are often understood not to evoke the same translocationality effect as do narrative fiction films and videos, at least this genre of productions about the Japanese American concentration-camp experience, regardless of their non-narrative elements, function within and sometimes in response to a dominant, primarily U.S. historical narrative. Thus, translocationality is brought about not by the internal cinema narrative, but by the ideological, historical one.

Arguably, cinema has a special seductive quality for Japanese Americans and others who have a transnational diasporic heritage—namely, the desire for and pleasure of translocationality, transpositionality, and transtemporality that cinema provides and that approximates the process of coming to terms with the history following migration. A sublimated, if not forgotten history, can thereby be summoned with ease, whether through self-named "fictions" or through documentaries, magically appearing before the spectator as a history oblivious to the individual labor, perseverance, and dedication necessary to produce it. For instance, although what we are seeing on video in *Something Strong Within* (Nakamura 1994) is a reproduction of personal home and camp footage (a compilation of original productions possibly taken at personal risk to the prisoners), the seamlessness of the text resulting from editing, mellifluous music, and the gathering together of these disparate fragments (historically and geographically) highlights the ease of production, not its double difficulty.

For Japanese Americans, as well as for other Asian Americans and people of color rarely represented compassionately in cinema, seeing Asian, Japanese, Asian American, and Japanese American bodies, spaces, places, and times on the screen may provide a unique and profound experience. Not only may the Japanese American body, itself, affirm identity, but Asian bodies projected onto the screen synecdochically imply the larger Asian American body politic—that is, a formidable, and perhaps exaggerated, presence within the larger public sphere of an Asian American body politic. Within a living room or other small space in which video images may appear, the effect may in fact be even more pronounced, because such images may appear to be so pervasive as to have invaded even the "personal" space of television. The public projection enhances the potential of community, creating a profound feeling of connectedness, as if a given moment can be shared across space, place, and time because of the shared experience among local theater spectators and people in their living rooms. Thus, cinema represents a transgressive mediated space in which time, space, and place can be collapsed, and the imaginary collectivization of Japanese Americans can be effected. From this perspective, viewers do not so much identify one on one with film characters, or, say, with a remarkable sound. Rather, cinema figures as the point of identification, with the projected sound and moving image as key elements in cinema's overall effect.

In short, I suggest that film consumption is a complex experience made up of various and ambivalent identifications associated with the process of coming to terms with individual and group identity and with relative social power relations within the cultural context of a racialized, capitalist, and colonial nation. I turn now to a discussion of the productions themselves.

The Missing and Now Found Subject of History

By no means will my analysis exhaust the possible connections that can be drawn between the theoretical sections of this chapter and the films and videos I will discuss, although a more detailed examination of Rea Tajiri's *History and Memory* will conclude this section. My brief discussion of these films in relation to the issues of transnationalism, racism, and ocularcentrism is meant to be provocative and to encourage a critical engagement with the films and videos. Discussions of the following productions are organized around not only specific concentration-camp themes, but also the resonant themes of family, masculinity and heroism, and women's role in the incarceration narrative.[16] In each category, I use one or two examples to illustrate how these topics begin to connect to the central issues of this essay.

Very often, directors of films about the incarceration are third-generation, or Sansei, Japanese Americans representing the concentration-camp experience of their parents, the Nisei. As a result of this relationship between subject and object of cinema, many films and videos focus on family. For example, two women and one man discuss their personal lives and families before, during, and after the camps in the fictionalized *Conversations: Before the War/After the War* (Nakamura 1986). These characters challenge traditional ocularcentrism by looking directly into the camera, but they paradoxically create a heightened sense of ocularcentrism for the spectator who is the object of the direct address. Michael Uno's full-length fiction feature *The Wash* (1988), which is based on Philip Kan Gotanda's play, addresses family tensions surrounding incarceration. Susan Inouye's fictionalized *Solo* (1989) revolves around a father's memory of his son being shot while running for a baseball beyond the barbed wire. Lise Yasui's Academy Award-nominated *A Family Gathering* (1988) and the longer version, *Family Gathering* (1989), address Yasui's search for her own Japanese American history. In both films, Yasui remains suspicious of her father's home movies, while nevertheless creating her own film. Midi Onodera's *The Displaced View* (1988) addresses the filmmaker's sexuality with regard to her family and incarceration. Nakamura's film *Wataridori: Birds of Passage* (1976) focuses on the first-generation, Issei, saga of happiness prior to incarceration and sadness resulting from it. Lucy Ostrander and Elizabeth Clark's educational film *Home From the Eastern Sea* (1990) focuses on Asian immigrant families, including the Hondas, a Japanese American family. Although *Home From the Eastern Sea*, like so many Asian immigrant documentaries, discusses the immigration experience, larger transnational issues, especially the politics behind the specific immigration to the United States, versus other parts of the world, and the reception of immigrants in the United States in relation to this global context, are not addressed. Moreover, distinct ethnic experiences tend to collapse into the general Asian subject of the film. The other films in this category tend to downplay the relationship between families and incarceration and larger transnational and racial issues.

In addition to family themes, many films and videos can be said to demonstrate a preoccupation with the return of the Japanese American man to history. This theme has four subthemes: the hero resister, the hero soldier, the hero father, and the hero artist. This theme of a man who emerges as a hero of the community appears to answer Frank Chin's call for "real" Asian Americans. Chin (1991, 76) suggests that Frank Emi, who resisted the military draft while being incarcerated, was the "kind of *Nisei* [Japanese American Citizens League] history says never was, and the kind the *Sansei* wish there had been as they suffer unique emotional problems because not one of their mother and father's *Nisei* generation had the guts to stand their ground and fight for their constitutional rights." Certainly, this is the theme of John de Graff's *A Personal Matter* (1992), which focuses on the hero Gordon Hirabayashi's personal struggle to fight the history of incarceration. Steven Okazaki's Oscar-nominated *Unfinished Business* (1984) focuses on the role of the heroes Hirabayashi, Minoru Yasui, and Fred Korematsu in the movement for redress; Okazaki's recent *American Sons* (1995) addresses masculinity in general, although it favors soldier themes. Loni Ding's two documentaries *Nisei Soldier* (1984) and *The Color of Honor* (1987); Wendy Hanamura's *Honor Bound: A Personal Journey* (1996); and Nicole Newnham's *Unforgettable Face* (1993) explore masculine heroism in war in detail. *Minoru: Memory of Exile* (Fukushima 1992) focuses on the Japanese Canadian filmmaker's father Minoru Fukushima. *Sam* (1973) is a film documentary focusing on the main character's imprisonment and his partner's atomic-bomb experiences. John Esaki's *Yuki Shimoda: Asian American Actor* (1985) and Alan Kondo's *I Told You So* (1974) focus on male artists.

By centering the masculine subject as hero, whether he is explicitly working for or against the U.S. government, all of these films draw upon a version of U.S. or ethnic nationalism. As Lowe (1991, 31) suggests in her discussion of Frantz Fanon, cultural nationalism and assimilation often go hand in hand. The "logic of visibility" may be confirmed, precisely because cinema provides what is longed for: a hero who counters the dominant racist society while doing so through appeals to "essentialized notions of precolonial identity"—in this case, a sexualized masculinity. Although Janice Tanaka's recent *Who's Going to Pay for These Donuts Anyway?* (1992) does not deal with well-known "heroes," it explores the loss and reappearance of her Nisei father and his and the rest of her family's role in living with their newfound history. Distinct from the other productions listed here, this video puts masculinity under scrutiny and constructs the absent father (Nisei) without a memory, then creates the history, demonstrates the forgetting, and projects a contemporary version of the masculine subject as an effect of history. The knowing spectator, who presumably has not forgotten the past, is invited to participate in filling in the lost history. Alternatively, if the spectator has lost memory, the film seeks to provide one for the subject.

Collectively, these films counter stereotypes of Japanese quietness, reserve, lack of agency, and lack of resistance. Thus, they counter traditional conceptions of Western and Eastern femininity as applied to Asian people, and through counter-example they illustrate the proud masculine heritage of Japanese Americans, despite the "emasculating" effects of concentration-camp experiences. The spectator is thus asked to celebrate the Japanese American man and thus to celebrate resistance against dominant history.

In contrast to masculine heroism, Allie Light and Irving Saraf's *Mitsuye and Nellie* (1981); Steven Okazaki's *Days of Waiting* (1989); Janice Tanaka's *Memories from the Department of Amnesia* (1989); Rea Tajiri and Pat Saunders's *Yuri Kochiyama: Passion for Justice* (1993); and Tajiri's recent full-length, fiction feature film *Strawberry Fields*

(1997) focus on women's role in the history of incarceration. Okazaki's Oscar-winning documentary film emphasizes contrasts of light, dark lighting, and shading to tell the story of the concentration camp-prisoner Estelle Ishigo, the white spouse of the now-deceased Japanese American Arthur Ishigo, while Tanaka focuses on her mother via an experimental, avant-garde approach, using non-narrative means to maintain suspicion of the medium of cinema. Ocularcentrism and the role of resistant cinema in challenging and transforming Western film conventions are therefore a preoccupation for Okazaki, who indirectly criticizes racialized color, and for Tanaka, whose excursus on the issue of "amnesia" in *Memories from the Department of Amnesia* is tantamount to a study of resistant spectatorship via nonlinear, non-narrative, and avant-garde video strategies. For Tanaka, in a process similar to the amnesia suffered by so many in the camps, the spectator slowly gains context within the video to be able to piece together an understanding of the video, and therefore of a fragmented, though now pieced together, history (Ono 1994).

One of the most salient productions about the incarceration is John Korty's Emmy-winning made-for-television movie *Farewell to Manzanar* (1976), which is based on the fictionalized autobiographical book of the same title by Jeanne Wakatsuki Houston and her husband, James D. Houston. This film loosely fits into the category on specific concentration camps. Another work focusing specifically on Manzanar is Nakamura's *Manzanar* (1971). David Tatsuno's *Topaz* (1997), an extended "home" film of incarceration, was inducted into the Library of Congress's National Film Registry in 1997.[17] Another production named *Topaz* (1987), by Ken Verdoia, is a traditional documentary of the camp. *Legacy of the Barracks* (Mohr 1994) and *Memories of the Camps* (Heman and Mohr 1992) both examine return pilgrimages to Heart Mountain. *Bitter Memories* (1975) and Scott Tsuchitani's *Meeting at Tule Lake* (1994) focus specifically on Tule Lake. Dianne Fukami's *Tanforan: Race Track to Assembly Center* (1995) focuses on imprisonment prior to the concentration camps. Many of these productions are compelling because of the found footage and factual images of camp sites, yet this compelling quality contributes to their ocularcentrism, and their rarity lend an aura of exaggerated facticity to them.

Conclusion

I would like to end with a discussion of one cinematic artwork that fits uneasily within the categories I have created for these films so far, in order to illustrate the importance of continued theorizing about cinema. I chose this video because it problematizes and does not fully reconcile many of the issues examined in this chapter. Specifically, Tajiri's *History and Memory* addresses the transnational, through Japanese newsreel and fictional re-enactments of the bombing of Pearl Harbor as spoken in Japanese. The video depicts the social and political conditions leading up to World War II and therefore does not reduce incarceration solely to a national context.

Further, *History and Memory* questions the U.S. nationalist position with respect to patriotism, inclusion in the nation of the United States, and the hypocrisy of imprisonment of Japanese Americans while asking them to go to war for the government. One way it does this is through a self-reflective foregrounding of clips from the 1942 Hollywood musical *Yankee Doodle Dandy*. A tragic irony is depicted here between film and social reality: The film's rhetoric of citizens collectively sticking together is placed in contradistinction to the fact that Japanese Americans, at the time of the film's premiere, were being instructed to leave their homes and enter concentration camps. In addition, an extended clip documents the musical's own tragically ironic juxtaposition of the lyrics, "We're all for one and one for all," against the black-and-white footage of African Americans standing at the base of the Lincoln Memorial, their backs turned toward the lighted ("whited") statue, with voices crescendoing to match the camera's position facing Lincoln from below and behind the African Americans, but above them. This Hollywood rhetoric not only positions African Americans against Japanese Americans, in the context of *History and Memory*, but also challenges government hypocrisy on two levels: 1) with regard to depictions of African Americans, who raise their voices up to and for the white, heroic patriarch, and 2) with regard to Japanese Americans, who, in context, are not the "we" who are "for all," but obviously the musically absent "they."

By addressing a non-binary racial formation, the video never calls for a specifically Japanese American or Asian American history. It counters dominant historical narratives and draws on Japanese American culture to tell its story. For instance, when Aunt Betsy tells the story about the day Japanese fighter pilots bombed Pearl Harbor, she says that her father gave advice in Japanese to a neighbor soldier on furlough. "*Shikataganai*," he said, which means, "Be strong. You'll be all right." And when the aunt tells a story of not being able to get lodging, the attendant asks about her race. She proudly replies, "Japanese American," which in this instance is used to deny her access to lodging. The video text does not linger on this specific identity, persisting instead in providing a family and community genealogy, clearly differentiating the experience of incarcerated Japanese Americans from, for example, the experiences of Native Americans whose reservation land was used to build a prison in which to house Japanese Americans. Thus, racial identity is placed into context, and while the collective identifying term "Japanese American" is spoken, individual, familial, and community life takes priority.

Finally, as Feng suggests, although the video relies on a logic of image as proof, it nevertheless puts into question what is seen, especially what is seen within a larger U.S. racial context. For example, the voiceover narration over Hollywood and Japanese documentary and fictional clips of the "Attack on Pearl Harbor" provides educational information about media production. The voice says,

> There are things which have happened in the world while there were cameras watching, things we have images for. There are other things which have happened while there were no cameras watching, which we restage in front of cameras to have images of. There are things which have happened for which the only images that exist are in the minds of the observers present at the time. While there are things which have happened for which there have been no observers, except for the spirits of the dead. [Tajiri 1991]

Here, the fictional quality of fictional and non-fictional footage of "real events" is questioned. The whiteness of the film stars in the narrator's sister's photos is questioned. Even the ability to represent the incarceration experience is ultimately questioned.

Nevertheless, a spectatorship that addresses the transnational, historically dialogic, and genealogical imaginary—while remaining critical of the context of Western ocularcentrism that in many ways overdetermines the possible visual resources available to people of color in and outside the United States—is not produced by this collective cinema, or even ultimately by *History and Memory.*

A close examination of each of the other thirty-six films and videos mentioned here might reveal that they, like *History and Memory,* have moments of transnational insight and multiracial and multicultural consciousness, as well as desires to decenter the primacy of the visual. These moments, as I have discussed with *History and Memory,* are in fact what I consider transformative about this collective cinema. Yet in the context of the historically grounded Japanese American spectator–subject who is repeatedly produced by these productions, even *History and Memory*'s more sustained challenge to that linear, unified history becomes only the boundary surrounding the absence that is now filled by this cinema.

I am not suggesting that the cinematic histories depicted are not true. Rather, I suggest that their logic is to produce a consumable history as counter-evidence to a lack, and to produce a spectator position, the point of which it is the text's obligation to demonstrate. The implication of this for this collective cinema is that this counter-evidence is possible only through visual images that tend to neglect or marginalize transnational and anti-racial contexts.

Japanese American cinema produces a history in which the spectator can be understood and does so by drawing on the larger narrative of Japanese American history—which until now was constructed as a lack—in order to stitch a narrative together as evidence of its own desire, thus recentering that version within history. The final effect is an exemplary text, which, in addition to being memory, is memorial, and arguably monumental, functioning as an iconic presence in place of a lack. Ultimately, however, what are produced are re/membering spectators, who now have a memory of trauma and can see themselves as members of a history and community created by cinema.

Especially in experimental documentaries, cinema simultaneously recognizes that films and videos can never be, and can never fully account for, lived reality, because lived reality always exceeds representations even as it cannot be understood outside of them (that is, beyond signification and narrative). Thus, in their longing for a history, these films and videos do maintain a certain level of anxiety over cinematic production that is effected through the figure of the spectator.

But this anxious longing may also be a preoccupation with an event that leads to a kind of narcissistic cultural encounter. Cinematic representations therefore can do nothing but, and nothing more than, remain anxious about longing for and producing a presence. A preoccupation with or fixation on producing a constitutive history of a peoples may necessitate a continuous anxiety about the legitimacy of presence.

This longing acknowledges the grass-roots margins from which these films and videos comment.

The anxiety about cinematic representation is articulated through the figure of the spectator. These questions, among many, underscore the problematics of representation that are evident in Japanese American cinema of incarceration, such as: Who actually sees these films and videos? What kind of history is constructed here, if it can be called history at all? And how does a film or a video depict history in a world in which identity is a strong determinant of being, when at the outset it denies its very power to represent?

Spectators, scholars, and artists should remain anxious about the histories and subjects produced here, because the transnational, racial, and ocularcentric contexts out of which productions emerge saturate the potential field out of which art emerges. That is, without a constant and committed theoretical understanding of the ways in which identity and history interrelate with powerful social forces beyond practices of representation, accounts of historical trauma will always fail to acknowledge the embeddedness of the social conventions at play and their effects on desires for identity.

Notes

Acknowledgments: I thank Sarah Projansky and Peter Feng for their insightful readings of this chapter and assistance in helping me locate relevant material. I also thank the University of California, Davis, for a Humanities Research Fellowship (1993) and the Faculty Research Grants (1993–96) that made this project possible.

1. I am thinking in particular of the early work by Stephen Heath (1981) and Kaja Silverman (1983) on the concept of "suture." Since then, scholars have revised this formulation, paying particular attention to social material relations (e.g., Mayne [1993] and Gaines [1986]).

2. For a recent discussion of "articulation" theory, see Slack (1996).

3. In his dissertation on Asian American cinema, Peter Feng (1996, 85) suggests that self-consciousness is central to the films and videos he examines. He writes, "These movies thus attempt to represent that which should have been represented—they must somehow depict the absence of depictions of the Internment, and that paradox is evident in an ambivalent attitude toward the processes of cinematic representation." See also, the discussion of skepticism in Japanese American cinema in Payne (1997).

4. See also the discussion of Appadurai's essay in Smith (1994).

5. Hall (1989, 72) writes: "Cultural identities are the points of identification, the unstable points of identification or suture, which are made, within the discourses of history and culture. Not an essence but a *positioning.*"

6. The U.S. government's mass imprisonment of Japanese Americans followed a thoroughgoing campaign orchestrated by various racist forces, many originating in California. Hence, the imprisonment was a response to an imaginary threat that Japanese Americans posed to the U.S. nation-state.

7. I use the term "projected" when discussing films and videos throughout this chapter for the following reasons: Although not all video images are projected, in public settings in which

videos are shown, they often are. Moreover, while a projector helps to "throw the image" onto a screen, the screen monitor approximates the effect of light doing so. Finally, video reproduction of original film is common in these productions.

8. For further discussion about empowerment based on ethnic identification, see Portes and Rumbaut (1990), especially Chapter 4: "From Immigrants to Ethnics." The authors suggest that the appeal of these categories is actually part of a democratic "incorporation." They write: "[T]he reaffirmation of distinct cultural identities—whether actual or invented in the United States—has been the rule among foreign groups and has represented the first effective step in their social and political incorporation. Ethnic solidarity has provided the basis for the pursuit of common goals through the American political system: By mobilizing the collective vote and by electing their own to office, immigrant minorities have learned the rules of the democratic game and absorbed its values in the process" (ibid., 141).

9. As Roediger (1991) and Lahti (1997) suggest, whiteness historically operated differently for different class groups.

10. See also Fong and Yung (1995–96) for a discussion of the complex relationship among desire, whiteness, and racial acceptance.

11. For example, the government's accession to the suffragist movement has been read as a response to the growing post-slavery power of African Americans (see Davis 1981a, 1981b).

12. Ideally, multiple emphases on individual, family, group, and community identities and histories and on that of the larger group (constituted as a reaction formation against dominant forces) would be preferable. In many cases, however, the genealogy of unique members and member groups becomes submerged into the (very often nationalist) history of the movement.

13. Throughout her book *Asian American Panethnicity* (1992, esp. 75–80), Yen Le Espiritu calls attention to Chinese American and Japanese American dominance in U.S. pan-ethnic social organizations.

14. This discussion of the "return of the gaze" hinges on that of panoptic power. Rather than being Foucault's object of the gaze, Japanese American cinema artists take up the camera, but do so recognizing the harmful way it was used against them. The existential question, however, is how to use the camera differently from the way it was used originally to fix us in the camera's eye.

15. For another theoretical approach to the study of this video, see Marks (1994).

16. This discussion does not address generic incarceration productions, such as those that would be aired on or made for national television, or those made primarily to educate people about the general facts about the incarceration experience. Nor does it address films and videos of which the incarceration experience is not a substantial or primary focus. This discussion also does not include films and videos documenting conferences, panel discussions, university talks, and other events; government productions; or videos and films that are not widely distributed.

17. I include Tatsuno's film because parts of it have been reproduced in Japanese American cinema about the concentration camps. Among the products that cite Tatsuno's film is Nakamura's video *Something Strong Within* (1994), which depends on found footage taken inside concentration camps in order to constitute a present text as exemplification of prison-camp life. *Something Strong Within* follows Nakamura's *Moving Memories* (1993) (which also is a compilation of home movies, but from the 1920s and 1930s). Whereas the history of Japanese American concentration camps argues that cameras were forbidden, *Topaz* and *Something Strong Within* constitute a presence in place of a lack—using cinema as counterfactual to the historical assertion of an absence.

Works Cited

Anderson, Benedict R. O. 1983. *Imagined Communities: Reflections on the Origin and Spread of Nationalism.* London: Verso.

Appadurai, Arjun. 1991. "Global Ethnoscapes: Notes and Queries for a Transnational Anthropology." Pp. 191–210 in *Recapturing Anthropology: Working in the Present,* ed. Richard G. Fox. Santa Fe, N.M.: School of American Research Press.

Chin, Frank. 1991. "Come All Ye Asian American Writers of the Real and the Fake." Pp. 1–92 in *The Big Aiiieeeee!: An Anthology of Chinese American and Japanese American Literature,* ed. Jeffery Paul Chan, Frank Chin, Lawson Fusao Inada, and Shawn Wong. New York: Meridian.

Davis, Angela Y. 1981a. "Racism in the Woman Suffrage Movement." Pp. 70–86 in *Women, Race and Class.* New York: Vintage Books.

———. 1981b. "Woman Suffrage at the Turn of the Century: The Rising Influence of Racism." Pp. 110–26 in *Women, Race and Class.* New York: Vintage Books.

Espiritu, Yen Le. 1992. *Asian American Panethnicity: Bridging Institutions and Identities.* Philadelphia: Temple University Press.

Feng, Peter. 1996. "Memories of Our Ancestors: Storytelling and Asian American Cinematic Autobiography." Ph.D. diss., University of Iowa.

Fong, Colleen and Judy Yung. 1995–96. "In Search of the Right Spouse: Interracial Marriage among Chinese and Japanese Americans." *Amerasia Journal* 21, no. 3: 77–98.

Foucault, Michel. 1979. *Discipline and Punish: The Birth of the Prison.* Trans. Alan Sheridan. New York: Vintage Books.

Gaines, Jane. 1986. "White Privilege and Looking Relations—Race and Gender in Feminist Film Theory." *Cultural Critique* 4: 59–79.

Hall, Stuart. 1989. "Cultural Identity and Cinematic Representation." *Framework* 36: 68–81.

Hamamoto, Darrell. 1996. Lecture, University of California, Davis, November 25.

Heath, Stephen. 1981. *Questions of Cinema.* Bloomington: Indiana University Press.

Lahti, Martti. 1997. "White Dirt." Paper, Society for Cinema Studies Conference, Ottawa, May 17.

Lowe, Lisa. 1991. "Heterogeneity, Hybridity, Multiplicity: Marking Asian American Differences." *Diaspora* 1: 24–44.

———. 1996. *Immigrant Acts: On Asian American Cultural Politics.* Durham, N.C.: Duke University Press.

Marks, Laura U. 1994. "A Deleuzian Politics of Hybrid Cinema." *Screen* 35, no. 3: 244–64.

Mayne, Judith. 1993. *Cinema and Spectatorship.* New York: Routledge.

Morse, Margaret. 1990. "An Ontology of Everyday Distraction: The Freeway, the Mall, and Television." Pp. 193–221 in *Logics of Television: Essays in Cultural Criticism,* ed. Patricia Mellencamp. Bloomington: Indiana University Press.

Ono, Kent A. 1992. "Representations of Resistance and Subjectivity in Japanese American Discourse." Ph.D. diss., University of Iowa.

———. 1994. "Modes of Distraction: Decentering History in Visual Representations of Japanese American Imprisonment." Ohio University Film Conference, Athens, Ohio, November 3.

———. 1995. "Re/signing 'Asian American': Rhetorical Problematics of Nation." *Amerasia Journal* 21 no. 1–2: 67–78.

Payne, Robert M. 1997. "Visions of Silence: *History and Memory* and *Who's Going to Pay for These Donuts Anyway*?" *Jump Cut,* vol. 41, 67–76.

Portes, Alejandro, and Rubén G. Rumbaut. 1990. *Immigrant America: A Portrait*. Berkeley: University of California Press.

Roediger, David R. 1991. *Wages of Whiteness: Race and the Making of the American Working Class*. London, New York: Verso.

Silverman, Kaja. 1983. *The Subject of Semiotics*. New York: Oxford University Press.

Slack, Jennifer Daryl. 1996. "The Theory and Method of Articulation in Cultural Studies." Pp. 112–27 in *Stuart Hall: Critical Dialogues in Cultural Studies*, ed. David Morley and Kuan-Hsing Chen. London, New York: Routledge.

Smith, Michael Peter. 1994. "Can You Imagine?: Transnational Migration and the Globalization of Grassroots Politics." *Social Text* 39: 15–33.

Wang, L. Ling-chi. 1995. "The Structure of Dual Domination: Toward a Paradigm for the Study of the Chinese Diaspora in the United States." *Amerasia Journal* 21, no. 1–2: 149–69.

Films and Videos Cited

Bitter Memories: Tule Lake. 1975. University of California Office of Media Services.

Curtiz, Michael. 1942. *Yankee Doodle Dandy*. Warner Bros.

De Graaf, John. 1992. *A Personal Matter: Gordon Hirabayashi v. the United States*. NAATA.

Ding, Loni. 1984. *Nisei Soldier: Standard Bearer for an Exiled People*. Vox Productions.

———. 1987. *The Color of Honor: The Japanese–American Soldier in WWII*. NAATA.

Esaki, John. 1985. *Yuki Shimoda: Asian American Actor*. NAATA.

Fukami, Dianne. 1995. *Tanforan: Race Track to Assembly Center*. NAATA.

Fukushima, Michael. 1992. *Minoru: Memory of Exile*. NAATA.

Hanamura, Wendy. 1996. *Honor Bound: A Personal Journey*. Filmakers Library.

Heman, Vic, and Mark Mohr. 1992. *Memories of the Camps*. ABC.

Inouye, Susan. 1989. *Solo*. No distributor.

Kondo, Alan. 1974. *I Told You So*. NAATA.

Korty, John, and Jeanne Wakatsuki Houston. 1976. *Farewell to Manzanar*. Made-for-television movie.

Light, Allie and Irving Saraf. 1981. *Mitsuye and Nellie: Asian American Poets*. Women Make Movies.

Mohr, Mark. 1994. *Legacy of the Barracks*. ABC.

Nakamura, Robert A. 1971. *Manzanar*. NAATA and Visual Communications.

———. 1976. *Wataridori: Birds of Passage*. NAATA.

———. 1986. *Conversations: Before the War/After the War*. NAATA.

———. 1993. *Moving Memories*. Japanese American National Museum.

———. 1994. *Something Strong Within: Home Movies from America's Concentration Camps*. Japanese American National Museum.

Newnham, Nicole. 1993. *Unforgettable Face*. NAATA.

Okazaki, Steven. 1984. *Unfinished Business*. NAATA.

———. 1989. *Days of Waiting: The Life and Art of Estelle Ishigo*. NAATA.

———. 1995. *American Sons*. NAATA.

Onodera, Midi. 1988. *The Displaced View*. Women Make Movies.

Ostrander, Lucy, and Elizabeth Clark. 1990. *Home from the Eastern Sea*. Filmakers Library.

Sam. 1973. University of California Extension Media Center.

Tajiri, Rea. 1991. *History and Memory: For Akiko and Takashige*. Electronic Arts Intermix.

————. 1997. *Strawberry Fields.* No distributor.

————, and Patricia Saunders. 1993. *Yuri Kochiyama: Passion for Justice.* NAATA.

Tanaka, Janice. 1989. *Memories from the Department of Amnesia.* NAATA.

————. 1992. *Who's Going to Pay for These Donuts Anyway?* NAATA.

Tatsuno, David. 1997. *Topaz.* No distributor.

Tsuchitani, Scott T. 1994. *Meeting at Tule Lake.* NAATA.

Uno, Michael Toshiyuki. 1988. *The Wash.* Academy Entertainment.

Verdoia, Ken. 1987. *Topaz.* KUED TV, Salt Lake City.

Yasui, Lise. 1988. *A Family Gathering.* NAATA.

————. 1989. *Family Gathering.* NAATA.

Glen Masato Mimura

8   Antidote for Collective Amnesia?
Rea Tajiri's Germinal Image

Our lives go on viscerally, austere, beneath our memories.
Janice Gould, "Doves" (1994)

From the early 1970s through the late 1980s, Japanese Americans successfully mobilized as a community to seek redress and reparations for their wrongful internment in concentration camps during World War II. Led by the Sansei, who came to political consciousness through the anti-racist and anti-imperialist struggles of the 1960s and 1970s, the movement's efforts culminated in the passing of the American Civil Liberties Act of 1988. Consequently, the U.S. government publicly recognized the injustice of its wartime incarceration of more than 110,000 Japanese Americans, officially apologized for its wrongful actions, and promised $20,000 in reparations to every internee still living.

In the latter years of this movement and in its aftermath, several important media works have been produced, ranging from conventional documentaries to more experimental pieces. They have been screened at various venues, from film festivals to classrooms and community centers, and broadcast nationally on public TV. For analytical purposes, these works can be divided roughly into two groups: in the first group are those—"revisionist" in their collective purpose—which document aspects of the internment experience that are either neglected or less well known by mainstream audiences; and in the second are works—more "meditative" in nature—that reflect on the continuing effects of the internment in daily life and personal history. Together, these films and videos powerfully enter, contribute to, and illustrate the increasingly complex public debate about historical representation that is taking place today in the universities as well as in popular culture. More specifically, the works in the first group are centrally concerned with broadening mainstream history—for example, by telling the story of the 442nd Regimental Combat Team, which was composed of Nisei men who were recruited out of the camps and became one of the most highly decorated units in U.S. military history. These works—most notably Loni Ding's *The Color of Honor: The Japanese American Soldier in World War II* (1988), Katriel

Schory's *Yankee Samurai* (1985), and in many respects Steven Okazaki's Academy Award-winning *Days of Waiting* (1988)—grapple most profoundly with the question, "Who is an American?" They also grapple with what the response to this question—caught up with issues of citizenship, loyalty, and betrayal—has meant for Japanese Americans.

My attention lies with the second group of works, however, whose shared formal and thematic features stray far from considerations of nationality, Americanism, and public identity. Rather, these works formally constitute themselves around the motif of memory—its absences, inconsistencies, revisions, repressions. They include Lise Yasui's *A Family Gathering* (1988),[1] Janice Tanaka's *Memories from the Department of Amnesia* (1991) and *Who's Going to Pay for These Donuts Anyway?* (1992), and Rea Tajiri's *History and Memory: For Akiko and Takashige* (1991). Made by the daughters of internment survivors, these works all examine the ways in which state-sponsored racial violence extends beyond the lives of its original victims to haunt following generations. The fundamental question these works collectively pose, therefore, is: How does the legacy of mass incarceration more than fifty years ago persist in the everyday experiences and memories of Japanese Americans—even among those who were born long after the event? In tracing the contours of subjectivity, these media artists' responses are concerned less with telling a story according to the existing terms of documentary authority than with the psychical experience of memories in the present, the traumas they simultaneously hide and reveal.

This chapter is drawn from a larger work in progress devoted to an examination of the four titles in the second group named above. Rather than risk oversimplifying these important works by condensing the lengthier assessment, however, I will outline the vexed nature of the historical moment in which they emerge, then focus my discussion on Rea Tajiri's video to illustrate the tenor and direction of my broader argument and analysis. If I belabor context here, I do so to demonstrate that the marginal cultural forms that tell these stories are determined not simply by the personal, idiosyncratic choices of the artists, but also by the weight of competing historical forces. In the aftermath of the Redress and Reparations movement, these artists' contemporary invocations of memory startlingly uncover unacknowledged yet deeply rooted family traumas, still-open wounds at the contradictory meeting ground of American racism and democratic promise.

The Uses and Limits of Americanism

Disappearances conducted by the FBI in broad daylight, yet disavowed by the broader public; Japanese Americans intensely loyal to the United States suspected of sedition, precisely because their proud patriotism is perceived as too sincere to be true; mass detention of a national minority; sanitized images of imprisonment, fabricated to undercut rather than underscore the atrocities imposed on its victims. . . . Summoned across more than thirty years of coerced silence, these and other examples of state-sponsored violence appear everywhere in the testimonies that the Redress and

Reparations movement has brought to public attention ("Rite of Passage" 1981; U.S. Commission 1997; Hansen and Mitson 1974). In other geopolitical and historical contexts, such experiences of political terror and intimidation might have found their best expression through the style and ethos of Latin American magical realism or through the kind of political satire found in Eastern and Central European literature (the novels of Gabriel García Márquez and Milan Kundera are exemplary here)—that is, through narrative forms forged under authoritarian or totalitarian regimes.

Yet this historical event took place in a capitalist nation that was, precisely at that moment, leading its allies in a war expressly in the interests of democracy against fascism. Then, for nearly the next half-century, it was orchestrating the advanced industrial countries in the Cold War against Soviet communism. The bitter irony here cannot be overstated, as the highest political offices and the military establishment conjoined systematically to revoke the rights and freedoms of Japanese Americans— and destroy more than sixty years of Japanese American community-building on the West Coast—in a nation that was ostensibly advancing the ideals of social equality and political freedom. Nor does the irony end there: During the twilight years of the Cold War, in seeking accountability for such state-sanctioned atrocities, the Redress and Reparations movement took on the rhetoric of official nationalism, arguing that the government had betrayed its own principles and therefore must make amends— in essence, appropriating the same language that had authorized the mass evacuation and detention little more than thirty years before.

This fact might not be curious if the movement had been led by former internees themselves, the vast majority of whom insisted on their rights as Americans and passionately demonstrated their loyalty in time of war. Instead, it was led by their children, whose political sensibilities matured during a complex period in which the moral authority and meaning of Americanism was deeply challenged. However, emerging external factors were shifting the popular political climate: Amid the late 1970s' oil crisis and during the ascendancy of Japanese economic power in the 1980s, pro-nationalist sentiment rapidly consolidated (the "Buy American" campaign, the rise of Japan-bashing, etc.). Consequently, liberal and much radical protest, which might have assumed a more caustic, anti-American tone ten years earlier, refashioned itself in Americanist rhetoric.[2] In contrast, political subjects in the Eastern bloc countries and in the underdeveloped client states in Latin America could not have imagined claiming the state's own language to name their oppression, having become accustomed to political systems that rule more explicitly by coercion than consent. Hence, the development of such radically anti-state cultural forms as *real maravilloso* and anticommunist satire.

In coming to voice in a nation long offering the illusion of free speech, however, Japanese Americans faced an altogether different burden. Of the countless experiences shaped by the internment, the scholarly accounts tend heavily to foreground the eminently American, redemptive figures of the selfless, loyal Japanese American soldiers; those who resisted in the camps or who protested their constitutionality; and, to a lesser degree, the conscientiously objecting No-No Boys. The two general syntheses of Asian American history—Ronald Takaki's *Strangers from a Different Shore* (1989) and

Sucheng Chan's *Asian Americans: An Interpretive History* (1991)—both concentrate significantly on these figures of ultimate, proven loyalty and conscientious resistance to animate their recountings of the internment drama. The painful yet dignified sacrifices of the soldiers are also patriotically affirmed in the very titles of the two prominent internment-related documentaries of the mid-1980s: *Yankee Samurai* (Schory 1985) and *The Color of Honor* (Ding 1988). Such exemplary stories have achieved visibility and prestige, no doubt, because the moral strength they illustrate so irreproachably appeals to popular democratic sentiment. And in part, these stories simply have been easier to document and identify, because they stand out from the more pervasively routine, everyday realities of camp life. But the elevation of these figures has also been fostered by the Sansei generation—again, politically spirited and empowered by the turbulent 1960s era and the driving force of the Redress and Reparations movement—whose rejection of then-prevailing accounts of cooperation and subsequent search for a dissident legacy almost inevitably privileged such heroic, therapeutic stories.[3]

Yet this point of view and its attendant rhetoric tended to scissor away some of the most severe and crucial issues from the fabric of history—that is, from the constellation of events that lay bare not only the causes, but also the less visible, ongoing effects—thereby implying that, after the apologies have been made and the solemn ceremonies have concluded, and after the ink has dried and the reparation checks mailed, we can all get on with our lives. However rightfully recognized and celebrated, the heroic stories of soldiers, protesters, and No-No Boys have inadvertently displaced and obscured the more commonplace, yet shamefully disavowed, experiences of madness, depression, alcoholism, suicide—the irrevocable damage caused by the mass incarceration of Japanese Americans.[4] The creative, critical act not simply of naming such suffering and unfreedom in the context of formally espoused freedom, but of investigating their devastating, lingering consequences, would require cultural forms altogether different from magical realism or literary-political satire. To give expression to these more problematic experiences—certainly not more painful or oppressive or unjust, but more problematic to represent—artists such as Lise Yasui, Rea Tajiri, and Janice Tanaka have turned to the more private, intimate languages available through autobiographical documentary film and experimental, or "art," video.[5]

Silence and Forgetting

Reflecting on oblique traces of Jewish memory in New York's Lower East Side, the cultural critic and anthropologist Jonathan Boyarin (1992, 1) writes: "Forgetting seems ghostly, not because it has no force or weight (it presses against us heavily and constantly, and it may yet do us in), but because we are so unused to naming it that even those of us who realize its danger usually prefer to speak for memory." His words usefully remind us that remembering and forgetting are inextricably tangled in subjectivity, perpetually struggling over the representation of the past. That is, more than an innocent, passive, gradual dissolution of memories, forgetting is one of the fundamental forces that dialectically constitutes memory (individual and collective), that intangibly yet relentlessly shapes not only its "content" but its very "form." In the case of Japanese Americans, the federal government actively attempted to cleanse the reality of mass detention from national memory.

Seeking to bury the traumatic experience themselves rather than suffer further abuse for its invocation, most Issei and Nisei refused to acknowledge the terrible episode of their history. Their collective disavowal transformed it into a taboo that was literally and symbolically unspeakable. Yet repression (psychical and political) always leaves traces, unintentional clues to that which it attempts to extinguish. In the wake of the consciousness-raising politics of the 1960s and '70s, the ever-present motif of silence in Japanese American history (and Asian American history more generally) has come to represent the heavy force of forgetting, its symptomatic gesture. Powerfully defined by the sum of Asian American literature as a crucial effect of racial and patriarchal oppression—censorship of the speech-acts that constitute our racial–ethnic identities[6]—silence therefore names not so much the objective fact of absolute, unrecoverable loss but rather the (detected) attempt to forget, to short-circuit the perpetuation of collective memory.

This pernicious, internalized force is evident everywhere in the works in question, from the Yasui family's constant, overt disavowal of the suicide of Lise's grandfather to the unconscious revisions or gaps in Tajiri's mother's memory. Yet these media works are ultimately concerned with the operations of their makers' memories: what they remember and how they come to know it. At least two prior commentators (Nornes 1993; Xing 1994) view Tajiri's video as advancing the positive and corrective powers of memory, gained through its recovery, against the mythologizing nature of official history. Jun Xing even names it "a subversive tool, challenging the dominant historical narrative and formulating a counter-cultural voice *based on the memories of Japanese Americans*" (Xing 1994, 95; emphasis added). To my mind, however, these works stage memory not as a truth against history's falsehoods, but rather as memory against forgetting. Or, more precisely, they stage memory against history not as the always available, continuous repository of folk knowledge and cultural stories, but as what Janice Tanaka expresses in *Memories from the Department of Amnesia* (1989) as that which negates the possibility of ever knowing things "as they actually happened" and that therefore incites speculation in the philosophical sense. The process of recovery therefore cannot simply be an act of summoning "what actually happened" versus the fictiveness of mainstream or dominant accounts. Remembering is itself a generative, creative, fictionalizing act.

Critical Postmodernism?

Certain stylistic features of the media texts I examine invariably draw comparisons to postmodernism. With all their apparent formal fragmentations and rhetorical diversities, refusals of narrative, and preoccupations with the power of the image—most especially Tajiri's—they may indeed even seem altogether exemplary. Yet rival critics also warn against the blanket authority of such definitions, at times pointing out how some (mostly white male) commentators bemoan, say, the postmodern disappearing act of history, ironically as racially oppressed communities are as much invested today as ever in history and in its recovery as a cultural resource. Hence, Paul Gilroy (1993, 42) challenges, Fredric Jameson "views post-modernism as 'the cultural dominant.' However, all the constitutive features of the post-modern that he identifies—the new depthlessness, the weakening of historicity, the waning of affect—are not merely absent from black expressive cultures but are explicitly contradicted by their repertoire of complete 'hermeneutic gestures.'"

The relationship of the works by Tajiri, Tanaka, and Yasui to postmodernism, however, may be even more complicated than that, as they are more or less caught up precisely with the "depthlessness," "weakening of historicity," and "waning of affect" that characterize, for Jameson, the dominant cultural climate in the overdeveloped countries. In other words, they all incorporate dominant cultural images, to the degree to which they implicate Japanese Americans, in order to comment on them. This much is obvious, as all three, in their own ways, offer rebuttals to the wartime hysteria that defined the racist representation of Japanese Americans in countless newsreels and photos and expose the mechanics of official image-making. Their shared posture in this respect might be called a critical postmodernism: They confirm the emergent reality that Jameson describes but, likewise, to critique rather than to celebrate the prevailing terms of postmodernism and to use postmodernism's own styles and "methods" to reinvestigate its eviction of the moral, political, and historical significance of the internment.[7]

Abé Mark Nornes (1993, 169–70) describes this deconstructive gesture in his review essay on *History and Memory*, insisting that "[Tajiri] argues that our conception of history—indeed our very memory—has become deeply dependent upon the image at the expense of those people excluded from the viewfinder." He further writes:

> One of the most spectacular sequences in the tape brings this point home by creating a montage of images that have mediated our historical conception of the attack on Pearl Harbor. . . . Unlike other parts of her tape, these disparate clips are edited together for a perfectly seamless reconstruction of the event, affording the shots the same one-to-one relationship to the historical event regardless of whether they are fictional or documentary (or Japanese or American) images. To encourage us to ponder the implications of these relationships, Tajiri superimposes the word "HISTORY" over the middle of the screen. [Ibid.]

Precisely—although one might wonder who the "we" ("us," "our") of these passages includes, and to what degree some viewers experience the force of these images in fundamentally different ways from others. Whereas the video itself articulates these images' unique and irrevocable consequences for Japanese Americans living in their legacy—when Tajiri says, "Our presence was our absence," *her* "we" does not include everyone—Nornes's non-specifying address only obscures them. Importantly, however, Nornes's essay offers the key that can get us out of this interpretive dilemma, even if it does not ultimately push this key toward its genuinely radical implications: "The centrifugal force of so many competing texts would threaten to fly into confusion, except, for all its heterogeneity, the tape still centers around a *germinal image*:

Tajiri's mother as a young woman splashing water on her face in a desert place (performed by the director herself)" (ibid., 168; emphasis added). Although for Nornes's analysis this "germinal image" figures paradoxically both as the absence and presence in his title, it also hints at the less obvious, but profoundly constitutive, force or activity of memory.

"Germinal Images"

In themselves, these memories represent sources of lasting pain across generations, referring back to brutal, even devastating experiences, in the family histories of the artists. Most immediately, each memory is first experienced by its subject as a sometimes dull, sometimes visceral, feeling of unknowing—as a psychical lack. Tellingly, each artist had created a "germinal image" that revises the not-known into something less disturbing, more edifying for its subject—an acceptable fiction that presides and covers over the black hole in memory—but that also invariably returns, slowly gnaws at its subject's psychical consistency, coherence, integrity. Note the simplicity and innocence of these images: for Rea Tajiri, the recurring image of her mother filling a canteen in the desert; for Lise Yasui, the enduring memory of her grandfather, Masuo, speaking long into the night during a family visit; and for Janice Tanaka, the "stabilizing" image of her uncle, the mediating figure between the memory of her mother and the haunting absence of her father.[8] In each case, something about the germinal image compels its beholder toward questions that critically revisit the family stories, their inconsistencies and omissions. Each artist's work therefore reconstructs and bears witness to her difficult adventure of recovery—an act simultaneously of discovery and invention.

Here is Tajiri's own account from the start of *History and Memory*. In the video, she speaks slowly, in clips, over the image she describes:

> *I don't know where this comes from*, but I just had this fragment, this picture that's always been in my mind. My mother, she's standing at a faucet and it's really hot outside. And she's filling this canteen and the water's really cold and it feels really good. And outside the sun's just so hot, it's just beating down. And there's this dust that gets in everywhere and they're always sweeping the floors [emphasis added].

The thirty-five minutes that follow take us through powerful sequences of still and moving images, and often reflective, autobiographical voiceovers. Where no images "exist" in history or appear on the screen, words move up blank screen-space, alternately meditating on the nature of images and verbally rendering a nonexistent image, often exercising the sort of creative license normally excluded from the rhetorical options available to documentary, but found everywhere in fiction and poetry. After one such description (starting "View from 100 feet above ground"), we read: "(*The spirit of my / grandfather witnesses / my father and mother as / they have an argument / about the unexplained / nightmares their / daughter has been having / on the 20th anniversary of / the bombing of / Pearl Harbor, the day that / changed the lives of 110,000 / Japanese-Americans. . . .)*" (italicized in original).

These words cast starkly onto the screen spar with, and stand in contrast to, the visualizations of official history everywhere and textually demonstrate Tajiri's assertion that "Our absence was our presence." They signify the metonymic "surface" war over historical representation by undermining the authority of the prevailing images that flow ceaselessly throughout the circuits of mass culture. But the making of the video is most crucially a journey for Tajiri, even a sort of pilgrimage, to find explanations for those uncanny nightmares that drew together a private family concern and a larger historical moment (the bombing of Pearl Harbor), and its associations with other half-recollections scattered throughout the text—all somehow vaguely spidering out from that germinal image. After retracing the places of her mother's detention, ending at the concentration camp at Poston, Arizona, Tajiri closes her video, speaking over the recurring image, *not* finally of her mother, of course—we now clearly see the kneeling figure's young face—but of the artist herself re-enacting the scene:

> My sister used to say how funny it was, when someone tells you a story, you create a picture of it in your mind. Sometimes the picture will return without the story. I've been carrying around this picture with me for years. It's the one memory I have of my mother speaking of camp while we grew up. I overhear her describing to my sister this simple action: her hands filling a canteen out in the middle of the desert. For years I've been living with this picture without the story, feeling a lot of pain, not knowing how they fit together. But now I've found I could connect the picture to the story. I could forgive my mother her loss of memory, and could make this image for her. [Tajiri 1991]

This conclusion enacts a profound reversal. The *video* image is actually not the germinal image—no longer is; never was—but is rather an image of closure, literally for the text and symbolically for Tajiri's own odyssey. It is the daughter's gift to her mother, a symbolic reconciliation that imaginatively restores the history of the internment to the narrative structure of personal memory and family history. The germinal image—the generative, starting-point image—was a mental picture visible only to her mind's eye, which she had been "carrying around . . . for years." It signified the psychical lack that inexorably drew in its subject's desire—"I don't know where this comes from," says Tajiri at the beginning of her video—a desire that then achieved imaginative expression and fulfillment through the self-willed retracing of her mother's forced journey, and through the making of the video, all through which she "could connect the picture to the story."

How does this process begin for Tajiri? Why does she begin to question in the first place? And how does this initial questioning become a personal quest? One of the video's most vivid images is a painted wooden bird Tajiri once came across among her mother's belongings. "No, no, no—grandma gave me that," she was told. "Put that back." An innocent enough childhood memory, except that several years later, while digging through some archives, she finds a photo of her grandmother in camp, in—what else?—a bird-carving class. This new fact stimulates old or forgotten suspicions, saturates with doubt everything she has learned: "I began searching for a history—my own history—because I had known all along that the stories I had heard were not true, and parts had been left out" (ibid.).

I remember having this feeling growing up, that I was haunted by something, that I was living within a family full of ghosts. There was this place that they knew about. I had never been there, yet I had a memory for it. I could remember a time of great sadness before I was born. We had been moved, uprooted; we had lived with a lot of pain. I had no idea where these memories came from; yet I knew the place [ibid.].

This extraordinary spoken passage follows the bird image; it is spoken over Tajiri's germinal image and trails into home-movie images of camp life at Topaz, Utah, that were surreptitiously taken by an inmate, Dave Tatsuno.[9] She begins searching for her own history and remembers haunting feelings—that her family knew a place, then that they "had lived with a lot of pain," then that she herself "knew the place." This hopscotching, imaginative will-to-power replicates across the topography of Tajiri's memory and beyond, the generative energy of that "compromise-formation" (its psychoanalytical name), the image of her mother filling the canteen. Where her radical doubt negates—the protective lies, denials, silence—her imagination props up disturbing ghost-images, stand-ins for the stories that "were not true," and the "parts [that] had been left out." Finally: "I began searching because I felt lost, ungrounded, somewhat like a ghost that floats over terrain, witnessing others living their lives and yet not having one of its own" (ibid.). Tajiri's quest across the landscape of her mother's detention was finally an act of self-recovery. By imaginatively restoring, through her image-gift, the unspoken history her mother sought to disavow, Tajiri releases them both by externalizing and rendering visible its defining power in video.

The Return of History?

In an essay rich with insights grounded in nearly two decades' worth of experience in media activism, the filmmaker Renee Tajima (1991, 24) levels this peculiar critique:

Japanese American filmmakers, in particular, seem stuck in reverse. Perhaps it is a function of catharsis, as the Nikkei assemble the various pieces of the story in order to release itself of the whole. . . . But by relegating Japanese American life to historical artifact, we are not confronting racism today; and we are failing to confront the tremendous changes in our own cultural identity.

Tajima's essay is arguably the best assessment to date of Asian American media in the post-Civil Rights era, yet the leap in logic here, from her speculative observations ("seem," "Perhaps") to her resolute response ("But"), seems to reproduce the "loss of historicity" that, Fredric Jameson (1984) argues, characterizes postmodernism. Contrary to Tajima's assumption, however—that the past is a dead letter that no longer exercises influence over the present—Tajiri's *History and Memory* (and in a different way, Tanaka's *Who's Going to Pay for These Donuts Anyway?*) illuminates how the effects of traumatic events can erupt—painfully, unpredictably—in the lives of those even a generation removed from its experience.

So history (or more precisely, historical violence) repeats itself not in the form of decisive, apocalyptic events so much as in the often undetectable return of the repressed in the routine patterns of daily life. This is, perhaps, the most basic lesson offered by the inquiry prompted by Rea Tajiri, Janice Tanaka, and Lise Yasui. In an era saturated by the postmodern obsession with nostalgia, resurrecting the salad days of an American innocence that never was, these media artists' video memories—radically generative, creative, and reflective—seek redemption not in the insufficient gestures of capitalist democracy (too little, too late), but in the renewed possibilities of critical, historical, and thereby collective consciousness.

Notes

Acknowledgments: My thanks to the Civil Liberties Public Education Fund for support in writing this piece, and to the editors, whose criticisms have greatly improved its clarity and coherence.

1. I refer to the fifty-seven–minute version of this film, which was produced in 1988 for the PBS series "The American Experience," and was subsequently nominated for an Academy Award for Best Short Subject. Funded by WGBH-TV, the Boston public station from which "The American Experience" originates, this version expands upon Lise Yasui's thirty-minute film, initially made for Temple University's program in film production. Prior to its national PBS broadcast, the shorter 1987 original had already won awards and critical acclaim on the festival circuit, including a Golden Globe at the San Francisco International Film Festival; a Golden Hugo in Chicago; and an invitation to the first international film festival ever held in Leningrad (Kessler 1993, 311–14).

2. I don't know of any writings that specifically examine this shifting relationship between rhetoric and protest in the post-Civil Rights era. This is simply my own observation. But to offer another example from the same period, the grass-roots Sanctuary movement in support of Central American refugees criticized U.S. presence and intervention in the region by appealing to American ideals of justice. Also, two notable left-liberal critiques of U.S. foreign policy published in the mid-1980s, the Food First Institute's *Betraying the National Interest* (Lappe, Moore, and Schurman 1987) and Jonathan Kwitny's *Endless Enemies* (1984), both argue that, by "betraying" American democratic principles, U.S. foreign relations were exacerbating economic instability and political conflict both globally and at home.

3. Roger Daniels' outstanding study, *Concentration Camps, North America* (1981), provides carefully researched, detailed accounts of in-camp resistance and military service (chap. 6) and of the court cases challenging the constitutionality of the internment (chap. 7). But in underscoring the more sobering, mundane reality of cooperation, Daniels also provides a more balanced view and context: "Without in any way minimizing the opposition among the evacuated people, it must be emphasized that the majority accepted, at least passively, almost all to which they were subjected" (ibid., 144). Published first in 1971, during the great Civil Rights struggles yet preceding the Redress and Reparations movement, his study further sheds light on the initially dominant, ameliorating view of the camp experience. However, prescient to my own concerns, it also illuminates the mostly attenuated, internalized conflict that is the internment's most painful, intimate, and enduring legacy: "Most of the existing literature about the camps stresses the cooperation and compliance of the inmates, thus perpetuating the basic line of both the WRA and the JACL. Like most successful myths, this one contains elements of truth. There was little spectacular, violent resistance; no desperate attempts to escape; even sustained

mass civil disobedience rarely occurred. But from the very beginning of their confinement, the evacuated people were in conflict, both with their keepers and with each other. These conflicts started even before the evacuation began, grew in the Assembly Centers, and were intensified in the concentration camps; *their effects are still felt in the contemporary Japanese American community* as the questioning and often angry members of the third, or Sansei, generation—many of whom began their lives behind barbed wire or in exile—question the relative compliance of most of their parents a quarter century ago" (ibid., 105–106; emphasis added).

4. Published twelve years after the end of the war—that is, before the passage of time could alleviate the hatred directed toward its subject or obliterate the wrecked community from its memory—John Okada's *No-No Boy* (1976; originally published 1957) powerfully captured the postwar trauma of the Japanese American community.

5. In his recent article on Janice Tanaka and Rea Tajiri, Robert M. Payne (1997, 67) observes: "The medium of video art arrives as especially well-suited to occupy a space at the intersection of documentary and the avant-garde. Video equipment's ease in portability and its reproduction of synchronous sound echo two hallmarks of *cinema verité*, making video a useful tool for the documentary. Meanwhile, video's ability to be operated by one individual and its low cost relative to film permit an intimacy of vision and directness of voice most closely-associated with the avant-garde."

6. King-Kok Cheung's *Articulate Silences* (1993) offers a more complex discussion of silence, concentrating on three writers, than I can provide here. While carefully showing the persistent efforts of Asian American literary expression to "break silences" imposed by the dominant culture, Cheung also insists on the important uses of silence in the works she considers—that is, their affirming poetic and political implications. For Cheung, in other words, silence is irreducible to its commonly defined status in much feminist and Asian American male criticism as an effect of oppression.

7. A lengthier commentary on postmodernism is not possible here. However, for the sake of comparison, one might briefly consider the neo-*noir* revival that has colonized the movie market in recent years, exemplified by the director Quentin Tarantino's retro style. His cinematic expressions of disco-era fashions and hairstyles, '50s-style diners, and pre-1980s pop music and cars do not simply make up the backdrop for the narrative action (itself likely mined and reassembled from prior genres). They have become visual objects in their own right. That is, they no longer serve to legitimize and authenticate the demands of narrative development. Rather, their stylistic attractiveness exists in and for itself, related to the storyline but not subordinate to it. So we find here the "ironic distance" characteristic of postmodernism, but rather than open critical scrutiny of the image, it functions to divorce style from content, to prop up the former as an autonomous object for symbolic consumption. Hence, no one cares whether Tarantino tells a good story; we care only that the film look good when it delivers the story. In resurrecting prior rhetorical devices, the Tarantino films drain the devices of their historical contexts and semantic values. "The past" exists for Tarantino not as a temporal fact or problematic but simply as a palette for cinematic styles in the perpetual present.

8. My discussion of Tajiri's image follows. For the sake of comparison, here are the disclosures by the other two artists. Lise Yasui (1988): "I had a favorite memory when I was young. My grandparents came to visit. My grandmother laughed a lot to herself and spoke to me in Japanese, as if I could understand. One evening I stayed up late, listening to my grandfather as he talked into the night. He seemed tired, and every now and then he'd look at me and smile. Later, I learned that my grandparents never made such a visit, that I never met my grandfather at all. The memory was one I'd made up, a creation drawn from all the stories I'd heard, and the images on my father's movie screen."

And Janice Tanaka (1992): "I felt like a ball rebounding between two canyons, my father and my uncle who, because of their non-presence, had become larger-than-life mythological figures. My father, whose name engendered such hurt and pain for my mother; and my uncle, who seemed to represent some kind of comfort for her—my uncle's image became the stabilizing factor in my own life."

9. Dave Tatsuno's *Topaz* (1996) is a home movie composed of footage taken illegally between 1942 and 1945, during the amateur filmmaker's incarceration at the Utah camp. It was one of the twenty-five titles added in 1997 to the National Film Registry of the Library of Congress. Following the famous Zapruder footage of President Kennedy's assassination, *Topaz* is only the second home movie to be selected for the registry, which now consists of more than two-hundred films.

Works Cited

Boyarin, Jonathan. 1992. "The Lower East Side: A Place of Forgetting." Pp. 1–8 in *Storm from Paradise: The Politics of Jewish Memory*. Minneapolis: University of Minnesota Press.

Chan, Sucheng. 1991. *Asian Americans: An Interpretive History*. Boston: Twayne.

Cheung, King-Kok. 1993. *Articulate Silences: Hisaye Yamamoto, Maxine Hong Kingston, Joy Kogawa*. Ithaca, N.Y.: Cornell University Press.

Daniels, Roger. 1981. *Concentration Camps, North America: Japanese in the United States and Canada During World War II*. Rev. ed. (originally published 1971). Malabar, Fla.: Robert E. Krieger.

Gilroy, Paul. 1993. "One Nation under a Groove." Pp. 19–48 in *Small Acts: Thoughts on the Politics of Black Cultures*. London: Serpent's Tail.

Gould, Janice. 1994. "Doves." P. 3 in *The Sound of Rattles and Clappers: A Collection of New California Indian Writing*, ed. Greg Sarris. Tucson: University of Arizona Press.

Hansen, Arthur A., and Betty E. Mitson, ed. 1974. *Voices Long Silent: An Oral Inquiry into the Japanese American Evacuation*. Fullerton: Japanese American Project, California State University, Fullerton.

Jameson, Fredric. 1984. "Postmodernism, or, the Cultural Logic of Late Capitalism." *New Left Review* 146 (July–August): 59–92.

Kessler, Lauren. 1993. *Stubborn Twig: Three Generations in the Life of a Japanese American Family*. New York: Random House.

Kwitny, Jonathan. 1984. *Endless Enemies: The Making of an Unfriendly World*. New York: Congdon & Weed.

Lappe, Frances Moore, Rachel Schurman, and Kevin Danaher. 1987. *Betraying the National Interest*. Food First Publication. New York: Grove.

Nornes, Abé Mark. 1993. "Our Presence Is Our Absence: *History and Memory*." *Asian America: Journal of Culture and the Arts* 2 (winter): 167–71.

Okada, John. 1976. *No-No Boy*. Originally published 1957. Seattle: University of Washington Press.

Payne, Robert M. 1997. "Visions of Silence: *History and Memory* and *Who's Going to Pay for These Donuts Anyway?*" *Jump Cut*, vol. 41, 67–76.

"Rite of Passage: The Commission Hearings 1981. Selected Testimonies from the Los Angeles and San Francisco Hearings." 1981. *Amerasia* 8, no. 2: 53–106.

Tajima, Renee. 1991. "Moving the Image: Asian American Independent Filmmaking 1970–1990." Pp. 10–33 in *Moving the Image: Independent Asian Pacific American Media Arts*, ed. Russell

Leong. Los Angeles: UCLA Asian American Studies Center, Visual Communications, Southern California Asian American Studies Central.

Takaki, Ronald. 1989. *Strangers from a Different Shore: A History of Asian Americans*. Boston: Little, Brown.

United States Commission on Wartime Relocation and Internment of Civilians. 1997. "Personal Justice Denied: Report of the Commission on Wartime Relocation and Internment of Civilians." Forward by Tetsuden Kashima. Seattle: University of Washington Press.

Xing, Jun. 1994. "Imagery, Counter-Memory, and the Re-visioning of Asian American History: Rea Tajiri's *History and Memory: For Akiko and Takashige*." Pp. 93–100 in *A Gathering of Voices on the Asian American Experience*, ed. Annette White-Parks, et al. Fort Atkinson, Wis.: Highsmith.

Films and Videos Cited

Ding, Loni. 1988. *The Color of Honor: The Japanese American Soldier in World War II*. NAATA.

Okazaki, Steven. 1988. *Days of Waiting: The Life and Art of Estelle Ishigo*. NAATA.

Schory, Katriel. 1985. *Yankee Samurai*. MPI Home Video.

Tajiri, Rea. 1991. *History and Memory: For Akiko and Takashige*. Electronic Arts Intermix.

Tanaka, Janice. 1989. *Memories from the Department of Amnesia*. NAATA.

———. 1992. *Who's Going to Pay for These Donuts Anyway?* NAATA.

Tatsuno, David. 1997. *Topaz*. No distributor.

Yasui, Lise. 1988. *A Family Gathering*. NAATA.

Elena Tajima Creef

9   The Gendering of Historical Trauma
in Internment-Camp Documentary:
The Case of Steven Okazaki's
Days of Waiting

Over the past fifty years, only four Hollywood films have represented the World War
II Japanese American experience. *Go for Broke* (Pirosh 1951), unique for its politically
progressive and sympathetic wartime portrayal of the all-Nisei 442nd regimental
combat team, pivots on the racial ambivalence of a white commanding officer, played
by Van Johnson, and the heroism of Japanese American soldiers.[1] *Bad Day at Black Rock*
(Sturges 1954), another liberal postwar film, features Spencer Tracy as an insurance
agent who investigates the case of a Japanese American killed by vigilantes just after
the bombing of Pearl Harbor. Although explicit references are made to Japanese Americans during World War II, this MGM studio film is centrally concerned with representing white racism. (Indeed, in her documentary *History and Memory* [1991], the
director Rea Tajiri cleverly reworks Tracy's search for the missing Japanese American
as an extended metaphor for the missing histories of Japanese Americans during the
war.) *Hell to Eternity* (Karlson 1960) was the first Hollywood film to include actual
scenes of Japanese American relocation and internment, but it is primarily focused
on a heroic white character. Guy, who had been adopted and raised by a Japanese
American family, is an adult when Japan bombs Pearl Harbor. Enraged by the internment of Japanese Americans, he joins the army and eventually uses his Japanese-lan-
guage skills to persuade the Japanese civilians and military on an isolated island to
surrender.[2] *Come See the Paradise* (Parker 1990)—only the second Hollywood film to
deal explicitly with the Japanese American experience of relocation and internment—
impressively portrays the details of life in the camps. But the film amounts to little
more than a deft manipulation of internment history as a photogenic backdrop for
an interracial romance between Japanese American Lily and her husband, Jack, a left-

ist, Irish American labor-union activist who attempts a heroic, but ultimately impotent, intervention to save his wife and family behind barbed wire.[3]

What is it about this chapter in American history that has been off-limits or deemed uninteresting for Hollywood representation? Why do the few films that deal with the subject—films crafted by white directors—suggest that Asian American history has little relevance for white spectators unless liberal white male heroes are central players in the script?[4]

In dramatic contrast, the history of the camps has been one of the most obsessively told stories in contemporary independent Asian American filmmaking over the past two decades. Among these filmmakers, its representation continues to be explored at the individual and collective levels of experience.[5]

One could argue that the silence surrounding the Japanese American internment experience was officially broken only during the powerful public testimonials of internees before the Commission on Wartime Relocation in 1981–82. Yet in many ways, individual and collective secrecy about the camps has continued to dominate its filmic representation through the 1990s. The playwright Philip Kan Gotanda (1990, 30) speaks to the profound nature of collective silence among internees and to its lasting impact on the Japanese American community: "Even though I wasn't born in Camp and we didn't talk about it much, it's still a very big part of my life. Whether you speak about the Camps or don't speak about them, the experience is passed on generationally. . . . It's a psychic scar, almost like an abused-child syndrome."

Jeanne Wakatsuki Houston echoes this observation when asked why she waited some thirty years to break silence in her autobiographical record of the internment, *Farewell to Manzanar* (1973). Before she recovered the memories (with the help of her husband and co-author, James Houston), she says, she had repressed her family's three-and-a-half years at camp "as if they were a dream" (Houston 1993). Houston claims that among internees, the internment experience operates much the same way that post-traumatic shock syndrome does in Vietnam veterans. She recalls that, during the public hearings she attended for reparation and redress, virtually every man and woman who stood up to give testimony about the war years cried on the stand. For many, the hearings signaled the first occasion in which they could finally speak about their experiences. In her poem "Thirty Years Under," Mitsuye Yamada (1992, 32) also writes that she was unable to confront her own memories regarding internment until several decades after the fact:

I had packed up
my wounds in a cast
iron box
sealed it
labeled it
do not open . . .
ever
and traveled blind
for thirty years.

The psychic trauma of camp memory crosses gender lines. Indeed, a worthwhile project might be to map the different ways that the stigma of silence and shame have shaped representations of men's and women's experiences in the camps.[6] Although a full exploration is beyond the scope of this discussion, I remain fascinated with a pattern of representation that can be identified in many contemporary Asian American works about the relocation and internment in which the female body is constructed as a site that mirrors the complex process of the dislocation of home, family, and identity.

The short story "The Legend of Miss Sasagawara" in Hisaye Yamamoto's *Seventeen Syllables* (1988) chronicles the title character's mental collapse in the camps. Deemed an eccentric artist, Miss Sasagawara crosses the boundary from respectable eccentricity to sexual deviancy under conditions of relocation and internment. She is then removed from the camps, disciplined, punished, and eventually returned, only to descend into madness. Joy Kogawa's *Obasan* (1982), a novel about Japanese Canadian relocation, also charts the complex, interlocking narratives of the historical trauma of forced removal combined with psychic and even sexual abuse, numbing two generations of women—the title character and the novel's primary narrator, Naomi Nakane—into silence and emotional repression. The poetry anthologies *Shedding Silence* (Mirikitani 1987) and *Camp Notes* (Yamada 1992) also record the traumatic legacy of the internment experience for the female body. Indeed, Mirikitani's poem "Breaking Silence" (much of it taken verbatim from her mother's congressional testimonial record) stands as one of the most powerful reclamations of Asian American women's "voice" in contemporary Asian American poetry.

Likewise, many independent Asian American films that deal with the history of the camps explore the effects of psychic and historical trauma and repressed memory on women's bodies. In the short experimental film *Memories from the Department of Amnesia* (Tanaka 1991), the filmmaker represents her mother's life as a series of emotional and physical abuses, abandonments, dislocations, mental breakdowns, diseases, and disavowals that are acted out on her body through the official dispossession of her home and property, her internment at Manzanar, the dissolution of her marriage to a spouse who is officially declared insane, her subsequent passing as "Chinese" as a mode of survival, and finally her painful rejection by her own mother. Although this film centers not on the camps but on Tanaka's process of grieving, it is noteworthy for the way that she stitches the events from her mother's war years into a broader narrative about being an alienated female subject of history.

The voiceover in *Memories from the Department of Amnesia* consists of shared family memories and stories that have been passed down through three generations of women—much like the scenes of remembering in *Mitsuye and Nellie* (Light and Saraf 1981). Among other things, this film dramatically stages what Gotanda (1990, 30) refers to as the intergenerational fall-out of Asian American silence. In one of the film's most moving moments, the poet Mitsuye Yamada's teenage daughter, Heddy, voices how her mother's years of "protective silence" backfired on the children:

For me, I always felt like I'm so young that nothing like that could ever happen to me. I guess I felt sheltered. . . . It was a shock to me when I found out [that Mitsuye] was protecting us from something I didn't even know was there. When I was going to school with the other kids—who were all Caucasian—I really had no awareness that I was Japanese. And a little bit later, there was a Korean girl in the class, and I felt embarrassed when I saw her and acknowledged that she was different. And then I realized that I was different, too. I saw her in a different way than I saw everyone else, and now that bothers me.

For Heddy, cut off from the knowledge of her family's history in the camps, historical erasure and protective silence beget symbolic racial erasure and a sense of shame when her own racial difference is mirrored uncomfortably in the body of an Asian classmate.[7]

History and Memory (Tajiri 1991) also draws on powerful autobiographical and archival materials in its treatment of the Japanese American internment experience. This film examines and critiques the gaps between official and mainstream Hollywood representations of the internment and the Tajiri family's partial recollection of it. Indeed, some of the most powerful moments in the film occur as Tajiri screens official wartime footage of the camps while recording her mother's response on film. In these scenes, the jarring disjunctions between an official historical record and fragmented personal recollection suggest that her mother may have forgotten many of the details of camp life, or that the official wartime records fail to reflect accurately the individual experience. Tajiri records her mother's struggle to recall the lost details from her experience in the camps while viewing "official" footage of scenes she does not remember: "What's this? Canteen? They didn't have a canteen in Salinas Assembly Center.... They had one in Poston. I don't remember this. My goodness, I don't remember this."

By weaving together Hollywood film clips and archival footage from the camps, Tajiri also highlights the gap between the representation of the camps and the more "photogenic" bombing of Pearl Harbor as recorded and reconstructed in popular American culture and historical consciousness. The facts that so much original film exists of the attack on Pearl Harbor, and so many more Hollywood films have been devoted to re-creating the events surrounding December 7, 1941, attest to the visual power of re-membering this history.[8] Tajiri frames her treatment of the disparity in the historical representation of these wartime subjects by foregrounding in *History and Memory* the spectacular power and nature of Hollywood films. These independent films not only define, but also make clear, just who is allowed to be a central subject for Hollywood's selective historical memory and who traditionally stands outside such representations as spectator and subject.

The Story of a White Woman in the Camps

One independent Asian American film, however, explores internment-camp history from the privileged position of white spectatorship. The Academy Award-winning documentary *Days of Waiting* (Okazaki 1988) narrates the history of the relocation and internment through the perspective of a white participant and observer—but with results that are radically different from those in Hollywood films. Okazaki breaks new ground with his representation of a white woman in the camps who undergoes a profound symbolic metamorphosis that is also bound up in a complex narrative of race, class, and gender subjugation.

Like other interracial spouses unwilling to break up their families, the artist Estelle Peck Ishigo followed her husband, Arthur Shigeharu Ishigo, into relocation.[9] While interned at the Heart Mountain War Relocation Camp in Wyoming, Ishigo made hundreds of sketches and watercolor paintings and composed the text for her book *Lone Heart Mountain*, which depicts scenes from the years that she and her husband spent in the camps. In contrast to other artistic portrayals of life in the camps, Ishigo's sketches and paintings of extreme weather conditions and her ghostly portraits of what she calls "shabby, shivering people" with patches on their clothes are among the most haunting images of life behind barbed wire during the war years (Ishigo 1972, 33). Because all cameras and recording devices were initially banned inside the relocation centers and camps, Ishigo—like many other interned artists—devoted her time to documenting the details of everyday life in paintings and sketches in order to give testimony through the power of the image.

In the opening pages of *Lone Heart Mountain*, Ishigo identifies herself as a white woman of European ancestry who sought official permission to remain with her Japanese American husband during evacuation and relocation. There are, curiously, no sketched self-representations of her anywhere in this text.[10] Instead, the initial autobiographical account of her life in the camps quickly turns into a meticulous visual record of the physical and spiritual processes of uprooting, relocation, exile, and degeneration of an entire ethnic community within which she quietly aligns herself yet all but disappears from view.[11]

In contrast to the autobiographical record, Okazaki inserts Ishigo visually into the historic picture in *Days of Waiting*. He is even more explicit about her symbolic self-erasure as a white woman and her subsequent "racial" transformation within this exiled community of color. The film is narrated in epistolary form from Ishigo's perspective and bears witness to the personal and collective effects of relocation, as well as to the postwar diaspora that the Japanese American community experienced.

Like other camp documentaries, *Days of Waiting* begins and ends with a series of shots that focus on derelict, abandoned camp buildings, toppled guard towers, desert landscapes, and the ever-present tumbled lines of barbed wire.[12] The visual gesture of returning to the ruined landscape of former relocation centers—or what I would call the culture of camp ruins—operates as a metaphor for buried Asian American history, suggesting a kind of archeology of memory in which the filmmaker digs up remnants of the past in order to render visible and give voice to camp histories that have otherwise been erased or silenced in collective American consciousness. (Films such as *Mitsuye and Nellie, History and Memory, Farewell to Manzanar,* and *Manzanar* [Nakamura 1971] also use the recurrent image of camp ruins as a trope that suggests the unearthing of historical memory and the breaking of silence).

In *Days of Waiting*, Ishigo's stark narrative—much of it gleaned directly from the pages of her *Lone Heart Mountain*—is told against sepia-toned archival footage of evacuation and relocation and against her family photographs, sketches, and paint-

PHOTO 9.1.   From *Days of Waiting* (1989), dir. Steven Okazaki. Photo: Mouchette Films. Courtesy of National Asian American Telecommunications Association (NAATA).

ings. Compared with the visual record of internee productivity and adaptability in Ansel Adams and Toyo Miyatake's famous camp photographs (Adams and Miyatake 1978), or with the "success stories" of autobiographical camp narratives such as Monica Sone's *Nisei Daughter* (1953), Daniel Okimoto's *American in Disguise* (1970), or even with Jack Matsuoka's cartoons in *Camp II, Block 211, Lone Heart Mountain* and *Days of Waiting* document the dark sides of daily life in the camps:

> We lived less than twenty-five miles from home but it felt like we were in a foreign land. We lived in horse stalls, and cheap shacks, surrounded by barbed wire and machine gun towers. Each day we stood in great long lines to get food. Once inside we ate hastily to

make way for the others hungrily peering in. There was rarely enough to eat. Later, we found out that our meat supplies were being diverted from us and sold outside of camp. [Okazaki 1989]

Both Ishigo and Okazaki include scenes that touch on political and social problems that occurred within the assembly centers and camps, such as job blacklisting and news censorship, corruption within the War Relocation Authority itself (in the wartime black-market sales of camp supplies), the break-up of the traditional Japanese structures of family and home life, youth gangs and unwanted pregnancies, depression, suicide, and even the harsh descent into poverty and homelessness that many of the internees faced in their postwar dispersal.

Yet what is perhaps most compelling in *Days of Waiting* is Okazaki's deft handling of Ishigo's gradual process of stepping into a symbolic Japanese American subject position, allowing "us" to see and feel through her eyes and her experience. From the beginning of the film, Okazaki is careful to mark Ishigo as a white woman who is unwanted, outcast, abused, and silenced, and who eventually learns to take refuge in a socially transgressive "outsider" identity within a community of color. The film documents her movement from runaway to street adventurer and, ultimately, to disowned daughter who falls in love and intermarries during a time when "it was against the law for a Caucasian woman to marry a non-Caucasian man in California" (ibid.). Further, in this film, the process of "othering" is specific to gender, as Ishigo's body is repeatedly marked as a site of marginalization, abuse, and exile:

My parents had not wanted children. They were too old and too busy to take care of a child. I guess I was a mistake. When I was 12, we moved to LA, and my parents sent me to live with a procession of relatives and strangers. It was an unhappy time. I was raped by one of my guardians, who threatened to put me into an institution if I told. Back then, people who caused trouble were put away. After high school I ran away from home. I roamed the streets alone looking for adventure. [Ibid.]

By "othering" this white woman in the camps, Okazaki avoids merely "othering" Japanese American camp history and experience for a white American audience. The process is gradual, beginning with Ishigo's marginalization from her family and from the white community and followed by her first experience of racist discrimination when she loses her job at the Hollywood Art Center after the bombing of Pearl Harbor because of her Japanese name. In her choice to align herself with her Japanese American husband, Ishigo undergoes a psychological and linguistic transformation of consciousness as she moves from an individual to a collective subject position:

Arthur and I were faced with the choice of separating or going into camps together. I could not desert him. I wanted to stay with him. No matter what happened, no matter where we were sent. We'd been married for thirteen years. Neither of us had ever felt a racial barrier and now society was trying to create one. It seemed like a foul musty thing dug up from the dark ages. . . . *We* were American citizens, but *we* were treated as though *we* were the enemy. [Ibid.; emphasis added]

Two-thirds of the way into Okazaki's film, the process of Ishigo's symbolic racial transformation is completed as she crosses the color line, renouncing "whiteness" as

a constructed category for race hatred, domination, and power, and steps symbolically into a "Japanese American" subject position:

> Strange as it may sound, in this lonely, desolate place, I felt accepted for the first time in
> my life. The government had declared me a Japanese. And now I no longer saw myself
> as white—as a *hakujin*. I was a *nihonjin*—a Japanese American. My fellow Heart Moun-
> tain residents took me in as one of their own. We all shared the same pain, the same joys,
> the same hopes, and desires, and I never encountered a single act of prejudice or dis-
> crimination. [Ibid.]

While Ishigo articulates her symbolic transformation from *hakujin* to *nihonjin*, Okazaki makes clear that this is a political rather than a literal shift in consciousness. His
choice of photographs and paintings clearly marks Ishigo as the conspicuous *"hakujin* with white hair" who is standing or sitting in the company and community of her
fellow internees. Yet the trauma of relocation and internment does not end when Ishigo and her husband are released from the camps. The film implies that the couple's
descent into poverty, and Arthur Ishigo's premature death from cancer, are the logical trajectories of the world war and postwar damage to which the couple, like so
many others, has been subjected.

Days of Waiting ends with at least two gestures of discovery and recuperation in
which the white female body dramatically stands as a sign of the historically damaged and repressed. We learn that in 1972—fifteen years after the death of her husband and twenty-seven years after she "had long ago given up hope that [their] story
would every be told" (ibid.)—Ishigo's artwork and manuscript were included by the
California Historical Society in the first show devoted entirely to remembering the
internment through the eyes of camp artists. Although Ishigo's work was discovered,
Okazaki makes clear that her body was not discovered—let alone retrieved—until
some ten years later, in 1983, when a group of former Heart Mountain internees
tracked her down "in a run down basement apartment in Los Angeles where she was
living on five dollars a week for food and had lost both her legs from gangrene [ibid.]."
Ishigo's body seems to echo the visual rhetoric of camp ruins, which are similarly
marked by the passage of time, abandonment, and neglect.[13] If we consider that the
film closes with a shot of the "real" Estelle—elderly and disabled in a convalescent
home, her gaze directed off-camera—we can argue that the story of this particular
white woman is both "rescued" and recuperated: It is brought from the margins of
history to its center and given "voice" by Okazaki's crew of Asian American filmmakers, who remind us that the history of Japanese American internment is also a
crucial chapter in white American history.[14]

Notes

1. *Go for Broke* is unique for its all-Japanese American casting of the Nisei soldiers and for
its careful distinction between the Japanese Americans on the mainland ("kotonks") and those
from Hawaii ("Buddhaheads"). While heroic, loyal Japanese Americans are represented here,
there is no mention of that most tabooed of Asian American wartime subjects, the "No No

Boys"—those Nisei males who anwered "no" to both Questions 27 and 28 on the "loyalty oaths" given to all internees. Question 27 asked draft-age males, "Are you willing to serve in the armed forces of the United States on combat duty, wherever ordered?" Question 28 asked all internees: "Will you swear unqualified allegiance to the United States of America and faithfully defend the United States from any or all attack by foreign or domestic forces, and forswear any form of allegiance or obedience to the Japanese emperor, or any other foreign government, power or organization?"

2. I am indebted to Darrell Hamamoto, who brought this film to my attention.

3. It should be noted that this film appeared briefly at the box office just as the Persian Gulf War began. Perhaps as a result of this poor timing, this film (critical as it was of U.S. wartime policy) lasted for only a few weeks before it was pulled from the theaters and rushed to video. For an excellent discussion of the race and gender politics in *Come See the Paradise*, see Kang (1993).

4. I find it interesting that in Deborah Gee's *Slaying the Dragon* (1988), John Korty, the director of the made-for-TV movie *Farewell to Manzanar* (1976), which is based on Jeanne Wakatsuki Houston's book of the same title (1973), mentions that the film was almost remade from the point of view of a white person. Korty points out, with irony, that this concept was initially touted by "one of the highest-ranking African American producers" in Hollywood, who was afraid that no one would relate to the story unless it was restructured along such white-centric lines. This is precisely the kind of narrative framing that seems to have appealed to Parker fifteen years later.

5. Some of the most notable independent films on this subject are *Manzanar* (Nakamura 1971), *Wataridori: Birds of Passage* (Nakamura 1976), *Conversations: Before the War/After the War* (Nakamura 1986), *Mitsuye and Nellie: Asian American Poets* (Light and Saraf 1981), *The Displaced View* (Onodera 1988), *Unfinished Business* (Okazaki 1984), *Days of Waiting* (Okazaki 1988), *The Color of Honor* (Ding 1988), *A Family Gathering* (Yasui 1988), *History and Memory* (Tajiri 1991), and *Who's Going to Pay for These Donuts Anyway?* (Tanaka 1992). Because it is Asian American in subject matter rather than directorial positioning, *Mitsuye and Nellie* also raises a question about the boundaries that constitute Asian American cinema.

6. In counterpoint to the heroic portraits of Japanese American internees by the photographer Ansel Adams, Dorothea Lange's War Relocation Authority black-and-white documentary work on Japanese American men and women as tragic subjects of relocation and internment come to mind. Likewise, the outstanding documentary *Who's Going to Pay for These Donuts Anyway?* (Tanaka 1992) bears closer examination because of the way that the filmmaker frames her own father as a moving case study of the brutalizing effects of relocation, internment, and imprisonment on the male body and psyche. The film tracks Tanaka's search for her father, who has not been seen by the family since the years just after the internment and is finally discovered in 1989 in a Los Angeles half-way house for the mentally ill. As an angry and politically outspoken young man in the camps, her father was beaten by the FBI, declared mentally ill, and institutionalized for more than a decade. The years of electro-shock, drug therapy, and trauma leave Tanaka's father painfully oscillating on screen between moments of extreme memory loss and lucid recollection.

7. A fascinating gendered discourse surrounds silence and speech in Asian American literature. For the deepest analysis of this topic, see Cheung (1993).

8. I actually question whether more film footage documenting the attack on Pearl Harbor exists than that documenting the relocation and internment of Japanese Americans (which can be found in the National Archives' collections). My guess is that because the events surrounding Pearl Harbor are given more weight, the archival footage is simply much more visible.

Internment, by contrast, is less photogenic in the official historical record. Indeed, the news coverage of the fifty-year anniversaries of the bombing of Pearl Harbor and the signing of Executive Order 9066 in 1991 and 1992, respectively, made these differences all too clear. A comparative media analysis is worthy of much more complete treatment than I can possibly provide here.

9. Although Ishigo mentions in her autobiography that many white people lived with their Japanese spouses in the camp at Heart Mountain, Wyoming, I am not aware of any one study that tabulates the numbers of Caucasians and other non-Japanese Americans who refused separation from their Japanese and Japanese American family members and were held in the camps. Yoneda (1983) and Houston (1973) include some discussion of this topic.

10. I place *Lone Heart Mountain* in the unique genre of visual autobiographies of the internment-camp experience. The very best in this category is Mine Okubo's *Citizen 13660* (1946). Other notable visual collections are Jack Matsuoka's *Camp II, Block 211* (1974) and Deborah Gesensway and Mindy Roseman's *Beyond Words: Images from America's Concentration Camps* (1987), which features outstanding selections of the work of camp artists together with oral histories.

11. Although Ishigo notes that there were a number of "blond, brown, and red-haired" internees in the camps, her black-and-white pencil and charcoal sketches depict only Japanese and Japanese American subjects. Her portraits are stark and lack the detail of individual faces, as if to signify the personal effects of relocation on a more abstract Japanese American community.

12. I am indebted to Glen Mimura for the insightful comment that the desert needs to be re-territorialized for its crucial role in Asian American history, because Asian American subjects have been erased from historical representations of the American West.

13. Although my discussion has focused on the representation of Estelle Ishigo, Okazaki also briefly depicts the body of Arthur Ishigo as another figure bearing the trace of historical trauma. In particular, the final scenes of the film record the dramatic physical transformation that occurs as Arthur Ishigo ages perceptibly in the camps while working as a full-time laborer. In Okazaki's narrative, Estelle Ishigo recalls that, when they "were first interned, [Arthur] was strong and alive." Yet, in "three-and-a-half years, he seemed to have aged twenty years. He grew morose and sentimental. In the evening he would sit quietly or play his bamboo flute, reminiscing and dreaming of what might have been" (Okazaki 1989). It is interesting that the final shot of *Days of Waiting* visually reverses the movement of Estelle and Arthur Ishigo's physical decline by returning to close-up images of the couple as children unmarked by hardship, loss, and trauma.

14. In my experience teaching *Days of Waiting* to undergraduates, I have noticed that this film triggers more reactions than any of the other independent films about relocation and internment. Occasionally, Asian American students have expressed outrage over what they initially perceive to be unexamined whiteness at the center of this film about Asian American history. Likewise, I have noticed that many white students find themselves deeply touched by Ishigo's story and deeply troubled by their own symbolic shift from mere spectators of internment history to participants in it through the spectacle of this white woman in the camps. The disparity in students' response raises complicated questions about the politics of racial representation and ownership of the historical gaze. To whom do historical representations of the internment-camp experience "belong"? *Days of Waiting,* after all, reminds us that individuals with as little as one-sixteenth Japanese blood were subjected to relocation and internment.

Works Cited

Cheung, King-Kok. 1993. *Articulate Silences: Hisaye Yamamoto, Maxine Hong Kingston, Joy Kogawa.* Ithaca, N.Y.: Cornell University Press.

Gesensway, Deborah and Mindy Roseman. 1987. *Beyond Words: Images from America's Concentration Camps.* Ithaca, N.Y.: Cornell University Press.

Gotanda, Philip Kan. 1990: "The Wash." Pp. 30–73 in *Between Worlds: Contemporary Asian-American Plays,* ed. Misha Berson. New York: Theatre Communications Group.

Houston, Jeanne Wakatsuki. 1993. "Remembering the Internment Camps." Lecture delivered at University of California, Santa Cruz, January 28.

———. 1973. *Farewell to Manzanar.* Boston: Houghton Mifflin.

Adams, Ansel, and Toyo Miyatake. 1978. *Two Views of Manzanar.* Los Angeles: Frederick S. Wight Art Gallery.

Ishigo, Estelle Peck. 1972. *Lone Heart Mountain.* Los Angeles: Anderson, Ritchie and Simon.

Kang, Hyun Yi. 1993. "The Desiring of Asian Female Bodies: Interracial Romance and Cinematic Subjection." *Visual Anthropology Review* 9, no. 1 (spring): 5–21.

Kogawa, Joy. 1982. *Obasan.* Boston: D. R. Godine.

Matsuoka, Jack. 1974. *Camp II, Block 211.* San Francisco: Japan Publications.

Mirikitani, Janice. 1987. *Shedding Silence.* Berkeley, Calif.: Celestial Arts.

Okimoto, Daniel I. 1970. *American in Disguise.* New York: Walker and Weatherhill.

Okubo, Mine. 1946. *Citizen 13660.* New York: Columbia University Press.

Sone, Monica. 1953. *Nisei Daughter.* Boston: Little, Brown.

Yamada, Mitsuye. 1992. *Camp Notes and Other Poems.* Latham, New York: Kitchen Table: Women of Color Press.

Yamamoto, Hisaye. 1988. *Seventeen Syllables and Other Stories.* Latham, New York: Kitchen Table: Women of Color Press.

Yoneda, Karl. 1983. *Ganbatte: Sixty-Year Struggle of a Kibei Worker.* Los Angeles: Resource Development and Publications, Asian American Studies Center, UCLA.

Films and Videos Cited

Ding, Loni. 1988. *The Color of Honor: The Japanese American Soldier in World War II.* NAATA.

Gee, Deborah. 1988. *Slaying the Dragon.* Women Make Movies.

Karlson, Phil. 1960. *Hell to Eternity.* CBS/Fox Video.

Korty, John. 1976. *Farewell to Manzanar.* Made-for-television movie.

Light, Allie, and Irving Saraf. 1981. *Mitsuye and Nellie: Asian American Poets.* Women Make Movies.

Nakamura, Robert. 1971. *Manzanar.* Visual Communications.

———. 1976. *Wataridori: Birds of Passage.* NAATA.

———. 1986. *Conversations: Before the War/After the War.* NAATA.

Okazaki, Steven. 1984. *Unfinished Business.* NAATA.

———. 1988. *Days of Waiting: The Life and Art of Estelle Ishigo.* NAATA.

Onodera, Midi. 1988. *The Displaced View.* Women Make Movies.

Parker, Alan. 1990. *Come See the Paradise.* CBS/Fox Video.

Pirosh, Robert. 1951. *Go for Broke.* Video Yesteryear.

Sturges, John. 1955. *Bad Day at Black Rock.* MGM/UA.

Tajiri, Rea. 1991. *History and Memory: For Akiko and Takashige.* Women Make Movies.

Tanaka, Janice. 1991. *Memories from the Department of Amnesia.* NAATA.

———. 1992. *Who's Going to Pay for These Donuts Anyway?* NAATA.

Yasui, Lise. 1988. *A Family Gathering.* NAATA.

Part IV

Exploring Form

Valerie Soe

---

10   Fighting Fire with Fire:
      Detournement, Activism,
      and Video Art

As someone who grew up with the activism and idealism of the 1960s and 1970s, but who came of age during the 1980s' "me generation" and the lowered expectations of the 1990s, I have seen direct political action wane among my peers. Confusion, conservatism, and ennui have replaced the sweeping social movements of thirty years ago, while electronic media's role in shaping popular mores has increased rapidly. More than ever, this country's values and opinions are drawn from mass media—television, advertising, and film.

Because of this shift in emphasis from direct action to mediated opinion-making, I feel that effective cultural change can be made through creative work in electronic media. As an artist and cultural worker, I attempt to critique and recontextualize popular culture and cultural assumptions. My work deals with issues found in a society in transition from a predominantly white European culture to one whose growing Latino and Asian populations affect and influence everything, from the food we eat and the music we listen to and the way we view the rest of the world. I am trying to create an alternative voice, one that has resonance, significance, and meaning for the culture existing outside the mainstream.

One strategy I have repeatedly employed in my work is the Situationist International's (SI) technique of *detournement*, in which all pop culture is fodder for recontextualized politicization. The SI, a radical cultural organization that was active in the May 1968 student demonstrations in France, espoused the recycling of pop-culture images for political ends. In their seminal essay "Methods of *Detournement*," the Situationists Guy Debord and Gil Wolman (1981, 9) proclaimed, "The literary and artistic heritage of humanity should be used for partisan propaganda purposes.... It goes without saying that one is not limited to correcting a work or to integrating diverse fragments of out-of-date works into a new one; one can also alter the meaning of those fragments in any appropriate way." By starting with images and methods from mainstream artistic sources and turning them around, *detournement* alters and revises the meaning and intent of even the most disposable popular culture.

This strategy became especially popular among artists and activists working in the United States in the late 1980s and into the 1990s. During those years, the Reagan and Bush administrations worked to undermine the progressive gains of the 1960s and 70s by restructuring the national economy by deregulating the financial and communications industries, dismantling funding for public education and the arts, and attacking social programs. The Reagan administration also learned to manipulate and outmaneuver dissenting voices by replacing the press conference with the photo op and by perfecting the art of "spin control," embedding the government's reading of events into all reportage.

At the same time, the administration effectively suppressed direct political action by conducting covert military activities in Central America. These furtive activities were acknowledged by the mainstream media only *post facto*, a strategy that fragmented or discounted organized opposition until after the damage has been done. Despite protests and lobbying by organizations such as the Committee in Solidarity with the People of El Salvador (CISPES), the media's willful ignorance of the war in Central America short-circuited widespread popular opposition to the conflict.

These deceptive tactics were most clearly demonstrated during the 1991 Persian Gulf War, during which mainstream media outlets such as CNN and the networks colluded, malevolently or not, with the U.S. State Department to ignore and thus stifle dissenting voices against the war. The media observer and analyst Norman Soloman (1992, 98) writes:

> One front-page pie chart, depicting the results of a New York Times/CBS News Poll, proclaimed that seventy-nine percent of the U.S. public wanted to "continue the bombing from the air" while eleven percent wanted "to start a ground war." People who did not favor either activity were reduced to nonexistence; the poll listed the remaining ten percent as "don't know" or "no answer." As outrageous as they were routine, such methods for discounting and discouraging antiwar views caused deep alarm among peace activists.

This deep alarm prompted activists and cultural workers to develop new means of dissent that exploit the influence and power of mass media and advertising. The visual artists Barbara Kruger and Adrian Piper challenged structures of power through their altered advertising and anthropological images. Film and videomakers such as Craig Baldwin (*Tribulation 99*, 1990), Greta Snider (*No-Zone*, 1993), and Phil Patiris (*The Iraq Campaign*, 1993) devised strategies of resistance that included *detournement* and recontextualization, using existing images from pop culture to critique political and social structures.

Asian American media artists have also taken to *detournement* as a creative strategy. Spencer Nakasako's *Do It on the Oriental* (1990) uses found footage exclusively for its succinct and scathing indictment of portrayals of Asians in Hollywood filmmaking. In this short compilation, Nakasako recontextualizes and removes from their original narrative structure stereotypical portrayals, such as early images of Anna May Wong's "dragon lady" roles in *Shanghai Express* (von Sternberg 1932) and *The Thief of*

Bagdad (Walsh 1940), World War II representations of evil Japanese soldiers in *The Good Earth* (Franklin 1937), and Gedde Watanabe's clownish Japanese caricature in John Hughes's *Sixteen Candles* (1984). He also uses the soundtrack to comment effectively on the imagery, juxtaposing American pop-music recordings such as Wanda Jackson's *Fujiyama Mama* (*I been to Nagasaki / Hiroshima, too / And what I did to them / baby, I can do to you*) and Carl Douglas's *Kung Fu Fighting* (*There were funky Chinamen / in funky Chinatown*) with equally inflammatory film clips of Asians as merciless killers and vampish prostitutes.

Nakasako wryly critiques misrepresentations of Asians and Asian Americans throughout U.S. pop-culture history by isolating and re-presenting these inaccurate images. Through rapid-fire re-editing and recontextualization, Nakasako uses ignorant and damaging images to comment on dominant culture's pathetic track record of sensitivity toward Asians.

Rea Tajiri's *History and Memory: For Akiko and Takashige* (1992) also uses appropriated images from Hollywood films, including *From Here To Eternity* (Zinnemann 1953) and *Bad Day At Black Rock* (Sturges 1955), as well as archival newsreel and educational-film footage. Tajiri juxtaposes clips from *From Here to Eternity* with newsreel footage to underline the similarities between factual and fictional representations of the bombing of Pearl Harbor. This allows Tajiri to point out the various means by which U.S. media shaped perceptions of the Japanese empire.

Tajiri suggests that Hollywood films with a more liberal bent can be just as unsuccessful in representing Asian characters by including clips from *Bad Day at Black Rock.* She critiques the film, which is an indictment of racism against Kimoko, a Japanese American character, by pointing out that Kimoko himself is never seen in the film. As Tajiri notes in her voiceover, "He never appears—not even a picture or a photograph" (Tajiri 1992). Thus, Tajiri suggests that even while examining the plight of a sympathetic Japanese American character, Hollywood filmmakers could not bring themselves to portray that character accurately and visually.

By using outtakes from the U.S. War Department's infamous propaganda film *Japanese Relocation* (1942), such as written slates and other informational titles, Tajiri illustrates the falsity of the government's version of the "facts," pointing to the deceit and paranoia used to justify the wrongful internment of Japanese Americans during World War II. Here Tajiri performs the ultimate *detournement*, using government-issue propaganda to expose the duplicity of the U.S. War Department.

Tajiri contrasts the inaccuracy of these "official sources" of information with images from the Japanese American community itself. She presents full-faced, fully realized images of Japanese Americans, including her personal family photographs as well as footage from David Tatsuno's Super 8 mm films, which were shot with a camera smuggled into the Topaz internment camp. With these images, Tajiri clearly depicts the visages that Hollywood and the War Department obscured or omitted, representing a community that was unseen in mainstream media.

In *Chinese Characters* (1986), Richard Fung also takes found footage and turns it to a more politicized end, this time using recontextualized images from gay Asian pornography as commentary on representations of Asian male sexuality. Countering these images are staged interviews with Asian men recounting their experiences with sexual and racial politics. In an essay on his work, Fung (1991, 67) acknowledges the need to reexamine and rework the stereotypes and misrepresentations found in the mainstream: "(Re)creating ourselves in our own terms requires constant reevaluation of the master narratives that have bracketed our lives. For this we need to understand the history and language of images, we must grasp this language and make it our own."

In this atmosphere of double meanings and deconstruction I, too, find *detournement* a useful strategy. In *"ALL ORIENTALS LOOK THE SAME"* (Soe 1986), I examine a common stereotype, taking the title phrase and inverting it to new effect. While a male voice drones the titular statement, my voice counters with a recitation of some thirty-five Asian American ethnic groups residing in the United States. That litany, combined with a series of head shots of distinct, individual Asian American faces, renders the title phrase untrue. The piece exposes the fallacy of the title's racist assumption, taking a tool of dominant culture and using it to dismantle its power and influence over cultural perceptions.

Picturing Oriental Girls: A (Re) Educational Videotape (Soe 1992; Photos 10.1 and 10.2) compiles clips from more than two dozen Hollywood films and television programs that portray stereotypical Asian women. The clips are from diverse sources, ranging from Josef von Sternberg's classic film *The Shanghai Gesture* (1941), with the lead

PHOTO 10.1.   From *Picturing Oriental Girls: A (Re) Educational Videotape* (1992), dir. Valerie Soe.

PHOTO 10.2.   From *Picturing Oriental Girls: A (Re) Educational Videotape* (1992), dir. Valerie Soe.

actress in yellowface wielding a gun in her mandarin-nailed grip, to the archetypal Hong Kong hooker film, *The World of Suzie Wong* (Quine 1960), and modern-day music videos, including the singer George Michael's *I Want Your Sex*, which features Asian women's bodies as drawing boards. The video recontextualizes and deconstructs these gems, mixing them up and highlighting repeated motifs such as women in high heels, masterful Asian masseuses, and Bond girls with fetishized long hair and long red fingernails. I have taken these fairly useless and potentially damaging representations and redeemed them, using them as social commentary.

Destiny (Soe 1991) similarly dissects the power structure by using manipulated footage of news broadcasts from the 1991 Gulf War. The piece lays a simple soundtrack over a found-footage panoply of talking heads, rocket diagrams, and maps of the Middle East. A young man recounts his experience at his workplace, a corporate office in Southern California, where he had casually mentioned his opposition to the war to a coworker named Destiny. His boss forcefully silenced his opinion and insisted that he refrain from discussing his views at work, an attitude that exemplified the muzzling of dissent—the most chilling aspect of the war at home. The young man's simple retelling of this unsettling experience, coupled with an ominous electronic-music track, counters the visual images of the official State Department version of the war, which were sanitized to minimize distress for prime-time viewers.

Here again, elements of the ruling hierarchy's arsenal—in this case, mass self-censorship and the government's sanitized crimes found on nightly news—are used to condemn and expose the controlling motivations of the ruling class. General Electric is both a prominent defense contractor and the parent company of NBC-TV; CBS-TV's board of directors shares members with such multinational corporate giants as Citicorp, AT&T, and Chase Manhattan Bank. These connections suggest conflicts of interest and intent in which the entities reporting the news are controlled by those who stand to gain from skewed reporting of the events. *Destiny* draws a parallel between the stifling of divergent points of view in the media and the intolerance of dissent in a workplace situation.

My most recent interactive installation, *Mixed Blood* (Soe 1992–94; Photo 10.3), not only reuses imagery from dominant culture's version of reality; it also integrates technology commonly used by systems of power, including computers, electronic signage, and multiple video monitors.

The piece deals with the subject of interracial sex in the Asian American community through text, interviews, found and archival footage, and quotes and statistics. I interviewed a number of concerned people on the topic, then interspersed the interviews with clips from classic miscegenist dramas, such as *Sayonara* (Logan 1957), *The Teahouse of the August Moon* (Mann 1956), and *Tai-Pan* (Duke 1986), all of which feature stereotypically subservient Asian women in erotic relationships with white men. Again, these images are edited to analyze their original intent and to recognize the pervasive influence that these images have had in shaping racial and sexual identity.

PHOTO 10.3.   From *Mixed Blood* (1992–94), dir. Valerie Soe.

Both *Sayonara* and *Teahouse* were released in the decade after World War II, and both prominently feature romances between American soldiers and Japanese women in postwar Japan. The cultural critic Gina Marchetti (1993, 134) notes that in *Sayonara*, Katsumi, one of the female Japanese characters "is shown performing her domestic tasks, cooking, serving guests, bathing her [Caucasian] husband, cheerfully and quietly.... [The film] sticks to accepted stereotypes about Asians, particularly Asian women, as passive, childlike, and servile."

In *Mixed Blood*, I *detourn* the original intent of *Sayonara* and similar Hollywood films by contrasting them with their modern-day legacy. For instance, on a visual clip from *Teahouse* of a geisha coyly serving tea to an American serviceman I juxtapose the voiceover of a mixed-race Asian American woman who wryly notes, "They always ask me: 'Are you part-Asian'—or, they say, 'Are you Oriental?'" (Soe 1992–94). Another Asian American woman laments, "He expected [me] to bring out the massage oil and walk on his back, and he was really disappointed when [I] didn't" (ibid.) while visuals show James Bond receiving a loving rubdown from an adept Japanese masseuse. An Asian American man similarly recounts, "Asian men are always portrayed as creeps, bad guys, and creatures" (ibid.), over television images of Ming the Merciless and the accused serial killer Charles Ng. In short, *Mixed Blood* points out the absurdity of the stereotypes' skewed visions by contrasting the reality of the interview subjects with the fantasy of the clips.

Mixed Blood also used a range of electronic media in its installation: Five monitors displayed two channels of video while a computer terminal invited viewers to respond to questions about the piece (Photo 10.4). An LED message board displayed these comments at the top of the piece. These electronic systems originated as commercial marketing tools and as products of defense research. The LED message board is a descendent of the famous moving electronic billboard in New York's Times Square and cousin to countless "silent radios" that present text displays of wire-service news and advertising in post offices across the country. Computer technology was first developed in this country by defense contractors such as the RAND Corporation and the Los Alamos Nuclear Laboratory. I have taken these devices and reoriented their purpose, using hardware designed to sell products and promote warfare and instead used them as elements of a creative work dealing with social concerns. The origins of the systems are unimportant—it is their ultimate application that matters.

In the past, some activists have hesitated to employ seemingly corrupt and sullied means and methods, such as video cameras, advertising images, and computers, whose geneses lie in harmful or manipulative industries. The cultural critic and noted Luddite Jerry Mander asserts in his infamous screed *Four Arguments for the Elimination of Television* (1978, 214): "The technology of television and the inherent nature of the viewing experience actually inhibit learning.... Very little cognitive, recallable, analyzable thought-based learning takes place while watching TV.... Television inhibits your ability to think."

In this time of historical flux, however, when mediated images control the ballot box and political demonstrations are staged for prime time, artists and activists realize the importance of mastering the most powerful tools available, regardless of their

PHOTO 10.4.   *Mixed Blood* (1994), installation view, Center for the Arts, Yerba Buena Gardens, San Francisco. Courtesy of Valerie Soe.

origins. Despite their beginnings as purveyors of the status quo, film and television programs, advertising, and electronic technology can be consciously critiqued and recontextualized and thus used for the greater good.

As an artist and cultural worker I feel an obligation to speak in the lexicon familiar to the greatest number of people, which at this point in history is the language of the mediated moving image. By taking control of modern technology and its idioms, I am defining and empowering those traditionally oppressed by such tools. Instead of carefully holding myself apart from potential corruption by distancing myself from the fray, I would like to be able to respond blow for blow, with intelligence and in an informed way, parrying with the weapons that are most able to make effective and lasting change.

Works Cited

Debord, Guy, and Gil Wolman. 1981. "Methods of *Detournement*." Pp. 8–14 in *Situationist International Anthology*, ed. Ken Knabb. Berkeley, Calif.: Bureau of Public Secrets.

Fung, Richard. 1991. "Center the Margins." Pp. 62–67 in *Moving the Image: Independent Asian Pacific American Media Arts*, ed. Russell Leong. Los Angeles: UCLA Asian American Studies Center, Visual Communications, Southern California Asian American Studies Central.

Mander, Jerry. 1978. *Four Arguments for the Elimination of Television*. New York: Quill.

Marchetti, Gina. 1993. *Romance and the "Yellow Peril": Race, Sex, and Discursive Strategies in Hollywood Fiction*. Berkeley: University of California Press.

Soloman, Norman. 1992. "Manipulating Minds." Pp. 96–101 in *War after War*, ed. Nancy J. Peters. San Francisco: City Lights Books.

Films and Videos Cited

Baldwin, Craig. 1990. *Tribulation 99*. Canyon Cinema, Other Cinema.

Duke, Daryl. 1986. *Tai-Pan*. No distributor.

Franklin, Sidney. 1937. *The Good Earth*. Metro Goldwyn Mayer.

Fung, Richard. 1986. *Chinese Characters*. Frameline Distribution.

Hughes, John. 1984. *Sixteen Candles*. Universal. MCA, Universal Pictures.

Japanese Relocation. 1942. U.S. War Department.

Logan, Joshua. 1957. *Sayonara*. Metro Goldwyn Mayer. Metro Goldwyn Mayer.

Mann, Daniel. 1956. *The Teahouse of the August Moon*. Metro Goldwyn Mayer. No distributor.

Nakasako, Spencer. 1990. *Do It on the Oriental*. NAATA.

Patiris, Phil. 1993. *The Iraq Campaign*. Modern Television.

Quine, Richard. 1960. *The World of Suzie Wong*. World Film Services. Paramount Pictures.

Snider, Greta. 1993. *No-Zone*. Canyon Cinema.

Soe, Valerie. 1986. *"ALL ORIENTALS LOOK THE SAME."* NAATA, Women Make Movies, Video Data Bank, Video Out Distribution.

———. *Destiny*. 1991. Video Data Bank.

———. 1992–94. *Mixed Blood*. NAATA, Video Out Distribution, IDERA.

———. 1992. *Picturing Oriental Girls: A (Re) Educational Videotape*. NAATA, Video Out Distribution.

Sturges, John. 1955. *Bad Day at Black Rock*. MGM/UA. Metro Goldwyn Mayer.

Von Sternberg, Josef. 1932. *Shanghai Express*. Paramount Publix. Paramount Publix, MCA.

———. 1941. *The Shanghai Gesture*. United Artists. Films Around the World, United Artists.

Tajiri, Rea. 1992. *History and Memory: For Akiko and Takashige*. Women Make Movies.

Walsh, Raoul. 1940. *The Thief of Bagdad*. United Artists. Kino International, Stokey Video, United Artists.

Zinnemann, Fred. 1953. *From Here to Eternity*. Columbia.

Jun Xing

| 11 | Hybrid Cinema by Asian American Women |

In her book *Woman, Native, Other* (1989, 1–2), the Vietnamese American filmmaker Trinh Minh-ha explores the meaning and nature of popular memory, storytelling, "truth," and history for women of color. In the tradition of oral history, she identifies a nonlinear, open-ended approach to history and knowledge. "The story never really begins nor ends," she proclaims, "even though there is a beginning and an end to every story, just as there is a beginning and end to every teller. . . . It appears headless and bottomless for it is built on differences. Its (in)finitude subverts every notion of completeness and its frame remains a non-totalizable one."

Experimental films and videos by and about Asian American women produced in the past few years exemplify the dynamics of the different kind of storytelling that Trinh describes. Among the most innovative and critically acclaimed are Valerie Soe's *New Year: Parts I and II* (1987) and *Picturing Oriental Girls: A (Re) Educational Videotape* (1992), Lise Yasui's *Family Gathering* (1988), Janice Tanaka's *Memories from the Department of Amnesia* (1989), Shu Lea Cheang's *Color Schemes: America's Washload in 4 Cycles* (1989), Trinh T. Minh-ha's *Surname Viet Given Name Nam* (1989), and Rea Tajiri's *History and Memory: For Akiko and Takashige* (1991). Indeed, using unconventional techniques and provocative cultural practices, these sophisticated experimental works by Asian American women address important issues of racial representation and challenge the conventions of commercial filmmaking (especially the Hollywood variety) in ways that are rarely possible in documentaries and dramatic features.[1]

For a long time, critics largely overlooked experimental films, possibly because of their topics and themes and their aesthetics. Within the white, male-dominated Hollywood tradition, Asian American women suffer a "double marginality," so to speak. Being independent and Asian, the artists are not only outside (and going against) the mainstream; they also are often pigeonholed into dealing only with ethnicity and

An earlier version of this chapter was printed in Jun Xing's *Asian America Through the Lens: History, Representations and Identity* (Walnut Creek, London, New Delhi: AltaMira Press, 1998).

gender-specific subjects. In contrast to Hollywood's sexist and exotic stereotypes of "Oriental" women, the works of these filmmakers focus on personal history, families, and everyday lives in the United States—which the audience-driven movie industry views as lacking broad public appeal. Further, avant-garde film is traditionally interpreted purely as a "personal" work of art, and its social dimensions are largely overlooked.[2] Avant-garde film criticism, according to P. Adams Sidney (1974), usually focuses on visual aesthetics but rarely engages discourses on gender, race, and ethnicity.[3] Although he made the observation more than twenty years ago, Sidney's statement still holds true. bell hooks (1996, 103) similarly writes about the situation among black filmmakers: "Avant-garde/experimental work is central to the creation of alternative visions. Yet when black filmmakers embrace the realm of the experimental, they are often seen as practicing elitism, as turning their backs on the struggle to create liberatory visions."

Minority filmmakers who attempt to use the experimental medium often find the criteria used to define the avant-garde too restrictive. For Trinh, for example, a film might be considered avant-garde "because it exposes its politics of representation instead of seeking to transcend representation in favor of visionary presence and spontaneity, which often constitute the prime criteria for what the avant-garde considers to be Art" (quoted in hooks 1996, 106). Although they share some discursive ground with the avant-garde tradition, the films and videos discussed in this chapter use alternative narrative techniques and cut across the constricting boundaries of the political, experimental, and documentary genres. Further, in contrast to the avant-garde tradition, this new hybrid cinema allows the films to become vehicles for the filmmakers' political statements (ibid.).[4] Cheang has commented on her personal experience: "Experimental film and video work expands the boundaries of conventional forms, using unusual structures or visual language, or approaching unlikely topics or themes.... By balancing an unusual formal structure with more immediate conceptual concerns I've been able to create accessible yet challenging work" ("[Video] World" 1988).

But the diversity of these filmmakers' experiences, techniques, and cultural practices poses a serious problem of acceptance.[5] As a result, these filmmakers are largely excluded from Eurocentric experimental-film criticism.[6] However, it is "by their marginality," as Trinh (1992, 250) puts it nicely in a different context, that these filmmakers "contribute to keeping the notion of 'experimental' alive, hence to resisting modernist closures often implied in the very label of 'avant-garde.'"

Taking this contradiction as a point of departure, this chapter examines Asian American women's experimental filmmaking as a new subgenre in Asian American cinematic discourse. It proposes that these Asian American experimental films and videos have subverted a major convention of mainstream filmmaking—its "realism"—and opened new discursive practices in the revision of the Asian American experience. They have "deconstructed" several key elements in filmmaking, such as the symbolic order of time and space, especially in documentaries (which allegedly possess a false sense of objectivity because of visible evidence, such as eyewitness interviews). In the end, the alternative discourse of avant-garde filmmaking has been turned into a different form of storytelling.

Avant-Garde Film as History

Discussions of historical film rarely take into account the experimental format. This neglect can be explained through both film criticism and historiography. "While films may be documentaries or fiction," the film historian Malcolm Le Grice (1997, 7) writes, "their essential form and language has been evolved to tell stories." Like other story-oriented media—the short story, the novel, the play, the opera—movies are judged mainly on the basis of how well they tell a story (Bywater and Sobchack 1989, 145). From its early beginnings in the French avant-garde tradition, experimental film has developed a cinematic form that is quite different from that of film drama, the dominant mode of cinema. Because our popular conceptions of meaning and critical language are derived from literary habits, most major cinema critics have a strong bias toward theatrical dramas, while overlooking the non-narrative format.

Further, consciously and unconsciously we think of history ("his [mankind's] story") as a narrative. In the historical analysis of film, as Robert Rosenstone (1988, 1174) writes, what probably come to mind are the "historical romances" and historical documentaries, both of which use common narrative conventions in that they attempt to "compress the past to a closed world by telling a single, linear story with, essentially, a single interpretation."

Although Hollywood narrative and the standard documentary are the most common forms of filmed history, the avant-garde has effectively engaged historical processes, as well. In his analysis of "the individual period" of the American avant-garde (1946–66), Fred Campter stresses the social dimension of experimental filmmaking. These "personal" works of art had a much broader agenda, Campter argues, and constituted a social challenge to the mass culture of conformity in the post-World War II decades (Campter 1986–87, 99–124). "It is no accident, for instance," Campter writes, "that a large proportion of the founding filmmakers were gay men, in an era when being publicly gay was itself considered an anti-social act of major proportions" (ibid., 101). Campter's insights illuminate the existence of a radical American avant-garde cinematic tradition, but the appreciation of its significance requires a new critical approach. In his book on film history, Pierre Sorlin (1980, 33) calls for the reading of significant "structural patterns" in historical films concerning formal techniques and structural relations: "Structural analysis is not a pure formalism," Sorlin points out, "nor a self-sufficient system: the structures do not exist by themselves, at least when we are working on a limited object like a film; they are conceptual models which help us in describing the organization and mutual relations of a particular complex whole." Although the "historical films" that Sorlin refers to are not necessarily avant-garde films, Sorlin's semiotic and structuralist emphasis on textual production is useful for our understanding of experimental films as history. It helps shift our critical attention from a film's historical accuracy or authenticity to its mode of representation (Musser and Sklar 1990).

Nowadays, one crucial question posed by contemporary cultural theoreticians, from Louis Althusser to Fredric Jameson, has to do with the specific relationship of cultural artifact to historical truth. How is one to account for the disparity between history and its representation, or between history and its lack of representation? The objectivity question, as hisorian Peter Novik calls it, has dodged historians since the beginning of the profession. In a similar way, documentary filmmakers have been pre-occupied with "authenticity" since Flaherty and Grierson, the fathers of the American and British documentary. Also, it is assumed that filmed and written history can be objectified and reified through "data" and "evidence." But the pursuit of objectivity in history often privileges the powerful at the expense of the powerless, because traditional history texts often reduce the "voiceless" subordinate communities and groups to "objects" of policies and "references" of the main stories (Grierson 1966, 145). This critique recalls Stuart Hall's idea of "taking representation apart"—in other words, opening the practice of representation in order to recognize how ideology and power attempt to fix meaning in a particular direction, and for particular ends and interests (quoted in Jhally 1997).

I now turn my examination to the seven films named earlier, which I term "hybrid films." These "reflexive" film texts will be analyzed to show how their avant-garde style violates the temporal and spatial conventions of commercial cinema and subverts the seductive power of "realism." Specifically, these films have challenged the cinematic language of cuts, fades, frame composition, and camera movement and have succeeded in creating their own forms of expression in re-presenting history.

Time and Subjectivity

In the Judeo-Christian tradition, time has been conceived as the medium of sacred history, and it has long assumed its own "objective" existence and linear character (Kern 1983, 33). As Johannes Fabian (1983, ix) put it, "Time, much like language or money, is a carrier of significance, a form through which we define the content of relations between the Self and the Other. . . Time may give form to relations of power and inequality under the conditions of capitalist industrial production." Along the same line of argument, Mary Louise Pratt (1985–86, 129) notes that anthropologists tend to represent racial and cultural Others as if they were living outside time, in a realm of spatialized stasis.

Under this reductionist logic, the Orient conceived in Western discourse is stagnant, passive, and feminine; it fulfills its role as the Other to the West (Said 1978, 1). The duality of Asian primitivity, or backwardness, and Western modernity has been recycled numerous times in Hollywood's representation of Asian Americans. A quote from the white cop Stanley White (Mickey Rourke) in *Year of the Dragon* (Cimino 1985) illustrates this point. At the beginning of the movie, White scolds a group of horrified Chinatown bosses: "I'm tired of Chinese this and Chinese that. Does the fact that bribery, extortion, and murder have been going on for a thousand years make it kosher? Well, this is America, which is two hundred years old, so you'd better adjust your clocks." Hollywood uses violence against women, arranged marriages, and other alleged Asian traditions as instances of Asiatic anachronisms. "The linear way in which we [Asian Americans] are taught to accept Eurocentric historical definitions and processes," writes Russell Leong (1991, xv), "also appears in the linking of our culture and history primarily to the experience of western domination."

In conceptualizing black film aesthetics, Teshome Gabriel (1988, 66) supports the idea of a subjective nomadic time of black cinema, in which "time is seen, observed and experienced as 'subjective'. . . . The central orientation points toward a 'cyclic' system wherein several time frames occur simultaneously." This so-called traveling aesthetics—or "migrant sensibility," as Salman Rushdie (1985) terms it—is not unique to black cinema. It informs Asian American films, as well. In the form of personal, family, and community histories, each of the works under discussion rejects the linear narrative and validates a traveling aesthetics, a subjective experience of time, in various ways. Tajiri's impressionistic experimental video *History and Memory*, for example, explores the gaps in both personal and popular memories. "I began searching for a story, my own history," Tajiri twice tells her viewers in the video, "because I had known all along that the stories I had heard were not true and parts had been left out" (Tajiri 1991, 9). Here, her own subjectivity is infiltrated by Hollywood images. In recuperating her own and her mother's memory, time in the film is compressed, expanded, and reversed at different points. For example, whereas her mother chose to "forget" Poston, Arizona, where she was interned during World War II, Tajiri is haunted by ghostlike memories of the site she has never seen. "There was this place that they knew about I had never been there," says the voiceover. "Yet I had a memory for it. There was a time of great sadness before I was born. . . . I had not [*sic*] idea where these memories came from. . . . Yet I knew the place" (ibid.).

Yasui employs a strikingly similar technique in *Family Gathering*. In the film's beginning, we hear Yasui speak nostalgically about a favorite childhood memory of her grandfather (the family member she investigates): how he comes to visit her family and how she stays up late, listening to him talk. But minutes later, she openly admits, "Later, I learned that my grandparents never made such a visit, that I never met my grandfather at all. The memory was one I'd made up, a creation drawn from all the stories I'd heard and the images on my father's home movies." By playing with personal memory, Yasui "introduces the idea that memory can be fabricated, made up of a patchwork of events and feelings which may or may not correspond to what actually happened" (Van Buren 1992, 56).[7]

This emphasis on personal memory over "historical" time coincides with the shift in focus from traditional history to genealogy. Traditional history, according to Michel Foucault (1977), produces continuities that "link events into a united, coherent story. . . . Writing genealogy, on the other hand, involves the recognition of disparity, of the dispersion of origins, and links, of discontinuities and contradictions." Organized around memory (itself a patchwork of events and feelings), the "stories"—or genealogic narrative, in Foucauldian terms—are often elliptical and fragmented, and sometimes even disruptive. Flashback, backtracking, repetition, and other cinematic strategies are used to break the sequential order. Soe's two-part video *New Year*, for example, is supposed to be a progressive coming-of-age story. The slow-paced progression of her childhood memory, portrayed through voice-over narration accompanied by drawings, is twice disrupted by intertitles: "Ching Chong Chinaman sitting on fence/trying to make a dollar out of five cents" and "Chinese/Japanese/Dirty Knees/Look at these Chinese Japanese/Dirty Knees." This disjunctive structure in the first part of the video breaks into a topical structure in the second part, based on Hollywood's five stereotypical representations of Asian Americans: "Japs, Slopes, and Gooks," "Fortune Cookie Philosophers," "The Worldwide Empire of Evil," "Geisha Girls and Dragon Ladies," and "Masters of Kung Fu." Each of these scrolling titles is followed by excerpts from Hollywood movies, wartime documentaries, television shows, and comic books. "The scenes and caricatures are shuffled, repeated, and run together without identification," writes Carole Gerster (1994, 195), "indicating that they are recycled stereotypes with interchangeable parts." The narrative structure of *Family Gathering* is also highly elliptical. Instead of unfolding in a clean and linear order, the film corresponds to the complex and meticulous process of Yasui's investigation of her family history, which involves "false starts; backtracking to pick up what was originally overlooked; reevaluating; and, ultimately, progression" (Van Buren 1992, 62).

In recent years, counter-memory—or popular memory, as some scholars call it—has become a powerful concept in cultural studies. Foucault, for one, discusses counter-memory in terms of genealogy. According to Foucault (1977, 139–40), genealogy "must record the singularity of events outside of any monotonous finality; it must seek them in the most unpromising places, in what we tend to feel is without history—in sentiments, love, conscience, instincts." George Lipsitz offers a different interpretation by emphasizing counter-memory's oppositional nature. Counter-memory, he asserts, "focuses on localized experiences with oppression, using them to reframe and refocus dominant narratives purporting to represent universal experience" (Lipsitz 1990, 213). In studying the aesthetics of Third Cinema, Gabriel (1989) demonstrates how popular memory negates an official history that "claims a 'centre' which continually marginalises [sic] others." Gabriel further argues that, "for popular memory, there are no longer any 'centres' or 'margins,' since the very designations imply that something has been conveniently left out" (ibid., 53–54).

Despite their apparent differences in emphasis, the three scholars agree that, as an alternative way to remember and forget (rooted in the personal, immediate, and particular), counter-memories create an autonomous cultural space for marginalized social groups. In other words, counter-memory calls our attention to the fact that history is a multilevel and plural-voiced narration, and a single level or voice is often privileged, depending on the preferences of the writer. It is precisely this notion of counter-memory that problematizes an easy writing of history and opens new critical spaces, allowing for the marginalized and silenced voices to be heard. Thus, personal memories have become an interventional tool for negotiation and mediation. As a victim of incarceration in relocation camps, for example, Tajiri's mother responds to her daughter's inquiry about her traumatic experience with painful self-denial. In a tape-recorded conversation between the two, the mother says:

No, that's the truth, I don't remember. . . . When you hear people on television and everything, how they felt and everything, I don't remember any of that stuff. All I remember is . . . when I saw this woman . . . this beautiful woman, young, you know, and uh, I thought to myself, why did this happen, you know? You can go crazy, you can go out of your mind, so you just put these things out of your mind, you know. [Tajiri 1991, 10]

Here, the boundaries between memory and invention, history and myth, never seem clear. The filmmakers decide to merge facts and memory, or the actual and the dreamed, because such a synthesis of techniques best presents their sense of self and their connections to their heritage.

Calling all her works "electronic reflections," Janice Tanaka (1991, 206) feels that memory does not work in a linear fashion: "Memories are not always an understood compilation of linear ideas," she writes. "They seem instead to be fragments of stored, synthesized, edited sensory stimuli; bits of personalized perceptions." Tanaka skillfully turned this fluid and fragmentary memory into visual concepts in *Memories from the Department of Amnesia*. The video's richly textured opening sequence is a good illustration: It consists of a deep-focus shot of a dazed and frenzied bicyclist circling inside a bar. By constantly changing angles, the restless camera creates a series of quick shots—a glance at the bar, a close-up of the turning wheel, and a long shot of a robed doctor advancing and retreating in a snowstorm. This dreamlike sequence becomes a metaphor that determines much of the video's thematic focus: the loss of Tanaka's mother, Yuriko Yamate, and the elusiveness of the filmmaker's memories. Tanaka's use of dissolves and repeated shifts between positive and negative images (transitions between color and black-and-white film stock) creates a multilayered visual text that reinforces the subjective nature of personal memory and its impact on history. This experimental style of editing links scenes together in an ahistorical fashion,[8] informing the film's overriding message that our sense of history exists only as our memory of the past flows through our own existence. As a result, narrative causality easily disappears in subjective reflections.

Trinh's feature-length film *Surname Viet Given Name Nam* also represents a radical break with the linear perspective. "Working in the realm of stories and popular memories," Trinh explains, "I was not interested in a linear construction of time, and I was not attempting to reconstruct any specific period of Vietnam history" (Trinh 1992, 208). To displace the notion of fixed time, she employs various strategies. For example, she intercuts staged interviews with five Vietnamese women with black-and-white news footage and photographs that obviously do not belong to the same time period as the voiceover. A case in point, which Trinh cited in an interview, is the juxtaposition of 1950s footage of the north–south movement of Vietnamese refugees with a young woman's voice reading a letter that she has written her sister. The young woman is reminiscing with her mother in Guam in 1975 about her refugee experience. In this scene, Trinh says, "the focus is neither on the plight of the refugees in the 50s nor on that in the 70s; rather, what seems more important to me is the specific nature of the problems women of many times and many places have to undergo—as women" (Trinh 1989, 209). In the ending sequence, images of a group of refugees floating on a raft in the sea during the 1950s become the background for off-screen comments on the contemporary problems of the "boat people." Thus, the film breaks up sequential time and creates "monumental time," with no beginning or ending (to borrow a concept from Julia Kristeva [1986]), in the women's stories. One voiceover in *Surname Viet* comments, "There is always the tendency to identify historical breaks and to say 'this begins there,' 'this ends here,' while the scene keeps on recurring, as unchangeable as change itself" (Trinh 1989, 56).

Juxtaposing images that are out of chronological order seems to be a common structural feature in almost all the works under discussion. Historical footage and contemporary events often occupy the same time and space. In *History and Memory*, Tajiri parallels the footage that she shot with found footage. In one scene in which she revisits the Poston barracks in Arizona, for example, she films the camp (or, rather, traces of the camp) as it is today, then intercuts these scenes with government photos showing the camp under construction in 1942. The most eloquent example might be this scene: As clips from the movie *A Bad Day at Black Rock* are playing, the text from an August 28, 1990, *New York Times* article scrolls into the frame: "Assemblyman Gil Ferguson, Republican Orange County, California, seeks to have children taught that Japanese Americans were not interned in 'concentration camps' but rather were held in 'relocation centers' justified by military necessity" (Tajiri 1991, 19). Soe's twelve-minute *Picturing Oriental Girls* uses the technique of incongruous juxtaposition to an extreme. In almost every sequence, quick movie clips are overlapped with written texts from various sources, such as mail-order–bride catalogues, men's magazines, and the movie *The World of Suzie Wong* (Quine 1960). The texts cleverly deconstruct, or subvert, the meaning of the collage of racist and sexist images by literally turning them upside down and against one another.

Counter-memory may not carry effective countercultural values for marginalized groups until it is related to the present. Put differently, popular memories are meaningful only insofar as they "teach us" about our current actions. In re-creating her family history, for example, Tajiri not only tries to rescue human memories. She also, and more significantly, tries to establish links between reminiscences about the past and present struggles. This existential theme is conveyed by the letter she reads from Uncle Shinkichi: "You asked what I thought I gained or lost from the evacuation. Gained? Very little except a unique situation that a very tiny percentage of the American public had ever explained. What I lost was my faith in the American Constitution and it is for that reason that I left the U.S. 43 years ago, a year after I returned from the war" (Tajiri 1991, 20).

Here, Tajiri formulates a historical narrative that not only attempts to reshape our memory of the past but can also inform the present political dialogue. In a sense, this struggle of memory against forgetting, as represented by the video, could become a source of community empowerment.

In addition to inventive camera techniques, these experimental artists have also used asynchronous sound to break the conventions of editing. A careful examination of the soundtrack of Soe's *New Year* reveals mismatches between graphic and sound at several points. A major break occurs when, for example, martial-arts fighting is heard on the soundtrack but no picture appears for two full minutes. In Trinh's *Surname Viet*, out-of-sync editing is more intricate. Playing with the so-called time-image format,[9] Trinh deliberately creates gaps among what is read, what is heard, and what is seen on the screen. "Not only does the text not always enter at the same time as the speech," the filmmaker emphasizes in an interview, "its shorter duration on the screen also makes it quasi-impossible for the viewer to hear and read at the same time without missing parts of both" (Trinh 1992, 208). This manipulation is further complicated, as Gwendolyn Foster (1997, 102) notes, by the "diegetic speech in both Vietnamese and English, sometimes translated and subtitled, and sometimes left deliberately 'untranslated.'" For Trinh, this kind of asynchronic editing becomes an inventive ideological and structural device to "displace the notion of fixed time and place" (Trinh 1992, 210).

In describing the symbolic order of time for women, Kristeva links female subjectivity to cyclical time (repetition) and monumental time (eternity). "As for time," says Kristeva (1986, 191), "female subjectivity would seem to provide a specific measure that essentially retains repetition and eternity from among the multiple modalities of time known through the history of civilizations." The filmmakers examined here have indeed adopted a circular or cyclical structure as an alternative to a self-enclosed linear narrative. This framework is best represented in Cheang's *Color Schemes*. Originally conceived as a multipart video installation, the tape uses three 1954 front-loading washing machines as a metaphor for the great American "melting pot" of ethnicity. In a re-enactment of the Last Supper, twelve performers, of various ethnic backgrounds, gather and discuss American history and racism inside the washing machines. We view this poignant image with the full knowledge of the fact that the four cycles—soak, wash, rinse, and extract—become the narrative structure of the film. In each cycle, a different historical theme is explored, from Chinese coolie labor to the genocide of Native Americans.

Yasui's cyclical narrative in *Family Gathering* is embedded in the content of the film largely through the attitudes of her father, Robert Shu Yasui, and her aunt and uncles toward her grandfather's suicide: from denial and hesitancy to acknowledgment. The way Yasui handles the gradual process of her kins' gradually coming to terms with their emotions is revealing. As Van Buren (1992, 62) observes: "The way in which Yasui frequently comes back around to the specific conversation about Masuo's suicide is a striking example of the cyclical nature of the film. She first alludes to Masuo's wrongful internment in the introductory narration of the film, then leaves the subject untouched for nearly half of the duration of the documentary. It is about three-quarters of the way through the film that she weaves her bit of narration mentioned earlier, in which she relates the climactic conversation with Robert and shows him explaining why many Nisei kept this information from her generation."

In comparison, Tajiri uses the technique of repetition to create a back-and-forth structure in *History and Memory*. The video's opening image, for instance, is a dripping outdoor water faucet. Then the sequence shows a close-up of a pair of hands holding a canteen in the middle of the desert. On numerous occasions, the film circles back to this beautifully composed sequence for at least two narrative purposes: First, it illustrates that personal memory is subjective and malleable; and second, it symbolizes her family's experience of dealing with the trauma of internment. For example, Tajiri's mother's struggle with her traumatic experience functions as an important subtext of the video. As a victim of incarceration in relocation camps, her mother uses "forgetting" as a defense mechanism for self-preservation. Working within the tradition of oral history, these Asian American female filmmakers have taken a nonlinear and open-ended approach in the stories they tell about their personal, family, and community histories.

Screen Space as Social Space

Western culture has long valued time over space. While time carries the meaning of a story, space often figures as its passive setting. In recent years, however, there is a growing recognition of the ideological construction of space, especially in theories of postmodernism. Edward Soja's book *Postmodern Geographies*, for example, calls for radical "spatial deconstruction by resituating the meaning of space in history and historical materialism" (1989, 73). "The 'East' is divided into 'Near,' 'Middle,' and 'Far,'" Ella Shohat and Robert Stam (1994, 2) write about the Eurocentric nature of spatial logic, "making Europe the arbiter of spatial evaluation, just as the establishment of Greenwich Mean Time produces England as the regulating center of temporal measurement."

   Indeed, the racial and cultural hierarchy in Hollywood is made up of relationships that are spatial as well as temporal. In his analysis of new black films, Manthia Diawara (1993, 11) points out that "spatial narration in classical cinema makes sense through a hierarchical disposition of objects on the screen. Thus space is related to power and powerlessness, in so far as those who occupy the center of the screen are usually more powerful than those situated in the background or completely absent from the screen." Indeed, the absence of minorities from the screen could be read as a symbol of their absence from society as constructed by Hollywood. Some scholars see a direct relationship between the geography of the world and the geography of the imagination (Blythe 1991). Said (1978, 1) defines the "imaginative geography" as a typical example of "Orientalism": "The Orient was almost a European invention, and had been since antiquity a place of romance, exotic beings, haunting memories and landscapes, remarkable experiences." As a creator of grand narratives and ideology, Hollywood has long used physical, social, and psychological "distancing" as strategies in its grotesque representations of Asians. Whether it takes the form of the yellow menace or the exotic image, this anti-Asian xenophobia has been frozen on the silver screen.[10] Asian locales in American films—from the mysterious Chinatown, USA, to the Vietnamese jungle—are presented as exotic tourist attractions and dangerous wildernesses for colonialist adventurers. In a symbolic sense, immigrants from Asia and their descendants can never claim America in the same way that their European counterparts have. As Eugene Wong notes in *On Visual Media Racism* (1978, 265), "The commonly held belief that Asian Americans are an alien collective living within a white American sea has become a popular cliché of self-perpetuating dimensions." This construction of space, which is symbolic as well as geographical, is an important aspect in Hollywood's representation of Asians.

Abjuring a straightforward documentary style, hybrid films and videos by Asian American women have sought to break up this spatial logic as it operates in artistic and social space. *Color Schemes*, for example, is a parody of public space in America. Both the setting of the laundromat and the wash motif inside the frame of the washers symbolize limited social space for ethnic minorities. While the laundromat is "a racially mixed gallery," the wash motif is analogous to the power-mediated racial conflicts in American society. As Cheang explains in an interview with *CineVue* (1989, 5): "When you do a wash, you separate whites and colors. The colors are always thrown in together with each other. . . . And that is the power structure that has us fighting each other. This is what the 'soak' cycle was to be about." Likewise, in the pool-table scene in the wash cycle, the pool balls are used "to represent assorted people of color, and how they are being banged around" (ibid.).

The video's framing effect is equally suggestive. The entire frame of the screen is folded and unfolded in a way that corresponds to each wash cycle in the machine. The washing-machine's door becomes the frame for Cheang's interviews, suggesting the spatial confinement that many racial groups experience. Interracial conflicts, Cheang argues, are rooted in the unbalanced spatiality of social life. "Minorities are the diverse colors constantly being thrown together by society," Cheang told *CineVue*, "without knowing each other and feeling very uncomfortable" (ibid.). The very concept of a homogeneous melting pot is dismantled in the film. On the surface, the washing process seems to imply assimilation, while the fading of color suggests the loss of individual identity. But Cheang's vivid characters defy the process, emerging as colorful and vibrant individuals. As semiotic imagery and ideologies, these representations play a powerful role in reshaping the spatial dimensions of American society.

Tanaka's highly geometric *Memories* has an equally significant but different spatial dialectic. In a surrealist manner, screen space becomes a symbol of Tanaka's inner struggles to retrieve her mother's life history in America. Out-of-focus shots, whip pans, and split screens are some of the spacing mechanisms that she uses. In the beginning sequence of a pedaling bicyclist, for instance, the filmmaker uses rapid zooms, and the screen frame is radically tilted, blurred, and deformed into surreal, exaggerated shapes. In a series of dissolves, the footage of the bicyclist cuts to a blank screen, soon to be occupied by a male physician in a surgical gown, which in turn cuts to a snowstorm scene. Through superimposition, the two figures become part of the same space. From this point on, the spatial dimension of the video settles into a split screen. Frame by frame, a series of small snapshot negatives of her mother develop into prints on the left; on the right, enlarged pictures, in a different order, appear, with thirty-six scrolling titles that identify the dates and events in Yuriko's life. While the past is represented graphically on the screen by the photographs, the filmmaker and her daughter are heard on the soundtrack reminiscing nostalgically about the woman. Thus, through experimental mise-en-scene and editing, Tanaka's contemporary perspectives and her mother's stories of the past come to occupy the same space at one time. As Marina Heung (1995) observes, three contradictions emerge in the sequence: the personal tragedies in the subtitles, the images of a smiling and radiant filmmaker and her daughter, and their light-hearted and loud voices. "This light-hearted and casual conversation runs counter to the mood and content of the subtitles," Heung writes, "as the two women laugh and giggle through their memories of Yuriko as a woman with a 'warped sense of humor,' a 'hot rod' who drove a Mustang, dated a lot of men, encouraged her family to eat arsenic-laced prune pits, and stored her wild outfits in a cedar trunk" (ibid., 101). These spatial devices are so effective that they lend credibility to the narrative by the family members. The occupation of screen space serves as a form of empowerment for them, as well.

Strikingly similarly, Soe's *Picturing Oriental Girls* skillfully employs several techniques, such as overlapping, cross-referencing, and ironic juxtaposition, to manipulate the screen space. For example, over the image of a geisha girl in a kimono from *The Teahouse of the August Moon* (Mann 1956), a quotation runs across the screen: "Asian women are renowned for their beauty, femininity, traditional values, and loving dispositions." The source of the quote (the Sunshine International Catalogue, a mail-order–bride business) reveals the irony of the citation.

Trinh's approach to spatial form, in comparison, is more conceptual than structural. As a filmmaker and a theoretician, Trinh seeks a broader reexamination of the ideological constructs of hierarchies, oppositions, and boundaries that are used pervasively in Western media. As in her earlier films, *Reassemblage* (1982) and *Naked Spaces—Living Is Round* (1985), the artist attempts to create "a hybrid place," or what she calls "interstitial space"—that is, "the space in between, the interval to which established rules of boundaries never quite apply" (Trinh 1992, 174). This "hybrid place" operates at several levels in her films. In formal terms, *Surname Viet* resists easy categories—documentary, narrative, and avant-garde. For instance, the viewer usually takes the staged or re-enacted "fake" interviews in the first part of the film as real, only to confront a series of on-site interviews with the same women but in the explicit context of the United States. This mixture of genres creates an unsettling situation for the viewers. As Trinh recalls the statement from a bewildered Vietnamese viewer: "Your film is different. I can't yet tell exactly how, but I know it's different from the documentary films I am used to seeing" (ibid., 146).

To expose the "object-oriented camera," Trinh experiments with the notion of "negative space" both on and off screen. For example, in many of the interview sequences in the early part of the film, the establishing shots are of women's bodies—with only segments shown. Talking heads literally become "headless." When the faces of the women do appear, the restless camera never stays on them. Instead, it pans across the screen, creating a series of blank screens. What is more, the framing effects heighten the importance of off-screen space. Very few "full-frame" images of the women appear. Half-face images are shown, with the screen edge cut right on the women's noses. Old photographs and stills, large and small, are framed with disproportionately large black space. Sometimes, lighting is extremely low-key and reinforces this dark screen space. The film's soundtrack is also interrupted with empty spaces (silences) or "sounding holes." The filmmaker relates all these strategies to the notion of the "Void" from Zen Buddhism: "People often don't even know what you are talking about when you mention the vitality of the Void in the relationships between object and non-object, or between I and non-I" (ibid., 142). This notion of the Void best explains Trinh's approach to spatial form.

One of the recurring motifs in the film is the critique of an essentialist identity, or what Trinh calls (1989, 95–97) "identity enclosure." The title itself is a pun and parody of the politics of naming a person, a nation, and a culture; it is taken from an anecdote in which an unmarried Vietnamese woman claims her marital status as being married to her country. What this means to female Vietnamese exiles in the United States becomes one of the film's subtexts. "I keep on thinking, despite our emigrating to the U.S.," as Kim, one of the actresses, says, "if our surname is Viet, our given name ought to be Nam—Vietnam" (Trinh 1992, 86). In "acted" interviews, Vietnamese women tell of war, exile, traditions, and daily lives from the shifting perspectives as women, mothers, wives, Vietnamese, and American. With the wedding ceremony as another motif of the film, women transform their identities from "lady, and maid, to monkey." In these pluravocal formulations of identity politics, "the self loses its fixed boundaries," says Trinh, and hybridization occurs in its place (ibid., 133). In its critique of women's oppression, the film is "directed toward the condition of women— whether in socialist or capitalist context, whether back home in the nation-space or over here in the community-space" (ibid., 196). For example, if the story of Kieu, a woman who sells her body to save her father's honor, serves as a critique of patriarchal structure in Vietnamese society, how does it relate to the Miss Vietnam pageant in the United States? Does the story signify the multiple exploitation of women's bodies? And what is the difference between sexual oppression on the one side and the commodification of sexuality on the other? *Surname Viet* thus reveals several issues, ideological as well as cinematic, in the conventional ordering of spatial form in commercial cinema.

In conclusion, these space-based techniques are used to reveal and link different forms of oppression that have been separated or suppressed in Hollywood. In other words, Asian American experimental filmmakers have opened up a new textual space in their films. Spatial narration has become a conduit to Asian womens' self-expression, a storytelling device that interrogates identity, memory, and Asian American ways of life. Taken together, their efforts, to borrow Foster's comments about Trinh's *Naked Spaces*, conflate "a number of theoretical attempts to reconstitute 'women's space'—for example, Laura Mulvey's 'lucid' space, Teresa de Lauretis' notion of off-screen space, Julia Kristeva's notion of the prelinguistic space of the chora, or Luce Irigaray's rereading of psychoanalytic 'lack' of a voicing of the female body" (Foster 1997, 100).

Historically, many of the techniques discussed in this essay can be found in the avant-garde tradition from the 1920s. As Kern has demonstrated in *The Culture of Time and Space*, the disjunctive impulse can be traced to several early twentieth-century art movements, such as the fracturing of time by the futurists and the fracturing of space by the cubists (Kern 1983, 33). Many of these strategies could also be seen in avant-garde films from the same period, such as Man Ray's *Retour à la Raison* (1923) and Fernand Léger's *Ballet Mécanique* (1924). The latter in particular employed similar disjunctive techniques, such as looped repeated action, flashes, black spaces between shots, and images fragmented by mirrors and cardboard cutouts. They may also be reminiscent of the New Wave filmmakers, such as Jean-Luc Godard in the

1960s. Borrowing the experimental techniques from those early twentieth-century visionary predecessors and the French New Wave directors, Asian American female artists have used their structural thrust not merely to create special aesthetic effects, but also to challenge the formulaic verisimilitude of Hollywood films.[11] hooks's recent call for African American filmmakers to go "back to the avant-garde" serves as further affirmation of the significance of experimental works by Asian American women:

> For too long black people and everyone else in this culture have been socialized to see the avant-garde solely as a marginal place where art that only a few understand resides. The time has come to rethink our assumptions. When we embrace the avant-garde as a necessary matrix of critical possibility, acknowledging that it is a context for cultural revolution, new and exciting representations of blackness will emerge. [hooks 1996, 107]

Indeed, Cheang, Soe, Tajiri, Tanaka, Trinh, and Yasui have used avant-garde techniques as a vehicle to approach both historical and social issues, literally turning this alternative discourse of the avant-garde into a different mode of "storytelling."

Notes

1. Although this chapter examines experimental films by Asian American women, the complex issue of how gender may interconnect with the aesthetics of these films is one that I cannot adequately treat here.

2. Renee Tajima (1991, 20) acknowledges that Asian American critics also have largely overlooked the avant-garde. The exception is Daryl Chin.

3. Sidney (1974, 407–408) declares, for example, that "[t]he structural film insists on its shape, and what content it has is minimal and subsidiary to the outline."

4. I use the term "hybrid cinema" in a broad sense, referring to films that depart from cinematic conventions, or what Burch (1990, 257) calls "technological image norms."

5. For a critique of film theory and practice, see Crusz (1985).

6. Trinh seems to be the only exception. Various reviews of, and articles and interviews about, her films have been published in journals and books. See, for example, the chapter on Trinh in MacDonald (1993).

7. Cassandra Van Buren's insightful essay on the film offers helpful points on its narrative structure, emotional texture, and soundtrack. Her ideas contribute substantially to my analysis of the film.

8. For more on this editing technique in visionary films, see Sidney (1974).

9. The time-image format refers to films in which the act of reading printed or written texts is a central viewing experience. For details, see Trinh (1991, 114–15).

10. Note, for example, in Joel Schumacher's *Falling Down* (1993), the rude and incongruous Korean grocer still carries the enigmatic image of an ungrateful sojourner in contrast to the image of the white man (played by Michael Douglas) as a patriot and natural heir to this white land.

11. Asian Americans are not unique in using experimental films and videos to make political statements. As Cheang says, "If you look at tapes now, you will find that a lot of experimental video makers are including a lot of social/political elements in their work. I think that's a very important element in the eighties. Conversely, you will find that tapes that deal with

very serious subject matter use what we might call experimental techniques" (quoted in "[Video] World" 1988, 7).

Works Cited

Blythe, Martin. 1991. "'What's in a Name?': Film Culture and the Self/Other Question." *Quarterly Review of Film & Video* 13, no. 1–3 (May–October): 205–15.

Burch, Noel. 1990. *Life to Those Shadows.* Trans. and ed. Ben Brewster. Berkeley: University of California Press.

Bywater, Tim and Thomas Sobchack. 1989. *An Introduction to Film Criticism: Major Critical Approaches to Narrative Film.* New York: Longman.

Campter, Fred. 1986–87. "The End of Avant-Garde Film." *Millennium Film Journal* 16–18 (Fall/Winter): 99–124.

"Color Schemes: *CineVue* Interviews Video Artist Shu Lea Cheang." 1989. *CineVue* 4, no. 1 (March): 5.

Crusz, Robert. 1985. "Black Cinemas, Film Theory and Dependent Knowledge." *Screen* 26, no. 3–4 (May–August 1985): 152–56.

Diawara, Manthia. 1993. "Black American Cinema: The New Realism." Pp. 3–25 in *Black American Cinema,* ed. Manthia Diawara. New York: Routledge.

Fabian, Johannes. 1983. *Time and the Other: How Anthropology Makes Its Object.* New York: Columbia University Press.

Foster, Gwendolyn Audrey. 1997. *Women Filmmakers of the African and Asian Diaspora: Decolonizing the Gaze, Locating Subjectivity.* Carbondale: Southern Illinois University Press.

Foucault, Michel. 1977. "Nietzsche, Genealogy, History." Pp. 139–64 in *Language, Counter-Memory, Practice: Selected Essays and Interviews by Michel Foucault,* ed. Donald F. Bouchard. Ithaca, N.Y.: Cornell University Press.

Gabriel, Teshome H. 1988. "Thoughts on Nomadic Aesthetics and the Black Independent Cinema: Traces of a Journey." Pp. 62–79 in *Blackframes: Critical Perspectives on Black Independent Cinema,* ed. Mbye B. Cham and Claire Andrade-Watkins. Cambridge, Mass.: MIT Press.

———. 1989. "Third Cinema as Guardian of Popular Memory: Towards a Third Aesthetics." Pp. 53–64 in *Questions of Third Cinema,* ed. Jim Pines and Paul Willemen. London: British Film Institute.

Gerster, Carole. 1994. "The Asian American Renaissance in Independent Cinema and Valerie Soe's *New Year.*" Pp. 187–96 in *A Gathering of Voices on the Asian American Experience,* ed. Annette White-Parks. Fort Atkinson, Wis.: Highsmith Press.

Grierson, John. 1966. *Grierson on Documentary.* Ed. Forsyth Hardy. London: Faber and Faber.

Heung, Marina. 1995. "Representing Ourselves, Films and Videos by Asian American/Canadian Women." Pp. 82-104 in *Feminism, Multiculturalism, and the Media: Global Diversities,* ed. Angharad N. Valdivia. Thousand Oaks, Calif.: Sage Publications.

hooks, bell. 1996. "back to the avant-garde: the progressive vision." Pp. 98–108 in *Reel to Real: Race, Sex, and Class at the Movies.* New York: Routledge.

Kern, Stephen. 1983. *The Culture of Time and Space: 1880–1918.* Cambridge, Mass.: Harvard University Press.

Kristeva, Julia. 1986. "Women's Time." Pp. 187–213 in *The Kristeva Reader,* ed. Toril Moi. New York: Columbia University Press.

Le Grice, Malcolm. 1977. *Abstract Film and Beyond.* Cambridge: MIT Press.

Leong, Russell. 1991. "To Open the Future." Pp. xi–xxi in *Moving the Image: Independent Asian Pacific American Media Arts*, ed. Leong.

Leong, Russell, ed. 1991. *Moving the Image: Independent Asian Pacific American Media Arts*. Los Angeles: UCLA Asian American Studies Center and Visual Communications, Southern California Asian American Studies Central.

Lipsitz, George. 1990. *Time Passages: Collective Memory and American Popular Culture*. Minneapolis: University of Minnesota Press.

MacDonald, Scott. 1993. *Avant-Garde Film: Motion Studies*. Cambridge: Cambridge University Press.

Musser, Charles and Robert Sklar. 1990. "Introduction." Pp. 3–11 in *Resisting Images: Essays on Cinema and History*. Eds. Robert Sklar and Charles Musser. Philadelphia: Temple University Press.

Pratt, Mary Louise. 1985–86, "Scratches on the Face of the Country." *Critical Inquiry* 12: 119–43.

Rosenstone, Robert A. 1988. "History in Images/History in Words: Reflections on the Possibility of Really Putting History onto Film." *American Historical Review* 93, no. 5 (December): 1173–86.

Rushdie, Salman. 1985. "Outside the Whale." *American Film* (January–February): 16, 70–73.

Said, Edward W. 1978. *Orientalism*. New York: Pantheon Books.

Shohat, Ella, and Robert Stam. 1994. *Unthinking Eurocentrism: Multiculturalism and the Media*. New York: Routledge.

Sidney, P. Adams. 1974. *Visionary Film: The American Avant-Garde*. New York: Oxford University Press.

Soja, Edward W. 1989. *Postmodern Geographies: the Reassertion of Space in Critical Social Theory*. New York: Verso.

Sorlin, Pierre. 1980. *The Film in History: Restaging the Past*. Oxford: Basil Blackwell.

Tajima, Renee. 1991. "Moving the Image: Asian American Independent Filmmaking, 1970–1990." Pp. 10–33 in *Moving the Image: Independent Asian Pacific American Media Arts*, ed. Leong.

Tajiri, Rea. 1991. Script for *History and Memory*. Chicago Video Data Bank.

Tanaka, Janice. "Electrons and Reflective Shadows." Pp. 206–207 in *Moving the Image: Independent Asian Pacific American Media Arts*, ed. Leong.

Trinh, T. Minh-ha. 1989. *Woman, Native, Other: Writing Postcoloniality and Feminism*. Bloomington: Indiana University Press.

———. 1991 *When the Moon Waxes Red: Representation, Gender and Cultural Politics*. New York: Routledge.

———. 1992. *Framer Framed*. New York: Routledge.

Wong, Eugene Franklin. 1978. *On Visual Media Racism: Asians in the American Motion Pictures*. New York: Arno Press.

Van Buren, Cassandra. 1992. "Family Gathering: Release from Emotional Internment." *Jump Cut* 37: 56–62.

"The [Video] World According to Cheang and Chong." 1988. *CineVue* 3, no. 1 (March): 7.

Films and Videos Cited

Cheang, Shu Lea. 1989. *Color Schemes: America's Washload in 4 Cycles*. Women Make Movies.

Cimino, Michael. 1985. *Year of the Dragon*. MGM/UA Home Entertainment.

Jhally, Sut. 1997. *Representation and the Media.* Media Education Foundation.

Léger, Fernand. 1924. *Ballet Mécanique.* Video Yesteryear.

Mann, Daniel. 1956. *The Teahouse of the August Moon.* MGM/UA Home Entertainment.

Quine, Richard. 1960. *The World of Suzie Wong.* Films Inc.

Ray, Man. 1923. *Le Retour à la Raison.*

Schumacher, Joel. 1993. *Falling Down.* Warner Home Video, Inc.

Soe, Valerie. 1987. *New Year: Parts I and II.* Women Make Movies.

———. 1992. *Picturing Oriental Girls: A (Re) Educational Videotape.* NAATA, Video Out.

Tajiri, Rea. 1991. *History and Memory: For Akiko and Takashige.* Electronic Arts Intermix

Tanaka, Janice. 1989. *Memories from the Department of Amnesia.* NAATA.

Trinh, T. Minh-ha. 1982. *Reassemblage.* Women Make Movies.

———. 1985. *Naked Spaces—Living Is Round.* Women Make Movies.

———. 1989. *Surname Viet Given Name Nam.* Women Make Movies.

Yasui, Lise. 1988. *Family Gathering.* NAATA.

Gwendolyn Foster and Trinh T. Minh-ha

12   Character Zone: A Conversation with Trinh T. Minh-ha

Gwendolyn Foster: A Tale of Love [Trinh and Bourdier 1995] transgresses the borders between narrative film and experimental film. I read it as a postmodern performative enunciation of a nineteenth-century Vietnamese poem, "The Tale of Kieu." How would you classify the film, if it even needs classification, and how do those people who have seen the film classify it? It has been positioned as your "first narrative film." How do you feel about that?

Trinh T. Minh-ha: Yes, no doubt, the term is not mine, and I don't consider *A Tale of Love* my first narrative film. One can see it as a natural extension of my previous work, or one can see it as a different kind of performance, a new trajectory in directions similar to those taken by my earlier films. These have always resisted the reductive binaries set up between "fiction" and "documentary" films.

GF: Exactly. This brings up the issue of categorization.

TMH: I've made it quite clear, in the writings and interviews published, that "experimental" is not a genre, and "documentary" does not really exist, since everything goes through fictional devices in film. Rather than reverting endlessly to these established categories, I would prefer to speak about different degrees of staged and unstaged material, or about different spaces of resistance—such as that of enriching meaning while divesting it of its power to order images and sound. I work with the tension these differences raise and the way they creatively or critically contaminate each other. This largely accounts for the difficulties my films kept encountering in many exhibition venues, including those that claim to support multicultural, independent, or alternative work. The films I've been making confront people in their nor-

An earlier version of this chapter appeared as "'A Tale of Love': A Dialogue with Trinh T. Minh-ha," *Film Criticism* 21, no. 3 (Spring 1997). Reprinted with permission.

malized need to categorize, to make sense and to know all. It is in this vein that *A Tale* also continues to frustrate easy consumption, although it certainly differs from the earlier films in its work process. For example, none of my previous films was scripted before the shooting, while in this film almost everything was scripted ahead of time, albeit in a form that was unusual for the actors and the crew.

GF: What was different about the way you worked with the actors and the crew on this film?

TMH: The script I gave them had all the scenes, with storyboards that showed all the camera positions and movements and the framings, as well as the lighting designs for each scene. But there was no set order to these scenes. I wrote them both as a director and as an editor, so I was leaving room for the scenes to build on one another during the shooting and to find their own order in the editing phase. Since I did away with sequential order, the planning was at times very frustrating for the key organizing members, including the script supervisor, who is traditionally the continuity person. Working with a large crew in a limited time frame makes it almost impossible to improvise and to operate outside the framework of traditional narrative filmmaking, in which the specific division of labor tends to become at times too rigid and constraining. However, most of the "department heads" of our crew had more than one role to fulfill, and I can't complain, because everyone did their best. The actors, for example, tried very hard to make their lines, their roles, and their precisely blocked movements seem natural despite the quite "unnatural" nature of the script. I myself had to shift ground radically and to conceive of the space of "improvisation" other than as a space of spontaneous formation. The openings offered should then be found elsewhere than in the dichotomy of unscripted versus scripted work.

GF: I could feel the real tension that existed between the performative forms. How did it feel to be directing in a different genre, even though it is a genre that comes out of your own tradition? Did you feel in some ways more free and in some ways more restricted in the making of *A Tale of Love*? I'm also very interested in the spare acting style of the film.

TMH: In some ways, it was certainly more restrictive. I used to have a crew of three to six people, maximum, and I was doing most of the work myself, including the camera and sound recording in remote rural contexts. Of course, the time was then my own. I shot whatever I saw or whenever the moment was ripe for shooting, and I shot it the way I looked at it through the lens. The indeterminate waiting and looking without using the camera was always part of the shooting. As soon as you start working with a crew of seventeen to twenty-five people, the space for improvisation is extremely limited. Because of budgetary constraints, I cannot afford, for example, what Godard can sometimes afford, which is to keep the actors for a certain length of time (he mentioned three to six months) so he can experiment and write his script from day to day as he works with them. Or, for example, the case of Robert Bresson, who asks his "models" (or non-actors) to perform their actions mechanically and exactly as he wants them, and then to repeat them until they no longer notice what they are doing. It is in this mechanical precision that he feels he can capture something "raw" (*matiere brut*) in his models. These are two examples of ways of reconceiving acting that I love, but I had a different situation and very different constraints. These constraints actually added to the film, because I learned to work with them and use them to my advantage.

Since experimentation cannot be equated with improvisation in this film, I was compelled to come up with a space of acting whose slightly denaturalized performance would hit on very different sensitive chords in our reception of narrative film. It was more a question, let's say, of performing with the unknown (what is veiled to our ear and eye) within the appearance of the known. As Alikan, the photographer, states in the film, here everything is performed for and nothing is really unforeseen. Freedom in a highly constructed space is a different kind of freedom, much less obvious and hence more easily mistakable for its absence. Yet it is in this space that elements unknown to myself, to the actors, and to the end product emerge in the moments of production and reception. Performing here is not simply evaluated according to how well an actor can portray the psychology and behavior of a given character. The intent is not to capture "natural" or naturalistic acting, but rather to capture what remains unforeseeable—for example, when one works with precision on duration. The overall choreography of the camera movement in the film is both exact and exacting. There is not a single shot-reverse-shot in the entirety of this feature-length film, and what may become perceptible when the camera stays fixed on two actors in dialogue, or when it passes by them in a mercilessly slow movement, is the very space of viewing and of performing. When the actors' slightest self-consciousness becomes visible to the spectators, the latter may also become conscious of their own moment of consumption of the "spectacle" or of the "scene" acted on screen for them, and hence the general discomfort that some of them have voiced.

GF: That seems to have added resonance within the context of this film because it is about a woman who, as a model, makes her living performing for the camera. This film is a meditation on performance and dramatic narrative, and I think it breaks open the boundaries of what we think of as performing, especially in performing a poem, and in a sense re-performing the poem "The Tale of Kieu."

TMH: Right, . . . yes, exactly.

GF: One could read the film in the traditional linear narrative fashion in the sense that it centers on a heroine, Kieu, who is in love with writing. She's investigating "The Tale of Kieu" and working as a model. But as the film unfolds, I see her as a figure who moves across narrative zones. I notice that she often gazes at the viewer and speaks to us as she actively deconstructs the very narrative that she embodies. Toward the middle of the film, the narrative drive of the film seems to become less and less linear. I'm referring to those sections of the film in which we watch her writing and

PHOTO 12.1. Kieuh (Mai Huynh) in *A Tale of Love* (1995), dir. Trinh T. Minh-ha and Jean-Paul Bourdier. Courtesy of Moongift Films.

daydreaming, thinking about writing and fantasizing. She makes me think of a "character zone," a very fluid zone in the sense that Mikhail Bakhtin used that phrase. Do you see her that way?

TMH: To some extent, yes. Most of the experimentation done in "narrative film" focuses on the structure of the narrative. Very few filmmakers have worked on the space of acting to stretch the dimension of the narrative. Marguerite Duras certainly contributed to calling into question narrative form by doing away with acting as impersonifying and representing. Her complex use of the voice (voiceover, voice off-screen; external, non-psychological, non-interiorized voices) in relation to blank spaces, love, death, desire, and their absence–presence through the actors' bodies is unique. It is more common among experimental filmmakers to rupture the narrative by using non-linear time and space, for example. But for me, since I've always worked at the limits of several categories, several narrative realms at once, it was not a question of simply rejecting linearity or doing away with the story.

GF: Yes, here we have many stories, many Kieus, and many levels of narrative. At the same time, there really is no unified narrative. It's very pleasurable to experience.

TMH: You start out with a story, and you realize, as it unfolds, that there's not really a story in the film. The thread created moves forward crisscrossed and interlaced by other threads until it breaks with its own linearity. Hence, a story is told mainly to say that there is no story—only a complex, tightly knit tissue of activities and events that have no single explanation, as in life. Of course, a number of viewers tend to catch immediately onto the relationship between Kieu, the protagonist, and Alikan, the photographer, because what they see above all is a conflict between genders, cultures, and economical and political positions (boss–employee; subject–object). The ideology of conventional narrative is, as Raul Ruiz puts it, based on the globalized central conflict theory, a theory that rules over both the film industries of the world and the political system of the United States as a dominant model nation. Fortunately, however, for other viewers and myself there is no real conflict in *A Tale*. Not only is the relationship with Alikan merely one among the three visualized in the film, but there are also many relationships other than the ones people tend to follow, especially those not dependent on actors and dialogue. Further, these dialogues are not real dialogues; they are written as story spaces that are peculiar to each role designed, and

PHOTO 12.2.   Kieuh (Mai Huynh) and Alikan (Dominic Overstreet) in *A Tale of Love* (1995), dir. Trinh T. Minh-ha and Jean-Paul Bourdier. Courtesy of Moongift Films.

despite their close interactions, they maintain their independent logic—not good versus bad logic, but only *different* ones.

Here the notion of a fluid "character zone" raised in your earlier question is very relevant. I am thinking more specifically of the movements of the characters across dream states and reality on film. I could talk in dichotomies and say they are the landscapes of a person in love: internal and external, past and present, mythical and historical, literary and filmic. I could also see these movements as inscribing a multiplicity of narrative threads and narrative interfaces. An example is the night scene (in an industrial setting) toward the end of the film, when Kieu is speaking to a man wearing a raincoat and a hat, whom we do not recognize as Alikan until the last line of the scene or until we see Kieu, in the next day shot, waking up (in Juliet's court) and uttering his name with surprise. The same day shot with Kieu drowsing off (in Juliet's court) is seen somewhere toward the beginning of the film. So many things have happened in the film during this lapse of time that a multitude of questions may be raised as to both the nature of that night scene (Is it a nightmare? A fantasy? A memory?) and the nature of the events that came before it (Was she telling herself stories all this time? Or was the daydream dreaming her?). No single linear explanation can account for these narrative interfaces in which performer and performance, dreamer and dream, are constituted like the two sides of a coin. One cannot say that she's simply moving in and out of fantasy and reality; rather, one can say that it's a different zone we are experiencing.

GF: As a viewer, I really like that sense of falling into that zone because it's indescribable and it makes you want to see the film again and re-experience the cracks and fissures in narrative and character. I was interested in the implications you make between writing and loving and the connection to the rhetoric around women as writers. In particular, I was thinking of some of the writing that has been done on women's writing, such as Hélène Cixous' "The Laugh of the Medusa." But it also made me rethink Plato's *Phaedrus*. Both speak specifically about writing, creativity, and romantic love and how they're very much tied to the body. I was struck by the ways in which you embodied and enacted these ideas in the film.

TMH: Well, I'm certainly glad to hear that, because although I do not expect viewers to be receptive to all the layers involved (I myself am still learning to articulate them), the fact that some viewers, yourself included, may be familiar with feminist writing would make all the difference. If we don't center our attention on this so-called conflict in the film, then there is a whole other narrative layer that may come to the front. This is the realm in which Kieu as a character shuttles between more than one identity and contributes to the afterlives of The Tale. No matter how non-illustrative the relation is, the film's present-day Kieu who lives as an immigrant in the States and does research on "The Tale of Kieu" is also embodying the poem's nineteenth-century Kieu who sacrifices herself for love. In that sense, she partakes in the life experiences of the thousands of all-time Kieus whom her aunt mentioned in the film. As with my other films, there are many forms of reflexivity in *A Tale*. And working with them means opening up to the possibility of engaging with infinity within the very finiteness of a constructed film space. Kieu's self-reflectivity and reflexivity constantly shift; the question is not simply that of doubling—one looks into the mirror and sees a reflection, or a double, of oneself—but that of one reflection reflecting another reflection to infinity. Kieu's reality here is in tune both with the boundless (or bounding) reality of love and with the radically reflexive nature of cinema and writing. It is this notion of shifting interface and reflection, with no side passing for the original, that really interests me, especially in working with voyeurism in this film.

GF: One of the things I really liked about the film is that it is obviously a meditation on the discourse around the politics of women and objectification and voyeurism. As a viewer, I felt engaged in a performance that was voyeuristic and that, at the same time, made me critique that place of voyeurism. This must be provoking all sorts of responses from audience members. Can you talk about that?

TMH: Yes, I think the film can offer the viewer a unique entryway when it is placed in the context of feminism. But if you miss that entryway, there are other possible ways to enter *A Tale,* because the voyeur has appeared quite prominently in a number of writers', filmmakers', and artists' works. One can look at the entire history of narrative in terms of voyeurism—how different forms of voyeurism are deployed in order to sustain narrative power, and how they are made to go unnoticed, especially among spectators who, unaware of their complicity as screen voyeurs, want to be "convinced" of what they see. In other words, the production of (unacknowledged) voyeurism and the consumption of realist narrative continue to feed on each other. It's difficult for me to tell right now how audiences are viewing the film because it has just been released. From the screenings I attended, its reception already oscillates between a very high discomfort and a very intense, enthusiastic response.

GF: Maybe even a bit of both. I do remember being a bit shocked that you were taking on what can be shown and what cannot be shown. I mean, we're looking at women being looked at, and with all the discourse around women being reduced to their object status of to-be-looked-at-ness, this is transgressive space that you're moving into. And it is clearly an important counter-strategy. It made me constantly ask myself questions such as, How is Trinh, as a woman filmmaker, different in her representation of voyeurism? How can I negotiate the many different narrative strands of the film with relation to the questions of voyeurism and spectatorship? How is this moving the discourse of pornography further beyond rigid moralistically defined ideals?

TMH: Right. Actually, the film does not really show nudity in a pornographic way, and it doesn't have any lovemaking scenes, for example. As a filmmaker has said it before, when it comes to lovemaking, all actors just start looking like all other actors. The way lovemaking scenes are realized on film remains quite homogenous throughout the history of commercial narrative. Knowing my background, it was perhaps unavoidable that you would ask how a feminist treatment of voyeurism could be different, but this is one way of approaching *A Tale*. I would say that the viewers' discomfort with it so far seems to be less easily locatable, perhaps because it takes time to articulate this discomfort, and there is no consensus among them as to where or what disturbs them. Some think it's the script; some, the lack of plot and unified storyline; others, the acting and the actors; and others yet, the explicit recognition of themselves being voyeurs.

A number of comments did focus on the acting, which some spectators find "hard to look at," "self-conscious," "distant," or "odd," or they simply "didn't like the style." Informed viewers have invoked similarities with the films of Jean-Marie Straub and Danièle Huillet or of Marguerite Duras. What seems striking in the more negative comments is the fact that viewers differ markedly in their opinions about the specific actors. The one they really have problems with is definitely not always the same (and this applies "democratically" to all five main actors of the film), and yet each sees in one, and only one, particular actor the unequivocal source of his or her discomfort. Several viewers have also divided the acting, in accordance with the setting and the characters, into three levels: more natural, more stylized, and in between the two, mid-stylized. By these comments, it seems likely to me that the viewer is uncomfortable because she or he feels some of the acute moments when the actors themselves are self-conscious. This is exactly what I was aiming for, although I was not sure what the exact outcome would be. *A Tale* does not fall squarely into the kind of film whose actors' deliveries sound deliberately read or monotonously flat, because the artifice is clearly exposed as such. A number of films work in that direction—Yvonne Rainer's films, for example. In my case, I was experimenting with different effects in a slightly different space, and I didn't want the scripted lines to sound distinctly "read." I would let the actors try to make their deliveries as naturalistic as possible because I knew that the "dialogues" I wrote could not be entirely naturalized, although what ultimately resists being naturalized remains undefined, and hence fascinating to me.

GF: So in a sense, you're acting as an ethnographer of performance itself. You are problematizing acting styles in ways that are questioning naturalistic expression. I'm thinking particularly of moments such as the one in which Kieu tells the photographer, Alikan, that what he really wants is a headless body. There's a sense, as a viewer, that she may not have said that (in any sort of reality or narrative construct that we're used to), but she's saying it in this film, and there's something disconcerting and abstract about the way she says it. How did the actors feel about delivering these lines? It must have been discomforting or maybe funny at points.

TMH: Actually, it seemed that what bothered them—or, at least, in the case of Dominic Overstreet, the actor who played Alikan—was not so much the lines themselves as the way they were written. He would repeatedly try to change the sentence slightly to make it more colloquial. At one point, I asked him to tell me on camera the problems he was having with the script. And he said that, for him, it wasn't really written in American English, the kind of English he's used to, it was written in British English. I was tickled to hear that because there is some truth to such a remark. I was taught English in Vietnam by British and British-educated teachers, and furthermore, both my personal assistant and the script supervisor speak British English. Yet I know the problem is not only to be found there; it also has to do with how, when, and where (in what situations) the lines are supposed to be delivered. Alikan is working with a model who "resists not having a head" and whose uncommon lines can leave both actors slightly at a loss as to finding the right tone and reaction for them.

GF: It's very active and self-reflective in a wonderful way. I was astounded at, and found great visual pleasure in, watching the scene in which the male photographer is blinded. I don't know whether that was an allusion, but it reminded me of something that nineteenth-century women writers do to heroes in Gothic romances. I was particularly thinking of *Jane Eyre.* I wondered whether you were making an allusion or whether I was just looking for connections to female writers.

TMH: This is a wonderful reading. But for me, this was not a direct allusion, because when I was creating it, I was doing it quite intuitively in relation to the whole context of voyeurism. It is important to note that in the scene you mentioned, both the man and the woman are blindfolded. The people working with me and some of the viewers who have seen the film have been really struck by the fact that for the first time neither can *see* the other.

GF: Yes, that scene is certainly one of the most transgressive images. It certainly destroys subject–object positionality as we know it. It is a staggering image. To look as a voyeur at both man and woman who are bound with the veil feels oddly powerful yet self-conscious, because we find ourselves surprised at our active gaze.

TMH: On the one hand, it is a rupture with domination by eye because only touching prevails here in the relationship between the man and the woman. And the sense of touch is heightened all the more when sight is hindered. Vision and visuality have long been the domain in which men's mastery is exerted, while the eroticism of the female body through touch is an area some feminists have reappropriated and theorized at length. On the other hand, one can say that the film is a trap for the gaze, and the gender line is not so clear-cut. Except for Alikan, the other voyeurs in the film are women, and as you mention, the scene we're discussing is one among those designed to call attention to the viewing space or to the spectator's own voyeurism. (If the actors can't see each other then, who's looking at them?) Finally, it is not just looking at the scene, but being put on the spot—the voyeur's encounter with his or her own gaze— that has the potential to make the viewers most uncomfortable, even though they may not recognize this and would rather find fault elsewhere.

GF: Perhaps because it's a new experience. We have not really seen images like this before, images that place us in a different kind of subjectivity with relation to our sense

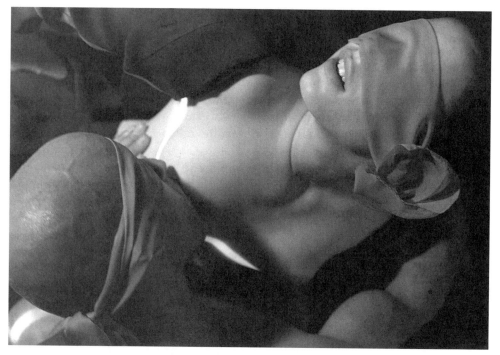

PHOTO 12.3.   From *A Tale of Love* (1995), dir. Trinh T. Minh-ha and Jean-Paul Bourdier. Courtesy of Moongift Films.

of voyeuristic pleasure. Other scenes have a resonance in their ability to render pleasure and discomfort in the viewer. I'm thinking of the scene in which Kieu takes the veil and puts it on herself. That seemed out of the ordinary.

TMH: Which one was that?

GF: At one point, Kieu seems to be taking a lot more control of her situation. She goes to work at the photo studio, and there she takes the veil and places it on herself. I think this happens immediately before she gets verbally assertive towards Alikan. She tells him he really wants only a headless body. This is interesting because immediately before this, when she enters the studio, she is flipping through a book of pornographic images of women. She's taking more and more of her body back, of her subjectivity back. I was very drawn to those scenes and also to the scenes between Juliet and Kieu in which they discuss the history of fragrances and love. I know there's some critical writing about fragrance and film and eroticism. For me, this is wrapped into the idea of writing and performing and romance.

TMH: In filmmaking, the two senses that are most privileged are the visual and the auditive. The other senses—touch, taste, and smell—are extremely difficult to solicit without falling into the order of meaning. One hears or looks at a film, but one can

PHOTO 12.4.   Juliet (Juliette Chen), left, and Kieuh (Mai Huynh) in *A Tale of Love* (1995), dir. Trinh T. Minh-ha and Jean-Paul Bourdier. Courtesy of Moongift Films.

only literally touch, taste, and smell a piece of celluloid. Perhaps it is necessary to return here to the notion of film as event rather than as mere spectacle. Instead of centering on the screen, the viewer's experience of film is also engaged in the extra-screen space—that is, the movie-house space or the immediate environment. I am reminded of a practice in Japanese Kabuki theater devised to heighten the audience's sensual experience of the play: With the extended notion of the stage and the many uses made of the passageways (*hanamichi*) that run through the audience, a play can, for example, have its "fragrant stamp," or its performance can be intensified at specific moments—such as at the last rites of a funeral, when the body of a beloved character is placed in a palanquin with a bowl of incense, and as the palanquin is carried through the audience, the theater slowly fills with the mournful fragrance.

This is quite a challenge for a filmmaker to convey through film, and unfortunately, one cannot aim for similar effects with today's movie-theater audiences (a public that is largely not initiated to the language of fragrance and its precise use in different rites and ceremonies). Most of us tend to minimize the sense of smell as well as the tools that qualify it. However, it seems that the time one becomes oversensitive and one's senses are wildly awakened despite oneself is when one is in the state of being in love. Since the film enacts this state, with all of its lucidity and its silliness, it is important to dedicate a large part of the film to the importance of smell. Andy

Warhol wrote a whole chapter on smell and perfume. What interests me is that you find perfume in all women's magazines. So in the film, it is through Juliet, who is the editor of a women's magazine, that one hears about how stories and fragrances can be created. When you see how inventively the creation of perfume in these women's magazines is written about, it's just amazing. It's a whole unexplored area, for me, of creativity.

GF: Another thing I am really interested in is the use of multiple voiceovers in the film. In the context of the discussion of disembodied knowledge and embodied knowledge, Kieu has a number of very active voiceovers presented within the context of the discourse of eroticism of headless women. I thought that was really funny and poetic. The film repositions the voiceover in search of a multiplicity of subject positions for Kieu. Did you make this choice while editing the film, or did you have those sort of ideas in your mind before you wrote it?

TMH: The lines Kieu read in voiceover were written with the script from the start (albeit on separate sheets to be recorded at the post-production phase), but I decided how and where they came in only when I built the soundtrack. As I've mentioned, the order of these lines was not set in advance. The film took form during the shooting and changed again during the editing. It was in the process of going from one form to another that the different designations of the voiceovers (the verse singing can be another indirect voice) emerged.

GF: One thing that should be noted is how the character Kieu stresses that the importance of Kieu (of the poem) is her resistance. Kieu forces us to think about the daily acts of resistance that so many women, particularly women who are read as "victims," perform. I find it significant that Kieu is walking along in front of strip clubs when we hear her voiceover reflecting on the morality of Kieu. What she says in her voiceover is as important as her actions. Within the context of the film, I get a sense that "The Tale of Kieu" is one of the most culturally significant poems of the Vietnamese diaspora. Why did you choose this poem?

TMH: It is a very important poem for the Vietnamese. I already touched on the figure of Kieu in one of my previous films, *Surname Viet Given Name Nam* (1989). It was then placed in the context of mythical, historical, and current women of resistance of Vietnam. Kieu's passion-driven life, marked by unremitting misfortunes and sustained by her sacrifice, endurance, and loyalty, has become the allegory for Vietnam's destiny. But if in *Surname Viet* the film's reflexive dimension is gradually brought out through a number of devices, and more explicitly toward the end in the comments of a voiceover, in *A Tale of Love* you don't have the explicit staging of any voice that stands outside "the story" to comment on it. In other words, there's no visible meta-discourse. That is discomforting for viewers who expect, as with my other films, to be informed more directly of the moves involved by a voice that pulls out from the film to reflect on it. I decided in this film that I would have none of that, so meaning, form, and structure evolve out of the tension among the filmmaker, the subject, and the viewer. As we've discussed, the reflexive dimension is both diffused in every narrative layer and concentrated in the treatment of voyeurism. This seems to have made film viewers even more uncomfortable.

Voyeurism is here further coupled with the aesthetics and politics of the veil. Of course, the veil and the headless female body are reflected in many ways in the film, both literally and metaphorically. Linked to voyeurism, the veil is framed in a whole fabric of relations. First, there is Alikan's love for everything that is veiled, including the *look* of the model. That the model should not "look back" while he shoots is certainly nothing new in photography (the naturalistic formula we all abide by when shooting on location is: "Don't look at the camera, just go on with your activities as if I'm not there"). Looking back is also commonly experienced as an act of defiance, a perilous act that is historically feared for its ability to divest the master of his power to possess and control. In many parts of the world, the unveiled woman is still the one who moves about "undressed." She who looks back rather than hides or is oblivious to her body and her sensuality is bound to provoke. And here we paradoxically link up with the other dimension of the veil: If Alikan uses all kinds of veiling devices, it is both to dispossess the model of her power to gaze and to prevent the image from falling into the realm of pornography (in pornography, the nude often looks straight—provocatively and invitingly—at the camera). The veil is oppressive, but it can also become a form of resistance—hence, the importance of the scene in which both man and woman are blindfolded and the necessity of also having women voyeurs in the film. The way we all partake in the politics and aesthetics of veiling is complex and often paradoxical.

The scene that you mentioned, having Kieu walking outdoors, is therefore very important for me personally. I've noticed, for example, how in certain Middle Eastern cultures—this should apply to other contexts across nations, as well—the streets continue to belong to men while the domestic realm remains women's domain. But this being said, I don't want to reiterate that binary opposition between public and private space as developed in certain feminists' work. Let's just say that since the street belongs to men, women have a different space. Whenever they go out into the street, for example, they do so only at certain hours of the day. The unspoken rule is that they shouldn't be seen too much in daylight and they shouldn't be seen at night; they should appear somewhere in between. This is what I've noticed in Yemen. Between 4 and 6 p.m., the women come out in the street completely veiled. This is the time of the day when their veiled silhouettes are seen moving outside against the walls of the houses. So, for me, the scenes of women walking outdoors at night, the scene of Kieu walking by herself and a later scene in which the camera pans along with women outside on the street, is also a way of gesturing toward the whole history of veiling. The dark of night itself is a veil. Even in progressive societies, a woman is not supposed to be alone outside in the street if she comes, let's say, from a well-to-do family or if she has been "properly educated." The night belongs, actually, to those on the margins: sex workers, drug users, secret lovers, and so on. So the scenes of women walking outdoors can be liberatory, but they also remind us of the values of society and the restraints it puts on women in their movement. For how is a woman walking aimlessly alone at night looked at?

GF: Even up until very recently, Western women weren't allowed to travel without a chaperone. That brings me back to the issue of the veil. In this way, the veil is actually someone who travels with you. The idea of taking back space is something that is important to me in a feminist performative context. I read Kieu as *"devenir femme,"* or "becoming woman" in the sense that French feminists use this term. Kieu has flashbacks or fantasy sequences in which she sees herself as a child. Were you staging a primal fantasy of mother–daughter recovery or were you doing something different here?

TMH: No. Actually, I was thinking more in the context of the tale or the poem itself.
The classical poem opens with a very famous scene in which Kieu goes to a temple. There she suddenly sees a desolated tomb and weeps over it, moved by the fact that nobody is really tending it. At night, the woman who was buried there comes

PHOTO 12.5.   Kieuh (Mai Huynh) in *A Tale of Love* (1995), dir. Trinh T. Minh-ha and Jean-Paul Bourdier. Courtesy of Moongift Films.

back to her. It is through this woman that Kieu becomes very conscious of the fact that she's a talented woman and that women with many talents are bound in life to suffer. She begins remembering signs from her childhood that foretold how she was going to suffer in life because of her beauty and her talent. The scene where you first see Kieu as a child precisely alludes to that part of the poem. But it can also work on another level, especially for people who are not familiar with the poem. I guess for those viewers, it evokes a physical and psychological response. In these memory scenes, the child is seen near a body of water. The element of water that runs through the film is very important; here, it is visually tied to the image of a naked Kieu playing freely and to Kieu's memories of home. This is again an intervention of women's space. Another device that I use here is the voiceover, the brief voice of memory. Instead of using a standard device such as a dissolve or a color change to signal the passage to fantasy or memory, I simply have her name being called by an off-screen voice. To hear one's name called by an ex-lover or by a relative can trigger unexpected memories or it can lead one to an immediate change of zone. One can enter and exit a zone by a smell, a sight, or a sound. So, yes, the scenes with the little girl introduce the viewer to the relationship between mother and daughter. This is tied to another thematic thread in the film between tradition and modernity; between the Vietnamese in the diaspora and the Vietnamese "at home" in Vietnam. The link between the two can be moving, warm, affectionate, and tense, burdensome, problematic. But either way, one cannot simply dispense with it. The mother figure is always present.

GF: This is a little bit off the topic, but I feel that you may be making a connection in this film between how people of the supposed "Third World" are lumped together in a space called "the Other" and the way in which romantic narratives break down our notions of an undifferentiated "Other." Kieu is very much like Kieu of the poem, and yet unlike her. And Juliet is also like and unlike Juliet of *Romeo and Juliet.* I like the way that you challenge categorizations. You challenge the notion of the "Other" just as you challenge our notion of self. This revolves around a questioning of the constructions of our essential love tales.

TMH: This is your own reading of the film. The film is made to invite such readings, so I'm very happy to hear them. But I would rather say that I was working with multiplicity. The letters Juliet receives, for example, indicate that even though people know Juliet does not exist, they still address their letters to "Juliet, Verona, Italy." The same can be said of "The Tale of Kieu," which every Vietnamese remembers, whether it serves the official narrative of the Vietnamese government or is carried on by the people who have exiled themselves from Vietnam. The verses have long been part of our daily expressions. Instead of saying how bad a person is or describing what kind of a person one is dealing with, for example, one just invokes the name of one of the typical characters in "The Tale" to communicate precisely what one means. It happens with all classes of people. Because the poem is written in a rhythm taken from Vietnamese proverbs and folk songs, people remember it very easily and they quote its verses as popular sayings. But for me, what remains most amazing is the fact that a whole people identify the destiny of their country with the love story of a woman. Kieu personifies Love. This is the link to Juliet and Romeo, for Kieu is not one heroine, not one character, but, as it is stated in the film, she's numberless. There are as many Kieus as there are talented women across generations whose destinies Kieu's story typifies. Kieu is a multiplicity, just as Juliet is a multiplicity. So for me, it's not so much a question of opposing the West to its Other or of correcting the gap between the Self and the Other. "Juliet" is a name that stands for a person; at the same time, she's a character in the film whose fiction evolves from another fiction. She's a symbol for love and a love site that is radically a multiplicity.

GF: I see what you mean. I guess what I was speaking of was the whole discourse of the essentialized notion of woman, which would mean that "Third World" stories cannot be spoken of in context of "First World" stories. And you really break that down by aligning *Romeo and Juliet* with "The Tale of Kieu"—not in distinct categorizations, but in ways that you can, at least, see parallels because people always quote *Romeo and Juliet*. People constantly refer to that love story, which, of course, has such a tragic ending. I'm drawn to the scene in which Kieu questions Juliet about her conception of romance. She says, "The problem with your love story is that it invariably ends in death or in marriage. You see, I prefer the less definite ending of 'The Tale of Kieu,' which ends in love and friendship." I was very interested in the idea of women's love and friendship in the film. The friendship between Kieu and Juliet is foregrounded. Their relationship is just as important as, if not more important than, the relationship between Kieu and Alikan.

TMH: Yes. I am happy you noticed that because, for me, the relationship between Juliet and Kieu is decisive. They move through different levels. At the beginning, it might seem as if their friendship is based on an editor–writer relationship, which is usually inequitable. Some viewers have rightly seen Juliet as a mentor or elder sister to Kieu, who is younger and an emergent writer. But I think they are equals in the sense that the performance space and the acting trajectory allow them to develop as equals.

GF: It's a relationship usually based to some extent on money and privilege, but in the film, it's a more even exchange; it is a fantasy relationship. The two women spend great amounts of time together, and Juliet speaks from her heart in ways that are really interesting to me. In other words, she says the unexpected. In reference to new ways of looking at acting, I'd like you to talk about the section of the film in which Juliet does a performative dance. It is very funny and unusual and self-reflective. It is during the scene when they're talking about *Romeo and Juliet*. Juliet stares directly at the camera and begins dancing. Her dance seems to be out of context. I was wondering why she suddenly begins doing those dance moves?

TMH: One aspect of my film work comes out very strongly with certain audiences and is totally lost on other audiences. That's the whole dimension of humor. To some extent, it may be because of cultural difference. When *Surname Viet Given Name Nam* premiered in San Francisco, half of the audience, the Vietnamese-speaking audience, laughed at certain parts, while the English-speaking audience laughed at other parts. They were almost never in sync, and some of the viewers were disoriented by that because they had the feeling they had missed out on something. Language seems to have played a role here. But then the reception of *Shoot for the Contents* (1991) was similarly disparate. It varied from audiences that were extremely serious and totally silent throughout the film to audiences in which people were laughing and giggling all along. The same thing seems to be happening with *A Tale of Love*. The very first small audience I showed it to—mostly programmers—were deadly serious with it, but when *A Tale* had a sneak preview with hundreds of people, they were largely laughing and giggling throughout the film. Many media makers and consumers tend to reduce humor to its most evidently comical connotation (the sitcom kind of jokes), but humor can be subtle, barely present, yet disturbing, tragic, anarchic, dissociative, moving, deconstructive, and so on. Humor is not only in what makes one laugh; it also lies in one's ability to respond (with humor). With humor, things always leak and, as you've seen, there is definitely a dimension to my films that is quite silly and that has no logical explanation.

GF: Another thing I wanted to talk to you about is something I'm interested in because I'm a filmmaker, and so is my husband. We have collaborated in both film and performance art, so I'm always interested in the nature of collaborative partnerships. Also, I have written a great deal on women filmmakers, many of whom have worked with their husbands in collaborative partnerships. Often one or the other tends to get sole credit for a project, because when one co-directs, when you give credit to both partners, often someone chooses who will get the credit—usually a film historian, curator, or archivist. And usually, that person will choose the male partner. For example, Elizaveta Svilova co-directed many of the Vertov films, and there are many, many other examples. I want to make sure that it is known that Jean-Paul Bourdier co-directed this film with you, and that you often co-direct. In Western culture, we tend to see the artist as an individual, and we have trouble with the notion of any kind of collaborative art. Would you talk a little about the nature of collaboration and your experience of collaboration?

TMH: Collaboration is a term that is highly esteemed among marginalized groups because there is a tendency to value collaborative work over individual work in contexts where it is almost impossible to escape the burden of representation. In a number of film collectives (the more successful ones were Sankofa and the Black Audio Film and Video Collective in the United Kingdom), a certain rejection of individual authorship may thrive. I think collaboration is a wonderful concept, but most of the time what happens in collaborative situations is that you end up having one person who directs, then the other people work with the director. Some of the solutions that collectives have come up with include having different members direct different films. But in the process, it usually becomes clear that you only have one or two directors on whom the members of the collective rely to "give direction" to a project. So unless one works with someone on equal ground, but whose areas of strength are radically different from one's own (even when situated in the same field), one cannot really talk about collaboration. Collaboration happens not when something is shared between the collaborators, but when something that belongs to neither of them comes to pass between them. This is what happens between Jean-Paul and me when we work together.

Not only did Jean-Paul take part in all of my previous films—he was consistently the co-producer, production designer, or art director—but we have also written two books on African architecture together. Even though he didn't have to design any specific setting for the films shot in Africa, we selected all the sites together. He did research for all the locations and had a major role in deciding at which site we would choose to film. He really has an eye for that. We have different strengths, though. Every time we encounter the same experience, we have totally different approaches to it. For example, during the shooting of *Naked Spaces* (1985) and of *Shoot for the Contents*, Jean-Paul's relationship to movement and space was certainly that of a passionate "eye-feeler" who sees and feels almost everything at once. As an architect, he apprehends space in its overall expanse and potential; receives it instantaneously in form, volume, plan, and structural capacities; and visualizes it effortlessly from a bird's-eye view. A building is immediately envisioned as time, age, trace. My relationship to space and the built environment is almost the opposite: blind, fragmented, temporal, circumstantial. I don't see through walls and roofs, so I move around unknowingly, and I'm always at a loss. Both relationships are necessary in filmmaking. So in *A Tale of Love*, which Jean-Paul co-directed, we decided to divide our roles accordingly: Jean-Paul would direct according to the script. Being the one who actually facilitated all the action during the shooting, he was the "true director." I was a very quiet director because I needed the space both to take in and to pull out from the whole process. The execution of ideas is not all that there is to filmmaking, of course, but one easily forgets that, especially when one is working with some twenty-five people, and everybody wants the director's attention. The fact that we co-directed the film really allowed me to have that space, to reflect on what was going on in the production process and how that might act on the editing and post-production of the material. More than with my previous films, Jean-Paul's production design and lighting design in *A Tale* play a decisive role in bringing out what I discussed earlier as being most stimulating—the sensual, nonverbal, unmeasurable dimension of the film.

Films and Videos Cited

Trinh, T. Minh-ha. 1985. *Naked Spaces—Living Is Round*. Women Make Movies.
———. 1989. *Surname Viet Given Name Nam*. Women Make Movies.
———. 1991. *Shoot for the Contents*. Women Make Movies.
Trinh, T. Minh-ha, and Jean-Paul Bourdier. 1995. *A Tale of Love*. Women Make Movies.

Eve Oishi

13   Bad Asians: New Film and Video by
Queer Asian American Artists

It is after midnight on an early fall night in 1995. I am walking through a darkened section of New York's East Village with my girlfriend when we pass a lighted storefront. Inside are rows of pool tables, each one surrounded by groups of young Asian American men and women, smoking, drinking, waving pool cues and beer bottles, and shouting curses and challenges across the room. The scene is startling, raucous, slightly seedy, and it reminds me of my father's descriptions of the pool halls frequented by Filipino bachelors back in Guadalupe, California, before World War II, places that held a certain fascination and danger for the more conservative Japanese Americans. "Bad Asian pool hall," I say and explain my theory about Good and Bad Asians. Good Asians embody the images and behaviors prescribed to them by white society. They are conservative and quiet supporters of the status quo. Good Asians don't hang out at pool halls. There is a white-supremacist fiction that Asian Americans are overwhelmingly interested in something called "saving face" and therefore will not do anything to call undue attention to themselves or their communities.[1] Therefore, any Asian American who makes noise, acts nasty, or in any way flouts the expectations of racist stereotype is a Bad Asian. Bad as in "badass." Bad as in anyone who does not covet white patriarchal approval; anyone who challenges racism, class oppression, sexism, homophobia; anyone who talks candidly about sex and desire.

Bad Asians are inherently threatening to hegemonic systems, but they do not always choose their oppositional status. Falling outside the boundaries of social approval and propriety is just as often the result of poverty, racism, language barriers, or the segregation of urban demographics. The gangs of young Cambodian kids that I used to encounter in my neighborhood in Philadelphia developed their badass street postures in response to the police harassment, racial tension and cultural alienation that they encountered daily rather than an expressed desire to challenge the dominant power structure. Bad Asians challenge and resist the status quo because they have already been excluded from it or oppressed, silenced, or limited by it.

Some examples of this phenomenon: I am flipping channels on my television and light upon an episode of one of the many *Star Trek* offshoots. An Asian man in Starfleet uniform is kneeling over a wounded white comrade. The wounded officer feebly exhorts the Asian man to leave him behind and save himself. But even though his life is in danger, he assures the white comrade that he will never leave his side. He will sacrifice his life if necessary before abandoning his duty to his friend. Good Asian.

At a community video screening, I discover a documentary on Yuri Kochiyama, a resident of Harlem and local activist for more than forty years. Kochiyama, who was interned with more than 100,000 Japanese Americans during World War II, became involved in the Japanese American redress movement later in life, as well as with the Black Panthers and the Young Lords. A still from the video shows a tiny, elderly Japanese American woman working the crowd at a rally for the political prisoner Mumia Abu-Jamal. Bad Asian.[2]

This chapter pays tribute to a new movement of Bad Asians—lesbian, gay, transgendered, and bisexual—in independent experimental film and video and to the movements that preceded them. Because the cultural status and image of Asian Americans is constantly changing—partly through the vicissitudes of history and partly through pressure from Asian Americans themselves—the avant-garde Asian American movement must also remake itself in order to remain challenging. I have heard these emerging young artists criticized for abandoning the politicized forms and priorities of their predecessors, but I believe that such criticisms are a fundamental misrecognition of the ways in which these artists have reinvented a political address. Their work continues the tradition of unruliness, outrageousness, and iconoclasm of earlier generations of Bad Asians, but different times require different strategies of attack. Because of the work of a diversity of aesthetic and political movements preceding them, the latest generation of media makers lays claim to a new store of images, attitudes, and technology, all of which come out of and respond to the specific cultural context of the late 1990s. The result is a body of work that pushes not only Asian American cinema but experimental cinema in general into the next century.

Over the past several years, there has been an explosion of independent film and video work by queer artists of Asian descent, partly in response to the relative accessibility and affordability of video production and distribution, and partly in response to the growing body of work that has already been produced by lesbian, gay, and bisexual Asian American artists. For example, out of 152 films shown at MIX: 10th New York Lesbian and Gay Experimental Film/Video Festival in 1996, about thirty-five were by Asian American artists. Similarly, out of seventy films by Asian American artists screened at the 1997 San Francisco International Asian American Film Festival, sixteen were by queer artists. At both gay and Asian American festivals, queer Asian Americans are currently making about 23 percent of the work.[3]

Because lesbian, gay, and Asian American artists have not had extensive access to the financing, production, and distribution sources required for feature-length films, some of the most exciting recent work has been short, independently produced and distributed, and often available only on the festival circuit. Sufficient critical attention still is not paid to queer artists and artists of color who are making theatrically released feature films, and almost none is paid to independent artists working in short, experimental media, largely because their work is often so difficult to see. One of the purposes of this chapter is to draw attention to this rarely seen body of work and to alert readers to the ways in which they can see it through university-organized screenings, private or group rental, and independent festivals.

The diversity of visual styles, formats, and modes of address in this wide body of work cannot be narrowly characterized in one chapter. The eight films and videos I will discuss can be seen as representing the breadth and scope of the entire field of experimental media because of their varied aesthetic and narrative strategies and because of the cultural and ethnic identities of the makers. The nine artists whose work I will look at are of Indian, Vietnamese, Chinese, Filipino, Japanese, and Anglo descent. Two of them are of mixed heritage. They are immigrants to the United States, U.S. born children of immigrants, and multi-generational American. They are working in black and white and color; in video, 16 mm and Super 8 mm film, and combinations thereof. Two pieces were made collaboratively, one by two South Asian makers, another by a white and an Asian American artist. The pieces range in style and tone from camp humor to lyrical autobiography to outrageous punk trash.

Nevertheless, despite the stunning variety of this work, common strategies and perspectives in these films and videos make it possible to identify them as representing a new movement in Asian American cinema, in queer Asian American cinema, and in experimental cinema in general, particularly in their awareness and treatment of racial identity and cultural representation. Unlike much earlier work by Asian American artists and queer artists of color, questions of ethnic and racial identity do not occupy the foreground of these works, although they are never absent or without influence. The artists about whom I write find their voices through a "perverse" identification and relationship with popular culture that uncovers, tweaks, and plays with the racialized fantasies, fears, and representations that make culture popular.

In order to understand fully the significance of these new interventions, it is important to examine the political and aesthetic traditions out of which they develop and to which they respond. The history of a politically committed, self-defined Asian American cinema developing in the 1960s and '70s, its movement toward mainstream access and institutionalization in the 1980s and early '90s, and the parallel emergence of an international body of work by lesbian and gay artists of color all depended on certain assumptions about the relationships between race and cinematic representation: Most generally, the role of oppositional cinema by people of color was to fill historical absences in representation and to counter distorted or nonexistent images of people of color in media, in queer communities, and in politics.

By looking more closely at these movements and their accompanying ideologies, one can better understand the ways in which the young artists I discuss both come out of these earlier traditions and employ a range of other cultural discourses in order to create a historically and aesthetically significant movement of their own. This movement articulates the particular sensibilities and desires of queer artists of color in the late 1990s and, I hope, signals the new directions to be taken within the entire field of independent and experimental film and video in the twenty-first century.

In her comprehensive essay "Moving the Image: Asian American Independent Filmmaking 1970–1990," Renee Tajima charts two foundational stages in the history of Asian American cinema. The first stage was born out of community-based, political-activist movements of the late 1960s and 1970s and drew its inspiration from the political and artistic developments of the same period: "the San Francisco State Strike, the Young Lords, the Black Power movement and the emergence of a new black cinema; the Chicano school blow-outs, the 1970 moratorium against the war, and the birth of the Chicano arts movement" (Tajima 1991, 14). Asian American artists were supported by newly formed, community-based media institutions such as Third World Newsreel, Visual Communications, and Asian CineVision. The films they produced were predominantly documentaries; they were overtly political (the nickname for the Visual Communications collective was "VC," after the Vietcong); and they were often characterized—either because of ideological conviction or economic necessity—by the rough, "anti-slick" aesthetic of much of the radical art scene of the period (ibid., 20–21).

These artists were Bad—directly confrontational, politically charged, and assertive in ways that took apart the common image of Asians and Asian Americans as the quiet, conservative "model minority." Besides the political and artistic innovations of their work, their very existence refused the cultural expectation of Asians as silent, docile, and "good"—an expectation in which a Bad Asian was an oxymoron.[4]

By the 1980s, according to Tajima, Asian American cinema had become decidedly more mainstream. Filmmakers began to gain access to broader avenues of distribution and production—public television, film schools, limited theatrical release—and, as a result, the focus and aesthetics of these films reflected the requirements of more polished, market-driven venues. Ironically, because narrative feature films reach a more general, mainstream audience, it is these films—such as Wayne Wang's *Joy Luck Club* (1993)—and not the earlier, more experimental work (even Wang's own films) that came to define the "Asian American experience" and its cinema for most white audiences. What Tajima does not mention is the fact that in the 1980s, the availability of the camcorder also made video much cheaper to produce, edit, and distribute, and many Asian American artists were continuing to produce political, "anti-slick" work for cable access and video collectives such as Paper Tiger Television and Deep Dish Television.[5] Although low-budget activist video is by definition marginal, the lack of attention paid to this work can to a large extent be understood through the institutional developments of the 1980s outlined by Tajima.

Daryl Chin, one of the few critics to talk about Asian American experimental media, chronicles the emergence in the 1970s of a hierarchical structure in the experimental film world that privileged white men such as Stan Brakhage as the most important and central artists of the "avant-garde." The programming and funding decisions that resulted from this hierarchy have helped to establish a "traditional experimental" canon and aesthetic (a paradoxical concept indeed) that remains largely white and male. Although a large number of Asian American artists were working in experimental forms at the time (Chin lists, among others, Yoko Ono, Tom Tam, Bruce and Norman Yonemoto, and Ruby Yang), these artists were often shunted over to the newly established venues for Asian American production, distribution, and screening, organizations that were not created to accommodate experimental works and found little room for them. As a result, artists such as those listed earlier who were

not directly addressing the "Asian American experience" or were working in experimental modes have fallen between the cracks of institutional formation and support
and are often labeled "obscure." Chin (1991, 223) says that "even within the margins
of an alternative practice, there is further marginalization, especially from the alternative media community."

The early 1990s witnessed a trend, dubbed the "New Queer Cinema" by the critics from the press and the academy. In an essay originally published in New York's
Village Voice, B. Ruby Rich describes the explosion of independent work by queer
filmmakers appearing on the festival circuit and in theaters. These films included
Derek Jarman's *Edward II* (1991), Tom Kalin's *Swoon* (1992), Gregg Araki's *The Living
End* (1992) and Laurie Lynd's *R.S.V.P.* (1991). Rich (1992, 31) writes, "All through the
winter, spring, summer, and now autumn, the message has been loud and clear: queer
is hot." Although widely varied, Rich writes, these films can be classified together
through a shared style:

> Call it 'Homo Pomo': there are traces in all of them of appropriation and pastiche, irony,
> as well as reworking of history with social constructionism very much in mind. Definite-
> ly breaking with older humanist approaches and the films and tapes that accompanied
> identity politics, these works are irreverent, energetic, alternately minimalist and exces-
> sive. Above all, they're full of pleasure. They're here, they're queer, get hip to them. [Ibid.,
> 32]

Despite the sense of possibility and range suggested by Rich, however, several
queer filmmakers of color responded to her article with hesitation. In a discussion published in *Sight and Sound*, the British artists Pratibha Parmar and Isaac Julien both point
to the exclusion of racial considerations in both the definition and the practices of
"New Queer Cinema."[6] Parmar writes:

> I am wary of talking about an overarching queer aesthetic, as my sensibility comes as much
> from my culture and race as from my queerness. In queer discourses generally there is a
> worrying tendency to create an essentialist, so called authentic, queer gaze. My personal
> style is determined by diverse aesthetic influences, from Indian cinema and cultural
> iconography to pop promos and 70's avant-garde films. [Parmar 1992, 35]

Julien (1992, 35) echoes this caution, saying, "But I still hold an ambivalent position
towards new queer cinema in terms of address. For most white queer filmmakers there
is no intersection of race."

The voices of Parmar and Julien represent the final historical strain that I want to
add to this genealogy—that is, film and video work by queer artists of color working in the United Kingdom, Canada, and the United States since the mid-1980s. This
expansive body of work includes Julien's *Passion of Remembrance* (made with the black
British film and video collective Sankofa in 1986) and *Looking for Langston* (1988), Parmar's *Khush* (1991), Marlon Riggs's *Tongues Untied* (1989), Richard Fung's *Orientations*
(1984), Ming-Yuen S. Ma's *Toc Storee* (1993), Valentin Aguirre and Augie Robles' *¡Viva
16th!* (1994), and Frances Negrón-Muntaner's *Brincando el Charco: Portrait of a Puerto
Rican* (1994). While differing greatly in style, format, and structure, all of these films

and videos respond directly to the historical and cultural erasure of queer people of color. Julien's *Looking for Langston* explores fantasy and desire using the poetry of Langston Hughes, one of America's most important black poets, whose homosexuality is often obscured or ignored in the official record; Ming-Yuen Ma's *Toc Storee* uses Chinese and Japanese myths to prove the existence and acceptance of homosexuality in Asian cultures. The other pieces move back and forth between talking-head interviews and experimental imagery to present and explore the lives and experiences of gay and lesbian people of color.

In general, these films and videos address the paradoxical situation for many queer people of color: communities of color that are hostile to the existence of homosexuality, and white gay and lesbian communities that are unsympathetic to the needs and concerns of people of color. Richard Fung (1991, 148) describes the ways in which white stereotypes of Asian men as impotent and effeminate have served to erase the presence of gay Asian men: "Whereas, as Fanon tells us, 'the Negro is eclipsed. He is turned into a penis. He *is* a penis,' the Asian man is defined by a striking absence down there. And if Asian men have no sexuality, how can we have homosexuality?"

What marks this body of work as a distinct movement is not only its historical placement in the period from the mid-1980s to the early 1990s, but also the fact that, despite radically different authorial styles, all of this work can be said to be ostensibly and explicitly *about* queer black, Latino, or Asian identity.[7] These films and videos can be seen as representing a certain committed identity politics necessitated by the state of queer cinema and activism, the politics of communities of color, and the alternative invisibility or demonization of queers and people of color within conservative political climates. The fact that a black gay filmmaker (Marlon Riggs with his documentary *Tongues Untied*) was singled out and denounced by Senator Jesse Helms in a sensationalist attempt to defund the arts illustrates the cultural context that motivated this work and to which it responds.[8]

While many younger Asian American artists are clearly affected by the work of filmmakers whose work deals with the experiences, contradictions, and pleasures of being queer *and* a person of color, the most recent work by new artists shows a movement away from film and video rooted in such overt identity politics in favor of an experimental aesthetic that responds to the more general influences of popular culture, American and international cinema, and queer culture in the age of AIDS. Although this work does not explicitly place questions of race and ethnic identity in its foreground, its critical engagement with the images and fantasies of contemporary American culture nevertheless exposes and comments on the racially charged subtext that lies beneath, supports, and constitutes popular culture in the late twentieth century.

Recent work by queer Asian American artists is radical in more ways than in its aesthetic practices. While the earlier work of straight and gay Asian American filmmakers is directly oppositional and unruly, challenging the stereotype of the silent, invisible, politically conservative Asian, this new work flouts another expectation of independent film and video—the expectation that the work of queer Asian American artists must address the issues of being queer and Asian American. Though individual artists such as Quentin Lee, Shu Lea Cheang, and Gregg Araki have been making experimental films with broader narrative and thematic concerns since the late 1980s, a decade later we can begin to see a broader movement developing among young Asian American lesbian, gay, bisexual, and transgendered artists, a movement that revises and advances the challenges of Bad Asians.

In *Love Song for Persis K.* (1995), David Dasharath Kalal creates a dreamy homage to the screen diva Persis Khambatta, the former Miss India who first appeared before American audiences in the 1980 film *Star Trek*. The piece begins by narrating the scene on July 26, 1978, ten days before the start of *Star Trek*'s production, when Persis has her head shaved for the part. Over a close-up of the bald Persis bathed in a blue screen, the narrator relates that "once shaved, her head's true shape emerged. It was wonderfully and strikingly lovely. Without her dark hair, she was, if anything, even more unusually beautiful." The video samples clips from Persis's films, isolating her image, framing it in abstract shapes, and drenching it in yellows, pinks and blues—the brilliant pastel colors that only video can render. Over the images, the narrator continues to tell the story of her life and career—her discovery by a talent agent, her modeling career, her entry as India's contestant in the Miss Universe pageant at age sixteen, her films in India and London. The narrative is interrupted by particularly campy lines from Persis's films: "It's not that you can't. It's that you won't. Like it, no. Understand, yes. But that's what makes you what you are."

The video medium is particularly suitable for these images, for aside from the surreal colors and special effects, the film clips evoke the aura of late-night television movies, of a devoted fan taping his idol's films and replaying the juiciest scenes. Kalal also signifies the fact that his fandom is linked to the particular desires and cultural influences of his adolescence in the 1970s: the musical score for the video is an a cappella woman's voice singing the Bee Gees' "More Than a Woman." (As the singer croons "more than a woman" over the image of Persis's bald head, the lyrics begin to morph into, "bald-headed woman. Bald-headed woman to me.")

Through the strikingly framed and enhanced images, Persis does indeed become "more than a woman." As the shaving of her head turns her into an extraterrestrial being, the apotheosis of her image, taken out of the context of the films in which they appear, turns her into an icon. One of the innovative practices of camp is to take femininity out of its context as a way to expose its inherently artificial and outrageous nature and to appropriate it for one's own fantasies. The manipulated images of Persis embody this abstraction, but she also embodies the anomalous image of an Indian woman as a sexual and powerful heroine. *Love Song* illustrates the appeal of a female diva to an adolescent gay man's imagination, an appeal that is intimately linked to ethnic identity and cultural identification. Although Kalal does not make explicit reference to his own queer or South Asian identity, his video hints at ways the imaginative influences of cultural divas such as Persis K. produce and shape a gay Asian American sensibility and aesthetic.

It is no accident that the work of the new Asian American media movement, which takes as its grist and fodder the raw materials of popular culture, is being made by queer artists. The queer theorist Eve Kosofsky Sedgwick traces the motivations behind childhood fascinations and obsessions with certain cultural texts like books, films, and

icons. Queer children, who already experience reality as a series of disjunctions, contradictions, and ambiguities, and who constantly find their desires and identifications
failing to match up with dominant expectations and behaviors, look for the affirmation of these experiences in cultural sources. In describing this practice of becoming
a "perverse reader" (or spectator), she writes:

> I think that for many of us in childhood the ability to attach intently to a few cultural
> objects, objects of high or popular culture or both, objects whose meaning seemed mys-
> terious, excessive, or oblique in relation to the codes most readily available to us, became
> a prime resource for survival. We needed for there to be sites where the meanings didn't
> line up tidily with each other, and we learned to invest those sites with fascination and
> love. [Sedgwick 1993, 3]

If queerness is, as Sedgwick relates, "the open mesh of possibilities, gaps, overlaps,
dissonances and resonances, lapses and excesses of meaning when the constituent
elements of anyone's gender, of anyone's sexuality aren't made (or *can't* be made) to
signify monolithically" (ibid., 8), then queer people of color experience several additional layers of dissonance, in relation not only to their sexuality but also to their racial,
cultural, and geographical positioning. *Love Song for Persis K.* is as much about the
critical perspective of a young, biracial, South Asian gay spectator as it is about the
eponymous diva, although both subjects construe, reinforce, and describe each other.
The feelings of displacement, disjunction, and alienation (literally feeling like an alien)
that accompany queer consciousness—particularly for people of color who apprehend
their reflections in the mirror of popular culture only in the most refracted ways—
can in a "perverse" way find expression in an actress who was chosen to play an extra-
terrestrial in an American film because her foreign beauty was already considered
"unusual" and "alien."

Paradice (1996), by Patty Chang and Anie "Super 8" Stanley, exposes the perversity that exists within the popular commodification of pleasure. The fifteen-minute,
Super 8 mm film is a vertiginous montage of "glamorous" images: a clasp of hands
opening boxes of gaudy costume jewelry, the neon lights of the Las Vegas strip, a spin-
ning roulette wheel, vacation brochures, a model plane crossing a map of the
Caribbean. Intercut with these images is the disjointed narrative of a motel-room
encounter between an Asian hooker (Chang) and a big spender (Stanley). Stanley
enters the room first, orders "room service": "I'd like to order some champagne. I don't
want anything cheap. I want it chilled. And a fancy ice bucket. No plastic." The order
arrives in the form of Chang, carrying an ice bucket. The two have sex, but when the
hooker realizes that she has been stiffed, she bashes the john with her stiletto heels
and storms out.

The soundtrack alternates between swinging big band and a recording of a telephone operator booking flights and cruises to Monte Carlo and the Virgin Islands for
such clients as "Lauren Bacall" and "Victoria Principal." "Don't be shy, sweetie. I'm
trained professionally to fulfill your caviar dreams," croons the operator as she books
another "passport package to paradise." The stock clichés and caressing tone of the
operator conjure up images of phone-sex operators selling fantasy scenarios to anony-

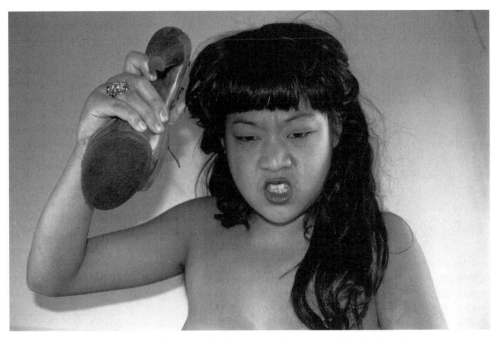

PHOTO 13.1.   From *Paradice* (1996), dir. Patty Chang and Anie Stanley.

mous callers. The muffled voices and the gritty quality of the Super 8 mm film create a contrast to the "glitzy" images being shown. The exuberant advertising for
America's leisure industries masks the seediness of our fantasies of "exotic escape"
through consumerism and Third World tourism. After Chang and Stanley have left
the motel room, the maid comes to clean up and finds the used condoms left behind.
This is the real story behind tourism's "caviar dreams"—paying someone for sex and
paying someone to clean it up. The next scene shows Chang on her way out of town
on a plane and Stanley putting the moves on a new Asian woman (played by the
filmmaker Julie Whang) in a bar: "Anything she wants. Give the girl a drink. Drinks
on me. Anything she wants."

In addition to being a shockingly clever indictment of the sleaziness of U.S. pleasure industries, *Paradice* is full of its own pleasures. Using humor, camp, and dead-on
editing, the filmmakers create their own jewel of a film. Like *Love Song for Persis K.*,
Paradice uses the outrageousness of camp to call gender out of itself. Stanley's character is composed of the "props" of masculinity—a dildo, a wad of bills, and an arsenal of pick-up lines. The interchangeable Asian women stand in for the product or
fantasy being purchased by the white consumer or tourist. Once again, although this
film is not ostensibly about queer or Asian identities, the parody of white heterosexual fantasy provides the setting for a subversive and raucous staging of queer sexuality. When we see a scene in which an Asian hooker services a white john, we are
actually watching two lesbians having sex—queer desire masquerading as heterosexuality.

The appropriation of popular culture and the transformative powers of camp take a different form in Machiko Saito's video *Premenstrual Spotting* (1997). The piece begins with nostalgic music over shots of family photos, a calm that is violently interrupted by loud, throbbing music and images of Saito dancing under strobe lights. We hear an audio clip of a man negotiating for sexual services and see another picture of Saito as a girl. In a series of monologues, the filmmaker describes her childhood sexual abuse by her father and her own evolving relationship to the sexuality that these experiences produced.

The images of the video are of Saito performing for the camera in her apartment—dancing, posing, lip-syncing, undressing, and stumbling around on the bathroom floor. Over the rapidly intercut images, she relates, "I'd get drunk, every night, out of my fucking mind, take off all my clothes and put on this elaborate fetish wear, run into the bathroom and sing show tunes. I used to pretend I was a big old fag in drag singing Sondheim on a stage somewhere."

Through the voiceover monologues, Saito describes how her mother's hatred for her daughter's body masked her denial of the abuse: "'I was much too tall for a Japanese girl,' she said. 'Freaky, deformed.'" The title of the piece refers to the depth of her mother's denial: "Premenstrual spotting" is the explanation she used to describe the blood coming from between her six-year-old daughter's legs. By dressing her daughter in tight, spangled costumes and forcing her to dance on stage, her mother vicariously lives out her own desire to perform, but her attempts to reshape her daughter's body into an acceptable, appealing feminine package become a collaboration with her abuse. "Somehow her dreams became my reality, and my reality became my father's fantasies."

Premenstrual Spotting is a testimony to the manifold ways that fantasy and reality create and transform each other, whether through the sexual exploitation of a child or an adult survivor's reclamation of her own desire. Saito's performance uses the props of this commodified, denaturalized femininity and reshapes it into her own powerful expression of survival. She wears her femininity as a masquerade—"like a fag in drag"—which underscores the artificiality of sexual desire and the shattering realness of its weight. The effects are inspiring (her lip-synced homage to survival, complete with silver lamé dress, mask, and fangs) and devastating (her nude body smeared with blood on the bathroom floor).

Premenstrual Spotting is a deliberate mess of images and sound. Saito uses skillful editing to convey the clashes and paradoxes of sexual identity. Breezy Broadway show tunes serve as ironic and dramatic counterpoints to the monologues and performances. She asks, "Where do you draw the line on where sexual expression turns to perversion? Or harassment to abuse? I don't know. But I do know now what sexual abuse is—for me. And sometimes I like it. I've learned to enjoy the things I once was ashamed of."

The video's density serves to illustrate the impossibility of cleanly separating pleasure from pain, harassment from abuse, sexual expression from perversion. In fact, it is the "perversity" of Saito's performances that transforms them into such cathartic expressions of sexuality, the recognition of sexuality as a space where meanings do not "line up tidily with each other," to return to Sedgwick's formulation. The influences of culture, memory, femininity, and desire are reshuffled and realigned. The songs from Broadway shows, formerly associated with torturous childhood performances, are recast as the joyous and defiant soundtrack of gay male culture. By dressing in silver lamé and lip-syncing show tunes, Saito assumes the drag of a drag queen, a mask that offers both a campy escape from femininity and a forceful reclaiming of it.

The integral ways in which all of these films and videos incorporate and engage with popular culture signal a shift in focus from earlier Asian American work. While earlier artists imagined their task to be the representation of subjects who have not been represented before, subjects who have been excluded from cultural representation,[9] these artists limn a cultural landscape of which queer, Asian American, and queer Asian American subjects have always been an integral part as audiences, consumers, desiring subjects, and misrepresented objects. This work starts from a position of immersion in, rather than exclusion from, popular culture. For queer Asian American spectators, even the absence of Asian images could become a space for critical imagination.[10]

The short video *Hindustan* (1995) by Gita Reddy and David Dasharath Kalal illustrates this point. The video presents a restaged version of Bing Crosby and Rosemary Clooney's song "Hindustan." The video opens with the sound of a gong and the image of an Indian woman's face (Reddy); the woman is raising her eyes seductively to the camera. But this stock-in-trade picture of exotic, "Oriental" femininity is quickly undermined: As she opens her mouth, the voice of Bing Crosby issues forth, crooning, "Here's a sort of tantalizing ditty. The tune is catchy and the words are witty. Could be it's a country or a city," while Rosemary Clooney's part is performed by a dapper South Asian man. The two lip-sync the song, a homage to Western clichés about the Orient, while the video runs through its own array of visual cliches—a peacock feather, a tourist's suitcase, a camera. Finally, we see "Bing" and "Rosemary" whirling around in a dance, but the woman is dancing with another woman and the man with another man. While the song continues to evoke the raptures of Hindustan, the two couples embrace and kiss.

By denaturalizing the performance of the song, Reddy and Kalal also expose the assumptions underneath its invention of Hindustan. The song's final lyrics, "Hindustan, where we met and the world began," suggest that, for Clooney and Crosby, the geographical region comes into existence only when the two lovers meet. It is their desire alone that creates the mythical place, a belief that constitutes and sustains colonialist fantasy. The video deconstructs the logic of this fantasy and, in doing so, opens up a space in which to stage a scene of queer desire, a scene that both appropriates the colonial prerogative of world-making for lesbian and gay subjects and locates queer subjects within the historical and geographical spaces of South Asia.

Work like *Hindustan* does more than uncover the presence of queer Asian subjects in popular culture. It performs an exposition of the process by which *all* identity is constructed through representation. As Stuart Hall writes:

> My own view is that events, relations, structures do have conditions of existence and real effects, outside the sphere of the discursive, but that it is only within the discursive, and

subject to its specific conditions, limits and modalities, do they have or can they be constructed within meaning. . . . This gives questions of culture and ideology, and the scenarios of representation—subjectivity, identity, politics—a formative, not merely an expressive, place in the constitution of social and political life. [Hall 1995, 224]

The films and videos I discuss offer examples and explorations of some of the "specific conditions, limits and modalities"—whether they be colonial discourses of escape and exoticization or a critical Asian American gaze—through which identity is created and given meaning. The "scenarios of representation" are not merely the places where racial and sexual identities are formed. They illustrate the fact that the process of identity construction depends on the collusion and cooperation of discourses of race, sexuality, gender, history, and national identity. The autobiographical video *First Year* (1996) by Trac Vu provides an evocative illustration of this process.

First Year is the first-person narration of the filmmaker's first year in America. The black-and-white piece begins with photos of a majestic Saigon, Vu's birthplace and the site of "lavish banquets and frugal generation, where only the certainty of kinship is what's passed down." Moving to California, his family settles in San Bernadino because of the opportunities for cheap housing. The narrow spaces and thin walls of their new apartment contrast with the opulence represented in Vietnam, enacting a reversal of First World–Third World distinctions in which America represents endless possibility and wealth. In Vu's narrative, Vietnam is pictured nostalgically as a time (more than a place) gone by, and despite its "lavish banquets," it leaves him no material legacy, only the connection of family.

Vu's inauguration into American life comes through the theme song from the television sitcom *Laverne and Shirley*. "It was the first English song I learned. I danced on the green shag carpet and wanted to live in Milwaukee." The theme song plays over still shots of the interior spaces of an apartment, evoking the stasis and boredom that the narrator describes.

First Year continues with a series of still shots of empty spaces—the public library, the bus station, the Kmart—as Vu describes shopping for bargains at Kmart and going to the library in search of books on homosexuality. Although most of the books he finds are "sociological studies from the '60s and '70s, finding their subjects pathologically doomed," the accounts of sexual encounters between men—coaches, priests, Times Square hustlers—serve as "instruction manuals" for Vu. He declares that "to this day I have never found better pornographic materials."

This account exemplifies the complex and contingent ways in which sexuality and desire are formed. Although they are not the origins of his sexuality, the clinical and voyeuristic accounts of homosexual pathology offer a shape, a language, and a fantasy life for his desires. Vu "learns" to be gay (as it is understood and experienced in the American context) even as he learns American music, language, and the importance of bargain hunting.

On one childhood shopping trip, he tries unsuccessfully to read a store sign. Despite his father's coaching, he is unable to pronounce the words "Wild West." Finally, his father gives up, assuring him that he will eventually get it. The final scene of the film is a shot of the expansive desert landscape of Southern California, dotted with windmills, moving past the windows of a car. A song in Spanish replaces the Vietnamese music of the opening scenes, and in a voiceover, Vu repeats the phrase "Wild West. Wild West. Wild West." The motion of the car and the windmills in this scene stand in contrast to the still photos of the rest of the film.

The effect of sudden movement offers a sense of possibility, while the music and voiceover echo the earlier nostalgic tone of the piece. He has finally "gotten it"—meaning that he has not only mastered the pronunciation of these difficult words, but he has also evolved a critical insight into the deeper topography of American culture. As demonstrated by the accompanying image and music, the words he has finally learned to speak, "Wild West," signify a romantic concept already long lost. Mexican music and the sight of windmills in a California desert signify other concepts: the harnessing of nature to power a city, the enclosure of Native Americans on reservations, the Anglo imperialism of Mexican land. The land of opportunity imagined by generations of immigrants is as much a fantasy as the open, unpopulated frontier that refuses to see the cultures (Mexican, Indian) that are already here.

In *First Year*, Vu has created a poignant and insightful picture of the way in which the multiple layers of the American cultural landscape—working-class consumer culture, social science, television, myths of the "New World"—overlap and merge into his autobiography. *First Year* is about "what's passed down" by American culture to its citizens, although no people appear in its landscapes. The formation of subjectivity, identity, and desire, particularly for immigrants who "begin" their lives in the United States, is as much about the legacy of a culture as it is about familial generation.

In *Maybe Never (But I'm Counting the Days)* (1996), Nguyen Tan Hoang places queer Asian American sexuality even more firmly within the context of popular culture. A charming, visually entrancing piece of eye candy on the surface, *Maybe Never* also offers an original analysis of the ways in which sexuality and erotic desire are passed down and acquired through culture. The video offers a litany of "nevers," lost chances, untried acts, unbroken taboos. Over nighttime footage shot from a car, we hear the muffled voices of men advertising their desires and preferences through a voice-mail service. As in *First Year*, the video's unstaged, external shots are unpopulated. Scenes of a street at night and at dawn evoke images of cruising for sex, leaving an encounter. When people do appear, they are seen only from the waist down. A shot of people walking through and gathering in crowds focuses on their legs and lower bodies, creating a feeling of distance and impersonal desire.

This is overlapped with the voiceover confessions of men and women, speaking in a variety of accents, listing a catalogue of "nevers": "I've never forgotten the pain of love," "I've never felt you deep inside of me," "I've never swallowed your cum," "I've never taken your breath away," "I never thought it would end this way," "I've never licked your pussy," "I never learned to pronounce your name," "I never know when to let go." The list is sexual and romantic, referring to both a lack of personal intimacy and erotic experience. Subsequent shots of condoms and gloved hands reinforce the implication that many of these experiences are about sexual practices and pleasures unavailable to a new generation of queer people, who are aware of the risks of unsafe sex and HIV, but the list also includes poignant reflections on failed relationships ("I never thought it would end this way") and cultural difference ("I never learned to pronounce your name"). The list chronicles the particular experiences and dilemmas of young gay men and lesbians, and although the "nevers" suggest chances lost, they also suggest experiences still to be tested. The parenthetical modification of the title, "But I'm Counting the Days," implies that regret and hope can exist together within the framework of desire.

A musical soundtrack of "never" songs adds irony and humor to the confessions. George Michaels laments, "I'm never gonna dance again"; Michael Jackson "never can say goodbye"; Elvis Presley croons, "It's now or never"; Dionne Warwick proclaims, "I know I'll never love this way again"; and En Vogue declares, "You're never gonna get it." With a strong dependence on the music to provide commentary, energym and nostalgic recognition, the video becomes an exuberant tribute to the genre of the music video. Against a background of vibrant primary colors, Nguyen positions young Asian American actors in various playful poses. The men and women mug for the camera using water pistols, cigarettes, and candy, all tongue-in-cheek metaphors and substitutes for sex. Replacing the list of forbidden acts is the humorous and sexy performance of a variety of alternative forms of flirtation, tension release, and self-pleasuring.

PHOTO 13.2. From *Maybe Never (But I'm Counting the Days)* (1996), dir. Nguyen Tan Hoang. Photo: Nodeth Vang.

In contrast to these campy, highly staged images are scenes, shot in grainy black and white, of young Asian American men and women recounting the stories of their first gay sexual experiences. Speaking directly to the camera in traditional talking-head documentary style, the subjects speak candidly and personally: "He said, 'Now you're gay.' I went down the hall to my room. My roommate was fast asleep in the next bed. I remember feeling nothing. Anticlimactic. Strange. Not sure what I was supposed to feel. Was I disappointed or relieved?"

While the cinema verité style of these confessions leads the viewer to accept the narrative as authentic, unstaged accounts, Nguyen quickly undermines our expectations. In the middle of one actor's story, a new voice takes over and continues to tell the same story. Another actor appears to repeat a phrase from the last account, stuttering and needing to check his script for the correct dialogue. A woman tells the same story but changes the sex of the person involved. Similarly, the credits reveal these same actors reading the scripted litany of "nevers," often stumbling over the words or giggling with embarrassment ("I've never fucked you up the ass with my black strap-on"). What appear at first to be unmediated autobiographical revelations turn into a deliberate overturning of expectation and a lesson in the way that sexual identity (as in *First Year*) is partly learned through popular cliché ("I know I'll never love this way again") and the repetition of standard, pre-scripted narratives (the story of the "loss of innocence" at the hands of an experienced partner).

Maybe Never restages a multitude of narratives about the loss of innocence and the changing nature of sexual fantasy and activity in the age of AIDS as well as the processes through which sexuality is constructed in this context. Although the question of Asian American identity is never specifically addressed, Nguyen's casting of Asian Americans as the objects of desire, the creators of fantasy, and the participants in erotic exchanges with one another produces a distinctive aesthetic that firmly incorporates Asian American bodies, perspectives, and imaginations within a contemporary sexual landscape of risk, desire, regret, and creativity.

Despite their immersion in the narratives and fantasies of popular culture, these artists are far from co-opted by it. By engaging with the forms and address of mainstream culture, they are taking both Asian American media and experimental media in general in new directions, widening the perspectives on dominant cinema's commentaries on race and representation as well as the formal, technical, and aesthetic means for expressing these perspectives. A particularly witty example of the critical appropriation of Hollywood cinema is *Back to Bataan Beach* (1995), by Ernesto Foronda, a short film that takes the form of a theatrical preview of coming attractions.

The film being advertised, *Back to Bataan Beach*, is a hilarious spoof of the Frankie Avalon and Annette Funicello beach-party movies of the 1960s. After announcing that "the following preview has been approved for all ages," the film begins with a map of Subic Bay in the Philippines. Martial music accompanies the arrival of American soldiers as they wade ashore to plant their flag on Bataan Beach (played by Southern California). The first sight that the soldiers encounter is a Filipino Jesus, complete with crown of thorns and cross, waiting to meet them, signifying that

PHOTO 13.3.   From *Back to Bataan Beach* (1995), dir. Ernesto M. Foronda, Jr.

although they may be imagining that they are planting their national flag on virgin territory, the legacy of Spanish imperialism has long since beaten them to it.

The second sight they encounter is a beach party in full swing. The trailer's cheesy announcer introduces us to "Frankie," "Annette," and the gang (this time with an all-Filipino cast). The promo continues with an exhaustive string of movie-trailer clichés: "Surfing Excitement!" "Burning Passions on Burning Sands!" "Young and Innocent Love!" "It's the movie everyone's been talking about! The movie your parents don't want you to see!" The masterly art direction, cinematography, and comic timing capture the look and tone of 1960s American popular films with a precision born of true fandom. Foronda calls *Back to Bataan Beach* one of his "in the closet films," and, as in *Love Song for Persis K.*, queer sexuality exists only in the quality of the filmmaker's cathexis to popular culture. If you don't blink, however, you may catch the scene in which a surfer boy directs a particularly loaded gaze at a juicy male backside.[11]

Filmed in "Glorious Flip-O-Rama," the film offers a satirical view of Filipino culture from a Filipino American perspective, a culture particularly Americanized through its saturation by Hollywood images and through military occupation. As the announcer promises "Girls! Girls! Girls!" the screen splits into three parts—colored red, white, and blue, respectively—each of which is occupied by a bathing beauty. The girls' swimsuits are replaced with a maid's uniform, a bridal gown, and a nurse's uniform, aligning the film's sensationalist marketing of sex and femininity with other international markets in which Filipino women are traded.

The trailer is complete with songs, dancing, sex, and even a pie fight. As the wacky pie-in-the-face sight gags build, the announcer exclaims, "We're not just nuts! We're Coco-nuts!"—an allusion to both the coconut-cream pies being tossed around and the pejorative epithet for brown people (Latino, Filipino) who are "brown on the outside, white on the inside." The adoration and mimicry of American popular culture is most effectively spoofed through its loving execution. But the accuracy of Foronda's parody serves to reverse the traditional colonial narrative, which privileges the perspective of white American culture's representation and analysis of Third World cultures. In *Back to Bataan Beach*, white American culture is turned into the subject of exploration—the strange "dark continent." White popular images such as John Wayne's World War II films and the *Beach Blanket Bingo* films are understood as coming out of and supporting a particular national and historical naïveté, an innocence that ignores and depends on U.S. colonialism in the Third World.

Replacing the "traditional" experimental cinema's assumptions that it must by definition remain separate from mass culture, Foronda's film is an example of new work that continues the critical project of breaking down the distinctions between "high" and "low" art, between "minority" and "majority" culture, between "straight" and "queer" sexualities, exposing the formal, ideological, and historical connections between the two.

A final example of this new direction in experimental cinema is *Facile* (1996), a short Super 8 mm film by Rajendra Roy. The fact that Roy is also the director of MIX: The New York Lesbian and Gay Experimental Film/Video Festival signals the centrality of work such as his to a new experimental aesthetic. Accompanied by a synchronized musical score on audio cassette performed by the band Fresh Fish, the film uses an ethnically mixed cast to re-enact memorable, and often appropriated images, from Italian neo-realist cinema to *Pulp Fiction* (Tarantino 1994).

Shot without a script, the "narrative" begins with an encounter on the street between a glamorous blonde and a masher. It moves to a rooftop cocktail party, sexual intrigue, a chase scene through an empty alley, an ambush and double-cross, and finally a murder. In true cinematic glamor, all of the characters wear dark sunglasses. The women wear scarves and the men narrow ties, as if they had just stepped out of a Fellini double feature.

The over-the-top acting and Roy's casting choices serve further to denaturalize the film's images. A bombshell in spiked heels and an enormous blonde wig is played by the Asian American artist Patty Chang. Anie "Super 8" Stanley also reprises her role from *Paradice* as the masher, and the New York drag legend Linda Simpson performs out of drag as Les Simpson. By appearing without his recognizable women's attire, Simpson performs a kind of double drag—man dressed as a woman dressed as a man, a reverse *Victor/Victoria* (Edwards 1982).

The movements of the camera, the gestures of the characters, the props, and the poses all reference so many different cinematic traditions at the same time that the resulting narrative highlights the pervasive extent to which these traditions plunder and copy one another's images. Contemporary Hollywood films do not even borrow from other films anymore. They borrow clichés that themselves were borrowed from other films. At one point, all of the characters take turns demonstrating the different ways to hold a gun in the movies—one-handed, two-handed, sideways, toward the camera, off-screen—creating a kind of instructional montage of cinematic gun history. Billed as "avant-garde made 'easy,'" *Facile* serves as both a critique and a celebration of the continuous recycling of visual images in the cinema and the powers and pleasures of appropriating them for oneself.[12]

All of this work marks a significant development in the history of visual media by Asian Americans and by lesbian, gay, bisexual, and transgendered artists. While an earlier generation of artists created a space, a market, and a tradition for queer Asian American film and video by directly addressing the issues of gay Asian identity in the United States (as well as Canada and Britain), new makers are producing work that understands racial and sexual identities as being formed out of and in conjunction with a larger set of cultural forces. Although race and ethnicity are never absent from this work, their presence is felt more as the foundation of an artistic sensibility, a sensibility formed out of an always racialized, always sexualized cultural landscape. Rather than challenging the status quo from a position of marginality, these filmmakers and video makers understand Asian American identity to be an integral part of American culture, a culture in which the construction and maintenance of white identity depends on the erasure of ethnic difference and visibility.

Notes

1. A large and growing body of sociological, anthropological, psychological, and fictional work supports this belief, often blurring the distinctions between Asians and Asian Americans. Of all this work, none is more egregious than Michael Crichton's 1992 novel *Rising Sun,* which uses a murder-mystery plot to warn Americans of Japan's corporate imperialism. The novel is rife with "explanations" of inscrutable Japanese culture, including the desire to "save face" and not to stand out in the crowd. Crichton raises the union of fiction and sociology to a new level by including a bibliography of texts on Japan at the end of his novel.

2. The video is Saunders and Tajiri (1994).

3. I must note that these figures are only rough approximations based on perusing the festival catalogues and trying to identify Asian American names, films with explicitly queer content, and work with which I was familiar. Obviously, the crudeness of my methodology leaves out a lot of titles that are not curated or billed as gay and a lot of artists with Anglo family names. Nevertheless, the sketchy review revealed surprising consistency both between the two festivals and between international and American work. Of the 104 titles shown in total at the San Francisco International Asian American Film Festival, twenty-one were billed with gay content or gay makers—also about a 20 percent ratio.

I limited my tally of work at the 1996 MIX Festival to films and videos made in 1995 or 1996 in order to assess the most recent state of production. The 1997 MIX Festival shows a slight decline in the percentage of artists of Asian descent. Out of 128 films and videos made in 1996 or 1997, about twenty are by Asian artists. Looking at the festival's first two years, however, the overall rise in Asian American work is dramatic. In 1987, when the festival was called the New York Lesbian and Gay Experimental Film Festival, there were no Asian American artists among the sixty-one films screened. The next year, 1988, included two filmmakers of Asian descent among sixty-three films.

4. The filmmakers' writings reflect this refusal to remain silent, uncritical and "good." In a letter addressed to "V.C. (Viet Cong)" in the same volume, Christine Choy (1991, 60–61) describes her work this way: "All my films are reflections of this 'jack-ass' society from the bot-

tom up. . . . I am not nice or kind, my issues are crude, there ain't much money in my types of films, funders always tell me there isn't much of an audience for this type of film, but they are wrong. . . . Look where my concepts come from, right between my legs. Be Cool." In the same volume, Curtis Choy (1991, 181) writes: "Now I ain't knocking nobody in particular (you fill in your own blanks), but check out the rags put out by different organizations. Who gets written up? Who gets left out? And what is success? Who defines it? Who needs it? Ain't it amazing how the answers all point in the direction of the mainstream money and honkie notions of success? Is public masturbation really good form?"

5. For a historical review of some of these video collectives, see Saalfield (1993).

6. Cherry Smyth also talks about the specific problems for lesbians within the aesthetic practices of the "New Queer Cinema." She writes that "[p]art of the problem of inventing a queer dyke cinema is the difficulty for lesbians of what Tom Kalin refers to as the 'revisionist aesthetic,' which pillages and pastiches a vast store of images stretching back to Genet and Cocteau. In seeking past movies to parody, lost images to reclaim, icons to glorify, dykes have always had less booty to raid. Thank god for Marlene, Greta and James Dean" (Smyth 1992, 39).

7. Although the focus of this chapter is on recent work that eschews direct and explicit discussions of race and sexuality, the strategies and focus of earlier work continue to have relevance for emerging queer artists. One of the most significant examples of this is the work of Christopher Lee and Elise Hurwitz, whose experimental documentaries *Trappings of Transhood* (1997) and *Christopher's Chronicles: Christopher Does Dallas—Chapter One* (1996) address the experiences and identities of transgendered people of color using visual innovation, autobiography, interviews, and the music of George Michael.

8. Pratibha Parmar (1993, 5) rearticulates this position, saying, "I do not speak from a position of marginalization but more crucially from the resistance to that marginalization. As a filmmaker, it is important for me to reflect upon the process through which I constantly negotiate the borderlines between shifting territories . . . between the margin and the center . . . between inclusion and exclusion . . . between visibility and invisibility. For example, as lesbians and gays of color, we have had to constantly negotiate and challenge the racism of the white gay community, and at the same time confront the homophobia of communities of color."

9. Fung (1994, 165) writes, "Given the historical misrepresentations of mainstream media, I am not surprised that most independent films and videotapes produced by North American men and women of Asian descent seek redress from white supremacy. They perform the important tasks of correcting histories, voicing common but seldom represented experiences, engaging audiences used to being spoken about but never addressed, and actively constructing a politics of resistance to racism."

10. bell hooks (1990, 3–4) describes this critical practice for black spectators: "Cultural criticism has historically functioned in black life as a force promoting critical resistance, one that enabled black folks to cultivate in everyday life a practice of critique and analysis that would disrupt and even deconstruct those cultural productions that were designed to promote and reinforce domination. . . . Our gaze was not passive. The screen was not a place of escape. It was a place of confrontation and encounter."

11. Foronda has just completed the second film in his "in the closet" series. *Dreamtime* (1997) uses science-fiction alien-invasion movies as the fantastic space in which a cast of sexually repressed characters can discover their buried desires.

12. Roy's video *O.J. Simpson My Father* (1995) similarly appropriated the popularly circulated narratives of race and violence around the O.J. Simpson trial as the backdrop for a creative meditation on queer sexuality and biracial identity.

Works Cited

Chin, Daryl. 1991. "Moving the Image, Removing the Artist, Killing the Messenger." Pp. 219–226 in *Moving the Image,* ed. Leong.

Choy, Christine. 1991. "Q&A." Pp. 60–61 in *Moving the Image,* ed. Leong.

Choy, Curtis. 1991. "Suckcess Above the Line: From Here to Obscurity." Pp. 181–84 in *Moving the Image,* ed. Leong.

Crichton, Michael. 1992. *Rising Sun.* New York: Ballantine Books.

Fung, Richard. 1991. "Looking For My Penis: The Eroticized Asian in Gay Video Porn." Pp. 145–68 in *How Do I Look? Queer Film and Video,* ed. Bad Object-Choices. Seattle: Bay Press.

———. 1994. "Seeing Yellow: Asian Identities in Film and Video." Pp. 161–71 in *The State of Asian America: Activism and Resistance in the 1990s,* ed. Karin Aguilar-San Juan. Boston: South End Press.

Gever, Martha, John Greyson, and Pratibha Parmar, ed. *Queer Looks: Perspectives on Lesbian and Gay Film and Video.* New York: Routledge, 1993.

Hall, Stuart. 1995. "New Ethnicities." Pp. 223–27 in *The Post-Colonial Studies Reader,* ed. Bill Ashcroft, Gareth Griffiths, and Helen Tiffin. New York: Routledge.

hooks, bell. 1990. *Yearning: race, gender, and cultural politics.* Boston: South End Press.

Julien, Isaac. 1992. "Queer Questions." *Sight and Sound* (September), 35.

Leong, Russell, ed. 1991. *Moving the Image: Independent Asian Pacific American Media Arts.* Los Angeles: UCLA Asian American Studies Center, Visual Communications, Southern California Asian American Studies Central.

Parmar, Pratibha. 1992. "Queer Questions." *Sight and Sound* (September), 35.

———. 1993. "That Moment of Emergence." Pp. 3–11 in *Queer Looks,* ed. Gever, Greyson, and Parmar.

Rich, B. Ruby. 1992. "New Queer Cinema." *Sight and Sound* (September), 30–34.

Saalfield, Catherine. 1993. "On the Make: Activist Video Collectives." Pp. 21–37 in *Queer Looks,* ed. Gever, Greyson, and Parmar.

Sedgwick, Eve Kosofsky. 1993. *Tendencies.* Durham, N.C.: Duke University Press.

Smyth, Cherry. 1992. "Trash Femme Cocktail." *Sight and Sound* (September), 39.

Tajima, Renee. 1991. "Moving the Image: Asian American Independent Filmmaking 1970–1990." Pp. 10–33 in *Moving the Image,* ed. Leong.

Films and Videos Cited

Aguirre, Valentin, and Augie Robles. 1994. *¡Viva 16th!* Valentin Aguirre (3356-A 16th St., San Francisco, CA 94114; tinobear@hotmail.com).

Araki, Gregg. 1992. *The Living End.* Academy.

Chang, Patty, and Anie "Super 8" Stanley. 1996. *Paradice.* Roychang Productions (mix@echonyc.com).

Edwards, Blake. 1982. *Victor/Victoria.* Metro Goldwyn Mayer.

Foronda, Ernesto. 1995. *Back to Bataan Beach.* NAATA.

Foronda, Ernesto M. 1997. *Dreamtime.* No distributor.

Fung, Richard. 1984. *Orientations.* Third World Newsreel.

Jarman, Derek. 1991. *Edward II.* Columbia Tristar.

Julien, Isaac. 1988. *Looking for Langston.* Third World Newsreel.

————, and Maureen Blackwod. 1986. *Passion of Remembrance.* Third World Newsreel.

Kalal, David Dasharath. 1995. *Love Song for Persis K.* Third World Newsreel.

————, and Gita Reddy. 1995. *Hindustan.* Third World Newsreel.

Kalin, Tom. 1992. *Swoon.* New Line, Image Entertainment.

Lee, Christopher, and Elise Hurwitz. 1997. *Trappings of Transhood.* Christopher Lee Productions (P.O. Box 14354, San Francisco, CA 94114).

————. 1996. *Christopher's Chronicles: Christopher Does Dallas—Chapter One.* No distributor (Christopher Lee, trannyfest@aol.com).

Lynd, Laurie. 1991. *R.S.V.P.* Frameline.

Ma, Ming-Yuen S. 1993. *Toc Storee.* Thirld World Newsreel.

Negrón-Muntaner, Frances. 1994. *Brincando el Charco: Portrait of a Puerto Rican.* Women Make Movies.

Nguyen, Hoang Tan. 1996. *Maybe Never (But I'm Counting the Days).* No distributor (Nguyen Tan Hoang, foreverlinda@yahoo.com).

Parmar, Pratibha. 1991. *Khush.* Women Make Movies.

Riggs, Marlon. 1989. *Tongues Untied.* Frameline.

Roy, Rajendra. 1995. *O.J. Simpson My Father.* Roychang Productions (mix@echonyc.com).

————. 1996. *Facile.* Roychang Productions (mix@echonyc.com).

Saito, Machiko. 1997. *Premenstrual Spotting.* No distributor.

Saunders, Pat, and Rea Tajiri. 1994. *Yuri Kochiyama: Passion for Justice.* Women Make Movies.

Tarantino, Quentin. 1994. *Pulp Fiction.* Miramax.

Vu, Trac. 1996. *First Year.* NAATA.

Wang, Wayne. 1993. *The Joy Luck Club.* Buena Vista.

Part V

Beyond "Nation": Diasporas and Hybrid Identities

Renee Tajima-Peña

---

14   No Mo Po Mo and Other Tales
of the Road

I have learned many lessons on the road. The most important one is, you've got to get out of the car and onto the pavement. I can remember countless times driving through new territory while scouting a film—the Skid Row alleys of downtown Los Angeles, a trailer park on Orlando's notorious Orange Blossom Trail, past the Harleys and pick-ups sporting Confederate flags along the Black Warrior River of Alabama. Each time, I am scared shitless. I feel the hostility as I drive by, staring out the window from the cocoon of my car. But, inevitably, I find that when I get out and walk around, talk to people face to face, they are no longer a frightening specter, an abstraction. In most cases, folks are folks, and in that simple act of human connection I begin truly to understand the place and the people.

For me, theory is like the car. It is a great way to navigate the intellectual road map— it gets you there. But once in a while, you've got to park that baby and get out into the world.

I was a guest lecturer at a film criticism course when the professor asked me to talk about the impact of theory on my filmmaking. I told the class that I had thought a lot of postmodern theory would be helpful, but by the time I figured out what people were saying, I had already finished making the film. My problem was not with post-modernism and the other fashionable theories of the time. It was with what seems to be the culture of theorizing, with its attendant language and insider references.

Listening to the jargon of cultural theory reminds me of the days when I was the only non-Chinese staff person at Asian CineVision, the media-arts center in New York's Chinatown. Every so often, I would hear my name amid a blast of Cantonese, and I would have no idea whether it was being taken in vain or merely being mentioned. I am not normally given to states of paranoia; I don't hear voices whispering from the bowels of the microwave, for example. It is just a matter of respect. I try not to represent people's lives on film using a language and style that the subjects themselves cannot comprehend. That would be arrogance, pure and simple. By the same token, I take offense at intellectuals' theorizing about artists in such a way that many artists cannot embrace, defend against, or *learn* from the discussion.

And that is the greatest tragedy of some contemporary trends in cultural theory. No doubt these theories are teeming with profound ideas and erudition. But the opportunity to teach and communicate, whether one's venue is the lecture podium, a textbook, or a film, has been squandered. I say this as a filmmaker who has fumbled along the sidelines of the cultural-theory road show for a number of years. This is a chronicle of that bumpy ride, through the production of two films made only ten years apart but during vastly different intellectual times: *Who Killed Vincent Chin?* (Tajima and Choy 1988) and *My America . . . or Honk if You Love Buddha* (Tajima-Peña 1997).

Higher Learning and the Making of *Who Killed Vincent Chin?*

Perhaps my formal education was too limited to comprehend it all—the ponderous cerebralism of the conferences, books, journals, and panels that clogged the arteries of cultural theory as it made its way through the 1980s and '90s. I never went to film, art, or graduate school; I endured my single film-criticism course at Harvard with the handful of other students of color, sitting at the back of the class shooting spitballs at the Eastern European avant-gardists on screen.

I began my career explicitly as a political filmmaker, having come of age during the 1970s. It was the height of the Asian American movement, when a highly effective triumvirate of academia, community activists, and artists moved the agenda forward. Each sector had a role in achieving racial justice and in the collective struggle to improve the lives of Asian American people in such areas as education, employment, health care, and housing. That synergy fueled the creation of early publications such as *Roots: An Asian American Reader* (Tachiki et al. 1991) and *Counterpoint* (Gee 1976); films such as *Hito Hata: Raise the Banner* (Nakamura and Kubo 1980); and, most important, any number of organizing struggles. The lines between the disciplines were not as sharply drawn as they are today. On any number of occasions, I would find myself marching against the anti-affirmative action Bakke decision, or organizing anti-apartheid demonstrations (Photo 14.1) with a picket sign in one hand and a camera in the other.

Living through that time made me a true believer in political theory and, in particular, in the power of theory and practice—understanding how systems, people, and history operate, extrapolating that understanding to my own microcosmic world and to principles of action, then revising theory based on concrete experiences.

I recently pulled out an old mimeograph from a study group I joined during my college years. It was one of several Marxist–Leninist formations that were driving forces behind the early Asian American movement and reflected the union of activists, academics, and artists. True, I was as naïve as I was enthusiastic about this new, semi-clandestine world of leftist politics. For example, one of my first questions to my study group was, "Do I have to marry someone in the party?" Worse yet was my blind, partisan flirtations with such dunderheads as Pol Pot, Mobutu, and the Gang of Four—a symptom of the Cold War sectarianism of these formations.

PHOTO 14.1.   Renee Tajima (left) with Fred Houn at an anti-apartheid rally. Courtesy of the author.

Yet in the immediate practice of organizing within Asian American communities, there was an impressive ideological lucidity, articulated in principles of action and borne out in the living fruit of the movement—any number of health-care centers, anti-racist legislation, ethnic studies departments, arts centers, and on and on.

In making *Who Killed Vincent Chin?* I relied on this grounding in political theory, primarily the internal colonial model that dominated thinking about Asian America during the 1970s. As an antidote to the assimilationist theories that dominated the post-war era, this model asserted that the American socioeconomic system relegated its racial minorities to positions of disfranchisement and exploitation. In other words, racial minorities existed in "colonies" inside the U.S. national borders in conditions much like those of traditional colonies of imperial powers such as England and France.[1]

In the fall of 1983, associate producer Nancy Tong and I made our first, two-month research trip to Detroit to look for the *Who Killed Vincent Chin?* story.[2] I had every confidence that, in the narrative of Asian American historical marginality, this one fit like a glove. Vincent Chin was killed during a time in which the Asian American political identity that was shaped during the 1960s and '70s was still appropriate. This is the Asian America I knew when I was coming up. We were relatively easy to define: We were predominantly Chinese, Filipino, Japanese, and American-born. We spoke a common language—English. We shared a similar labor and immigration history and an identity as a historically oppressed racial group.

Nancy and I arrived at night at our motel, just outside the deceptively protective confines of Detroit's Renaissance Center. We were carjacked at gunpoint and lost all of the paper research we had compiled to that point. Maybe it was a prophetic moment. Now working from scratch, we had to rely on intuition, old-fashioned detective work, and talking to primary sources. Inevitably, it was the uncovering of ambiguities of the case, rather than didactic analyses, that intrigued me. Was Chin's death the result of a barroom brawl or a racial assault? The subjective factors of intent—what went on in the mind of the defendant—rather than physical evidence forms the crux of criminal civil rights (and today, hate crime) prosecutions. In a racialized society the interpretation of intent is inevitably colored by the experience and racial position of the judge, the juror, the viewer. As a result, *Who Killed Vincent Chin?* is concerned far more with dissecting these gray areas of the story than with the ideological clarity of a traditional advocacy documentary.

In another sense, the thematic approach of the film was in conflict with the doctrine of people's art, influenced by the cultural revolution in the People's Republic of China, which was influential in the Asian American movement during the 1970s. For example, the standard narrative line for politically correct leftist art would document the people's struggle and their ultimate triumph over oppression. *Who Killed Vincent Chin?* ends with ambivalence. In the parting shot, Lily Chin has lost the civil rights prosecution against her son's killer, Ronald Ebens, but she makes one last, tearful plea for justice (Photo 14.2). It is unclear whether this is internal strength or futile yearning. For me, then, theory was not a blueprint for making the film; it was a standard by which to question and challenge my artistic investigation.

The more doctrinaire pressures regarding political art were fading by the early 1980s anyway. What was most notable about Asian American aesthetic theory at the time was its paucity. There was little in the way of Asian American film theory; Asian American independents had largely extrapolated from other cinema movements, such as the Third Cinema of Latin America and alternative cinema of color in the United States. What remained from the 1970s was the sense that we as Asian American artists were building a pan-Asian American culture from scratch.

As a result, I felt a great deal of both freedom and desperation in the task of locating an "Asian American" artistic strategy for the making of *Who Killed Vincent Chin?* The idea of an Asian American sensibility has always been problematic. Ever since the beginnings of the political-identity movement, we've strained under the burden of aesthetics, following the political–cultural footprint of Third World nationalist movements within and outside America. As Wittman Ah Sing, Maxine Hong Kingston's Tripmaster Monkey, bemoaned: "Where's our jazz? Where's our blues? Where's our ain't-taking-no-shit-from-nobody street-strutting language?" (Kingston 1990).

I, too, was obsessed with the search for an Asian American equivalent to African American and Latino cultural forms. And so, as a teenager, I bought a beat-up thrift-store *koto*, fashioned Asian American-version *daishiki*'s from twenty-five-pound rice bags, made a pilgrimage to Japan. Ultimately, this search for an Asian American aesthetic, in the cultural-nationalist tradition, proved fraught with perils. The material conditions of our lives as Asians in America has never been reduced to a singular cul-

PHOTO 14.2.   Lily Chin responds to a federal appeals court jury's decision to overturn Ronald Ebens's conviction: "I want justice for my son. I want justice for all." Courtesy of Renee Tajima-Peña.

tural experience, or even to a duality between East and West. The artificial trappings of the roots journey didn't make sense. Here in the United States, Asian Americans have never had the land base and regional history to sustain an aesthetic in the way that we think of Afro Caribbean, African American, or Tejano cultures, for example. Hawaiian culture is an exception—and the Hawaiian way is probably the closest we'll ever get to having an Asian (Pacific) American culture. Asia the homeland is simply too huge, too diverse as a singular aesthetic source. So many languages, so many religions, so many rhythms. Our forebears brought them all, then a new generation was born in America, then another, and another and another. What is left and what becomes that which is Asian American?

Therefore, I felt that my greatest stylistic challenge was dealing with the uneven baseline of cultural reference points between Asian and non-Asian viewers. How do you articulate the experience of a marginalized group, with its particularities and minutiae, for a mainstream audience? How do you disrupt the center and realign the notion of universality? Is an Asian American film aesthetic a realistic goal?

Ultimately, defining Asian American culture didn't make sense until I looked back at my own upbringing. What was organic to me, what was intuitive? As a third-generation Asian American, there was nothing in my life of the biculturalism common to the conventions of immigrant literature; rather, there was an eclecticism defined by Carlos Montavais's *la cultura de necesidad*. I came of age in the fervent California mix of the Asian, the African American, the Mexican American, and the western. I watched a lot of television and was immersed in R&B, soul, and rock music. By nature I had an affinity to white male writers such as Jack Kerouac, Charles Bukowski,[3] John Fante, and Raymond Carver (although I never would have admitted it in my cultural-nationalist days). Meanwhile, living at home with three generations, the legacy of Japanese migration, displacement, and family was etched into my memory.

As a filmmaker, I slowly discovered an artistic home in this eclecticism, these multiple identities. There was freedom in never having to learn the *koto*. The freedom is not only to embrace the plurality of these influences, but to search more deeply into the meaning of Asian America as a dynamic, ever-changing organism. Being a Japanese girl existing in such a pluralistic milieu simply seemed oddball when I was a child, too outside the mainstream to affirm in art. But today, I find increasingly that *la cultura de necesidad* more accurately defines the American character as much as it defines my individual and ethnic experience and artistic strategies.[4]

These influences have played out in my work. First, I have tried to give my films a populist veneer—that is, infiltrating a marginalized culture into a mainstream consciousness by using conventions of entertainment, such as the murder story (*Who Killed Vincent Chin?*), the humor and Americana of a road trip (*My America*), the drama of a family reunion (the works in progress *Kansas, Doi Moi* and *La Reunion*). In the making of *Who Killed Vincent Chin?* I began to apply a literary and narrative sensibility to nonfiction filmmaking that would negotiate this specificity and marginality. Although *Who Killed Vincent Chin?* has no overt narration, its dramatic structure and fractured storytelling approach is based on *Rashomon* (Kurosawa 1950) merged with the parallel narrative lines of *Hill Street Blues* (Bochco 1981–87), one of my favorite television shows at the time. In addition to the tabloid murder elements of the drama, the literary approach was intended as a palatable vehicle for guiding the audience into the uncharted territory of Asian American civil rights issues.

Likewise, the iconography I wanted to use as the cultural roadmap for the film surfaced organically—Motown; Dinah Shore's exuberant, standing-on-top-o'-the-world exhortations ("See the USA in your Chevrolet!"); the prevailing sense of America-ascendant. It was how I connected to Vincent Chin and to his convicted killer, Ron Ebens, having the shared experience of coming of age in America's go-go years, when car was king, then coming face to face with the United States in its decline. I remember very clearly as a child the meat crisis and the gas crisis and the recession of the 1970s, realizing that our entitlement as Americans—that heady feeling of being in a three-ton V-8 monster tooling down the highway with Wolfman Jack blasting on AM radio—wasn't going to last.

Dazed and Confused on the Road to Asian America

Who Killed Vincent Chin? was made during a time of great change in Asian America—the waning days of the civil rights era and the escalating wave of new immigration. As the reforms of the Immigration and Nationality Act of 1965 were implemented, we found ourselves undergoing a population explosion in numbers and diversity, especially during the 1980s. From a tiny, invisible minority, Asian Americans became the fastest-growing racial group in the United States. Once overwhelmingly Chinese, Filipino, and Japanese in ethnicity, we came to represent more than fifty nationalities. We are now a foreign-born majority, with great differences in our histories and back-grounds, ranging from multimillionaires to indigent refugees. Needless to say, we were left with one hell of an identity crisis.

During the same period of the 1980s, the Asian American movement itself, still dominated by Japanese and Chinese Americans, entered a period of consolidation and pro-fessionalization.[5] The trend had both benefits and hazards. Academics got tenure, artists got grants and galleries, activists got elected, and we all got a modicum of respectability. Some may argue that we were co-opted. Yet our potential influence and effectiveness also expanded. An Asian American film may now be seen by millions. I found a collection of Asian American books at a tiny border-town library in the predominantly Mexican American Rio Grande Valley.

It was about this time that I began to receive invitations to speak on panels about deconstruction, re-imaginings, gazes on races, and the Other postcolonial reality—presumably as their Asian American–female–filmmaker participant. The hosts were primarily white-run institutions within the art world and academia, and among avant-garde filmmaking and feminist circles, and the events were funded by new "multicultural" monies from public agencies and foundations. The many institutions of color that had been doing multicultural work long before it became fashionable did not have the same inside track to these funds. Among artists of color, much grumbling was directed at tokenism, opportunism, and, more important, theoretical and ideological carpetbagging. Coco Fusco articulated the contradictions wrought by the new multicultural vogue in *Screen*'s "Last Special Issue on Race":

> What is not always addressed in the policy discourse of multiculturalism is the segregat-
> ed division of labour in which, more often than not, white arts institutions provide struc-
> tures of control in which white intellectuals theorise about racism while ethnic film and
> video producers supply "experiential" materials in the form of testimony and documen-
> tary, or in which the white intelligentsia solicits token Third World intellectuals to theo-
> rise about the question—that is, the problems of the "other"—for the white intelligentsia.
> These divisions contribute to the continuation of cultural apartheid regardless of the mul-
> ticultural veneer. [Fusco 1988, 82]

I was just out of college at the time, still in my twenties and neither intellectually prepared nor intellectually mature enough to grasp the larger theoretical skirmishes that were brewing. Amid the rhetorical battles over psychoanalytic theory versus historical materialism, canons and margins, most of the filmmakers of color I knew were simply worried about scraping a few thousand dollars together to make a movie. I resented white people getting colored money to theorize about their interpretation of our plight; loathed the high-falutin' terminology and references. In retrospect, I wish I had had the patience and training at least to ground myself in the basic cultural-theory texts, but the alien milieu turned me off to the whole enterprise.

Meanwhile out in the real world, as leftist intellectuals split hairs and wallowed in gobbledygook, the right was marching on, taking over the opinion pages, school boards, and Congress, wielding by comparison a decidedly populist vernacular. When the 1980s rolled into the '90s, the massive and spectacularly diverse wave of new Asian immigration fractured the scrupulously constructed Asian American political identity of the civil rights generation.

I count myself as a part of this generation—dominated by Chinese and Japanese Americans who had come of age during the Third World mobilizations of another era. We were caught off-guard by the transformation of Asian America that was brought on by this new immigration. I remember filming in Chicago at a conference of Chinese dissident students soon after the Tiananmen Square massacre. Having been weaned on the social movements of the 1970s and their critique of American hegemony and political hypocrisy, I was rankled by the students' veneration of the United States as the mecca of democracy. "Are you kidding?" I thought. "Democracy and freedom? America the racist state? America, where freedom of speech, the meritocracy, and individual opportunity are all myths?"

Of course, it was my naïveté speaking. The war in Southeast Asia, the poverty and tyranny of Third World underdevelopment, the exigencies of life-and-death struggle when it exists in your backyard—these had all been abstractions for me, a student activist living in the comforts of American prosperity and privilege. I have been pondering this naïveté ever since the conference in Chicago—this gulf between my own narrow Asian American experience and that of the new Asian immigrants and refugees.

It hit me once again in 1992 during the Los Angeles riots, with the upsurge of tension between Korean immigrants and African Americans. The hostility disrupted my worldview of non-white racial solidarity, shaped from the moment I devoured *The Autobiography of Malcolm X* (1975) at age ten and sharpened through years of Third World coalition work. I was well schooled in the meaning of the black and brown racial rebellion. But I had little comprehension of what it means to be a Korean immigrant working the day-to-day grind in the city's poorest communities. Dealing with the distrust, the hostility, the violence. My historical memory was of the internment camps and Civil Rights Movement, not Japanese aggression and postwar destitution.

Not too long ago, I interviewed a Vietnamese refugee, Mr. Cao, who showed me his immigration documents. I noticed his birthdate and pointed out to him, "I'm exactly two months older than you!" Without looking up from his papers, he simply said, "But you have been very lucky." Mr. Cao had lost eleven years in a prison camp, where he was tortured and often literally confined to a box. He has a young child in Vietnam whom he has never seen, and has been separated from his family for five years. With the arrival of the new wave of Asian refugees and immigrants, the global realpolitik of race and economy is no longer an abstraction. It is here, in your face. There is little of the romance and clarity I relished when we were *here* and they were over *there*.

As history charged through Asian America, I found myself ill-equipped as a filmmaker to grasp the meaning of this transformation. I missed the guidance of the activist–academic–artist communion that had begun to fade into professional specialization. Getting tenure, grants, and galleries and getting elected had its price in terms of time and energy. At least, that was the case for me as a filmmaker. Apart from the tasks of production, an independent filmmaker is a schlepper, publicist, copywriter, graphic designer, researcher, fundraiser, bookkeeper, paralegal, exhibitor, lecturer, and marketing specialist. On top of that, you have to do something to earn a living. I ran an organization and freelanced as a film critic, a print editor, and a programmer.

For me, Derrida, Lacan, Foucault, and the like weren't going to get read on the F train to work or in the waiting room at the dentist's. Then there were the legions of adherents and interpreters, who referenced theorists I had never read, often writing or speaking in that secret language I had never learned. There was no *Postmodernism for Dummies*, no Cliff Notes for the post-pedagogical. Besides, I wondered, if these theorists were out to demolish the hegemonic foundations of Eurocentrism, why did they sound so . . . French?

No Mo Po Mo and the Making of *My America*

Armed with my blank slate, I decided to go out on the road and see for myself what the changes in Asian America were all about. I ended up filming *My America . . . or Honk if You Love Buddha*. I wanted to make a road movie because I had discovered America as a child traveling the country (Photo 14.3), and I was influenced by the tradition of the American road narrative, specifically the careering travel style and observational posture of Jack Kerouac's *On the Road* (1955) and the outsider's quest for humanity along the peripheries in Carlos Bulosan's Depression-era novel *America Is in the Heart* (1943). In my own journey, the road is a metaphor for the Asian American experience—that is, the exuberant promise of the American landscape, juxtaposed with the loneliness of being considered a foreigner at home. Will we ever truly belong in America?

Like an algebra problem, the process of finding an answer is often more important, and intriguing, than the result. Similar to Wayne Wang's filmic journey through Chinatown in *Chan Is Missing* (1982), that of *My America* leads to these different territories—historical, emotional, socioeconomic, personal—that define Asian America and its surroundings. It is a dense, complex landscape—ranging from empirical demographic data to subliminal media messages, romance, public policy, and family legend. Therefore, as metaphor, the road is traveled not only literally in the film. Memory is carved into place, in the subjects and in the past, and personified by the central character, the iconoclastic actor and former Beat Generation painter Victor Wong—a fellow traveler, only allegorically speaking—who preceded me along the social history of Asian America (Photo 14.4).

I hoped the film would work on different levels. Because *My America* was for television, and given my populist leanings, I wanted to be able to reach a broad (not necessarily Asian) audience. At the very least, I hoped that Joe Sixpack in the American heart-

PHOTO 14.3.   The filmmaker on the road in America. Photo: Calvin Tajima.

land, wherever that may be, would recognize our fundamental humanity in our lives, stories, humor, and tragedies. That is why the film is constructed around the narrative convention of tales from the road, with humor and irony mediating the nuance of social and political themes. For example, my visit with Yuri Kochiyama and her husband, Bill (who died soon after the production), in Mississippi, which recalls the World War II experience of the 442nd Battalion and internment camps, is presented as a love story.

Yet there is the possibility of reading more deeply into the text. The fortune-cookie maker Chung Y. Choi is a man with five jobs and a comic vision of the Model Minority gone haywire. But on another level, his single-minded devotion to entrepreneurial riches underscores the dilemma between the acquisitive side of the American Dream and the social covenant of the American ideal. As the filmmaker–narrator asks, "Are we here with visions of liberty and equality, or to take the money and run?" Is it enough to improve our lives and take care of our families? Or do we have a deeper role in the struggle for democracy and in the public life of the nation? After encountering the sheer range of Asian American experiences on the road, I realized that the question was not, "Who are we as Asian Americans?" but rather, "What are we here to do?"

When I was growing up during the 1960s and '70s, the end of ethnicity was defined as assimilation—how would we as Asian Americans fit into the mainstream? With the demographic changes wrought by the post-1965 immigration reforms and the culture wars of recent years, there has been a paradigm shift. The more I traveled, the more it

PHOTO 14.4.   Fellow traveler Victor Wong at home in Sacramento, California.
Photo: Quynh Thai.

seemed that we could no longer look at Asian Americans as marginal to the larger society. They are playing a central, activist role within the fabric of the republic.

Gary Okihiro sets that theoretical foundation in his book *Margins and Mainstreams*
(1994) by arguing that the "marginal" peoples of the United States have actually been
a pivotal force in moving democracy forward through their struggles against oppression (unfortunately, a book I read after I had finished the film). I found that this ideal
was embodied in many of the people I met on the road, such as the Kochiyamas and
Alyssa Kang, a young Korean American activist. They have taken their struggles as
a moral imperative to commit their lives to the fight for justice—not just justice for
Asian Americans, but "Justice for all," as Lily Chin demands at the close of *Who Killed
Vincent Chin?* The idea of "Justice for all" embodies a new vision for progressive
Asian Americans who have been searching for an ideological and moral anchor for
collective action.[6]

The two found media clips I use in *My America* are indicative of this changing paradigm. In the first third of the film, there is a clip of a white actor in yellowface from
a '50s-era propaganda film about the Japanese. That is the screen Asian I remember
as a child. On screen we were either invisible or, more often than not, not even truly
Asian. In the final third of the film, there is video of Oklahomans in the immediate
aftermath of the bombing of the Murrah Federal Building. In the face of this right-

wing, anti-democratic violence are people of all races working collectively to comfort and protect one another. And there, in the midst of all that is going on, is an Asian woman saving a child of another race.

Lisa Lowe (1998, 7) has written: "Although the law is perhaps the discourse that most literally governs citizenship, United States national culture—the collectively forged images, histories, and narratives that place, displace, and replace individuals in relation to the national polity—powerfully shapes who the citizenry is, where they dwell, what they remember, and what they forget." Similarly, the image of that woman in Oklahoma, central to this simultaneously terrifying and uplifting American scene, was a powerful, symbolic visual metaphor for me—the agency of an Asian American recorded at a historic event fraught with larger meaning.

One reason I used a personal approach in the film is that, for better or worse, I found little in the way of the collective thinking that existed during the 1970s to provide theoretical guidance for the production. It was very much a seat-of-the-pants, visceral response to what I experienced on the road. However, I found the cultural theories of eclecticism from authors such as Coco Fusco and the approach of other Asian American artists such as Jon Jang, the film's composer, to be affirming of my own experience with Asian American filmmaking and influential in the film's subtext of music, Americana, humor, and vision of Asian America.

I tried to take the idea of connecting the organic, cultural synapses of Asian American experience in my earlier films a step further in *My America*. As a chronicle of my personal responses to the American cultural landscape, both in memory and in the present tense of being on the road, the film deals with political identity in that it is a conscious search for Asian America. But it is also a cultural document because of the subconscious—listening to and seeing American lives as one eclectic highway. Though the conventional notion of an aesthetic, a sensibility, begs for commonality, in the case of Asian Americans—indeed, for all Americans in modern society—the commonality is difference.

I took an unusual route in the making of the film by showing the rough cut in public screenings around the country. Some of these showings were in the context of academic conferences; consequently, I was directly exposed to certain theoretical sensibilities in cultural studies. I was struck by the dissonance between the concerns of the Asian Americans I was encountering during filming and some theorists who were ostensibly engaged in issues of race and ethnicity. Similarly, on the road, I was constantly dismayed by my own insularity.

I think that art or scholarship is always a matter of pushing boundaries. And what can be more important than pushing one's own frame of reference and constituency past our familiar intellectual or aesthetic environs? For me, that has come to mean filming outside the cocoon of the Asian American coastal metropolises. *Who Killed Vincent Chin?* took me to Detroit. *My America* took me to such places as Orlando, Florida; Duluth, Minnesota; and New Orleans. My next film will be shot primarily in Kansas. I do this because I find it so comfortable at "home"—in the warm embrace of colleagues, audiences, like-minded people in the art–filmmaking–academic circuit. The technology and economy of filmmaking mean that it is easier to live in the big cities, such as New York, Los Angeles, and San Francisco. These cities are also populated by the heaviest concentrations of Asian Americans, as well as artists. It's synergy, it's heaven. It's also incredibly parochial.

Moving outside of one's boundaries influences who you film, what you film, the very questions you ask. In the production of *My America*, I spent time with a Hmong garment worker in Duluth, Pang-ku Yang (Photo 14.5). Meeting her family, eating in her home, listening to the story of her journey from Laos to Thailand to Minnesota, I realized that all of the identity questions I had been immersed in sounded quite frivolous. I had thought of asking all of the subjects on the road, "What is an Asian American?" But with Pang-ku, I couldn't even spit it out. Don't get me wrong: The question of identity is a critical one. But my questions were not Pang-ku's questions.

I believe the distance that results from staying within our cocoons keeps us from finding and understanding the questions that require our immediate attention and responses. I, for one, was embarrassed that we Asian American filmmakers did not break the story of the Thai garment workers in El Monte who were virtually enslaved by Asian American factory owners. The local news broke that story. We used to have our ears to the ground; we used to know what was going on in our communities. Recently, I attended a national gathering of Asian Pacific American labor activists. It was an exhilarating event. Immigrant workers have been the vanguard of renewed energy and ideas in an otherwise declining American labor movement. There was only

PHOTO 14.5.   Pang-ku Yang (right) and her husband, Xia Yang, in Duluth, Minnesota. Photo: Quynh Thai.

one camera there—that of the veteran filmmaker Loni Ding, of course, who in twen-ty-five years has been unstoppable.

In order to step beyond my boundaries, I have had to try to communicate with people outside my own range of experience. Filmmaking has its own language—the challenge is to not let it get in the way of the viewers' comprehension or connection to the work. I find that the greatest danger in certain contemporary theoretical practices is that you never really have to *talk* to people. You can create a film entirely from artifacts, text, and found images. You can write an epic tome based purely on the same. But I find that if I don't get out and talk to people and truly interact, I start to believe my own press. As a filmmaker of color, I have given a great deal of lip service to the notion of underserved audiences and the production of relevant film programming. The working assumption is that I, as a product of the underserved community, know best how to serve it. On the one hand, it is the basic problem of essentializing race (you can't imagine how hard it is for me to spit that one out). Frankly, no matter where artists come from, once we are artists in this society we are of an intellectual class. In the case of filmmakers, we are of a professional class. And for all of the reasons I have cited—where we live, who we associate with, our class *affiliations*, our boundaries—it is easy to get out of touch.

By the same token, I don't think one can truly understand issues of cultural production and representation without some sense of the realities of practice. Theory leaves out critical factors such as luck, cash flow, and flexible production staffing, and scholars can be deluded by the mythology of the auteur, especially when they venture into the perilous realm of critiquing intention and processes. I had a recent experience with graduate students who were steeped in the study of race and representation. They wanted to tail me for a day to see what a filmmaker does. But I felt that if they really wanted to learn about cultural production, they should actually do a small project of their own. I assigned them a simple video production—to film non-citizen, legal immigrants who were threatened with loss of public assistance because of welfare-reform legislation. More specifically, the immigrants were elderly and disabled—the most vulnerable portion of the population other than children.

The students made time to meet and discuss the possibility, but I could never get them actually to leave campus and dive into the process. It is a pity, because all manner of ethical, political, and artistic questions arise from the conception of such a project, and I have never seen a book that could truly describe these complexities and nuances. Even at the very start, as you plan interviews and initial filming, you have to ask: Who is the audience? How will the final product be used? Who's Rolodex do you use to find interview subjects? Do you go through a county social worker, an advocacy group, family contacts, or the INS? Or do you hang around the neighborhood? Although the focus is on immigrants, will your intended audience tolerate subtitles or voiceovers? What kind of "audition" criteria do you use to choose subjects? Are they photogenic? Articulate? Are these valid criteria when filming this type of story? Will the media exposure leave your subjects vulnerable to detection by welfare authorities? Can they legally agree to be filmed, especially those who are mentally disabled? If they are housed in a board-and-care facility, what kind of access will you have? If they are home-bound in a small room, how many crew people can you fit in the room? What lens will you use to get a sense of the cramped space? Is there natural light? Is there a noisy, central air-conditioning unit that can't be turned off? And with each of these questions, there are sub-questions.

There was a time when Asian American studies always had a community component, and perhaps this notion is returning. I had another recent, and intriguing, classroom visit with an Asian American studies course at UCLA taught by the filmmaker John Esaki.[7] Each student actually produces his or her own video, filmed within an Asian American community. One student asked me an apparently simple, practical question that had surfaced during her production; it was, in fact, full of complex implications that I could not answer immediately and am still thinking about. She was filming a project with older, Filipino male subjects who did not respect her because she was a young woman. What should she do? Indeed what *should* she do? She could find more amenable subjects, but then she would lose the perspectives of these men, and consequently the subtext of patriarchy. She could film their response to her, in all their patriarchal honesty, using a personal approach. But would that divert from the main issues? She could use a surrogate interviewer, she could lie to them, she could coddle them, she could use all types of manipulation. Is the product, then, more important than the process? Do the ends justify the means? By diving in there and engaging with living, breathing subjects, she confronted critical issues of representation that the earlier group of graduate students forfeited.

Yet practical experience alone would not necessarily lead her to the culturally sensitive, oppositional filmmaking strategies intended by the course. Implicit in the quandary are intellectual and ethical questions surrounding the workings of social hierarchies and how art intervenes with those hierarchies. What is the context of these men's lives as immigrants and workers in the United States, and how does it intersect with traditional values and prejudices? How can the representation of the men through interviews and visual material convey this multilayered understanding? Will the cultural assumptions or the film's intended audience mask or illuminate these contexts?

There are perils to practice alone. A few years ago, I was filming Asian American gangs for the documentary *Jennifer's in Jail* (Tajima 1995). One young man made me an offer he figured no filmmaker would refuse—the chance to film a drive-by shooting in progress. From a solely professional standpoint, there is no question of the cinematic power and drama this type of footage would provoke. There are also a host of considerations. Should one camera be set up in the car and one in sight of the victim? Will the crew be in danger? What are the legal ramifications of liability, protection of minors' privacy, recording evidence of a crime?

I could go on and on with these practical concerns, posed as they are within a moral and intellectual vacuum—clearly, filming and thereby participating in a drive-by shooting would constitute moral and intellectual bankruptcy. It would sensationalize, not illuminate, the problem of teenage alienation and violence in the Asian

American community. Of course, the bottom line is, I would be party to the taking of a life. The scenario may sound extreme, but media now penetrates every aspect of life and death. More and more, production decisions are governed by the amoral principles of commerce and competition. The bitter satire of Paddy Chayefsky's *Network* (Lumet 1976) is now edging on reality.

By contrast, social-change filmmaking demands an overarching, humanistic vision and intellect in concert with artistic practice. Traveling to campuses across the country during the past year, I found that this spirit has persevered in places such as Esaki's class, however overshadowed it has been by the sexier trends in cultural studies. Recently, the San Francisco-based group Asian Women United—composed of activist professionals and faculty from the University of California, Berkeley—asked me to make a film on immigrant workers that will be a kind of *Grapes of Wrath* for the new millennium of globalized low-wage labor. With its prolific history of print and media production dealing with community issues,[8] the AWU keeps cranking it out regardless of intellectual fashion by keeping its ears to the ground and working in concert with artists and community organizers.

I believe that Asian American filmmaking can be enriched with a return to the collective spirit of engagement among artists, scholars, and activists, unfettered by the parochialism of overspecialization—not as nostalgia for the 1970s, but as a force in seizing what Lowe has called "the power of culture." On the road through Asian America—I imagine a cultural theorist would navigate the road signs. A politico might worry about maneuvering among the other drivers. A filmmaker would concentrate on the view. It makes sense to get together behind the wheel, because, after all, the goal of social-change filmmaking is to move that baby forward.

Notes

1. For a good basic introduction, see Liu (1976).

2. Vincent Chin was a Chinese American draftsman in Detroit who was killed by a white Chrysler foreman in the midst of the auto recession and the U.S.–Japan trade wars. The case became the first federal civil rights criminal prosecution involving Asian Americans and a national cause celebré.

3. Bukowski narrated my film *The Best Hotel on Skid Row* (Davis, Choy, and Tajima 1991).

4. For more about this idea of cultural eclecticism, see Tajima (1991).

5. See Espiritu (1992).

6. This idea is eloquently framed in Chin, Cho, Kang, and Wu (1996), a call for Asian American support of affirmative action. The paper's authors are law professors.

7. The course is a part of the UCLA Asian American Studies Ethnocommunications Program, founded by Esaki and Professor Robert Nakamura. Both are alumni of an affirmative-action program of the same name at the UCLA film school during the 1970s, which was the training ground for key members of the Visual Communications collective.

8. Other Asian Women United films include *Slaying the Dragon* (Gee 1980), *From Dust to Threads* (Lo n.d.), *Four Women* (Ding 1982), and *Art to Art: Expressions by Asian American Women* (Soe 1993).

Works Cited

Bulosan, Carlos. 1943. *America Is in the Heart: A Personal History.* 1973 repr. ed. Seattle: University of Washington Press.

Chin, Gabriel, Sumi Cho, Jerry Kang, and Frank Wu. 1996. "Beyond Self-Interest: Asian Pacific Americans Toward a Community of Justice: A Policy Analysis of Affirmative Action," http://www.sscnet.ucla.edu/aasc/policy/.

Espiritu, Yen Le. 1992. *Asian American Panethnicity: Bridging Institutions and Identities.* Philadelphia: Temple University Press.

Fusco, Coco. 1988. "Fantasies of Oppositionality—Reflections on Recent Conferences in Boston and New York." *Screen* 29, no. 4 (fall): 80–93.

Gee, Emma, ed. 1976. *Counterpoint: Perspectives on Asian America.* Los Angeles: Asian American Studies Center, UCLA.

Kerouac, Jack. 1955. *On the Road.* New York: Viking.

Kingston, Maxine Hong. 1990. *Tripmaster Monkey: His Fake Book.* New York: Vintage Books.

Leong, Russell, ed. 1991. *Moving the Image: Independent Asian Pacific American Media Arts.* Los Angeles: UCLA Asian American Studies Center and Visual Communications, Southern California Asian American Studies Central.

Liu, John. "Towards an Understanding of the Internal Colonial Model." Pp. 160–68 in *Counterpoint,* ed. Gee.

Lowe, Lisa. 1998. "The Power of Culture." *Journal of Asian American Studies* 1, no. 1 (February): 5–29.

Okihiro, Gary Y. 1994. *Margins and Mainstreams: Asians in American History and Culture.* Seattle: University of Washington Press.

Tachiki, Amy, Eddie Wong, and Franklin Odo, with Buck Wong, ed. 1991. *Roots: An Asian American Reader.* Los Angeles: Asian American Studies Center, UCLA.

Tajima, Renee. 1991. "Moving the Image: Asian American Independent Filmmaking 1970-1990." Pp. 10–33 in *Moving the Image,* ed. Leong.

X, Malcolm, with Alex Haley. 1975. *The Autobiography of Malcolm X.* New York: Ballantine.

Films and Videos Cited

Bochco, Steven. 1981–87. *Hill Street Blues.* NBC.

Davis, Peter, Christine Choy, and Renee Tajima. 1991. *The Best Hotel on Skid Row.* Home Box Office.

Ding, Loni. 1982. *Four Women.* Asian Women United.

Gee, Deborah. 1988. *Slaying the Dragon.* NAATA.

Kurosawa, Akira. 1950. *Rashomon.* RKO Pictures.

Lo, Louise. n.d. *From Dust to Threads.* Asian Women United.

Lumet, Sidney. 1976. *Network.* United Artists.

Nakamura, Robert, and Duane Kubo. 1980. *Hito Hata: Raise the Banner.* NAATA.

Soe, Valerie. 1993. *Art to Art: Expressions by Asian American Women.* Asian Women United.

Tajima, Renee. 1995. *Jennifer's in Jail.* Lifetime Television.

Tajima, Renee, and Christine Choy. 1988. *Who Killed Vincent Chin?* Filmakers Library.

Tajima-Peña, Renee. 1997. *My America . . . or Honk if You Love Buddha.* Sai Communications.

———. Forthcoming. *Kansas, Doi Moi.*

———. Forthcoming. *La Reunion*.

Wang, Wayne. 1982. *Chan Is Missing*. New Yorker Films.

Theodore S. Gonzalves

---

15   "Unashamed to Be So Beautiful":
         An Interview with Celine Salazar
         Parreñas

The filmmaker Celine Salazar Parreñas represents a young cohort of cultural producers who offer works that complicate paternalistic aesthetics. Informed by interventions made in feminist filmmaking and cultural theory by Julie Dash, Trinh T. Minh-ha, Theresa Hak-kyung Cha, and Michele Wallace, among others, as well as by Philippine social-protest filmmaking signaled by the likes of Lino Brocka, Parreñas's work cuts against the grain of the Filipina–Filipino American community's insistence on "positive" images. In 1992, Parreñas and three other filmmakers—Ernesto Foronda, Pancho Gonzalez, and John Castro—founded the activist media collective SINE-GANG. The name plays on two registers. The first references the culinary metaphor of a staple soup of the Philippines, *sinigang*. The second combines two terms, "cinema" and "gang," recalling a time that all four were working on one another's films. That is, nutrition equals production: We eat what we are.

What follows is a conversation with Parreñas about her film work and production. In her works, a series of Filipina-centered narrations, Parreñas highlights the weaknesses of the stories we've told one another, while holding out for the possibility of building on the strengths of organizing meaningful, collective works. I also point to her function as an editor of sorts: Encompassing a range of activity, including encouraging artists' forums and collectives, she has taken on some of the task of anthologizing and organizing contemporary creative artists in ways similar to the foundational work drafted by Oscar Peñaranda, Luis Syquia, and Sam Tagatac in the 1970s [Peñaranda, Syquia, and Tagatac 1975].

Theodore S. Gonzalves: Your historiographical intervention is a decidedly feminist one—targeting what has putatively been a male-centered historiography. How do your films comment on the writing of ethnic histories?

Celine Salazar Parreñas: In my life around teaching, making, and theorizing in film, I am most concerned with looking at how power works in relationships among people—how people are affected by and act within larger structures of the state, government, corporations, nations. What is not told in the larger official story of globalization and transnational border crossings of multinational corporations? Where are the people? Where are their bodies? How do people move, organize, and resist every day in oppressive conditions? More precisely, how do people act in the unavoidable interstices of race, class, gender, and sex? People are not always heroic. Decisions are never easy. I hope to explore how people cope with their conditions, whether they are intellectuals, party girls, or single parents. I am most compelled by how people handle their power, how they exert it on others, and how they experience it as exerted over them.

At first, the way that Filipina women were told to me in history, as ornamental and as secondary to men as actors, led to my need to recover a more meaningful legacy around gender and race identities for both men and women. Also, the thrust of Filipino and other ethnic histories as masculine—that is, the rendering of racial freedom as the restoration of a lost manhood through castration—left women to be passive, powerless, and uninspiring. In other words, the established idea of racial movement and freedom as penile erection never got me off. Women's versions within the racial experience are too complicated and powerful a legacy. I found the lives of women, as well as my own life, negated, and I felt that as a loss to everybody. So at this point in my short career, I have been obsessed with women—Filipina women and their sexuality, specifically—as the site where I talk about power relations as a way to speak to people about particular experiences in the world we live in. That is, to speak about the contemporaneous situation of diaspora, migration, anti-immigrant nativist positions, and the ever-changing face of America as brown and woman.

In *Mahal Means Love and Expensive* [1993], my first short film, I explore the drama surrounding a Filipina woman's body and sexuality in terms of her postcolonial subjectivity. Filipinos come from a very intense and complicated place—colonialism, forced complicity, stalled revolution, suffering, slavery. In the struggle for freedom, the country's experience of colonization and defeat is imaged as the body of a woman raped by the Spanish, the Japanese, and the Americans. How do women translate and transform this idea of her body as "country"? Her memory, a map of that history of her body as property of nation and another's narration, contradicts how she owns the experience of her sexuality and her own sense of self-certainty and self-consciousness. In this film, I enter the space of sex as a site of power relations, a space where identities work each other out and where pleasure complicates "victim" identities. I explore a Filipina woman's resistance in terms of making a living space of her own: an embrace of "bad" womanhood and a contradictory experience of her body against national narration.

In my first film, I was very fortunate to collaborate with the artist Papo de Asis as visual consultant. He is a Filipino painter and was really my very best teacher, the one who taught me the pleasure of making a postcolonial visual language in film. His paintings of women screaming, screeching impassionately, expressed the woman in the film. Papo's paintings capture the extra that funks out of the colonial experience beyond forced complicity to our own subjugation or simple victimization to how we are transformed by that colonizing experience into a new configuration. I think it is one that recognizes how colonialism required coping and a new self-making to avoid certain death. That form of resistance involves fantasy, music, song, dance, and everyday movements of the body that express limit, contradiction, and desire for life.

In *Her Uprooting Plants Her* [Parreñas 1995], three Filipina immigrant sisters run a fantastic *sari-sari* store in downtown Los Angeles. I designed the film to be shot in a set that would be constructed with the objects that folks thought constituted their Filipino identity. The cast and crew constructed such a fantastic space made up of donations from every possible Filipino store, home, and family they could find. We filled the place with comics called *Gossip* and *Megastar* and a fictional magazine *Hip Flip*. Folks brought their favorite foods (corned beef, choconut, Goldilock's, SPAM); a "dirty" ice-cream truck, like the ones in the streets of Manila; woven fans; and other "Filipiniana" found in the ethnic markets and gift stores. I wanted the actors and crew to examine what constituted their sense of self in the historical moment of our collective, particular diasporas. The set was an installation, a freezing of our identities in motion.

This film was made during the ten-year anniversary of my family's immigration to the United States, not as a simple linear narrative of progress of events but as a chart of our losses and our transformations. I wanted to make a film that would mark the fissures of migration. In my family, identity is a movement and migration in different directions. It is not necessarily a movement away from memory, tradition, and

PHOTO 15.1.   Celine Salazar Parreñas (right) and Dawn Suggs on the set of *Her Uprooting Plants Her* (1995), dir. Celine Salazar Parreñas. Photo: Eugene Ahn/Media West Photographic.

culture; rather, it is toward a plurally directed diaspora: continuous rootings and uprootings, or home-making and unmaking. We all migrate to different places ten years after we land here. So even if we are in the same room sharing the same blood, we hold different memories and different experiences of migration and settlement.

I needed to gather this heterogeneity and have that flood the film. I rehearsed and brought together thirty of my family members on the set made by the principal actors and crew to gather where and who we were in that moment in history. I asked questions such as, Where is home? Who is family? The answers shocked us all. The parents who had begged relatives for space in cramped houses were saddened to hear that, for their children, home was any roof over one's head—a car or a garage. The kids were surprised to hear parents discuss where they wanted to be buried—the United States? the Philippines? Mexico? They talked about Mexico as a version of the Philippines but much closer to the united States. The story was based on these moments and confrontations and the distances between family members that happened on our way to making a new home.

In the latest film, *Super Flip* [Parreñas 1997], I was tripping on the photographs from the book *Filipinos: Forgotten Asian Americans* [Cordova 1983]. The men photographed in Watsonville and Seattle, mostly agricultural workers, looked directly into the camera from the fields. I noted their camaraderie, their context of work and hard labor, their staggered poses, their strong sense of style, their very presence in the history and identity of this country. Proud and painful stories. I wondered where the women were. There definitely were few, one woman to thirteen men, approximately. But their lesser presence does not justify invisibility. Why are they so gratuitously there, in occasional group shots sitting over the steaming pot of rice? Too insignificant to photograph? The representation in these photographs, of a very male history, looked very much like my own world today.

I looked around in San Francisco and Los Angeles where the scene of young Filipinos, which also involved lots of educated and privileged Flips like me, so evidently involved large numbers in the visible low-wage sector: McDonald's, hotels, etc. In Los Angeles and San Francisco, I interviewed a number of young Filipinos: students, stockboys, activists, actors, retail clerks, customer-service representatives, technical workers, and hotel and restaurant workers to get a sense of how they lived. I was most attracted to how a number of these contemporary young Filipinos author their lives in the very same sites where Filipinos in the '20s and '30s found "living" space: the pool halls, taxi dances, and so on, particularly in San Francisco. I was compelled by their visibility in the city: in the buses, in the streets, and in the clubs as hyper-stylishly visible but with less substantial voice and visibility in the city. So I sought to speak with people about all this, then I constructed a narrative based on some of my interviews. Furthermore, I worked this narrative over through the actors and photographer, designer, etc., who helped me come up with a version of things in the film *Super Flip*, which ended up being about a Filipina hotel maid and cafe waitress who cleans up her life.

Super Flip is a story around Gloribel and Porma, two young Filipino Americans. They came here from the Philippines in their childhood years, never finished community college or barely did, married each other while they were in their teens, do not speak Tagalog much, and live in San Francisco's South of Market or Mission district, in a basement warehouse apartment. Porma works as a stockboy and as a car valet; Gloribel works as an exoticized waitress who wears her national costume among other women of color in a hip white socialite cafe that celebrates multicultural diversity. She also works as a maid in a hotel, sweeping sidewalks and scrubbing floors like a contemporary Filipina Cinderella. At night, Porma club hops, a star in the scene, and verifies his manhood by "conquering" other women. When she is upset, Gloribel shops like Imelda [Marcos], agent of hyper-consumerism. They eventually destroy and confront each other with their hungers and displacements. I set up this scenario to talk about how power operates in this relationship, how they cope with their disfranchisement in society, and how they exert power over each other. I wanted to write Filipino life as it explodes and implodes in its complexity.

These issues of power, resistance, and freedom that revolve around race, gender, sex, and class most interest me in film. How do people cope with their displacement everyday? With drink, dance, and song? Is it sufficient to understand them as coping

PHOTO 15.2.   From *Super Flip* (1997), dir. Celine Salazar Parreñas. Photo: Chris Hutchins.

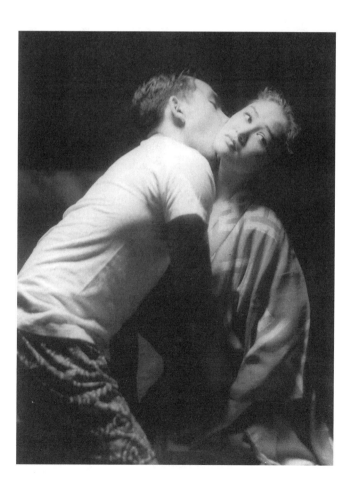

mechanisms that must be understood in their war-torn context? I question how these people handle their power. Do they perpetuate slave mentalities or write new identities? What does Porma do with the power, albeit little, that he does have? In the film, the racial-gendered targeted man of color chooses to abandon his wife and sacrifice her to his patriarchy, a freedom dependent on the slavery of women. And the woman chooses to save herself from her own mess in the face of uncertainty. I hope the film tells a story that conveys all the powerful feeling and fighting spirit around lives that are not frequently visible on film. I hope *Super Flip* shows lives that have always been fully in the United States. Filipinos have been living in the place others dismiss as the margins, the very site where the story of this country can be told better than the same old, same old stories.

TSG: Your films take place in Los Angeles and San Francisco, imagined Californian strongholds of traditionally male-centered narrations of Filipina–Filipino America. When you say "lives that have always been fully in the United States," I am reminded of those powerful visions by the visual artist Carlos Villa, whose works challenge the identities so often paraded about on T-shirt designs and in cultural festivals and marketing campaigns. Your works share that uncompromising attitude of refusing that sort of heroism. Villa affixes small brass plates into coffin-like objects—providing an informal catalogue of behaviors, desires, and failings—that read "SELF-LOATHE," "MASTER BAITING TRICKS," "ALL DRESSED AND READY," and so forth.[1]

Your films use poetry throughout the script work. It seems that the vocabularies of the films carry a poetic cadence. Could you describe the relationship you see between poetry and film?

CSP: Poetry, unlike film, is cheap. Just you and a piece of paper sitting in a corner. Writing about the emotion or event first helps me identify why I even want to isolate this moment as saying something worth the money it takes to shoot it in film. Poetry clears the road for me to make a film, from beginning to end and then round again because it captures the flavor and mood of the event in a few lines, without the expense of money, just spending time. Poetry is quick and easy: All it requires is attention to drama, which is what is found in life, people, and relationships.

Poetry isolates drama precisely. It threads moments in my everyday life into shots, scenes, and sequences in a film. The process of selecting image, moment, and emotion in poetry requires the writing of exact objects, bodies, things and physical expressions in everyday movements, choreography and situations. I am forced to identify exactly what makes people feel, whether it's the jacket with the repulsive smell from a sordid primal scene or the Prada bag for 80 percent off that pathetically constitutes your sense of purpose. Poetry, like film, is not just ideas—you cannot shoot an idea—but the identification of things I need to shoot to garner certain emotions. Writing a film in poetry focuses the film and filters out the extraneous through the hard work of seeing, feeling, and delving into life with one's full attention.

And to devote yourself to a sustained concern for drama helps the making of a film. Although the film may actually have been born long ago, at several different moments and places in life, I grasp it as its own object through the writing of a poem. In a sense, my films are raised through poems: images, words, feelings, tone, mood—exactly what constitutes a film for me. Writing the film in poetry as a long-time, everyday process brings the film out of the imagination into a physical, actual, and material realm. For me, poetry is the caress and the love that bursts into film.

Film and poetry both aim to arrest and make life. First, I find moments that reveal it, then I shoot it in hope of sustaining it. Filmmaking is an act of life-making, for the makers and the viewers. But film, unlike poetry, is a genre that requires a bigger production than just me, sitting in a corner with my pen and paper. Film is struggle with a hunger for tactics and strategies if it is to be born. In this struggle, I take the power that comes from poetry to help me navigate through the roughness of film production. Poetry is in the content of film, but it also is a mechanism that sustains me when producing the film. Poetry helps me when the making gets tough. If it's not the generator dying and I gotta borrow power from someone who doesn't know, doesn't care, or simply hates me and my agenda and wants to get in my way, it's another problem. Perhaps, editing the film months later, I've forgotten why I am making this film or am too confused by what I shot. So poetry is spirit in the sense of resistance, soul and heart.

Poetry is purpose in filmmaking; it whips me into shape. I take a poem, something precise and strong, a poem with a lot of risk, as strong as death—from something by the Filipino poets Jeff Tagami and Jessica Hagedorn to others such as Cherrie Moraga, Li Young Lee, and Sharon Olds. I take their words to focus me in my work of bringing a group of people together, each with a different job—the art, the sound, the photography, the actors, the light—as I direct their work so that we can capture drama and beauty in film from our labor. Poetry is what gets the film done and what guides and strengthens me in the directing process. In the circus of filmmaking, as a director, I must be able to clarify for everyone why we are working. Poetry, a single powerful line, gives me the clarity to fight anyone who gets in the way of the film, or to get money so I can finish the film, or to focus the actors and crew who bring the film life. I orchestrate all elements of the filmmaking process by using the power of poetry like a whip. I take the strength of poems, and they help me remember precisely why I found this idea important enough to risk my money, health, and time to make it into a movie.

So poetry begins, sustains, and completes my films. Yet it is important to say a certain kind of poetry, as well, toward a certain kind of filmmaking that is simply not satisfied with making beauty, and that would be enough. I like the idea offered by Gettino and Solanas of the Third Cinema school of making films—that films are acts of beginnings rather than products of consumption, an end or closure.[2] I hope that my own films are "acts which begin," new spins on old ways of thinking about the world we live in. To rock the view a little, maybe to open up new ways of thinking about the problem, whether it is women and work, women and the family, and Filipinos anywhere and everywhere.

TSG: Ella Shohat and Robert Stam suggest something of a link to your dissatisfaction with "making beauty" as if "that would be enough" when they identify that aesthetic of hunger. It's more than simply justifying the often bare-boned look of independent films, but tied, I think, to Kidlat Tahimik's colorful metaphor of making films with one cup of gasoline at a time—scarcity driving the production design, an explicit link between your works and Third Cinema.[3]

On other methods and pre-production work—of interviewing Pinays, of telling their stories; reportage, montage, collective biographies—could this be a kidnapping of Bulosan's concept of collective biography making? What do you consider some of the important lessons concerning this aspect of your work—that is, the pre-production methodological footwork of gathering oral histories and documenting life stories, work environments, social networks, and so forth? How is ethnography important to the filmmaking process?

CSP: I am uncomfortable with the idea of making a "collective biography" for "my people." As if that is possible without stepping on someone's feet! My own toes have suffered enough from others standing on them as they speak for a gendered me under the banner of a masculinist community. I do not intend, nor is it possible for me, to speak across the power inequalities in our community, even if people persistently put the noose on my neck. No, thanks! I do not speak for others. Damn, folks would jump me for that. What I am concerned with and committed to is analyzing the structural location of race, class, and gendered subjects in the web of power relations. As a filmmaker, I hope to theorize an analytics of speaking for a community rather than simply speak for a community.

What I mean by this is that I use interview and direct observation as an interrogation of my assumptions and not as a way to represent the story of all Filipina women. As if there were such a homogenous entity as Filipina women. I am concerned with Filipina women and hope not to homogenize their heterogeneity, so I interview. Interviewing functions as a major organizing principle in producing film for me in the same way that Anna Deveare Smith [1994] bases her work around a community, not for a community. I talk with and observe people to make my representations and images accountable to a truthful place—for example, how a disproportionate number of miscarriages occur for women who work as maids, and how shopping and dressing are coping strategies for folks who are mostly seen as workers. The authoring is mine, however. I do not aim to speak for anyone; I aim to speak *about* and *from* a place where I am immersed as a Filipina among a heterogeneous community of Filipinos in San Francisco and Los Angeles.

I author my films. Through them, I hope to make a cultural contribution to how Filipinos are understood and perceived as an entity. I hope to intervene in the homogeneity of our representations. Because I speak through my films, I am directly responsible as their author. It is I who directs the crew to represent the homes, surroundings, and the look of the locations (pool halls, discos, etc.). However, I do not mean to discount the speaking power of other objects and people caught in my acts of representation. I monitor my version of truth by comparing it with the lives of others. A commitment to historical research and discussion with living subjects within the field are musts in my filmwork, which I consider to be a certain form of social action, practice, and theory. I hope to speak from a place informed by personal struggle, a view that is tested and challenged by those who are different from me.

TSG: On other filmmaking processes and collective work, on disarming the general: Could you describe the role of the "director as general"? In other forums, you have challenged this authoritative mode of directing. And related to this: What were you trying to accomplish with the public forum and conversation series hosted by SINE-GANG in bringing together cultural producers, painters, filmmakers and video makers, writers, and so forth? What are the significant lessons derived from working in a collective? In other words, what is at stake in collective media-arts activism? What kinds of strategies are used?

CSP: On disarming the director as general? Yes, to a certain extent. Hollywood production processes are definitely reworked within a form of filmmaking constrained by money and resources. And because my films come from within Asian American communities—at the very level of story and production—the film is also informed by community building. This is a thing that I am authoring from what I know and hope for, and I gathered people who understand my hopes in a coalition kind of spirit and politics. As such, community is a central voice of the film, and community shows up in the organization of the film. It is, after all, a bunch of people of color who hunger deeply for fraught, complex, chaotic images making our very own. But the question of disarming the director as general must also be answered with a big "No." I claim the authority of the director; otherwise, nothing will get done. Film cannot happen without bodies, departments, positions, labor. What I mean is that the operations of my own production crew reflect my training in a Western film school and my films do not fall outside the way the industry functions as a hierarchized business. Especially as a brown woman speaking within such a white male industry, there is nothing romantic or real about my giving up directorial power in the sense of telling people what to do. But, indeed, I inform the directorial role with a different sensibility, as someone who identifies the realm of representation as struggle in racial, feminist, and other ways. So I unquestionably emphasize that I am, with the help of my friends, the author of the thing. I bear responsibility for how and what is said, made, framed, edited, and shown to the world in this film. Within this context, it is interesting that some responses to my work involve the need to point out the skills of those I hire to help me make the film. Particularly, some male viewers want to emphasize that men helped me or that it was actually the men who authored my film. It amazes me that there are still folks who cannot handle a woman telling men what to do or a woman saying something about men or representing men in a feminist work. This is why I must tell these folks in a very clear and firm way: my spirit, my idea, my script, my money, my hustle, my authorship, my work, mine female Filipina mine. I have been very fortunate that I rely on the greatest of friends who help me produce the film (almost all women), the director of photography (a man), the production designer (a woman). . . . It is really absurd to list this, because the crew was amazingly diverse in terms of race, class, sexual orientation, and gender. But it does amaze me that there are folks who cannot get over it. Go ahead and go make your films. All points of view and situations should be welcome and should be recognized. Making a film is hard enough.

And yes, it is healthy and fabulous to organize the film as much as possible as a coalition. You help me; I help you. This has seriously enabled my own making. My films are training grounds for making film production education accessible. Working with inexperienced filmmakers takes up double the time and energy but is worth the goal of sharing skills. The place to begin discussing this idea of coalition is through the organization that we (Ernesto Foronda and Pancho Gonzalez, et al.) started at the UCLA Film School, SINEGANG. It's a media-activist group in which we help one another make films and drama productions, and we are committed to organizing large-scale forums to talk about art and culture as a viable political strategy for addressing social-justice issues.

We were not satisfied with working in creative production without making an active intervention in the discussion about that production. It was important to situate our work within and against the work of other cultural producers. How did cultural activism and artistic production participate within social movements or "national" liberation struggles, if at all? We wanted to make a space in which to discuss the historical, political, and social meanings of our work. How are we in conversation, if at all, with our "communities"? What are we doing? What are we trying to do?

We organized yearly forums to which we invited prominent Filipino artists, such as the playwright Jeannie Barroga; the painter Manuel Ocampo; the television programmer Claire Aguilar; the poets Jeff Tagami, Shirley Ancheta, and Catalina Cariaga; and the filmmakers John Castro, Dan Tirtawinata, and Michael Magnaye to discuss their process as artists. We advertised these large forums all over the Filipino community. In Los Angeles, we did outreach all the way to Long Beach, at Filipino restaurants and grocery stores as well as on campuses. In San Francisco, we organized a community premiere for *Super Flip* in the same way. More than five hundred people attended the theater that night. The discussions at our forums went on all night, and they fed and fueled our work in a very serious way. They took me as a filmmaker outside the comfort of my editing room, where I slept on the floor for days on end with a supply of underwear, cigarettes, and water in my office. Things happened and externalized, for sure: There were confrontations between folks beyond the theoretical, so that important places were reached in the discussion. At the *Super Flip* premiere, the theme was very much about the "Death of the Filipino Macho," wherein the patriarchs in the audience could not come to grasp the different place new young people are coming from. This is a more intersectional approach for talking about Filipinos. The cast and crew, predominantly strong female activists as well as artists and academics, understood Filipino experiences not just racially, but also in the way that they intersect with other social categories and experiences. But it was the gender and sex analysis that was the problem.

I welcome the collision between generations, gendered positions, and differences among the crowds. I welcome the dialogue, particularly among folks who are committed to social justice. The meeting across differences was ultimately productive. But the short-sighted complaints were very much about a demand for positive images, especially for men. This is a very regressive political move that doesn't serve any of us—to return to a unified notion of community that enabled us once but never truly was. I feel that the anger from the predominantly male sector and the counter-argument from women, young and old, and from feminist men ultimately was about cultures and resistances in collision. Some folks ultimately felt uncomfortable with a Filipina speaking about Filipinos in an anti-homogenizing way. I think it was terrifying for many people who want to hold on to the romantic notion of a unified movement. But in my films, the men and women are both bad and good, and we can still struggle for recognition across our disagreements. I work to address Filipinos in a complex way, because our lives are terribly and truthfully complex. I do not want to, and cannot, render Filipinos as cartoons. That would be much more damaging for us.

Notes

1. See Gonzalves (1996, 6–7).
2. The essays in Pines and Willemen (1989) are a useful introduction to the subject of Third Cinema anti-colonial film movement and practice.
3. See Shohat and Stam (1994, 256–60). On the Filipina–Filipino filmmaker Kidlat Tahimik, see Hodel (1984), Zimmerman (1992), and Mirella (1987).

Works Cited

Cordova, Fred. 1983. *Filipinos: Forgotten Asian Americans.* Dubuque, Iowa: Kendall/Hunt.

Gonzalves, Theodore S. 1996. "Memories of Overdevelopment: Contemporary Art in the Philippine Diaspora." Exhibit Review. *Godzilla West* (Fall).

Hodel, Ramon. 1984. "Papier-Maché Capitalism." *Bridge* 9, no. 2: 26, 35.

Mirella, Loris. 1987. "Kidlat Tahimik's *Perfumed Nightmare.*" *Polygraph* 1, no. 1: 57–66.

Peñaranda, Oscar, Luis Syquia, and Sam Tagatac. 1974. "Introduction to Filipino-American Literature." Pp. 37–54 in *Aiiieeeee! An Anthology of Asian-American Writers,* ed. Frank Chin, et al. New York: Anchor.

Pines, Jim, and Paul Willemen, ed. 1989. *Questions of Third Cinema.* London: British Film Institute.

Shohat, Ella and Robert Stam. 1994. *Unthinking Eurocentrism: Multiculturalism and the Media.* New York: Routledge.

Smith, Anna Deavere. 1994. *Twilight—Los Angeles, 1992 on the Road: A Search for American Character.* New York: Anchor Books.

Zimmerman, Patricia. 1992. "Benevolent Assassination." *Afterimage* 20, no. 1 (Summer): 6–10.

Films and Videos Cited

Parreñas, Celine Salazar. 1993. *Mahal Means Love and Expensive.* Visual Communications and Sinegang (www.sinegang.org).

————. 1995. *Her Uprooting Plants Her.* Visual Communications and Sinegang (www.sinegang.org).

————. 1997. *Super Flip.* Visual Communications and Sinegang (www.sinegang.org).

Gina Marchetti

16 *The Wedding Banquet*: Global Chinese Cinema and the Asian American Experience

According to *Variety, The Wedding Banquet* (Lee 1993) was the most "commercially successful" film of 1993 (Klady 1994). Given its modest budget, recouping production costs did not prove difficult; therefore, a greater percentage of the film's gross could be counted as profit, thus outstripping *Jurassic Park* (Spielberg 1993), which was released the same year. However, *The Wedding Banquet* also proved itself a critical success, winning accolades from reviewers as well as the prestigious Golden Bear award at the Berlin Film Festival. A commercial success in Asia and an "art house" favorite in the United States, *The Wedding Banquet* found an enthusiastic audience around the globe.

The Wedding Banquet tells the tale of Gao Wai-tung (Winston Chao), a gay man living in New York City with his lover Simon (Mitchell Lichtenstein). Wai-tung's family presses him from abroad to settle down and get married. Spurred by his father's stroke, Wai-tung agrees on a "green card" marriage of convenience with one of his tenants, Wei-wei (May Chin), a starving artist from Shanghai. When Mr. and Mrs. Gao (Sihung Lung and Ah-Leh Gua) arrive from Taiwan, they are appalled by the quickie, city-hall wedding between their son and Wei-wei. An old army acquaintance of Mr. Gao's, who runs a restaurant in New York, insists on giving the couple a proper wedding banquet. Wai-tung and Wei-wei have intercourse on their wedding night, and Wei-wei becomes pregnant.

As Mr. Gao stays on in New York to recover from a second stroke, all of the plot's complications surface and find resolution: Simon threatens to leave Wai-tung but finally stays. Wei-wei threatens to have an abortion but finally decides to keep the baby and asks Simon to be the "co-father." Wai-tung comes out to his mother but agrees to keep his sexual orientation a secret from his father. Mr. Gao "comes out" to Simon and tells him that he knows Simon is his son's lover and accepts it, but asks that Simon keep this knowledge from Wai-tung. *The Wedding Banquet*, then, ends "happily." Wei-wei gets a green card and a family. Wai-tung gets a "son" and keeps his lover. Mr. and Mrs. Gao see the continuation of their family line through the anticipated birth of a grandchild as they leave to return to Taiwan.

Although the basic narrative is straightforward, *The Wedding Banquet* proves difficult to classify. In fact, perhaps part of the reason for the success of *The Wedding Banquet* comes from a fundamental contradiction concerning its classification. On the one hand, it fits easily into several categories, and therefore can be marketed to a variety of audiences as an Asian film, a Chinese film, a Taiwanese film, an Asian American film,[1] a Chinese American film, a New York Chinatown film, a "green-card" story, a popular comedy, a melodrama, an "art" film, a gay film, an "ethnic" family film, or a "multicultural" feature designed to raise the consciousness of viewers. On the other hand, *The Wedding Banquet* may have been able to find an audience because it defies all of these classifications and the political configurations connected with many of them. In other words, just as the film appears to applaud the tenderness of a gay romance, the plot twists to uphold the values of the traditional, extended family. Just as the narrative seems to take a radical turn toward celebrating women's autonomy, very bourgeois notions of class and family culture intrude to shore up decaying values. While the film may hint that sexuality and sexual orientation are socially constructed fictions, those fictions determine the "happy ending" promised by the comedy.

Ang Lee (a.k.a. Lee Ang),[2] from Taiwan and educated in the cinema at New York University, has established himself internationally with films that feature family and romantic relationships. *Sense and Sensibility* (1995) and *The Ice Storm* (1997) have received wide acclaim. His earlier work includes *Pushing Hands* (1992), on Chinese immigrants in the United States, made before *The Wedding Banquet*, and *Eat Drink Man Woman* (1994), on contemporary life in Taiwan, made after *The Wedding Banquet*. With *The Wedding Banquet*, he proved himself adept at orchestrating the various threads of transnational production and distribution. *The Wedding Banquet*'s polyglot script ambitiously deals with the edges of the New York gay subculture, characters from the Republic of China (Taiwan) and the People's Republic of China, the solid middle class, and the margins of the illegal working classes. With this film, Lee demonstrates an ability to bring ethnic issues and issues of sexual orientation into the mainstream. One of the characters in the film remarks, "This is a cross-cultural event. Everything goes." It can be argued that the film works for its various audiences because of this overload of "difference" rather than in spite of it.

This analysis looks closely at *The Wedding Banquet* in the transnational context of its production and reception in order to elucidate the ways in which it straddles the borders that outline the various American and global Chinese communities it treats.[3] By looking at the film in the context of Asian American screen culture, this chapter explores the edges of that classification and the elusive nature of identity in an increasingly complex global culture industry.

China, Taiwan, and Chinatown

Ang Lee calls *The Wedding Banquet* a "comedy about identity" (Central Motion Pictures Corporation 1993). Indeed, the film does seem to have a certain relationship to the director's own sense of identity, particularly Lee's sense of himself as the child of those displaced by the outcome of the Chinese civil war in 1949. Lee characterizes himself as follows: "To me, I'm a mixture of many things and a confusion of many things. . . . I'm not a native Taiwanese, so we're alien in Taiwan today, with the native Taiwanese pushing for independence. But when we go back to China, we're Taiwanese. Then, I live in the States; I'm a sort of foreigner everywhere. It's hard to find a real identity" (quoted in Berry 1993, 54).

If the search for *The Wedding Banquet*'s identity begins at the very beginning of the film, the first credit listed for Central Motion Picture Corporation provides the initial entry into the movie's production history. As John Lent (1990, 68) points out: "Central Motion Picture Corporation is the largest producer of motion pictures in Taiwan. Owned by the government and controlled by the Cultural Department of the Kuomindang [KMT], CMPC's structure includes a board of chairmen with a general manager in charge. . . . CMPC now expects young directors intending to make a company-funded film to prove its marketability, including overseas."

While government funding from the Republic of China might conjure up martial-law policies precluding the treatment of homosexuality and serious intercourse between the mainland and ROC citizens, *The Wedding Banquet* stands as a successful document of a thaw. A homosexual and a mainlander (from the People's Republic of China) have intercourse (quite literally). The film is a meeting of strange bedfellows on all levels. Taiwan and the mainland meet; the PRC and the ROC agree to a symbolic marriage. However, that marriage is false, based on deceptions, a play to "pass" for straight and to get that ever-elusive green card and all it means as a ticket to the American Dream.

To begin with the often quoted observation by Fredric Jameson that all literature from the Third World (and Jameson does include Taiwan–China in that category) by necessity is "national allegory" (Jameson 1986), then *The Wedding Banquet,* extending the argument from literature to film, can be looked at as involving a national allegory. Given the financial involvement of the ROC government in this particular case, the investment of Lee in a narrative of China as a nation, from a particular Taiwanese perspective, may not be too far-fetched.

From this standpoint, details of the script stand out for those viewers invested in reading the film as a political allegory. Indeed, parts of the dialogue in Mandarin concerning relations between Taiwan and the mainland are not subtitled, so that the political allegory is highlighted for Mandarin-speaking viewers and considerably lessened for the English speakers.[4]

From the credit sequence, the voiceover of Mrs. Gao reminding her son of his failure to get married and produce a son reveals other details. For example, she mentions Mr. Gao's retirement from the army and the fact that he went to Taiwan with the KMT forces at the end of the civil war. Later, Mr. Gao reminds his son that the entire family was wiped out during the war. (Although it could have been during the fighting with the Japanese, there is the implication that communist forces overran the family.)[5] Still later in the film, Mrs. Gao mentions that she, too, went to Taiwan after 1949, so the entire family finds itself in that ambivalent category of exiles–conquerors–liberators with the KMT forces and their supporters.

Because of this, Wai-tung's decision to settle in America is over-determined ideologically. His settling in the United States takes him away from direct family pressure to lead a heterosexual lifestyle. However, his decision to settle abroad also takes him away from the uncertainties of Taiwan's status as a nation and the further uncertainties of his own position as the offspring of the 1949 "mainlanders." While the Hokkien-speaking majority of Han Chinese were also "mainlanders" at some point, centuries of living on the island, which has gone through a series of foreign conquests (most notably, its roughly fifty-year occupation by Japan), makes separatist sentiments run very strong. Only recently have these sentiments been allowed expression in Taiwan.[6]

While some feel that these second-generation KMT mainlanders have been assimilated into the mainstream of Taiwanese society, others note a difference and a certain tendency for many of these well-educated, well-to-do children of the KMT forces to settle abroad. In the 1940s, then, Mr. Gao found himself in a situation similar to his own son's. As the script reveals, Mr. Gao joined the KMT forces not simply out of political fervor to rid the country of the Japanese (and, implicitly, the communists), but also because he, too, was fleeing from an arranged marriage. Only years later did Mr. Gao settle down to "do his duty" and produce an heir for the otherwise extinct Gao family. Like his father, Wai-tung, has a political and a personal reason to leave China (mainland and Taiwan) behind.

Wai-tung, in his marriage of convenience, fulfills a political desire for national integrity. The marriage reunites Taiwan with the mainland, leaving the Hokkien majority (and the even more marginal, non-Han aborigines) completely out of the picture. A great deal of nostalgia and a certain amount of melancholy are associated with the KMT old guard. Even after retirement and a stroke, Mr. Gao sticks to his old, military routine of brisk morning exercise. He, Mrs. Gao, and Wai-tung speak fondly of an old army servant who is still attached to the family as cook and housekeeper. The appearance of Old Chen (Tien Pien) as a successful restaurateur in New York City, who still feels uncomfortable sitting in the presence of his former army commander, confirms that these old relationships continue. Actually, both Mr. Gao and Old Chen's experiences with America have turned their initial relationship of superior to subordinate on its head. However, Old Chen still bows to Commander Gao, and he only reluctantly shakes his hand (a gesture too intimate and familiar for their former relationship).

One of the most significant nails in the coffin of KMT authority came with the United States' recognition of the PRC as "China." While economic and other ties continued (including significant military connections), political legitimacy fell by the wayside. In this case, Old Chen has abandoned the "sinking ship" to make a successful go at life in New York. His bankrolling of the wedding banquet pays tribute to the industry of ROC citizens abroad. While treating the old political guard with respect, the film makes clear that this is the respect shown to an already dead regime. Old Chen's bow to Gao, and Gao's forcing Chen to shake his hand, concretizes the melancholic sentiment associated with their relationship. The future is away from the old politics, away from the old countries, away from the old guard, in an America dedicated to making money. As in Wai-tung's case, Old Chen's future and continued prosperity lie outside of both Chinas.

In a somewhat Confucian turn, the national–political and the familial–private get confused. Confucius took the patriarchal family and its hierarchy of members as a metaphor for the ideal state ruled by the emperor and kept intact by a series of duties and obligations between superior and subordinate. Similarly, *The Wedding Banquet* tries to keep intact a vision of the traditional, heterosexual family, even when it is revealed as an utter sham. Just as the KMT in Taipei tried to continue the impossible illusion that it would return to the mainland as the ruling party of a united China, all the principals of *The Wedding Banquet* do their best to put forward a face of the "traditional" heterosexual family.

To continue with the allegory a bit more, in any intercourse between the two Chinas (embodied by Wai-tung and Wei-wei), America (Simon) plays a critical role. America ambivalently brings the Chinas together (i.e., Simon suggests the marriage of convenience to Wai-tung as a way to solve both his and Wei-wei's problems) and pushes them apart (i.e., Simon threatens to leave Wai-tung when he learns that his lover has had sex with Wei-wei, which, in turn, pushes a lovelorn Wai-tung to distance himself from Wei-wei, the cause of the problem). As both Mr. and Mrs. Gao learn about Wai-tung's homosexual relationship with Simon, each comes to accept Simon in his or her own way. Mrs. Gao, using Wei-wei as an interpreter, tries to make sense of Simon's complex family (since it is now intimately connected to her own).[7] Mr. Gao more simply gives Simon a *hong bao,* a traditional red envelope filled with cash, to show that he is an accepted part of the Gao family. America may not be to everyone's liking, but allegorically it is accepted, in this case, as a bedfellow.

Wei-wei, as the final element of the allegory, embodies the PRC—or, rather, the ROC vision of the mainland. She is multiply marginalized and subordinated in the film—that is, as a woman, as an artist, as an illegal alien, as working class, as coming from economically underdeveloped and politically "backward" Communist China. To a wealthy and militarily and technologically advanced Taiwan, she plays the poor mainland relation. Throughout the film, a lot of the verbal play revolves around her national origin. Playing the peasant to Wai-tung's landlord, her first words to Wai-tung in the script are, "This floor has been liberated." She is called *"tong zhi"* (comrade) jokingly, and, as she straddles Wai-tung on their wedding night, she proclaims, "I'm liberating you." The nature of this "liberation" remains uncertain: Is Taiwan, the wayward province, returned to the motherland, or is Taiwan, the bourgeois, decadent (homosexual) spawn of intercourse with America, returned to a "true," "Chinese" (heterosexual) path? Or is Wai-tung, ironically, really "liberating" Wei-wei from communism?

The allegorical dimension of *The Wedding Banquet* extends beyond the national, however, into the realm of ethnicity. The film's logo, for example, is an artificially created "triple happiness" character. The usual Chinese character for matrimonial bliss is a double *"xi"* (the character for "happiness"). In other words, this film presents a new version of the "double" happiness of marriage by adding a third element. The comic dimension of this nonsense character would not be lost on any literate Chinese viewer, and it serves as a reminder that this film has a transnational Chinese dimension. In other words, this national allegory is also an ethnic allegory, investigating the meaning of being "Chinese" beyond national affiliation.[8] Despite all the forces acting against a sense of Chinese tradition (embodied by the family over the nation), this allegory still manages to bring together a divided China by working with, rather than against, feminism, homosexuality, cultural imperialism, and the diaspora. However, this vision of a China elevated beyond the PRC and the ROC, reconciling communist and capitalist, fertile, and producing a new generation to erase historical differences, remains a comic vision, easily laughed at, ridiculed, and dismissed.

This allegorical reading of *The Wedding Banquet* tells only part of the story—that is, it favors a view of the KMT as a fading relic and the future of a united China on American terms. However, *The Wedding Banquet* offers other entry points into its interpretation. In fact, as the box office outside Taiwan demonstrates, many viewers of the film probably ignored elements of its national allegory for a reading that favors the perspective of a more globalized audience.[9]

To move from the modern national allegory to the postmodern fiction, the slippage between comedy and melodrama becomes telling in the film. The film's tone varies greatly. In one scene, Wai-tung finds Mr. Gao slumped in a chair. An extreme close-up shows Wai-tung putting his finger under his father's mustached nose to check his breathing. A close-up of Mr. Gao's still, vulnerable, aging face and another of Wai-tung's concerned expression follow. Then, Mr. Gao suddenly awakes, and the mood lightens again. As this moment shows, *The Wedding Banquet* does not shy away from presenting darker emotions and possibilities that are associated with the melodrama rather than the comedy.

Even as these changes of tone mark shifts between genres, another question can be posed: Slippage between what kind or kinds of comedy and what kind or kinds of melodrama? Is *The Wedding Banquet* a sex farce involving classic cases of mistaken identity and a few rounds of "musical beds"? Is it a gay comedy for straight audiences, like *La Cage aux Folles* (Molinaro 1978) and its American equivalents? Is the film a social satire on prevailing sexual mores? Is it a "romantic" melodrama, a family melodrama, or an "ethnic" family melodrama?[10] If, generally speaking, both the comedy and the melodrama work to keep heterosexuality and the patriarchy going, with a "successful" mating achieved after obstacles are overcome and progeny produced, then *The Wedding Banquet* need not be too firmly placed in one genre or the other. Its narrative resolution satisfies the aims of both. Rather, the question becomes whether anything exists in the film that exceeds the boundaries of allegory and genre.

On Photos, Phones, and Pictures of the Closet

Can *The Wedding Banquet* be looked at as camp? If so, is there a point of address in the film that can be said to target an "implied" gay viewer? Or does the film presuppose a straight audience by advancing a voyeuristic gaze onto an exotic, homosexual world for a "sympathetic," but decidedly "Other," spectator?

One Taiwanese commentator on the film laments the fact that no "gay mentality" exists in *The Wedding Banquet*, which the reviewer sees as a testing of traditional Chinese values in an alien environment rather than as a statement on gay life.[11] Indeed, the film's director, Ang Lee, married with children, does not identify himself as "gay."[12]

A few comments posted on the World Wide Web cover a range of perspectives by gay viewers. Gary Nygaard (1995) expresses the following view:

> I had heard good word-of-mouth about it, so eagerly I rented *The Wedding Banquet* within days of its appearance in video stores. But as I watched this film, which is billed as a gay comedy, I became uncomfortable and increasingly angry. . . . The lesson here, then, is that gay relationships must compromise themselves and bow to traditional, straight values and family structures. . . . Part of me can understand why this picture would catch on. The characters are generally likable—even the father, who I believe is the villain of the piece—and the film's tone is light with just enough emotional depth to engage. For a straight audience, the premise and the resolution are pretty non-threatening; and for a gay audience hungry to see gay and lesbian characters in the movies, this film does present "good-guy" gay men. But it makes me very sad that *The Wedding Banquet* has been so popular because, ultimately, I see it as a film that pretends to portray the lives of gays in a positive light, while really reinforcing old homophobic ideas and attitudes. Whether or not that was the filmmaker's intent, we don't need yet another movie which distorts us and demeans us.

Another review takes the opposite point of view:

> My favorite movie of all time has to be *The Wedding Banquet*!!! . . . An *absolute must* see for *any* in an Asian/Caucasian cross-cultural gay relationship, and a wonderfully entertaining comedy even if you're not :-). [DarkWhite n.d.]

Yet another gay viewer saw the film less as a campy comedy and more as a family melodrama:

> When I first saw the film, I was quite moved by it, especially the family relationships it portrays. I think that is something that is often ignored in straight perceptions of queers— family relationships actually do mean something to us. So I was very moved by mama's trying to understand what Wai-tung's life was, and father's quiet accepting of Simon's importance to his son. I think there is some universality there. [Anonymous 1997]

To begin again at the beginning with the opening credits for the producer and scriptwriter, Ted Hope and James Schamus have been involved with a number of projects involving gay issues, including *Poison* (1991) by Todd Haynes, as well as pieces on Roy Cohn, work by the lesbian filmmaker Jan Oxenburg, and more. Their production company, Good Machine, favors foreign art films and independent American gay–lesbian productions. *The Wedding Banquet* could fit into either camp. There seems to be enough in the text, too, to merit a careful consideration of an address to queer (particularly gay male) viewers.

One of the homoerotic visual themes begins in the opening scene. Wai-tung is introduced through a series of shots focusing first on close-ups of exercise-machine gears and pulleys and moving to shots of his body parts, with the emphasis on straining, sweat-drenched muscles. When looked at in the context of film history and its representation of the body as spectacle, these images tend to invite an erotic contemplation.[13] These shots can be taken as an invitation for a gay gaze at Wai-tung's semi-nude body. Other moments support this invitation to look pleasurably at men's bodies. In one scene after the wedding, for example, Wai-tung and Simon, thinking everyone else is out of the house, try to sneak in an afternoon sex romp. They kiss in the foyer and take off each other's clothes on the way upstairs. However, this brief respite from the closet ends abruptly when the two discover Mr. Gao upstairs.

These moments of possible gay erotic contemplation find themselves undercut or countered in various ways throughout the film. For example, the opening scene also includes the plaintive voiceover cassette letter from Mrs. Gao to her son, begging him to find a bride. Likewise, if there is an invitation to look at men as erotic spectacle, there is also a very open invitation to look at women in a similar way. Two bodies are "built up" in *The Wedding Banquet*: Wei-wei as the object of a presumably male heterosexual gaze and Wai-tung as the object of a presumably male homosexual gaze.

Wei-wei (played by a popular Taiwanese music personality who is unquestioningly taken as "attractive" by the public) enters the film with a series of shots that are strikingly similar to those that introduce Wai-tung. Living in an overheated loft, Wei-wei cools down with a sponge bath and a bottle of liquor. Like Wai-tung, she is introduced to the viewer through a series of moistly provocative, scantily clad body parts, and the mood is set with a blast of romantic Taiwanese pop music. Her disheveled appearance softens with the hazy, warm yellow-orange lighting used to convey a sense of "heat" in the flat. Throughout the remainder of the scene, she flirts with Wai-tung, trying to barter her painting, called *Heat*, for that month's rent.

In his business suit and tie, Wai-tung no longer holds center screen as an object of erotic contemplation. Wei-wei takes over that role, and Wai-tung, sweating and clearly uncomfortable in her presence, offers the possibility of straight identification for the viewer. In fact, it is this play with Wai-tung as a locus of identification for a heterosexual contemplation of Wei-wei that provides the specular working out of the plot's apparently irreconcilable incongruities.

Both scenes introducing Wai-tung and Wei-wei feature a split between the display of the male and female body, respectively, and a soundtrack with a less sexual and more sentimental bent. This split—between the carnal and the emotional, symbolized by the split between the body–spectacle and the voice–melodrama—continues throughout the film. Human relationships are organized around photographs (still images that construct and freeze a particular way of looking at things) and the telephone and tape recorder that connect disembodied voices (causing a split between the carnal and the sentimental). The drama revolves around the play between visual and aural (mis)communication.

The Wedding Banquet is a film about the "closet," defining the closet, constructing the closet, legitimizing the closet, coming out of the closet, staying in the closet, hiding behind the closet, and exposing the closet. As Jack Babuscio and others have pointed out,[14] camp humor revolves around issues associated with gay men's closeted lives, including a sense of irony, theatricality, and delight in surfaces. This aesthetic sensibility resonates with a life revolving around "false" appearances and a public "straight" persona needed to survive in the workplace, in the traditional family, and within a homophobic straight world. In *The Wedding Banquet,* both phones and photos serve to construct and deconstruct the closet.

For example, telephones in the film both illustrate gay intimacy and enable the closet to exist and adversely affect that intimacy. Wai-tung's love for Simon is introduced through a phone conversation. Their first screen kiss occurs after the two, sitting side by side, have a phone conversation to test the portable phone Simon has given Wai-tung as a gift. Also, Simon's decision to stay with Wai-tung is visualized through a shot of his tenderly replacing the receiver on the phone hook for an exhausted Wai-tung, who has fallen asleep in mid-conversation. However, the telephone also enables the closet to function. Mr. and Mrs. Gao's presence is felt in Wai-tung and Simon's relationship, long before the plane arrives from Taiwan, through long-distance late-night calls that interrupt the couple's sleep.[15]

The telephone, then, helps to create a gay relationship that can be disembodied and sentimentalized, but that can also, perhaps on a more positive note, be free of a perception of gay sexuality as "only sex"—that is, as unemotional, cold, and sterile. The telephone brings characters together and underscores their isolation and ignorance of each other's emotions. However, it is also important to note that the telephone enables the closet to function for Wai-tung. Disembodied communication allows for the distance necessary for the closet to keep going.

Scenes featuring still photographs punctuate the film and serve both to reaffirm Wai-tung's gay identity and to keep that identity in the closet. For example, when Wai-tung, Simon, and Wei-wei learn that the Gao parents will appear in New York for the wedding, they all do a lot of "house cleaning." Shown through a montage marked as conventionally comic by the use of up-beat, non-diegetic brass music played over the short takes, the construction of the closet is depicted primarily through the exchange of photographs. A photo of a nude Wai-tung is replaced with a photo of him in his Taiwan national service uniform.[16] Intimate photos of Simon and Wai-tung are replaced with photos of a distant-looking Wai-tung and Wei-wei. The scene comes to a climax with the unfolding of calligraphy scrolls in rapid succession. Gay New York has been replaced pictorially by ROC nationalism and Chinese tradition.

Later, in a striking shot, the camera takes the perspective of these scrolls (created by Mr. Gao) as they are admired by Wei-wei and the rest of the family. Wei-wei has a long speech in which she details the merits of the scrolls, their relationship to various schools of Chinese calligraphy and their overall aesthetic significance. The film viewer looks at her looking at the camera (scrolls) and admires her admiring the viewer–camera–scrolls. She becomes the visual, aural, and dramatic cynosure of the closet as she wins over all commanded by her gaze—including the silent scrolls symbolizing Chinese order, tradition, a father's loving handiwork, and, implicitly, heterosexual patriarchy. Mr. Gao comments that her expertise far exceeds Wai-tung's in this area, and he, as well as the scrolls–camera–viewer, is won over. Her voice and vision have legitimated the closet.

Wei-wei's association with the traditional connoisseur's eye finds its parallel in Simon's association with the eye of the modern photographer. During Wai-tung and

Wei-wei's civil marriage ceremony at the court office, Simon takes on the role of photographer. He snaps pictures during the comic ceremony in which the nervous Wei-wei mangles the English wedding vows. Afterward, Simon rushes ahead of the rest of the family to take a group photograph. As the camera (the spectator's vision) shows Simon's view through the viewfinder, and the shot goes in and out of focus as Simon presumably fiddles with the lens, Mrs. Gao melts into tears. Simon's photographic documentation of the wedding, to show the closet to U.S. immigration and the Gaos' circle back in Taiwan, is disrupted.

Later, Simon's role as the gay eye on the marriage is usurped by a professional photographer. Indeed, Simon becomes blind to the transformation of the closet into a constructed and artificial, but surprisingly functional, heterosexuality. When Wai-tung, Simon (now in the role of "best man"), and the photographer approach the elaborately outfitted Wei-wei before the wedding banquet, a snap of the camera shutter underscores Wei-wei's desirability as the "beautiful" bride. A close shot of Wai-tung shows an interested look; Simon, in the background, remains oblivious. The presumed libidinous significance of Wai-tung's look finds further confirmation in a knowing glance and wink at Wai-tung from one of Wei-wei's bridesmaids. As Wei-wei has been built up to be a bride and her position has been captured and confirmed by the photographic eye, Wai-tung falls into line as the groom by taking on the specular position of the heterosexual viewer (a position underscored by the legitimizing presence of the fictitious still photographer). He looks, sees a conventionally constructed image of female desirability, and identifies with the straight way of seeing.

The construction of the heterosexual couple continues during a montage sequence that features the requisite studio shots of the bride, groom, and wedding party. The montage begins with the professional photographer orchestrating the composition of the shots, moving the couple into a series of clearly awkward poses. A succession of still photos follows, including clichéd poses of the bride smiling in close-up, the couple looking at each other, the family all smiling (with Simon), and the couple positioned in silhouette against a sunset. The soundtrack of "light," up-tempo, nondiegetic pop accompaniment underscores the artificiality of the photos and encourages an ironic distance from the usual sentiments surrounding the "happy" institution of marriage and weddings. Each cut is accompanied by the sound of an old-fashioned camera shutter and flash bulb, again bringing attention to the constructed, mediated, and artificial nature of the sights captured by the camera. Finally, the bride wilts in one shot, composes herself in an awkward pose, and the last photo becomes the flash of a white screen used as a transition. Wei-wei literally has been bent out of shape to become the blushing bride for the camera's eye.

Throughout the rest of the film, photographs continue to function as visual emblems for the closet. When Wai-tung and Simon attempt to have sex, for example, a cut away to a shot of a framed photo of the bride and groom in their living room bears the visual reminder that they can no longer be themselves in their own home. In the bedroom Wai-tung now shares with Wei-wei, an oversize portrait of the bride and groom dominates the mise-en-scène. The wedding photos on the walls of the closet close in.

The earlier scenes featuring the house cleaning and the studio portraits were presented as comedic, with a welcoming entry for a gay viewer to take an ironic view of the artifice of the closet and the excesses involved in its pictorial construction and legitimization. Later in the film, these same images take on a darker significance, from this perspective, as they overpower the characters within the mise-en-scène.

Still later, after Wai-tung comes out to his mother, photographs take on a sentimental and manipulative function. Mrs. Gao takes out a photo album with pictures of Wai-tung as a baby to show to the pregnant Wei-wei. Her tears liberally rain down as she tells her daughter-in-law of the trauma of Wai-tung's cesarean birth, the pain of learning that she could not have other children, and the terror involved in raising a premature, sickly son when her husband was constantly away from home because of his military occupation. The black-and-white photos appear only briefly to punctuate a scene that focuses primarily on Mrs. Gao's face, gestures, and voice. The photos function as physical evidence of her sentiment used to manipulate Wei-wei into sympathizing with her, identifying with her as an enduring mother, and finally capitulating to her wish for Wei-wei not to have an abortion. Although the effect is not immediate, the photos seem to do the trick. Sentiment and melodrama win out over camp irony. The photos exclude a gay way of seeing.

The final, parting scene at the airport also features photographs. Wai-tung, Wei-wei, Simon, and Mr. and Mrs. Gao all look at the wedding photos together. The camera frames them all, like a family portrait, looking at the photo album. Sentiment turns back around to laughter as they look and laugh at a photo from the wedding banquet in which Wei-wei mistakes a kiss from a toddler for a kiss from Wai-tung. Focusing in on that photo of that moment underscores what brings this "family" together and legitimizes it—that is, the assurance of its continuation through Wei-wei's "son."

If all pictures imply a way of seeing,[17] and ways of seeing imply a perspective on what is viewed and an invitation for the spectator to identify with the perspective constructed by the artist–photographer, then that identification implies an identity—that is, an identification with an identity marked by ethnicity, nation, gender, sexual orientation, and so on. In *The Wedding Banquet*, these photographs show the shifting nature of identity and identification and the contradictions inherent in those shifts. Photos documenting gay life give way to an ironic picture of an artificial closet that becomes a constructed heterosexual desire that metamorphoses into a trap and finally dissolves into sentiment and an improbable nostalgia (that points to a bright and utopian future).

Myths of the Rice Queen and the Asian Gay

If the photographs that punctuate *The Wedding Banquet* underscore any single point, it is that the camera both creates and excludes. As the closet emerges, gay life recedes. Because of this, it becomes important to look at what is not shown in *The Wedding Banquet* and the implications of these exclusions.

When the structure of the film is examined closely, a polarization of characteristics becomes apparent. All of the gay characters in the film are Caucasian men—with the crucial exception of Wai-tung. All of the Asian characters in the film are presented as heterosexual—again with the exception of Wai-tung. In other words, the film posits a not-so-subtle division in which a figure such as Wai-tung, who is both Chinese and gay, becomes an anomaly. Gay Asian Americans, gay Chinese, and all gays of color have a single representative in the figure of Wai-tung. Or, to put it another way, gay Asians disappear into the character of Wai-tung. More than any other character in the film, Wai-tung stands as a symbol of a postmodern merger and erasure of identity. Avowedly homosexual, he falls for a woman and impregnates her. He upholds a Chinese tradition of filial piety and duty and still manages to keep his male lover. Is he gay? Is he heterosexual?[18] Is he traditionally Chinese? Is he modern and "American"? All of these remain impossible to answer completely as an entire community drops out of the picture. Singular and atomistic, Wai-tung can have no identity, because he has no fellows in the film. As a community of gay Chinese (Americans) drops out of the picture, so, too, does a key political element of the film.

In this case, the interracial nature of Wai-tung's relationship with Simon is crucial for the maintenance of the closet and for the preservation of a sense of Chinese ethnicity cleansed of any history of homosexuality. Although Wai-tung denies being "led" into a homosexual life by Simon when he comes out to his mother, the film does little to support any notion of a history of gay life in Asia and Asian America. Wai-tung must go outside of China, Taiwan, and Chinatown to find "someone compatible." Because of this, a polarization of the terms "Chinese" and "homosexual" can be maintained, along with a feeling that Wai-tung is a "unique" case (and a case fairly easily persuaded to be "Chinese," and therefore "heterosexual," at least on occasion).

From this perspective, the montage scene in which the closet is constructed for Mr. and Mrs. Gao's benefit can be looked at in another way. As the calligraphic scrolls unfurl, Wai-tung steps out of his ethnic closet and comes out as "Chinese." When he plays at being "straight," it is for the benefit of his Chinese acquaintances and family. When placed within the gay world, Wai-tung eats pizza, drinks wine, and has only Caucasian acquaintances. His ethnic identity is swept under the rug.

The consequences of this erasure of gay Asians branch off in many different directions. As the single gay Asian in the film, the figure of Wai-tung can counter extratextual stereotypes without spelling out the multitude of negative qualities associated with racist and homophobic depictions in the mass media. However, as the film works to counter stereotypes, it also moves away from addressing points of genuine concern. One of these areas involves racism within the gay community and a more general perception of gay Asians as "effeminate."

The Wedding Banquet moves away from this entire issue by feminizing the Caucasian partner in the gay relationship. In contrast to Wai-tung, Simon plays a more effeminate role. He cooks; wears an apron, clingy black tank tops, and jeans; and his earring is prominently displayed. He has the "nurturing" job of physical therapist and takes it upon himself to organize Wai-tung's emotional and familial life (e.g., through suggesting his marriage to Wei-wei and filling her in on all the intimate details of the household's domestic routines for the immigration interview, giving presents to Wai-tung's parents, and helping to cook and care for the aging couple). Simon is "out" to his own family and has no problems with public displays of his sexual orientation (e.g., a peck on the cheek from another gay friend, distributing gay-pride literature, etc.). Wai-tung, on the other hand, sticks to business suits and invites Simon to dinner at a restaurant rather than cooking himself.

Wai-tung's enactment of the "masculine" role in his relationship with Simon goes against stereotypical assumptions about gay Caucasian–Asian relationships. Indeed, gay Asians have complained about racism in the gay community by generally citing the presumption on the part of some Caucasian gays that Asian gays will play a more "subservient" role.[19] According to an anonymous white, gay viewer of the film involved in a relationship with an Asian man: "I think the filmmaker was at most trying to neutralize the Rice Queen motif. And I think he was trying to get beyond stereotypes. In a way, it would almost be more interesting to see a film dive into those issues head on, because it is certainly a relevant issue, both for rice queens and queer Asians" (Anonymous 1997).

The "rice queen," then, may be looking for someone more like Simon than Wai-tung. Erasing the "type" from the film allows the closet to function within the narrative. If Simon were Asian, the closet would collapse, because his "queerness" could not be attributed to cultural differences (e.g., all white Americans must be a little "odd") by the Gao family.

If Wai-tung were more like Simon and Simon more like common perceptions of the "rice queen," the narrative would strain under a different burden. Simon flatters a certain segment of the audience. Given a cinematic history dominated globally by images of Asian men as (generally heterosexual and) rapacious or impotent and effeminate,[20] this presentation of a character like Wai-tung as heterosexually potent and characteristically not "masculine" has a certain appeal.

However, when placed within that same cinematic history of the representation of Asian men in the cinema, *The Wedding Banquet* really does not step radically away from the currently popular depictions. Is Wai-tung the homosexual that different, for example, from the homosexual (and bisexual or otherwise feminized) characters in *The Last Emperor* (Bertolucci 1987), *Farewell My Concubine* (Chen 1993), *Double Happiness* (Shum 1994), and *M. Butterfly* (Cronenberg 1993)? Within a popular history of Asian men depicted as eunuchs, domestic servants, and, more recently, transvestites, Wai-tung has company as he occupies what Rey Chow has called a "feminized space" within world culture: "China exists as an 'other,' feminized space to the West, a space where utopianism and eroticism come into play for various purposes of 'critique'" (Chow 1991, 32).

When the West looks at itself through China (a position certainly available in this film, which may or may not be "from Taiwan" or may or may not be "from America"), opportunities for critical understanding sometimes emerge. Although Wai-tung may well play the "good Chinese son" gone bad in the corrupt West for a Taiwan and overseas Chinese audience, he occupies a different role and "space" for the non-Asian viewer. As a double "other" (homosexual and Asian), Wai-tung becomes, in his marginalization within the dominant American mainstream, surprisingly free to embody a utopian dream of erotic liberty coupled with a cultural critique of homophobia, racism, and ethnocentrism. He becomes a liberal call for tolerance within the American "melting pot" without any dramatic political consequences. Indeed, in his false marriage to Wei-wei, he domesticates and "feminizes" a potentially more potent source of social chaos.

Constructing the Heterosexual—Who's "Queer" Here?

Films such as *The Wedding Banquet* have a certain "art house" following in Europe and America; it must not be forgotten that *Ju Dou* (1990), *Red Sorghum* (1987), and *Raise the Red Lantern* (1991), all three by Zhang Yimou and starring Gong Li, have also been hits in this same international art-film circuit. When China's feminized space is not occupied by a homosexual man, women emerge as victims of Chinese tradition.[21] From this perspective, Wei-wei can be looked at as fulfilling another part of this fantasy. However, as with the case of the contradictory and ultimately indeterminate presentation of Wai-tung's sexuality, Wei-wei's sexuality also ambivalently critiques and upholds very conservative, patriarchal notions.

From the outset, Wei-wei is not a "victim" of traditional patriarchy but a "victim" of its dissolution. Going back a step to the political dimensions of the film as a national allegory, Wei-wei represents a "feminist" mainland, liberated from the "feudal" and Confucian principles embodied by Mr. and Mrs. Gao. Alcoholic, illegal, fired from a series of low-paying jobs, an unsuccessful artist, Wei-wei needs rescuing. Her "liberation" has led her away from home, hearth, and the stability of marriage. The "green-card" marriage offers her the hope of legal status and freedom from the constant fear of deportation. Also, as she moves into Simon and Wai-tung's basement to establish cohabitation for the immigration office, the film presents her as settling in very comfortably, away from the heat and dreariness of her warehouse loft–slum home. Her salvation rests in her embourgeoisement. Fired because of a misunderstanding with Wai-tung at the outdoor cafe where she worked as a waitress, Wai-tung has freed her, inadvertently, from the presumed dreariness of her working-class job. She can now concentrate on her unappreciated work as an abstract painter, a suitable "hobby" for the "housewife" she plays for immigration and the Gao parents. Wai-tung, the slum lord–husband, delivers on a promise of material comfort and "freedom" not for, but from, the working classes. Prosperous and aloof, Taiwan holds out the same promise for the mainland—that is, the promise of a bourgeois China.

Just as the wedding constructs Wai-tung as a heterosexual groom, it constructs Wei-wei as a bourgeois bride. She must be as completely transformed as Wai-tung in the process, leaving behind her feminism and her working-class roots. For example, the scenes preceding the wedding banquet comically construct Wei-wei to enable her to play the role of the bride. A montage, accompanied by up-tempo accordion music, shows the bride's hair shampooed, facial mask peeled off, hair curlers in place, eyelashes and lip gloss applied. A full-face close-up of the completed bride ends the scene.

In the next scene, her mainland friends surround Wei-wei, in full bridal-party regalia. One remarks in English, "Man, they really piled on the rocks"—referring to the Gao's elaborate and extensive bridal gifts—as she helps organize the bride's jew-elry. The dialogue switches to Mandarin, and Mrs. Gao says Wei-wei is "beautiful." When Wai-tung and the rest of the groom's party enter, a medium long shot shows the completed bride as she stands up to display her gown. A traditional Chinese "double happiness" decoration on the wall doubles up with the voluminous skirt and veil of Wei-wei's Western gown to underscore the cross-cultural power of the spec-tacle. As mentioned earlier, Wai-tung fits into the space created for him as viewer of this spectacle, an overdetermined locus of Chinese and Western visions of hetero-sexuality and bourgeois patriarchy.

Throughout the banquet scenes, Wei-wei continues to evolve into the type of woman that all wedding banquets are supposed to create—a bride desirable enough to overcome the groom's inhibitions. In this case, her desires need only be slightly redirected. Earlier, after going though a litany of her recent affairs and their unhap-py outcomes, she laments that she always seems to be attracted to "cute," gay men. With this comment, the script opens another can of worms. Is Wei-wei unhappy with straight men because she is a feminist and unhappy with their chauvinism? Are gay men somehow more "sympathetic" because they don't have all the privileges asso-ciated with heterosexuals? Is she not quite "straight" herself and, thus, looking for something "feminine" in (wo)men?

The film, like Freud, closes off all these questions by redirecting Wei-wei's libido into motherhood. The wedding prepares all for this redirection of energy with a series of games and rituals. A young boy jumps on the wedding bed for good luck, and, later, the blindfolded bride mistakenly picks him as her groom when he kisses her cheek. The couple tries to nibble at the same bobbing chicken head as an excuse to kiss. The wedding guests noisily clamor for lengthy, public kisses. Garters fly, and liquor flows. All of the sex games designed to "humiliate" the bride and groom, and bind them together with lots of liquor and loosened inhibitions, serve to soften up the couple for the marriage bed. In the final send-off, the last guests agree to leave only after the couple is naked under the bed covers and all their clothes are on the floor beside them.

At one point, a Caucasian man tells his Caucasian girlfriend that he thought the Chinese were meek and quiet. A Chinese male guest overhears and says: "You're wit-nessing the results of thousands of years of sexual repression." Actually, they are wit-nessing the results of a centuries-old collection of practices that traditionally deliver the same result—the consummation of the marriage. Although this may be taken for granted under the mystification of romantic love and marital bliss, it is an event that proves to be none too easy in cases of arranged marriage. In this case, Western and Chinese nuptial traditions come together to create a bride and groom who can con-summate the marriage. Although Wei-wei and Wai-tung appear to be a very modern "odd couple," are they really that different from others, such as Mr. Gao, who went into battle to avoid an arranged marriage? Would the same tricks of the trade have worked on him if he had not been able to escape into the KMT army? If *The Wedding Banquet* were set in the Qing Dynasty or earlier, could a similar outcome be imagined? With a patriarchal emphasis on sons and the continuation of the family line, who could deny the head of the household his lover (male or female, courtesan or concubine) if he otherwise did his "duty" for the family? Here, the radical multiculturalism of the interracial, transnational ménage à trois falls back into a very conservative sense of Chinese ethnic tradition and values.

Madame Butterfly in New York City

In this case, the modern rebuilding of Chinese patriarchal relations rests on the self-sacrifice of women. Wei-wei provides a modern twist on old "Madame Butterfly" themes.[22] The appearance of Wu Ren Ren/Little Sister Mao (Vanessa Yang) makes this association explicit. A computer date sent to Wai-tung from Taiwan, Ren Ren fits the impossible bill of speaking five languages, being a professional opera singer, and having a Ph.D. (Her only short-coming is that she has only one doctorate; Wai-tung had demanded two.) After accidentally running into Wei-wei, who is working in a cafe where the two have come for a drink, Wai-tung is "outed" by Wei-wei. Ren Ren then tells her secret. She has a Caucasian boyfriend, and her family does not approve. In this sense, she is like Wai-tung, involved in an illicit interracial affair. At the end of the sequence, Ren Ren sings Cio-Cio San's famous aria from Puccini's *Madama Butterfly*.[23] As she fades out of the plot, a new parallel develops—not between Ren Ren and Wai-tung, but between Cio-Cio San and Wei-wei. Like Cio-Cio San, Wei-wei sacrifices herself to bear a child for a man who does not love her.

Wei-wei suppresses her libido in the continuation of the Gao family line. Although materially better off, she has sacrificed her freedom for this exclusively maternal role. The feminist, "liberated" by Mao and the communists, falls back into the feudal role of a woman in a loveless, arranged marriage, whose only comfort is her son (or sons). In this respect, the film's construction of an accepting multicultural environment, in which heterosexual and homosexual, the ROC and the PRC, China and America come together in harmonious intercourse, is constructed on the ruins of feminism. Wei-wei must accept her mother-in-law's tearful statement that men and children still must "count for something" in a woman's life.

The melodrama of women's sacrifice, glossed over by a comedic tone, underlies *The Wedding Banquet*'s narrative structure. As in other postmodern texts, the blurring of genres underscores a blurring of identity and politics. Feminism, gay rights, and Chinese ethnic identity cannot exist simultaneously within *The Wedding Banquet*. Something must "give" for the narrative to work. In this case, feminism collapses. However, the choice seems somehow arbitrary—part of a postmodern sensibility rather than any genuine misogyny or anti-feminist sentiment. In other postmodern, nostalgic reconstitutions of an imaginary past within a contemporary environment, entire histories of colonialism, racism, and capitalism are conjured up, ground up, and reconfigured in similar ways. Within postmodern culture, radical and reactionary postures coexist within fictions that make it impossible to discern unequivocally a moral high ground for any political position.

Is There an Asian American in the Text?

When watching *The Wedding Banquet,* another comedy–melodrama set within the Chinese American community may come to mind: *Flower Drum Song* (Koster 1961), which has many of the same themes that appear in *The Wedding Banquet.* For example, both movies contain an aging son reluctant to marry, generational conflicts, and a "happy ending" in an arranged marriage. Lee, then, is not working in an arena alien to commercial Hollywood. On the contrary, some of *The Wedding Banquet's* appeal to more general audiences most likely comes from a familiarity with films that provide a voyeuristic entry into sequestered ethnic American ghettoes. The non-Chinese viewer can remark, along with the Caucasian guests at the wedding, about an ignorance of Chinese customs and practices while enjoying the exotic spectacle of the banquet.

In this case, that vision is limited in some interesting ways. Just as Hokkien speakers, upwardly mobile mainlanders, "out" Asians, and others have no place in *The Wedding Banquet,* the Asian American experience presented also has some blind spots. No one goes to New York's Chinatowns in lower Manhattan (primarily Cantonese-speaking from Hong Kong and Guangdong Province) and Queens (primarily Mandarin- and Hokkien-speaking from Taiwan). Immigration problems occur off-screen. No INS raids are depicted. No deportation proceedings are shown. Immigration tests are prepared for but never shown being taken. Wei-wei goes from job to job off-screen, for the most part. Searching for a job without a green card is not shown; employer–employee relations within the illegal labor force move to the fringes of the text. No mainland artists are mugged in Times Square doing portraits for tourists. No sweatshops or massage parlors appear. No racists threaten any of the characters with violence. The edginess of Wei-wei's existence at the fringes of the Asian American community is not a principal part of the events depicted in the plot. Much the same thing happens to Wei-wei's environment as happens to Wai-tung's. The illegal, working-class immigrant and the gay Asian become isolated as oddities rather than being embraced as members of a community.

Asian America is out of the allegorical picture, too. Wei-wei's fetus unifies China; it does not represent a new generation of Asian Americans. Wai-tung and Wei-wei continue to be Chinese, part of a greater China rather than part of a Chinese American community (let alone an Asian American body politic). Ang Lee describes his own experience of being Chinese in New York as follows:

> Of course, I identify with Chinese culture because that was my upbringing, but that becomes very abstract; it's the idea of China. My generation of Chinese has always felt that way. And the sentiment of being Chinese is different in New York than it is in Taiwan or in China. Wherever you come from, whether it's China or Hong Kong or Taiwan, in New York, you're just Chinese; it's sort of generalized and merged, and people are drawn to each other by that abstract idea of being Chinese. In that way, it was natural to me to include all the different Chinese in New York City in the film, because that's a reflection of my life, a mixture of language and characters, it's kind of natural to me. [Quoted in Berry 1993, 54]

The Wedding Banquet is not unique in its playing out of fantasies about the overseas Chinese for a mixed Asian and Western audience. In fact, there has been a boom in recent years in films set in American or European Chinatowns, usually produced by Hong Kong or Taiwanese concerns.[24] Like *The Wedding Banquet*, most of these films deal less with the development of an Asian American identity among Chinese immigrants than with the creation of a transnational sense of Chinese identity. With the exception of Wayne Wang's feature films on the Chinese American community (e.g., *Chan Is Missing*, 1982; *Dim Sum*, 1985; *Eat a Bowl of Tea*, 1989; and *The Joy Luck Club*, 1993), few of these films have received critical attention as Asian American films. In this respect, as indebted as the film is to its Taiwanese roots and despite its apparent inattention to many critical issues facing Asian Americans, *The Wedding Banquet* did receive attention as more than a Chinese film about the overseas community. Indeed, as daring as its treatment of homosexuality is from the standpoint of a traditionally conservative Taiwanese film culture, *The Wedding Banquet* may be even more daring in its ability to bridge the gap between Chinese film and Asian American film culture. Clearly, it is a film filled with surprises.

The final narrative "surprise" of the film occurs toward the end. Simon and Mr. Gao are outside, on the waterfront, doing Mr. Gao's physical therapy. Mr. Gao says "Happy Birthday" in English to Simon and gives him a *hong bao* filled with cash. Simon has a triple surprise: Mr. Gao speaks English; Mr. Gao knows that he and Wai-tung are gay lovers; and Mr. Gao accepts the homosexual relationship. With Simon, the viewer is also "surprised" by Mr. Gao's modernity. The old KMT officer has always been part of a modern, hybridized, transnational, transcultural world. He just never let "us" (the viewer—both East and West) know. According to Chow (1991, 28):

> What is missing from the preoccupation with tradition and authentic originariness as such is the experience of modern Chinese people who have had to live their lives with the knowledge that it is precisely the notion of a still-intact tradition to which they cannot cling—the experience precisely of being impure, "Westernized" Chinese and the bearing of *that* experience on their ways of "seeing" China.

Finally, Mr. Gao is as "modern" as Wai-tung is "traditional." Categories collapse, and identity becomes problematized. Old Gao has a "modern" face with a "Western" voice.

Produced, distributed, and marketed within a transnational matrix of economic, political, cultural, ethnic, and linguistic relationships, *The Wedding Banquet* does not posit a singular position for an abstract, "ideal" viewer. Non–Chinese-speaking viewers miss untranslated dialogue as well as plays on the Chinese language and customs. References to "Act Up" are most likely lost on a mainstream audience outside America or unfamiliar with the gay community. Rather than attempting to create a homogenized audience that could conceivably understand everything, *The Wedding Banquet* simply hopes for enough overlap not to lose anyone along the way.

This overlap has certain ideological ramifications. Types need to be broad enough to be recognizable, but not offensive. Political issues need to be broached, but kept safely within the realm of a utopian (and thus, fantastical) fiction. Behind the live-ly multicultural mix, an organizing principle emerges that builds its liberal vision on the erasure of the experiences of feminists, gay Asians, and other voices of the Asian American community. Within a transnational cinema with a multicultural, cosmopolitan vision of diversity, hierarchies of power and structures of silence still exercise a heavy burden on the emergent desire for social change, harmony, and understanding.

Notes

Acknowledgments: I thank the many people who provided valuable input while I was writing this chapter, including all those who attended "Screening China Globally: Gender and the Construction of Diasporic Identities," Teaching Asia Through Film, University of Pittsburgh, May 4, 1996 (particularly my host, Sheldon Lu, whose work on transnational Chinese cinema provided inspiration for this article); those who attended my presentation at the University of Oklahoma, Norman (particularly Joanna Rapf for her helpful comments on the sound comedy), in February 1997; the members of the Curriculum Transformation Project 1996 Faculty Study Group, "Globalization, Gender, and Culture," University of Maryland; the editors of this volume; and Yang Ming-yu, Yeh Yueh-yu, Tad Doyle, and Seth Silberman.

1. For a definition of Asian American filmmaking and its relationship to Asia and Asian film, see Feng (1995) and Francia (1990).

2. The film's title is *Hsi Yen* in the Wade-Giles system, and *Xi Yan* in pinyin. Given that the film is a Taiwanese production, the Wade-Giles system will be used for the transliteration of proper names (unless they are more commonly rendered in another system of romanization). Individuals differ in their preferences for the rendering of their names; Lee Ang is sometimes Ang Lee, for example, inverting surname and given name. The most commonly seen rendering will be used in this chapter.

3. Fine articles on *The Wedding Banquet* have appeared since I wrote this chapter. Some cover some of the same ground explored here. For more information on the film in relation to the filmmaker's other works, see Dariotis and Fung (1997). For more on *The Wedding Banquet* as a queer text, see Chiang (1998).

4. The most striking illustration of this is in the scene in which Mr. Gao blesses Wai-tung and Wei-wei's union as a coming together of Taiwan and the mainland. The English subtitles do not translate the political dimension of the speech.

5. This implication is stated directly in the program booklet.

6. In film, 1989 marked the first major feature to broach any critique of the KMT and its policies: *A City of Sadness* (directed by Hou Hsiao-hsien). Since then, a number of films have variously criticized the KMT version of Chinese–Taiwanese relations. See Chiao (1996).

7. In contrast to the Gaos' fevered attempt to keep the extended family going under any circumstances, Simon represents a common Chinese view that one of the principal ways in which America proves itself inferior to China is in its failure to take the institution of the family seriously. Hence, Mrs. Gao is fascinated by Simon's estranged biological father, stepfather, and various types of siblings. Wei-wei, in exasperation, finally stops translating when Simon gets to a half-brother killed in Vietnam.

8. A lot of scholarship has been generated on "Greater China" and an evolving sense of being ethnically Chinese in the modern world. See Tu (1994).

9. Indeed, critics of Jameson have pointed out many of the shortcomings of his conjecture that all Third World texts are "necessarily" national allegories. See Ahmad (1995). In this case, I would say that *The Wedding Banquet* can be taken as a national allegory and as a "postmodern" commercial product, while Jameson tends to see this as an either–or proposition in the article mentioned earlier. Jameson takes a different tack in his look at the Taiwanese film *The Terrorizer* (Yang 1986); see Jameson (1992).

10. What I would term the "ethnic" family melodrama involves those films which deal with domestic tensions within an American family marked as "Other" due to ethnic difference. This has been a staple of the Hollywood sound film since *The Jazz Singer* (Crosland 1927) and usually involves multigenerational conflicts, unassimilated parents (usually mothers), economic difficulties linked to ethnic associations, romantic tensions involving cross-cultural misunderstandings, and so on. The Asian American ethnic family melodrama has been quite evident recently in films such as *The Joy Luck Club* (Wang 1993), among other features.

11. Wang (1993). My thanks to Yang Ming-yu for providing this review and its translation. The term "gay mentality" appears in English in the review, pointing to a tendency to look at "gay life" as "Western" or "foreign."

12. Noted in Berry (1993). For more on Lee and his work, see Ma (1996) and Rayns (1993).

13. The classic article on the operation of the gaze and the representation of the body is Mulvey (1995). While the spectacle of the woman's body has been assumed as a staple of classical cinema, several genres gaze at the male body as spectacle, including Hollywood action adventure and gay porn.

14. For a complete explication of the closet and its meaning in film, see Babuscio (1977), Russo (1981), and Dyer (1990). For a theoretical examination, see Sedgwick (1990).

15. Wei-wei also has a long-distance telephone relationship with her family in Shanghai. The only glimpse given of this relationship and of conditions on the mainland comes in a brief conversation in Shanghaiese. The family has moved into a new flat (with the rapid modernization of the city, many families have moved into new housing in satellite areas in the past few years), and only a few words that nothing is new or wrong are exchanged before the conversation is interrupted by wedding preparations. Just as Wai-tung's family has no idea about his sex life, Wei-wei's family knows nothing about her green-card marriage to a homosexual. The telephone really does little to further communication, while it functions as a means to add to the sense of irony and miscommunication cultivated by the film.

16. All men in Taiwan are required to do a stint in the armed forces. The image conjures up both this masculine rite of passage and the family's military connections.

17. Berger (1972) might note something similar.

18. I am reluctant even to broach the idea of "bisexuality," because it is so foreign to *The Wedding Banquet*. The implication, at the end of the film, is that Wai-tung is not bisexual and will not consider continuing a sexual relationship with both Wei-wei and Simon. Rather, Wei-wei has implicitly given up sex to become the mother of Wai-tung's baby—a point underscored in her conversation with Mrs. Gao about the possibility of Wai-tung's getting in touch with his "straight" side after the birth of the baby. Wei-wei says she's certain that that will not happen. In other words, she accepts that Wai-tung's sexual orientation will always be toward men.

19. This has been brought up by filmmakers and video makers—for example, Nguyen Tan Hoang's *Seven Steps to Sticky Heaven* (n.d.)and Richard Fung's work on Asians in gay pornography. See also Fung (1991). For a listing of films and videos on Asian gay–lesbian themes, see http://www.tufts.edu/%7Estai/QAPA/films.html.

20. See Wong (1978) and Kashiwabara (n.d.).

21. There have been many wonderful critiques of the reception of these films outside China. See Lu (1996) and Chow (1995).

22. See Heung (1997) on the modern Madame Butterfly and Marchetti (1993).

23. For a useful synopsis of the opera, see http://classicalmus.com/bmgclassics/opera/operabutterfly.html.

It is important to remember that Puccini's version was not unprecedented, but based on the play by Belasco which had been based on the short story by John Luther Long, himself inspired by the work of French author Pierre Loti. However, it is Puccini's version that still seems to resonate most deeply in current references and retellings.

24. It is impossible to list all the films that have taken advantage of American and European locations to tell stories about the overseas Chinese. See Law (1992) for an excellent collection of essays on the topic.

Works Cited

Ahmad, Aijaz. 1995. "Jameson's Rhetoric of Otherness and the 'National Allegory.'" Pp. 77–82 in *The Post-Colonial Studies Reader,* ed. Bill Ashcroft, Gareth Griffiths and Helen Tiffin. London: Routledge.

Anonymous. 1997. Electronic interview with the author. July.

Babuscio, Jack. 1977. "Camp and the Gay Sensibility." Pp. 40–57 in *Gays and Film,* ed. Richard Dyer. London: British Film Institute.

Berger, John. 1972. *Ways of Seeing.* London: BBC and Penguin.

Berry, Chris. 1993. "Taiwanese Melodrama Returns with a Twist in *The Wedding Banquet.*" *Cinemaya* 21 (Fall): 52–54.

Central Motion Picture Corporation. 1993. Publicity book: *The Wedding Banquet* by Ang Lee. Taipei, n.p.

Chiang, Mark. 1998. "Coming Out into the Global System: Postmodern Patriarchies and Transnational Sexualities in *The Wedding Banquet.*" Pp. 374–96 in *Q and A: Queer in Asian America,* ed. David L. Eng and Alice Y. Hom. Philadelphia: Temple University Press.

Chiao, Peggy. 1996. "White Terror and the Formosa Incident: Introspections on Recent Political Film from Taiwan." *Cinemaya* 32 (spring): 22–24.

Chow, Rey. 1991. *Woman and Chinese Modernity: The Politics of Reading Between West and East.* Minneapolis: University of Minnesota Press.

———. 1995. *Primitive Passions: Visuality, Sexuality, Ethnography, and Contemporary Chinese Cinema.* NY: Columbia University Press.

Dariotis, Wei-ming, and Eileen Fung. 1997. "Breaking the Soy Sauce Jar: Diaspora and Displacement in the Films of Ang Lee." Pp. 187–220 in *Transnational Chinese Cinemas: Identity, Nationhood, Gender,* ed. Sheldon Hsiao-peng Lu. Honolulu: University of Hawaii Press.

DarkWhite. n.d. "Review of *The Wedding Banquet,* dir. Ang Lee," http://www.users.on.net/darkwhite/movies.htm.

Dyer, Richard. 1990. *Now You See It: Studies on Lesbian and Gay Film.* New York: Routledge.

Feng, Peter. 1995. "In Search of Asian American Cinema." *Cineaste* 21, no. 1–2 (Winter–Spring): 32–35. (Also http://www.lib.berkeley.edu/MRC/InSearchofAsian.html.)

Francia, Luis. 1990. "Asian Cinema and Asian American Cinema: Separated by a Common Language." *Cinemaya* 9 (Fall): 36–39.

Fung, Richard. 1991. "Center the Margins." Pp. 62–67 in *Moving the Image: Independent Asian Pacific American Media Arts*, ed. Russell Leong. Los Angeles: UCLA Asian American Studies Center and Visual Communications, Southern California Asian American Studies Central.

Heung, Marina. 1997. "The Family Romance of Orientalism: From *Madame Butterfly* to *Indochine*." Pp. 158–83 in *Visions of the East: Orientalism in Film*, ed. Matthew Bernstein and Gaylyn Studlar. New Brunswick, N.J.: Rutgers University Press.

Jameson, Fredric. 1986. "Third World Literature in the Era of Multinational Capitalism." *Social Text* 15 (Fall): 65–88.

———. 1992. *The Geopolitical Aesthetic: Cinema and Space in the World System*. Bloomington: Indiana University Press.

Kashiwabara, Amy. n.d. "Vanishing Son: The Appearance, Disappearance, and Assimilation of the Asian-American Man in American Mainstream Media," http://www.lib.berkeley.edu/MRC/Amydoc.html.

Klady, Leonard. 1994. "Pix' Profit Picture Present Surprises." *Variety*, January 10–16, 13.

Law, Kar, ed. 1992. *Overseas Chinese Figures in Cinema*. Hong Kong: The 16th Hong Kong International Film Festival.

Lent, John A. 1990. *The Asian Film Industry*. Austin: University of Texas Press.

Lu, Sheldon. 1996. "Postmodernity, Popular Culture, and the Intellectual: A Report on Post-Tiananmen Cinema." *boundary* 2 23, no. 2 (Summer): 139–69.

Ma, Sheng-mei. 1996. "Ang Lee's Domestic Tragicomedy: Immigrant Nostalgia, Exotic/Ethnic Tour, Global Market." *Journal of Popular Culture* 30, no. 1 (summer): 191–201.

Marchetti, Gina. 1993. *Romance and the "Yellow Peril": Race, Sex, and Discursive Strategies in Hollywood Fiction*. Berkeley: University of California Press.

Mulvey, Laura. 1975. "Visual Pleasure and Narrative Cinema." *Screen* 16, no. 3 (Fall): 6–18.

Nygaard, Gary. 1995. "Review of *The Wedding Banquet*, dir. Ang Lee." January, http://www.athena.net/~lavsalon/book_reviews-95.html.

Rayns, Tony. 1993. "*Xiyan (The Wedding Banquet)*." *Sight and Sound* 3, no. 10 (October): 56.

Russo, Vito. 1981. *The Celluloid Closet: Homosexuality in the Movies*. NY: Harper and Row.

Sedgwick, Eve K. 1990. *Epistemology of the Closet*. Berkeley: University of California Press.

Tu, Wei-ming, ed. 1994. *The Living Tree: The Changing Meaning of Being Chinese Today*. Stanford, Calif.: Stanford University Press.

Wang, Chi Cheng. 1993. "Review of *The Wedding Banquet*, dir. Ang Lee." *Min Sheng Daily* (Taiwan), 4 March, 31.

Wong, Eugene Franklin. 1978. *On Visual Media Racism: Asians in the American Motion Pictures*. New York: Arno Press.

Films and Videos Cited

Bertolucci, Bernardo. 1987. *The Last Emperor*. Columbia Pictures Corporation, Artisan Entertainment.

Chen, Kaige. 1993. *Farewell My Concubine*. Buena Vista/Miramax Films.

Cronenberg, David. 1993. *M. Butterfly*. Warner Bros.

Crosland, Alan. 1927. *The Jazz Singer*. Warner Bros.

Haynes, Todd. 1991. *Poison*. Bronze Eye Productions.

Hou, Hsiao-hsien. 1989. *City of Sadness*. Artificial eye/3-H Films/Era International.

Koster, Henry. 1961. *Flower Drum Song*. Universal International.

Lee, Ang. 1992. *Pushing Hands.*

———. 1993. *The Wedding Banquet.* Central Motion Picture Corporation/Good Machine.

———. 1994. *Eat Drink Man Woman.* Central Motion Picture Corporation.

———. 1995. *Sense and Sensibility.* Mirage/Columbia.

———. 1997. *The Ice Storm.* Good Machine/Fox Searchlight Pictures.

Molinaro, Edouard. 1978. *La Cage aux Folles.* United Artists.

Nguyen, Tan Hoang. *Seven Steps to Sticky Heaven.* No distributor.

Shum, Mina. 1994. *Double Happiness.* Fine Line Features.

Spielberg, Steven. 1993. *Jurassic Park.* Universal Pictures.

Wang, Wayne. 1982. *Chan Is Missing.* New Yorker Films.

———. 1985. *Dim Sum: A Little Bit of Heart.* CIM/Orion Classics.

———. 1989. *Eat a Bowl of Tea.* American Playhouse/Columbia.

———. 1993. *The Joy Luck Club.* Hollywood Pictures/Buena Vista.

Yang, Edward. 1986. *The Terrorizer.* Central Motion Picture Corporation.

Zhang, Yimou. 1987. *Red Sorghum.* Xi'an Film Studio.

———. 1990. *Ju Dou.* Tokuma Communications/Chinan Film.

———. 1991. *Raise the Red Lantern.* Orion Classics.

Julian Stringer

17 Cultural Identity and Diaspora in Contemporary Hong Kong Cinema

The reader will be forgiven for questioning whether this chapter really belongs in a collection of articles on Asian American screen cultures. After all, my title clearly states that I intend to write about Hong Kong cinema, and Hong Kong cinema is not the same thing as U.S. cinema. If I am not going to focus on the work of Asian Americans, what business does this chapter have being here? My response takes the form of two arguments. First, the Hong Kong films I want to look at are intimately related to the screen life of Asian Americans. Second, that these same films are significant because they represent Asian American screen identities that are in the process of formation.

To illustrate these two points, it may be enough simply to observe how the Hong Kong and U.S. film industries already interrelate across a number of levels of influence. Consider the crossover of production personnel. While Chinese and Western filmmakers have long been in the habit of traveling to each other's shores (especially after the Asian American star Bruce Lee achieved international prominence in the early 1970s), the traffic has intensified markedly in recent years. More specifically, as the July 1, 1997, deadline for China's resumption of sovereign control over Hong Kong crept ever nearer, more and more Hong Kong filmmakers made the United States their home. The case of director John Woo is well known (*Hard Target* [1993]; *Broken Arrow* [1994]; *Face/Off* [1997]), but there is more to the U.S.–Hong Kong film connection than just him. These days, going to the mall just wouldn't be going to the mall without the promise of a new Jackie Chan movie (*Rumble in the Bronx* [Tong 1996b]; *Police Story 3: Supercop* [Tong 1996a]; *Police Story 4: First Strike* [Tong 1997]), and in addition to working with Woo on *Hard Target,* the action star Jean-Claude Van Damme has made films with the Hong Kong directors Ringo Lam (*Maximum Risk* [1996]), and Tsui Hark (*Double Team* [1997]). Actress Maggie Cheung auditioned for a part in *Heat* (Mann and Smithee 1995) but didn't get it; her colleague Sylvia Chang was offered the same role but didn't want it. And as I was writing this chapter, one of Hong Kong's greatest stars, Chow Yun-Fat, was making his Hollywood debut in

The Replacement Killers (Fuqua 1998), and another top name, Michelle Yeoh, had just appeared in the James Bond film *Tomorrow Never Dies* (Spottiswoode 1997).

Within the bustle of such activity lie the seeds of an emergent Asian American cinema. Although this cinema may still be limited to the action-movie genre, the links that connect Hong Kong to Hollywood have already been recognized and welcomed by both mainstream industry personnel and Asian American media workers. For example, while the former honored Jackie Chan with an MTV lifetime award in 1995, the members of the Asian American Arts Foundation (a fund-raising organization in the San Francisco Bay Area) extended their own welcome to Chow Yun-Fat by presenting him with a Transpacific Award during their annual ceremony in 1994. During his special appearance at the Center for the Arts Theater in San Francisco's Yerba Buena Gardens, Chow rubbed shoulders with such celebrated Asian Americans as the author Maxine Hong Kingston and the artist Ruth Asawa.

In addition to this crossover of talent, recent Hong Kong titles as generically and stylistically diverse as *Alan and Eric—Between Hello and Goodbye* (Chan 1991), *A Better Tomorrow II* (Woo 1987), *Comrades, Almost a Love Story* (Chan 1998), *Eight Taels of Gold* (Cheung 1989), *Farewell China* (Law 1991), *The Master* (Tsui 1991a), *My American Grandson* (Hui 1991), *Once Upon a Time in China and America* (Kam-Bo 1997), *Siao Yu* (Chang 1995), and *Twin Dragons* (Lam and Tsui 1992) have made the experiences of Asian Americans part of their very subject matter. Such films explore related questions. What are the constituent features of Hong Kong's new postcolonial identity? How has mass migration and displacement affected this sense of identity? What can the United States offer traveling Chinese?

These works do not resemble the kind of Asian American cinema that some people have already begun to identify and celebrate, but they do anticipate the formation of new Asian American screen cultures. Each of these titles can be read as a map, a guidebook offering advice to prospective overseas Chinese about the skills they need to possess in order to get on in the new world. In other words, they anticipate what a future cinema may look like. (And as Mandarin becomes Hong Kong's next official language, the Cantonese vernacular may yet live on in the cinematic diaspora.) If nothing else, the exploration of such thematic material presents filmmakers with a practical link to Asian Americans working inside the U.S. film industry, and hence with the possibility of securing work through the manipulation of new channels of cooperation and funding.[1] The phenomenon also exhibits a marked circularity. Many of the filmmakers who established or benefited from Hong Kong's post-1979 "New Wave" were themselves educated in the United States (Allen Fong, Tsui Hark, Mabel Cheung). Their successors are now well placed to lead Hong Kong's productive infiltration into the American film industry.

The historical fact of mass migration has, crucially, also set the seal on the consolidation of an active Hong Kong fan culture across the United States. Fueled by the obsessions and resources of those who have brought their city's movie madness with them, these subcultural consumers are transforming the marketplace. Main Street video shops now stock the odd kung-fu title and Chinese ghost movie, and in addition to articles in specialist magazines, mass-market publications such as *The New York-*

er and *Time* carry features on key films and stars.[2] Put these various clusters of activity together and it is not hard to see how the Hong Kong film diaspora will play a key role in determining the direction some Asian American screen cultures are likely to move in over the next few years.

At the same time, however, it should also be recognized that the migration of Hong Kong residents alone does not fully account for the increasing popularity of Hong Kong films in the mainstream U.S. marketplace. The distribution of titles to other Asian societies with large migrant streams to the United States, such as China and Taiwan, should also be acknowledged, as should the popularity of Hong Kong action stars among African American audiences.[3] Most significantly, interest in Hong Kong movies is growing among many Asian Americans who grew up in the United States. Spurred by the work of Asian American programmers, Hong Kong film festivals are springing up on more and more college campuses, and Asian Media Access, an Asian American nonprofit organization operating out of Minneapolis, is striking new prints of contemporary classics to meet the demand. This phenomenon is explored in *Beyond Asiaphilia* (1997), a short video by the Asian American director Valerie Soe. Juxtaposing Soe's own autobiographical experiences with interviews with a number of Asian American men about their avid interest in Hong Kong movies, the video makes explicit connections between the reception of Hong Kong cinema in the United States and the recognition and formation of Asian American identities.

The significance of such cultural practices, then, cannot be established solely through a consideration of the changes brought about by the spread of the Hong Kong diaspora. The reception of Hong Kong cinema in the United States should not be separated from larger questions of Asian American history. As recent work on immigration trends makes clear, any discussion of Asian American identity needs to take into account a range of economic, political, and cultural factors that are linked to the global restructuring and integration taking place across the Pacific Rim as well as within the United States (Ong, Bonacich, and Cheng 1994; Hamamoto and Torres 1997). These factors have contributed to the conditions necessary for the mass acceptance of Hong Kong movies in the United States.

Although this is not the place to go into great detail about what these extremely broad and complex factors are, three in particular should be mentioned. First, the end of the Cold War in 1989, and the Tiananmen Square massacre in June of the same year, generated new and unforeseen relationships among Hong Kong, China, and the United States. Second, the spread of transnational capitalism and the proliferation of global media and instant electronic technology have eroded established cultural boundaries, allowing Hong Kong's popular culture to make deep inroads into American society. Third, the construction of pan-ethnic Asian American alliances in the United States offers an environment that is supportive of cultural artifacts that express the diversity of the Asian American experience (Espiritu 1992).

These reconfigurations have focused attention on the dynamics of Asian American identity. According to L. Ling-Chi Wang, much previous social-science research on the subject worked within a dual paradigm that conceptualized Asian Americans as

PHOTO 17.1.   From *Beyond Asiaphilia* (1997), dir. Valerie Soe.

subject to both racial exclusion and oppression through strict assimilation to Anglo-American norms, and through residual loyalty to an imagined homeland (Wang 1995, 159). Against this reductive schema, Wang advances the proposition that Asian American identity should be represented through an alternative paradigm—one that fully recognizes the legitimacy of the cultural assets and values that immigrants bring to the United States and the integral part they play in its vision. This paradigm must also recognize that Asian Americans are entitled to all the rights and privileges promised in the Declaration of Independence and in the U.S. constitution. In addition, changing global conditions need to be understood as a continuous influence on the formation of Asian American identities: "*Under the new paradigm, racial exclusion or oppression and extraterritorial domination converge and interact in the Chinese American community, establishing a permanent structure of dual domination and creating its own internal dynamics and unique institutions*" (ibid.; italics in original).

In another recent article, Wang further problematizes the dual structure of assimilation and loyalty by probing the importance of the concept of "roots" for diasporic Chinese societies. He offers a typology of how the term has been signified within Asian American and Anglo-American locations. To summarize these briefly, the concept of the *sojourner mentality* refers to the image of Chinese as aliens, strangers, pariahs, and outcasts; *total assimilation* assumes that Chinese Americans come to regard the need to be accepted by white society as their primary obsession; *accommodation* means the forced settling down in a foreign land and public adoption of its lifestyle (e.g., the situation that some Chinese students faced in the United States after Tiananmen) and differs from *assimilation* in that

its terms are worked out by Chinese themselves; *ethnic pride and consciousness* seek to lib-
erate Chinese Americans from the dual domination of racial oppression and extraterritorial domination through the development of a distinct Chinese American identity, one
rooted in experience and a belief in a community with shared interests and a common
destiny in the United States; and, finally, *the uprooted* refers primarily to those elite overseas students who decide, for a variety of reasons, not to return to their countries of origin. Many of these elites then opt for *accommodation* in the new environment (Wang 1991).

The mapping of such a typology suggests the complexity of images of migration
to the United States in Hong Kong cinema, as well as the diversity of issues that are
potentially opened for Asian American audiences in the act of reception. Indeed,
when considering the increasing popularity of Hong Kong movies in the United
States, one might start by asking how the terms of Wang's paradigm are reflected in
the ways that individual titles explore questions of migration and arrival.

Three recent films from Hong Kong introduce the subject of migration to the United States in order to suggest how they signify Asian American identities in the process
of formation. The films are *An Autumn Tale* (Cheung 1988), *Full Moon in New York*
(Kwan 1990), and *Rumble in the Bronx* (Tong 1996b). After noting these films' engagement with issues of cultural identity and displacement, I will offer a short critique of
what some critics consider their aesthetic and political limitations.

In each of these three titles, the United States is imagined as what Stuart Hall (1994,
401) calls "the third term"—namely, a cultural space, neither Chinese nor European,
where East meets West and new identities are negotiated. This "third term" encom-
passes two different ways of thinking about "cultural identity." On the one hand, it
gestures toward a shared culture, "a sort of collective 'one true self,' hiding inside the
many other, more superficial or artificially imposed 'selves,' which people with a
shared history and ancestry hold in common" (ibid., 393). On the other hand, there
is a "second, related but different view of cultural identity. This second position recognizes that, as well as the many points of similarity, there are also critical points of
deep and significant *difference* which constitute 'what we really are.'. . . Cultural identity, in this second sense, is a matter of 'becoming' as well as of 'being.' It belongs to
the future as much as to the past" (ibid., 394).

These three films open "the third term" as a space for the formation of Asian American identities by exploring two interrelated themes—namely, the specific nature of
Hong Kong's postcolonial situation and the diverse aspirations and experiences of
Chinese immigrants to the United States. Clearly, new identities are being negotiated here within a different cultural space because of Hong Kong's own stature as a
global city. When local citizens are already participants in the international economy,
old structures of domination no longer apply. *An Autumn Tale, Full Moon,* and *Rumble* work to establish common ground between the old and new worlds by putting
questions of travel and arrival into dialogical engagement with each other. This is not
a case of "culture clash" or the assimilation–loyalty binary so much as it is the exploration of a variety of in-between social positions. In other words, the films concern
themselves with the subtle teasing out of similarities and differences among Chinese,
Chinese American, and Asian American subjectivities.

A quick plot summary of each title should help illustrate the appropriate dramatic situations. *An Autumn Tale* concerns Jennifer (Cherie Cheung), a Hong Kong student enrolled in acting classes at New York University and the problems she faces in the United States. Living in a poor neighborhood, she receives help from her cousin, a former sailor and Chinatown community leader named Sam Pan (Chow Yun-Fat). The two become more intimate with each other after Jennifer discovers that her "Westernized" boyfriend from Hong Kong, Vincent (Danny Chan), has discovered "free choice" and begun to date an Asian American woman. However, Jennifer and Sam Pan do not consummate their relationship. When Jennifer finally takes a job on Long Island—with the implication that she will hook up once more with the economically mobile Vincent—Sam Pan is left to face a bleak future alone in Chinatown. A final scene reunites Jennifer and Sam Pan, but the meeting is revealed as nothing more than a fantasy projection (hers? his?).

In *Full Moon,* three Chinese women meet and strike up a friendship. Lee Jieu (Maggie Cheung) is a lesbian real estate speculator and restaurant owner from Hong Kong; Wang Hsiung Ping (Sylvia Chang) is a politically savvy actress from Taiwan; and Zhao Hong (Siqin Gaowa) is a newlywed from Shanghai with a boorish Chinese American husband and a desire to bring her mother to the States. The three women endure numerous confrontations and misunderstandings, but they soon come to respect and share the strategies each has chosen for survival within the Big Apple's inhospitable terrain.

Rumble opens with the arrival of Keung (Jackie Chan) from Hong Kong for a three-month visit to his Chinese American relatives in New York. Keung soon befriends the new owner of his uncle's former supermarket, Helena (Anita Mui), as well as a member of the local street gang, a young Asian American woman named Nancy (Francoise Yip). While helping out at the supermarket and looking after his family, Keung gets in trouble with the hoodlums and ends up in a number of fights. Later, though, Keung and the gang cooperate with each other to defeat a bunch of murderous diamond thieves.

These three films, in different ways and with different degrees of success, represent Hall's two conceptions of cultural identity as the struggle between "being" Chinese and "becoming" Asian American (Feng 1996). In *An Autumn Tale,* for example, the fact that Jennifer and Sam Pan occupy different class positions affects the formation of their Asian American identities. Although both live in Brooklyn and mix with whites, Latinos, and African Americans, Jennifer's command of English and deployment of middle-class social skills enables her to move to the suburbs of Long Island by securing a job as a babysitter for the daughter of a rich Asian American woman, while Sam Pan is left to mingle and fight with the neighborhood Chinese gangs. His experiences frustrate him: "You talk all yes talk, I talk all no talk," he complains to one white policeman. Jennifer is able to establish a new identity with her university friends without assimilating to white norms. Despite his aspiration to "get the green card, then the gold card," Sam Pan has no means to move out of Chinatown. When he picks Jennifer up from the airport in the opening scene, Sam Pan amuses himself by speaking in Japanese, precisely because the African American cop who moves him along cannot distinguish among different Asian people. Indeed, by the time Jennifer leaves him, Sam Pan appears to have lost all hope of individuality—he will shout "I AIN'T NO YELLOW COW!" at cops for the rest of his days. (In an iconic moment, familiar from so many other Hong Kong movies, the smile has been wiped off Chow Yun-Fat's face.) It is significant, however, that while Jennifer opts for accommodation in her new environment, Sam Pan's situation is all the more poignant for being left unresolved. By the end of the film, his cultural identity cannot be defined easily within the parameters of Wang's typology. Sam Pan's experiences could form the basis of a new ethnic pride and consciousness, or they could lead to his stigmatization via the terms of the sojourner mentality. The very openness of these different possibilities suggests the presence of "the third term."

Jackie Chan dramatizes the process of "becoming" Asian American through the development of his transnational star image, which has now taken on a global orientation. In *Rumble,* as in all of his recent work, Chan functions first as a repository of Chinese cultural values overseas, and his position as a charming intermediary between warring factions ("Don't you know," he implores a gang of toughs, "you are the scum of Society?") provides a perfect metaphor for this transnational success. Yet Chan is a highly ambiguous figure. His image appeals differently to different audiences, whose responses again suggest the opening up of "the third term" for his Asian American fans.

Consider four aspects of *Rumble.* First, part of the film's interest lies in the fact that, although the codes of decency and loyalty trotted out in the script suggest traces of the logic of Chinese extraterritorial domination, the narrative (unusual for a crossover U.S. hit) nowhere suggests its binary opposite—assimilation to white norms. Second, the fact that music by a variety of African American artists was added to the soundtrack for U.S. release suggests a conscious attempt to appeal to black audiences.[4] Third, although Chan's image combines not just the moral conviction that comes from a perfect coordination of mind and body but also a raging sexuality, it is telling that the love interest in this and other Jackie Chan films distributed in the United States is rather tentatively, and confusingly, split. In *Rumble,* he is set up with Helena, then with Nancy, but neither romance is developed conclusively. Although this narrative strategy—the hero is allowed to fight but not fuck—is certainly common in the martial-arts genre, it also plays very neatly into the U.S. mainstream media's stereotyping of Asian American men as asexual beings. Finally, however—and most importantly—the interviews in *Beyond Asiaphilia* testify to how some Asian American spectators resist such stereotypes by relishing the physical display and sexual power of Chan's body.

Themes of sexual power and performance, and of the adoption of a new identity as necessary for the process of survival in the United States, are also picked up in *Full Moon.* During one memorable scene, Hsiung Ping auditions for the role of Lady Macbeth, but she is turned down by a white male casting director, who bleats, "What makes a Chinese woman, or a Japanese woman, think that she can play Lady Macbeth?" (Even with Hsiung Ping's excellent command of English, she significantly is not referred to here as an Asian American; it is also signfcant that, like the black cop in *An Autumn Tale,* the man patronizingly conflates two completely different Asian cultures.) After describing the singularly vicious brutalities that a certain Chinese empress inflicted on her enemies, Hsiung Ping, a hint of disgust around her mouth, retorts, "With an ancestor like the empress, don't tell me I cannot play Lady Macbeth!"[5]

Part of the negotiation of issues of cultural identity and displacement in these films involves an exploration of the gap between the imaginative potential offered by travel to the new world and the humdrum fact of arrival. In *An Autumn Tale,* Sam Pan paints a picture of the Brooklyn Bridge for Jennifer because she cannot afford a room with a real view. Later, as she drives across the bridge with Vincent, the painting is framed next to its original referent, suggesting the distance between fantasy and reality. This sense that a potential space exists between the articulation of existing and emergent identities is further emphasized in *Full Moon.* For example, there is the moment when Zhao Hong, after talking with Ah Jieu about geomancy, attempts to bring the good *chi* of New York City into her high-rise apartment by opening all of its windows. After she has done so, a reverse shot takes us outside, and a slow zoom pulls back to reveal her living space as just one small box among many others. How many stories lie untold behind so many closed curtains? Kwan punctuates the narrative with brief shots of city exteriors, which, in addition to offering viewers the visual memory of another dazzling skyline (Hong Kong's), generate an uncanny feeling of complete stasis. Even when camera movement is used, it produces an unusual effect. When a crane shot traverses an empty street, the movement is executed in slow motion, approximating how an unfamiliar space may appear ominous and strange to the newcomer.

As a number of historians have noted, since the mid-1960s real-estate investment has promised to allow urbanized Chinese societies in the United States the chance to grow and, hence, to allow Asian American identities to flourish within the sanctuary of "ethnic enclaves" (Kwong 1987). *Full Moon* exhibits a significant thematic focus on real-estate investment among Chinatown denizens. However, as Sam Pan's experiences in *An Autumn Tale* testify, the reality is that overseas Chinese more often than not end up trapped and exploited within economically depressed ghettos. The main characters in Kwan's film struggle to move out of their own "ethnic enclaves," but this is not presented as a simple case of assimilation to mainstream values. From "little Hong Kong" to Manhattan, *Full Moon* opens a potential space where a new paradigm of identity can be formulated. The film recognizes that Asian Americans occupy all parts of the social- and economic-class spectrum and so cannot be typed in any casual manner.[6]

Rumble occupies an in-between social status by the very fact that it is itself something of a hybrid. Distributed state to state by New Line Pictures, but rush-released to meet a Chinese New Year deadline, the film does more than just exhibit a duality of languages (English and Cantonese) on its soundtrack. The movie works as a synthesis of the Hong Kong action film and the U.S. juvenile-delinquency picture. The Chinese family and business obligations that so often make their way into Jackie Chan star narratives are placed back to back with a wild assortment of marginalized and multiracial characters, making the whole package play like an updated version of *Rebel Without a Cause* (Ray 1955). The new Chinese kid on the block is taunted until he fights back, a younger man idolizes his friend, and there is even a nighttime chicken run (performed this time not by two car-driving buddies on a desolate hillside but by two young urban women on motorbikes). Such scenes illustrate the range of social alliances that open in the process of negotiating different Asian American identities.

To return to Hall's other definition of cultural identity, however, it is also possible to see how each of the three films tries to construct a shared identity among people of Chinese descent. That is to say, there is a simultaneous attempt to locate a spiritual core of "Chineseness," a collective "one true self" that remains apart from mainstream U.S. culture. The narratives describe various ways in which overseas Chinese are interpellated into the United States at the same time that they construct representations of "true Chineseness." And yet, because these titles locate examples of what the subaltern studies scholar Partha Chatterjee calls an "inner domain of national culture" in different places, the fact that such notions of extraterritorial domination coexist simultaneously with global cultural dynamics is highlighted.

For Chatterjee, the "inner domain" of a postcolonial national culture is the colonial subject's "essential" spiritual and cultural identity, the "outer domain" the Western-style material culture that is resisted:

> The material is the domain of the "outside," of the economy and of statecraft, of science and technology, a domain where the West had proved its superiority and the East had succumbed.... The spiritual, on the other hand, is an "inner" domain bearing the "essential" marks of cultural identity. The greater one's success in imitating Western skills in the material domain, therefore, the greater the need to preserve the distinctiveness of one's spiritual culture.... Nationalism declares the domain of the spiritual its sovereign territory and refuses to allow the colonial power to intervene in that domain.... The colonial state, in other words, is kept out of the "inner" domain of national culture, but it is not as though this so-called spiritual domain is left unchanged. In fact, here nationalism launches its most powerful, creative and historically significant project: to fashion a "modern" national culture that is nevertheless not Western. [Chatterjee 1993, 6]

It may come as no surprise that, as a metaphor for the uniqueness of being Chinese, a sensitivity to the delights of food surfaces in each film, and that this sensitivity is then contrasted with the blandness of "American" cuisine. Sam Pan teaches Jennifer how to cook proper ginger soup; Ah Jieu owns a Hunan restaurant (but one that specializes in Peking Duck!); and Keung helps out at the local Chinese grocery store. However, it is worth drawing attention to two other subjects explicitly tied into this "inner" culture.

In *An Autumn Tale*, the Chinatown gambling den provides Sam Pan with his retreat from trouble and strife. A spate of gambling films dominated the Hong Kong box office during the late 1980s, and these scenes of Chow Yun-Fat trying his luck with the arbitrary fates dealt out at card games—flaunting his wad before losing the lot—foreshadow the same actor's later incarnation as the "God of Gamblers" (*God of Gamblers* [Wong 1989] and *God of Gamblers Returns* [Wong 1995]). As linked to economic and class mobility, the aesthetics of gambling are based on chance and luck rather than on work and achievement. Mabel Cheung's decision to include such a location in a movie about Asian Americans in the Big Apple raises a number of issues—about the restructuring of economic relations between Hong Kong and New York, about the hopes and disappointments that accompany overseas migration, and about how gambling in Chinatown can itself provide the cause of nothing but trouble and strife.

In *Full Moon*, the emphasis is more on the body as the site of core identities. The focus in Kwan's film is on the politics of sex and romance. The three protagonists first meet at Lee Jieu's restaurant, where, after taking one look at the menu, Hsiung Ping accuses Jieu of adapting Chinese dishes to Western tastes. Jieu, who has been trying to evict Hsiung Ping's white boyfriend from one of her apartments, spits back that, no, Hsiung Ping herself is the Chinese dish offered up for American tastes. This concern with the racial and ethnic politics of sexuality later finds its boldest statement in Kwan's visualization and celebration of Chinese gayness. Hsiung Ping tells Zhao Hong about the mainland's long tradition of homosexuality, a tradition that the film insists has been suppressed and needs representing. Such rhetoric encourages sympathetic subcultural reception practices, just as the film as a whole encourages people from distinct Chinese societies to learn to live with their own differences. What is being validated is the very diversity of a community with shared values and a common destiny in the United States.

Now, a short critique of what might be considered the aesthetic limitations of these films. In his work on the postcolonial dynamics of modern Hong Kong cinema, Ackbar Abbas notes that the exploration of spatial and temporal issues has been a central and impressive concern—witness the use of time travel and reincarnation narratives, the balancing of multiple diegetic spaces in titles such as *Rouge* (Kwan 1987), *Iceman Cometh* (Fok 1989), *Center Stage* (Kwan 1991), *The Reincarnation of Golden Lotus* (Law 1989), and *Song of the Exile* (Hui 1990). These films distinguish themselves through brilliant use of multiple temporal frameworks (Abbas 1997; Stringer 1997). Such manipulation of space and time allows these films to travel internationally by galvanizing art cinema and film festival audiences. In addition, these films have drawn attention to the importance of issues of social mobility and fantasy to Hong Kong's own historical situation.

By contrast, Hong Kong films that imagine the United States and Asian American identities are noticeably less likely to take on board such spatial and temporal issues. The ability to imagine another time and another place presupposes the ability to be socially mobile, to be able to move on to someplace else. *An Autumn Tale, Full Moon,* and *Rumble* exhibit a lack of mobility across space and time, a diegetic stasis that indicates a fundamental inability to imagine the coexistence of other times and other places. Abbas implied this when he made the observation that, next to films such as *Rouge* and *Center Stage,* some of the Hong Kong film industry's "attempts to be 'international'—by using a foreign city as background, for example, as in Clara Law's [*sic*] well-regarded *Autumn Story*, a film about Hong Kong Chinese in New York made in the late eighties—may strike us as awkward and provincial" (Abbas 1997, 28).[7]

This criticism cuts two ways. Abbas has elsewhere suggested that Hong Kong cinema's recent love affair with high-tech special effects and spectacle enables the formation of its unique postcolonial identity ("a postcoloniality that precedes decolonization" [ibid., 6]). "This interest in special effects suggests not only that the Hong Kong cinema has caught up with the new technologies; more importantly, it now places the filmic action in a new technological, and by implication, transnational space" (Abbas 1996, 298). Innovative and fantastic special effects please diverse international audiences and promote Hong Kong's film industry as technologically more advanced than that of the People's Republic of China. More than that, the effects help open up what Abbas (echoing Hall) calls "the third space,"—"where East and West are overcome and discredited as separate notions, and another space or a space of otherness is introduced" (ibid., 300). Against these standards, the three films I have been looking at must be branded aesthetically impoverished and found wanting. By the time he made *Rumble,* not even Jackie Chan could push his body to perform the stunts he was able to do as a younger man; *An Autumn Tale*'s final fantasy scene is noticeably lackluster, a matter of a simple, "impossible" change from day to night in the space of one shot; and *Full Moon* has none of the subtlety of some of Kwan's earlier and later work.

Yet it seems to me that Abbas misses an important point here: Hong Kong films about the United States and Asian Americans are working with a set of concerns that resonate in the act of *reception* as much as they resonate textually. The "third space" they aim to introduce may be another space, or a space of Otherness, but is also a very specific geographical location—in this case, New York. This space is not just presented as a site for the allegorical disappearance of Hong Kong cultural identity. It also functions as a location for the mapping out of potential Asian American identities. For this reason, it is somewhat unfair to compare the promise of a new space imagined in Hong Kong with the reality found by filmmakers who have traveled on location to the United States. When Sam Pan beats up the owner of a Chinese restaurant in *An Autumn Tale,* for example, the scene undoubtedly appears "awkward and provincial" when compared with the sensational kung-fu dramas that Abbas writes about, such as *Once Upon a Time in China* (Tsui 1991) and *Ashes of Time* (Wong 1994). But because the stunning visual compositions conjured up in these two movies would be out of place in Brooklyn, Cheung suggestively stages her fight scene for what it is—namely, a low-budget parody of a similar interethnic fight scene from *The Godfather* (Coppola 1972).

Or, to give another illustration, when Jennifer first reaches New York, she is advised by Vincent to take advantage of all that the new world has to offer. "Now you're here," he tells her, "you should experience different lifestyles and broaden your horizons." Later, as Jennifer and Sam Pan discuss their lives while strolling along the shore of Long Island, Jennifer repeats this advice in the form of an assertion that she wants to travel and see the world. For Sam Pan, however, the search is over. "I've been everywhere," he says, smiling. "I want to stay here and open a restaurant facing the Atlantic Ocean." The point this exchange is trying to make is clear: Sam Pan may not get to fulfill his dream because, unlike Jennifer, he can't speak English, he is structurally excluded from New York's capitalist miracle, and he has no white friends. Yet by offering a highly tentative fantasy in its very last moments, the film suggests that Sam Pan may yet come to embody an alternative paradigm of Asian American identity.

The creative exploration of such themes should not be confused with a failure of nerve or lack of experimentation on the part of traveling Hong Kong filmmakers. Compared with other recent titles from the settlement, these three films do not strike the viewer as particularly eye-popping or gut-wrenching because they use a very down-to-earth style to locate very down-to-earth material. While concerned with the diasporic consciousness of Chinese people who have made it to the new world, they do not imagine the United States as itself a place of mobility. This contradiction can be read as anxiety over the threat of assimilation and over the loss of an "essential" "inner domain"—a "one true self"—within the dynamics of migration and postcolonialism. The attractions of *An Autumn Tale, Full Moon,* and *Rumble* pull in different directions. On the one hand, their narratives dramatize how the immigrant may lose social mobility and monetary power once she or he arrives in Uncle Sam's backyard. On the other hand, they do this productively by exploring some of the forms that Asian American identities may take.

The most successful recent films from Hong Kong construct a new localized subjectivity through an imaginative manipulation of formal questions, opening a space where transcultural identities may flourish after 1997. Films that imagine the United States sacrifice this in favor of a flattening out of imaginative potential. Aspiring to explore similarities and differences within and between Chinese, Chinese American, and Asian American identities, they expose audiences to the migrant's own experiences and to her or his own vulnerability and lack of opportunity, as well as to the ethnic pride and consciousness that bonds Asian American communities. Some critics might conclude from this that traveling Hong Kong filmmakers have yet to find ways to integrate themselves into the United States in the manner that Hong Kong star culture has managed to transform U.S. film culture and retain its own "inner" self-identity. However, I would not want to put the blame on unimaginative filmmakers. Rather than perceiving this strategy as a symptom of a short-term artistic retreat, it can be viewed instead as the difficult, but necessary, first step in the long-term project of moving beyond outdated paradigms. Comparing these few titles about Asian American identities with other contemporary movies from Hong Kong, one finds that, although the Chinese diaspora is presented far more imaginatively and fluidly than the realities of Asian American life itself, Asian American cultural identity is still being explored in all of its diversity.

Finally, even if it is true that some titles distributed in the United States do not offer the fascinations and pleasures of effects and spectacle, does this really matter? The indications are that Asian American audiences are using Hong Kong cinema for their own purposes. Fantasies and meanings are being created in the act of reception. As Alvin Lu explains in *Beyond Asiaphilia,* "For a while it was, like, 'Oh, there's no Asians in Hollywood,' but now it doesn't matter. You can just watch Hong Kong movies!" The possibilities opened by such moments of pan-ethnic appropriation are worth support and further consideration.

Notes

Acknowledgments: Thanks to Sandra Liu and Darrell Hamamoto for their extremely detailed and generous advice on an earlier draft of this chapter.

1. Wayne Wang, for example, worked with the Hong Kong director Allen Fong on *Life Is Cheap . . . But Toilet Paper Is Expensive* (1990) and with the actress Maggie Cheung on *Chinese Box* (1997).

2. See Ansen (1996), Corliss (1996), Dannen (1995), and Wolf (1996).

3. Yvonne Tasker (1993, 21–23) has noted the influence of Hong Kong cinema on such "blaxploitation" movies as *Black Belt Jones* (Clouse 1974) and the Warner Bros./Shaw Brothers *Cleopatra Jones* series. More recently, my friend Tobias Nagl pointed to the sampling of Hong Kong movies by contemporary rap crews (e.g., Wu-Tang Clan, Ol' Dirty Bastard's "Return to the 36th Chamber: The Dirty Version"). Nagl also reports that Hong Kong productions have blockbuster status in Kingston, Jamaica, where Jet Li is a superstar.

4. This observation is based on viewing the Hong Kong and U.S. versions of the film. Mark Gallagher ignores this aspect of Chan's star appeal in his article "Masculinity in Translation: Jackie Chan's Transcultural Star Text" (1997).

5. In a similar fashion, Jennifer's personal development in *An Autumn Tale* is charted through her progress as an actress. Her adoption of a "successful" identity of accommodation is tied to the creative transformation of her professional life.

6. It is worth drawing attention to the interconnectedness of Kwan's vision. As a Chinese director, he recognizes the existence of Asian American identities as they cut across class and national boundaries. As a gay man, he perceives the existence of similarly expansive homosexual communities.

7. See also Lynn Pan (1992, 63): "On the whole, Hong Kong filmmakers have portrayed the world of the Chinese abroad as little more than a kind of transplanted Hong Kong, with the adopted country acting merely as a backdrop."

Works Cited

Abbas, Ackbar. 1996. "Cultural Studies in a Postculture." Pp. 289–312 in *Disciplinarity and Dissent in Cultural Studies,* ed. Cary Nelson and Dilip Parameshwar Gaonkar. London and New York: Routledge.

———. 1997. *Hong Kong: Culture and the Politics of Disappearance.* Minneapolis: University of Minnesota Press.

Ansen, David. 1996. "Chinese Takeout." *Newsweek* (February 19), 66–69.

Chatterjee, Partha. 1993. *The Nation and Its Fragments: Colonial and Postcolonial Histories.* Princeton, N.J.: Princeton University Press.

Corliss, Richard. 1996. "Go West, Hong Kong." *Time* (February 26), 67.

Dannen, Fredric. 1995. "Hong Kong Babylon." *New Yorker* (August 7), 30–39.

Espiritu, Yen Le. 1992. *Asian American Panethnicity: Bridging Institutions and Identities.* Philadelphia: Temple University Press.

Feng, Peter. 1996. "Being Chinese American, Becoming Asian American: *Chan Is Missing.*" *Cinema Journal* 35, no. 4 (Summer): 88–118.

Gallagher, Mark. 1997. "Masculinity in Translation: Jackie Chan's Transcultural Star Text." *Velvet Light Trap*, vol. 39 (Spring), 23–41.

Hall, Stuart. 1994. "Cultural Identity and Diaspora." Pp. 392–403 in *Colonial Discourse and Post-Colonial Theory: A Reader,* ed. Patrick Williams and Laura Chrisman. London: Harvester Wheatsheaf.

Hamamoto, Darrell Y., and Rodolfo D. Torres, ed. 1997. *New American Destinies: A Reader in Contemporary Asian and Latino Immigration.* London and New York: Routledge.

Kwong, Peter. 1987. *The New Chinatown.* New York: Hill and Wang.

Ong, Paul, Edna Bonacich, and Lucie Cheng, ed. 1994. *The New Asian Immigration in Los Angeles and Global Restructuring.* Philadelphia: Temple University Press.

Pan, Lynn. "Chinese Emigres on Screen." 1992. *The 16th Hong Kong International Film Festival: Overseas Figures in Chinese Cinema.* Hong Kong: Urban Council, 59–64.

Stringer, Julian. 1997. "Centre Stage: Reconstructing the Bio-Pic." *Cineaction* 42 (February): 28–39.

Tasker, Yvonne. 1993. *Spectacular Bodies: Gender, Genre, and the Action Cinema.* London and New York: Routledge.

Wang, L. Ling-Chi. 1991. "Roots and Changing Identity of the Chinese in the United States." *Daedalus* 120, no. 2 (spring): 181–206.

———. 1995. "The Structure of Dual Domination: Toward a Paradigm for the Study of the Chinese Diaspora in the United States." *Amerasia Journal* 21, no. 1–2 (Winter–Spring): 149–69.

Wolf, Jaime. 1996. "Jackie Chan, American Action Hero?" *New York Times Magazine* (January 21), 22.

Films and Videos Cited

Chan, Peter. 1991. *Alan and Eric—Between Hello and Goodbye.* No distributor (U.S.).

———. 1998. *Comrades: Almost a Love Story.* Rim (U.S.).

Chang, Sylvia. 1995. *Siao Yu.* Central Motion Pictures.

Cheung, Mabel. 1988. *An Autumn Tale.* No distributor (U.S.).

———. 1989. *Eight Taels of Gold.* No distributor (U.S.).

Clouse, Robert. 1974. *Black Belt Jones.* Warner Bros.

Coppola, Francis Ford. 1972. *The Godfather.* Paramount.

Fok, Clarence Yiu Leung. 1989. *Iceman Cometh.* Golden Harvest.

Fuqua, Antoine. 1998. *The Replacement Killers.* Columbia Pictures.

Hui, Ann. 1990. *Song of the Exile.* No distributor (U.S.).

———. 1991. *My American Grandson.* No distributor (U.S.).

Kam-Bo, Sammo Hung. 1997. *Once Upon a Time in China and America.* Film Workshop/Oliver Stone Production.

Kwan, Stanley. 1987. *Rouge.* No distributor (U.S.).

———. 1990. *Full Moon in New York.* No distributor (U.S.).

———. 1991. *Center Stage.* Swift Distribution (France). No distributor (U.S.).

Lam, Ringo. 1996. *Maximum Risk.* Columbia Pictures.

———, and Tsui Hark. 1992. *Twin Dragons.* Miramax.

Law, Clara. 1989. *The Reincarnation of Golden Lotus.* No distributor (U.S.).

———. 1990. *Farewell China.* No distributor (U.S.).

Mann, Michael, and Alan Smithee. 1995. *Heat.* Warner Bros.

Ray, Nicholas. 1955. *Rebel Without a Cause*. Warner Bros.

Soe, Valerie. 1997. *Beyond Asiaphilia*. Oxygen Productions (U.S.).

Spottiswoode, Roger. 1997. *Tomorrow Never Dies*. MGM/UA.

Tong, Stanley. 1996a. *Police Story 3: Supercop*. Dimension Films (U.S.).

———. 1996b. *Rumble in the Bronx*. Buena Vista Pictures (U.S.).

———. 1997. *Police Story 4: First Strike*. New Line Cinema (U.S.).

Tsui, Hark. 1991a. *The Master*. Paragon Films.

———. 1991b. *Once Upon a Time in China*. Film Workshop.

———. 1997. *Double Team*. Columbia Pictures.

Wang, Wayne. 1990. *Life Is Cheap . . . But Toilet Paper Is Expensive*. No distributor (U.S.).

———. 1997. *Chinese Box*. Trimark.

Wong, Jing. 1989. *God of Gamblers*. No distributor (U.S.).

———. 1995. *God of Gamblers Returns*. No distributor (U.S.).

Wong, Kar-wai. 1994. *Ashes of Time*. Scholar Productions.

Woo, John. 1987. *A Better Tomorrow II*. Cinema City.

———. 1993. *Hard Target*. Universal.

———. 1996. *Broken Arrow*. Twentieth Century Fox.

———. 1997. *Face/Off*. Buena Vista.

Distributors

The following is a partial list of addresses, telephone and fax numbers, and Internet addresses for distributors of the films and videos cited in this volume. The list focuses on organizations that distribute independent works; contact information for major film studios, therefore, are not included. Information for works distributed by individual filmmakers is included in the Films and Videos Cited list at the end of the chapter in which the work is discussed. All addresses are in the United States, unless noted otherwise.

Documentary Educational Resources
101 Morse St.
Watertown, Mass. 02172
Phone: 617-926-0491; 800-569-6621
Fax: 617-926-9519
http://www.xensei.com/docued/

Electronic Arts Intermix
542 W. 22nd St.
New York, N.Y. 10011
Phone: 212-337-0680
Fax: 212-337-0679
http://www.eai.org/

Filmakers Library
124 East 40th St.
New York, N.Y. 10016
Phone: 212-808-4980
Fax: 212-808-4983
http://www.filmakers.com

Frameline
346 Ninth St.
San Francisco, Calif. 94103
Phone: 415-703-8650
Fax: 415-861-1404
http://www.frameline.org

IDERA
#400-1037 W. Broadway
Vancouver, B.C., Canada V6H 1E3
Phone: 604-732-1496
Fax: 604-738-8400
http://www.vcn.bc.ca/idera/
welcome.htm

Japanese American National Museum
369 W. First St.
Los Angeles, Calif. 90012
Phone: 213-625-0414; 800-461-5266
Fax: 213-625-1770
http://www.janet.org/janm

National Asian American Telecommunications Association (NAATA)
   346 Ninth St., 2nd Floor
   San Francisco, Calif. 94103
   Phone: 415-863-0814
   Fax: 415-863-7428
   http://www.naatanet.org

Sai Communications
   22D Hollywood Ave.
   Ho-ho-kus, N.J. 07423
   Phone: 800-343-5540
   Fax: 201-652-1973

Third World Newsreel
   545 Eighth Ave., 10th Floor
   New York, N.Y. 10018
   Phone: 212-947-9277
   Fax: 212-594-6417
   http://www.twn.org/index.html

Video Data Bank
   112 S. Michigan Ave.
   Chicago, Ill. 60603
   Phone: 312-345-3550

Video Out International Distribution
   1965 Main Street
   Vancouver, B.C., Canada V5T 3C1
   Phone: 604-872-8449

Visual Communications
   120 Judge John Aiso St.
   Los Angeles, Calif. 90012
   Phone: 213-680-4462

Women Make Movies
   462 Broadway, Ste. 500
   New York, N.Y. 10013
   Phone: 212-925-0606
   Fax: 212-925-2052
   http://www.wmm.com

About the Contributors

ELENA TAJIMA CREEF is Assistant Professor in Women's Studies at Wellesley College, where she specializes in Asian American Studies. She is currently working on a book about Asian American visual culture.

PETER X FENG is Assistant Professor of English and Women's Studies at the University of Delaware. He sits on the editorial board of the *Journal of Asian American Studies* and is currently completing a book-length study of Asian American cinema.

GWENDOLYN AUDREY FOSTER is Associate Professor in the Department of English at the University of Nebraska, Lincoln. Her books include *Women Film Directors: An International Bio-Critical Dictionary* (1995), *Women Filmmakers of the African and Asian Diaspora: De/Colonizing the Gaze, Locating Subjectivity* (1997), and *Identity and Memory: The Films of Chantal Akerman* (1999). Her forthcoming book is *Captive Bodies: Postcolonial Subjectivity in Cinema*. She is Joint Editor of *Quarterly Review of Film and Video*.

THEODORE S. GONZALVES is a doctoral candidate in Comparative Culture at the University of California at Irvine. He has taught literature, film, politics, history, and ethnic and cultural studies at several colleges and universities. His musical work has been featured in concerts and recordings; he also continues to work on film and musical-theater projects. His dissertation focuses on the cultural history of a performance genre and American ethnic historical consciousness.

DARRELL Y. HAMAMOTO is Associate Professor in the Asian American Studies Program at the University of California, Davis. He has written extensively on the dominant corporate-controlled media, but now devotes his energy to advancing Asian American cultural politics. Hamamoto founded the Asian American Para-Literature Archive at UC Davis and is president of Yellow Entertainment Network (YEN), which will feature Asian American programming.

LINDSEY JANG is a director, writer, and cinematographer who received his M.F.A. in film-video production from the University of Southern California. He wrote and directed the short narratives *Non-Endowment Care* and *Flames in the Heart*, and the experimental film *Frogs*. He is the director of the documentaries *No Evidence* and *Stolen Ground*.

CYNTHIA LIU, an independent scholar and writer, holds a Ph.D. in English and an M.A. in creative writing, both from the University of California, Berkeley. Her dissertation, supported partly by a Woodrow Wilson Women's Studies grant, examines gender and sexuality in literature and film by post-World War II Chinese Americans.

SANDRA LIU is a doctoral candidate in Ethnic Studies at the University of California, Berkeley. Her dissertation explores how capitalism, politics, and spectacle affect Asian American film audiences and the production of Asian American feature films.

GINA MARCHETTI is Associate Professor in the Department of Cinema and Photography at Ithaca College. She sits on the editorial board of *Jump Cut* and is the author of the book *Romance and the "Yellow Peril": Race, Sex and Discursive Strategies in Hollywood Fiction*. Her current research involves transnationalism and screen culture in Hollywood and Asia.

GLEN MASATO MIMURA is Assistant Professor of Asian American Studies at the University of California, Irvine. His research examines visual media—turn-of-the-century photography, recently restored silent film, experimental video—produced by Asian Americans as a neglected dimension of American cultural history. He is a recipient of a National Fellowship 1997–98 from the Civil Liberties Public Education Fund.

EVE OISHI is Assistant Professor of Women's Studies at California State University, Long Beach. She is working on a book titled, *The Memory Village: Fakeness and Authenticity in Asian American Fiction, Film and Video*. She has curated film and video programs for Outfest: Los Angeles Gay and Lesbian Film Festival; the Philadelphia International Gay and Lesbian Film Festival; and for MIX: The New York International Lesbian and Gay Experimental Film/Video Festival.

KENT A. ONO is Associate Professor in the American Studies Program and in the Asian American Studies Program at the University of California, Davis. His research on critical and theoretical analysis of media—print, film, and television—focuses on representations of race, gender, sexuality, class, and nation. He is co-editor of *Enterprise Zones: Critical Positions on Star Trek* (1996) and co-authored *Shifting Borders: Rhetoric, Immigration, and California's "Proposition 187."*

CELINE SALAZAR PARREÑAS works in film production, theory, and poetry. She is pursuing a Ph.D. in Modern Thought and Literature at Stanford University. She received her M.F.A. in Film Directing and Production from the UCLA Film School. She has taught in the Ethnic Studies Department at the University of California, Berkeley, and in the Cinema Department at San Francisco State University. Her dissertation, "Specters of 'Asian Woman,'" has a feature documentary component.

VALERIE SOE is an artist and writer living in San Francisco. Her work has been exhibited widely in this country and abroad, and she has won many awards, including a